SKILLS for Success
Premium Media Site

Improve your grade with hands-on tools and resources!

- Master *Key Terms* to expand your vocabulary.
- Prepare for exams by taking practice quizzes in the *Online Chapter Review.*
- Download *Student Data Files* for the application projects in each chapter.

And for even more tools, you can access the following Premium Resources using your Access Code. Register now to get the most out of *Skills for Success!*

- *Student Training Videos* are instructor-led videos that walk through each skill in a chapter.*
- *BizSkills Videos* cover the important business skills students need to be successful—Interviewing, Communication, Dressing for Success, and more.*

*Access code required for these premium resources

Your Access Code is:

Note: If there is no silver foil covering the access code, it may already have been redeemed, and therefore may no longer be valid. In that case, you can purchase online access using a major credit card or PayPal account. To do so, go to **www.pearsonhighered.com/skills**, select your book cover, click on "Buy Access" and follow the on-screen instructions.

To Register:

- To start you will need a valid email address and this access code.
- Go to **www.pearsonhighered.com/skills** and scroll to find your text book.
- Once you've selected your text, on the Home Page for the book, click the link to access the Student Premium Content.
- Click the Register button and follow the on-screen instructions.
- After you register, you can sign in any time via the log-in area on the same screen.

System Requirements

Windows 7 Ultimate Edition; IE 8
Windows Vista Ultimate Edition SP1; IE 8
Windows XP Professional SP3; IE 7
Windows XP Professional SP3; Firefox 3.6.4
Mac OS 10.5.7; Firefox 3.6.4
Mac OS 10.6; Safari 5

Technical Support

http://247pearsoned.custhelp.com

Photo credits: Goodluz/wrangler/Elena Elisseeva/Shutterstock

SKILLS
For SUCCESS

with Microsoft®
Excel 2013

TOWNSEND | CHANEY ADKINS

PEARSON

Boston   Columbus   Indianapolis   New York   San Francisco   Upper Saddle River
Amsterdam   Cape Town   Dubai   London   Madrid   Milan   Munich   Paris   Montréal   Toronto
Delhi   Mexico City   São Paulo   Sydney   Hong Kong   Seoul   Singapore   Taipei   Tokyo

Library of Congress Cataloging-in-Publication Data
CIP data on file with the Library of Congress.

Editor in Chief: *Michael Payne*
Executive Editor: *Jenifer Niles*
Editorial Project Manger: *Carly Prakapas*
Product Development Manager: *Laura Burgess*
Editorial Assistant: *Andra Skaalrud*
Development Editor: *Toni Ackley*
Director of Business & Technology Marketing: *Maggie Leen*
Marketing Manager: *Brad Forrester*
Marketing Coordinator: *Susan Osterlitz*
Managing Editor: *Camille Trentacoste*
Project Manager: *Debbie Ryan*
Senior Operation Manager/Site Lead: *Nick Sklitsis*

Operations Specialist: *Maura Zaldivar-Garcia*
Senior Art Director: *Jonathan Boylan*
Text and Cover Designer: *Jonathan Boylan*
Director of Media Development: *Taylor Ragan*
Media Project Manager, Production: *John Cassar*
Full-Service Project Management: *Jouve North America*
Full-Service Project Manager: *Kevin Bradley*
Composition: *Jouve*
Printer/Binder: *Quad Graphics/Eusey Press Inc.*
Cover Printer: *Lehigh-Phoenix Color/Hagerstown*
Typeface: *Palatino LT Std Roman 10/12*

Credits and acknowledgments borrowed from other sources and reproduced, with permission, in this textbook appear on appropriate page within text.

10 9 8 7 6 5 4 3 2 1
ISBN 10: 0-13-314800-9
ISBN 13: 978-0-13-314800-8

Contents in Brief

Table of Contents

Contributors

We'd like to thank the following people for their work on Skills for Success:

Focus Group Participants

Rose Volynskiy	Howard Community College	Lex Mulder	College of Western Idaho
Fernando Paniagua	The Community College of Baltimore County	Kristy McAuliffe	San Jacinto College South
Jeff Roth	Heald College	Jan Hime	University of Nebraska, Lincoln
William Bodine	Mesa Community College	Deb Fells	Mesa Community College

Reviewers

Barbara Anderson	Lake Washington Institute of Technology	Deb Fells	Mesa Community College
Janet Anderson	Lake Washington Institute of Technology	Tushnelda C Fernandez	Miami Dade College
Ralph Argiento	Guilford Technical Community College	Jean Finley	Asheville-Buncombe Technical Community College
Tanisha Arnett	Pima County Community College		
Greg Ballinger	Miami Dade College	Jim Flannery	Central Carolina Community College
Autumn Becker	Allegany College of Maryland	Alyssa Foskey	Wiregrass Georgia Technical College
Bob Benavides	Collin College	David Freer	Miami Dade College
Howard Blauser	North GA Technical College	Marvin Ganote	University of Dayton
William Bodine	Mesa Community College	David Grant	Paradise Valley Community College
Nancy Bogage	The Community College of Baltimore County	Clara Groeper	Illinois Central College
Maria Bright	San Jacinto College	Carol Heeter	Ivy Tech Community College
Adell Brooks	Hinds Community College	Jan Hime	University of Nebraska
Judy Brown	Western Illinois University	Marilyn Holden	Gateway Technical College
Maria Brownlow	Chaminade	Ralph Hunsberger	Bucks County Community College
Jennifer Buchholz	UW Washington County	Juan Iglesias	University of Texas at Brownsville
Kathea Buck	Gateway Technical College	Carl Eric Johnson	Great Bay Community College
LeAnn Cady	Minnesota State College—Southeast Technical	Joan Johnson	Lake Sumter Community College
John Cameron	Rio Hondo College	Mech Johnson	UW Washington County
Tammy Campbell	Eastern Arizona College	Deborah Jones	Southwest Georgia Technical College
Patricia Christian	Southwest Georgia Technical College	Hazel Kates	Miami-Dade College, Kendall Campus
Tina Cipriano	Gateway Technical College	Jane Klotzle	Lake Sumter Community College
Paulette Comet	The Community College of Baltimore County	Kurt Kominek	Northeast State Community College
Jean Condon	Mid-Plains Community College	Vivian Krenzke	Gateway Technical College
Joy DePover	Minneapolis. Com. & Tech College	Renuka Kumar	Community College of Baltimore County
Gina Donovan	County College of Morris	Lisa LaCaria	Central Piedmont Community College
Alina Dragne	Flagler College	Sue Lannen	Brazosport College
Russ Dulaney	Rasmussen College	Freda Leonard	Delgado Community College
Mimi Duncan	University of Missouri St. Louis	Susan Mahon	Collin College
Paula Jo Elson	Sierra College	Nicki Maines	Mesa Community College
Bernice Eng	Brookdale Community College	Pam Manning	Gateway Technical College
Jill Fall	Gateway Technical College	Juan Marquez	Mesa Community College

Alysia Martinez	*Gateway Technical College*	Jeff Roth	*Heald College*
Kristy McAuliffe	*San Jacinto College*	Diane Ruscito	*Brazosport College*
Robert McCloud	*Sacred Heart University*	June Scott	*County College of Morris*
Susan Miner	*Lehigh Carbon Community College*	Vicky Seehusen	*MSU Denver*
Namdar Mogharreban	*Southern Illinois University*	Emily Shepard	*Central Carolina Community College*
Daniel Moix	*College of the Ouachitas*	Pamela Silvers	*A-B Tech*
Lindsey Moore	*Wiregrass Georgia Technical College*	Martha Soderholm	*York College*
Lex Mulder	*College of Western Idaho*	Yaacov Sragovich	*Queensborough Community College*
Patricia Newman	*Cuyamaca College*	Jody Sterr	*Blackhawk Technical College*
Melinda Norris	*Coker College*	Julia Sweitzer	*Lake-Sumter Community College*
Karen Nunan	*Northeast State Community College*	Laree Thomas	*Okefenokee Technical College*
Fernando Paniagua	*The Community College of Baltimore County*	Joyce Thompson	*Lehigh Carbon Community College*
Christine Parrish	*Southwest Georgia Technical College*	Barbara Tietsort	*University of Cincinnati, Blue Ash College*
Linda Pennachio	*Mount Saint Mary College*	Rose Volynskiy	*Howard Community College*
Amy Pezzimenti	*Ocean County College*	Sandra Weber	*Gateway Technical College*
Leah Ramalingam	*Riversity City College*	Steven Weitz	*Lehigh Carbon Community College*
Mary Rasley	*Lehigh Carbon Community College*	Berthenia Williams	*Savannah Technical College*
Cheryl Reuss	*Estrella Mountain Community College*	David Wilson	*Parkland College*
Wendy Revolinski	*Gateway Technical College*	Allan Wood	*Great Bay Community College*
Kenneth Rogers	*Cecil College*	Roger Yaeger	*Estrella Mountain Community College*

What's New for Excel 2013

With Office 2013, Microsoft is taking the office to the cloud. The Skills for Success series shows students how to get the most out of Office 2013 no matter what device they are using—a traditional desktop or tablet.

Whether you are tapping and sliding with your finger or clicking and dragging with the mouse, Skills for Success shows you the way with the hallmark visual, two-page, easy-to-follow design. It covers the essential skills students need to know to get up and running with Office quickly, and it addresses Web Apps, touch screens, and the collaborative approach of Office 365. Once students complete the Instructional Skills, they put their knowledge to work with a progression of review, problem-solving, and challenging, end-of-chapter projects.

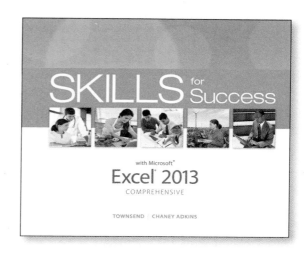

What's New for Office 2013

Coverage of new features of Office 2013 in an approach that is easy and effective for teaching students the skills they need to get started with Microsoft Office.

Skills Summary—new summary chart of all the Skills and Procedures covered in the chapter makes remembering what was covered easier!

Application Introductions—provide a brief overview of each application and put the chapters in context for students.

Student Training Videos—new, author-created training videos for each Skill in the chapters!

Application Capstone Projects— Chapter 4 and Chapter 10 conclude with a capstone project. These will also be grader projects in MyITLab.

Web Apps Projects (formerly Collaboration Project)—use a variety of the web apps available at the end of Chapter 4 and Chapter 10. Also includes an online "On Your Own" project to let students try an additional project.

Additional Grader Projects—two new grader projects based on the Skills Review provide a broader variety of homework and assessment options; written by the book authors.

New Training and Assessment Simulations—written by the book authors to provide enhanced one-to-one content match in MyITlab.

SkyDrive Coverage—included in the Common Features chapter.

MOS mapping—located on the Instructor Resource Site and provides a guide to where the MOS Core exam objectives are covered in the book, on the Companion Website, and in MyITLab to help students prepare to ace the exam!

A Microsoft® Office textbook that recognizes how students learn today

Skills for Success

with Microsoft® Excel 2013 Volume 1

- **10 × 8.5 Format**—Easy for students to read and type at the same time by simply propping the book up on the desk in front of their monitor

- **Clearly Outlined Skills**—Each skill is presented in a single two-page spread so that students can easily follow along

- **Numbered Steps and Bulleted Text**— Students don't read long paragraphs of text; instead they get a step-by-step, concise presentation

- **Broad Coverage of Skills**—Gives students the knowledge needed to get up and running quickly

Two Page Chapter Introduction—Briefs students on what is important and sets the stage for the project they will create

File Summary— A quick summary of the files the students need to open and the names of the files they will turn in

Outcome—Shows students up front what their completed project will look like

Clock—Tells how much time students need to complete the chapter

Student Training Videos for each Skill in the chapter provide a personal, instructor-led walk through

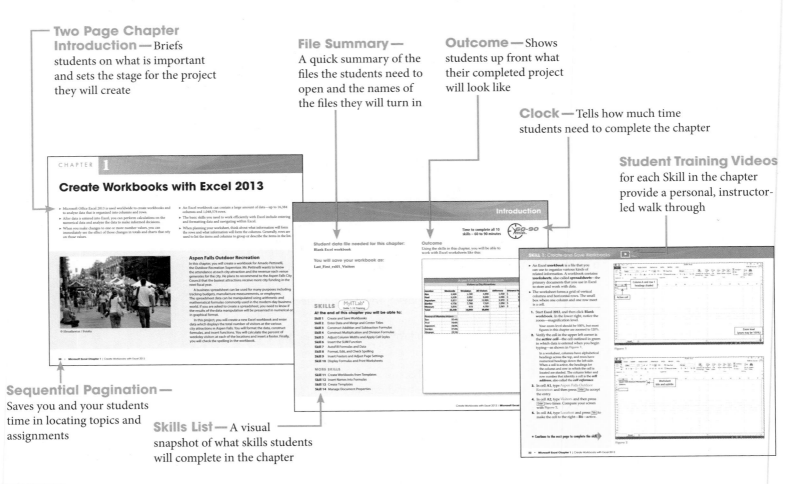

Sequential Pagination— Saves you and your students time in locating topics and assignments

Skills List—A visual snapshot of what skills students will complete in the chapter

Skills for Success

Written for Today's Students — Skills are taught with numbered steps and bulleted text so students are less likely to skip valuable information

Two-Page Spreads — Each skill is presented in a concise, two-page spread to give students the visual illustration right with the steps—no flipping pages

Colored Text — Clearly shows what a student types

Larger Screen Images — Provide a view of the full ribbon and include concise callouts for easy reference

Done! — Students always know when they've completed a skill

Hands-On — Students start working on their skills from Step 1

More Skills — Additional skills included online

New BizSkills Videos — Covering the important business skills students need to succeed: *Communication, Dress for Success, Interview Prep,* and more. Available for Chapters 1-4 only.

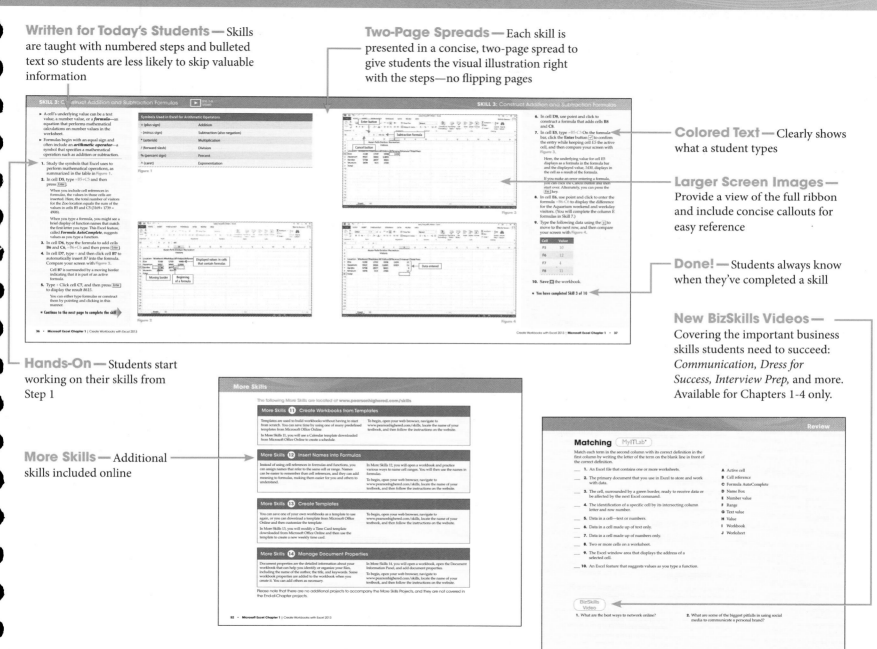

Skills for Success

End-of-Chapter Material — Several levels of review and assessment so you can assign the material that best fits your students' needs

NEW Skills and Procedures Summary Chart — Provides a quick review of the skills and tasks covered in each chapter

A stronger progression from point and click to practice, and to critical thinking.

NEW MyITLab grader project — Covers all 10 skills (homework and assessment versions)

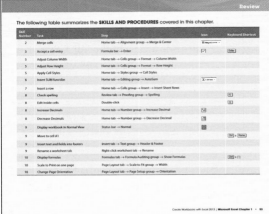

From Point and Click to Critical Thinking	
Skills 1–10 Guided learning	Annotated linear steps that tell "*where* to click" and *why*.
Skills Review Guided practice	Linear steps that tell them "*where* to click" one more time.
2 Skills Assessments Independent practice	Linear steps that tell them "*what* to click" but not necessarily where.
Visual Skills Assessment Non-linear problem-solving	Students determine their own steps to create the document shown in the figure and described in the directions.
My Skills Transfer of skills	Students transfer their skills to a different scenario—a personal document, instead of business document.
Skills Challenge 1 Apply skills to fix problems	Typically a document that needs "fixed" by apply the skills in the chapter. The problems are described in a way that the *challenge* is deciding how to fix the problems, not figuring out what the directions mean or how it will be graded.
Skills Challenge 2 Conduct research to solve a problem	Typically a project that requires some research to determine the content of the document. Directions are written in a way that the *challenge* is deciding what to say and how best to format the document, not figuring out what the directions mean or how it will be graded.

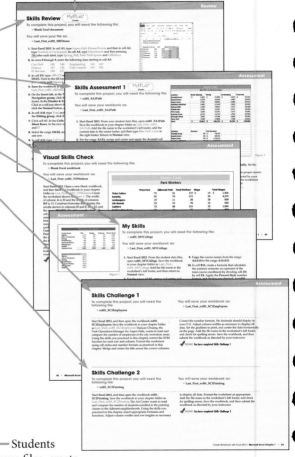

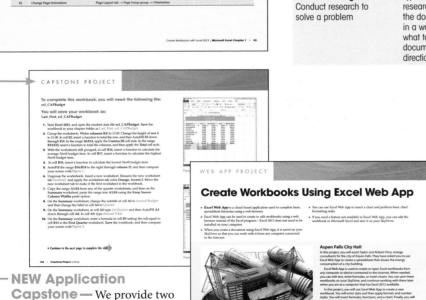

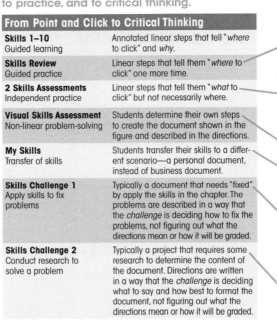

Web App Projects — Students use Cloud computing to save files; create, edit, and share Office documents using Office Web Apps; and create Windows Live groups. Also includes an online "On Your Own" project to let students try an additional project.

NEW Application Capstone — We provide two comprehensive projects that cover all of the Skills in Chapters 1-4 and Chapters 5-10. Also available as Grader projects in MyITLab.

Skills for Success

MyITLab [MyITLab®]

Skills for Success combined with MyITLab gives you a completely integrated solution:

- Instruction, Training, & Assessment
- eText
- Training & Assessment Simulations
- Grader Projects

Student Videos!

Student Training Videos — Each skill within a chapter comes with an instructor-led video that walks students through each skill.

(BizSkills Video) — Cover the important business skills students need to be successful—*Interviewing, Communication, Dressing for Success,* and more. **Available for Chapters 1-4 only**.

Student Data — Files are all available on the Companion Website using the access code included with your book. Pearsonhighered.com/skills

Instructor Materials

NEW Application Capstone Projects — Two projects cover Skills from Chapters 1-4 and Skills from Chapters 5-10. Also available as MyITLab grader projects

NEW MOS map — Guides you and your students to coverage of the MOS Exam objectives for each application

Instructor's Manual — Teaching tips and additional resources for each chapter

Student Assignment Tracker — Lists all the assignments for the chapter; you just add in the course information, due dates, and points. Providing these to students ensures they will know what is due and when

Scripted Lectures — Classroom lectures prepared for you

Annotated Solution Files — Coupled with the scoring rubrics, these create a grading and scoring system that makes grading so much easier for you

PowerPoint Lectures — PowerPoint presentations for each chapter

Audio PPTs — Provide an audio version of the PowerPoint presentations for each chapter

Prepared Exams — Exams for each chapter and for each application

NEW Detailed Scoring Rubrics — Can be used either by students to check their work or by you as a quick check-off for the items that need to be corrected

Syllabus Templates — For 8-week, 12-week, and 16-week courses

Test Bank — Includes a variety of test questions for each chapter

Companion Website — Online content such as the More Skills Projects, Online Chapter Review, Glossary, and Student Data Files are all at www.pearsonhighered.com/skills

All Student and Instructor Materials available at our Companion Websites ... pearsonhighered.com/skills

About the Authors

Kris Townsend is an Information Systems instructor at Spokane Falls Community College in Spokane, Washington. Kris earned a bachelor's degree in both Education and Business, and a master's degree in Education. He has also worked as a public school teacher and as a systems analyst. Kris enjoys working with wood, geocaching, and photography. He commutes to work by bike and also is a Lewis and Clark historical reenactor.

Margo Chaney Adkins is an Assistant Professor of Information Technology at Carroll Community College in Westminster, Maryland. She holds a bachelor's degree in Information Systems and master's degree in Post-Secondary Education from Salisbury University. She teaches computer application and office technology courses, both online and in the classroom. She enjoys athletic activities, gardening, and traveling with her husband.

A Special Thank You

Pearson Prentice Hall gratefully acknowledges the contribution made by Shelley Gaskin to the first edition publication of this series—*Skills for Success with Office 2007*. The series has truly benefited from her dedication toward developing a textbook that aims to help students and instructors. We thank her for her continued support of this series.

SKILLS
For **SUCCESS**

with Microsoft®
Excel 2013

Common Features of Office 2013

- ▶ Microsoft Office is a suite of several programs—Word, PowerPoint, Excel, Access, and others.
- ▶ Each Office program is used to create different types of personal and business documents.
- ▶ The programs in Office 2013 share common tools that you use in a consistent, easy-to-learn manner.

- ▶ Common tasks include opening and saving files, entering and formatting text, and printing your work.
- ▶ Because of the consistent design and layout of the Office applications, when you learn to use one Microsoft Office application, you can apply many of the same techniques when working in the other Microsoft Office applications.

© spaxiax / Fotolia

Aspen Falls City Hall

In this project, you will create documents for the Aspen Falls City Hall, which provides essential services for the citizens and visitors of Aspen Falls, California. You will assist Janet Neal, Finance Director, to prepare a presentation for the City Council. The presentation will explain retail sales trends in the city. The information will help the council to predict revenue from local sales taxes.

Microsoft Office is a suite of tools designed for specific tasks. In this project, the data was originally stored in an Access database. You will use Excel to create a chart from that data and then use PowerPoint to display the chart to an audience. Next, you will use Word to write a memo to update your supervisor about the project's status. In this way, each application performs a different function and creates a different type of document.

In this project, you will create a new Word document from an online template and open existing files in Excel and PowerPoint. You will write a memo, format an Excel worksheet and update chart data, and then place a copy of the chart into a PowerPoint presentation. You will also format a database report in Access. In all four applications, you will apply the same formatting to provide a consistent look and feel.

Time to complete all 10
skills – 60 to 90 minutes

Student data files needed for this chapter:

cf01_RetailChart (Excel)   cf01_RetailData (Access)
cf01_RetailSlides (PowerPoint)

You will save your files as:

Last_First_cf01_RetailMemo (Word)
Last_First_cf01_RetailChart (Excel)
Last_First_cf01_RetailSlides (PowerPoint)
Last_First_cf01_RetailData (Access)

SKILLS

At the end of this chapter you will be able to:

Skill 1   Start Office Applications
Skill 2   Create Documents from Templates
Skill 3   Type and Edit Text
Skill 4   Save Files and Create Folders
Skill 5   Apply Themes and Format Text
Skill 6   Preview and Print Documents
Skill 7   Open and Save Student Data Files
Skill 8   Format Worksheets
Skill 9   Copy and Paste Objects and Format Slides
Skill 10 Format Access Reports

MORE SKILLS

Skill 11 Store Office Files on SkyDrive
Skill 12 Use Office Help
Skill 13 Send Files as E-mail Attachments
Skill 14 Optimize Office 2013 RT

Outcome

Using the skills in this chapter, you will be able to
work with Office documents like this:

Aspen Falls City Hall

Memo

To:	Janet Neal
From:	Your Name
cc:	Maria Martinez
Date:	July 1, 2014
Re:	Sales Revenue

As per your request, the *Retail Sales* slides will be ready by the end of today. I will send them
to you so you can insert them into your presentation. Let me know if you have any questions.

CF 1-1
VIDEO

▶ The way that you start an Office application depends on what operating system you are using and how your computer is configured.

▶ Each application's Start screen displays links to recently viewed documents and thumbnails of sample documents that you can open.

1. If necessary, turn on the computer, sign in, and navigate to the desktop. Take a few moments to familiarize yourself with the various methods for starting Office applications as summarized in Figure 1.

One method that works in both Windows 7 and Windows 8 is to press ⊞—the Windows key located between [Ctrl] and [Alt]—to display the Start menu or screen. With Start displayed, type the application name, and then press [Enter].

2. Use one of the methods described in the previous step to start **Word 2013**, and then take a few moments to familiarize yourself with the Word Start screen as shown in Figure 2.

Your list of recent documents will vary depending on what Word documents you have worked with previously. Below the list of recent documents, the *Open Other Documents* link is used to open Word files that are not listed.

■ **Continue to the next page to complete the skill** ▶

Common Methods to Start Office 2013 Applications	
Location	**Description**
Start screen tile	Click the application's tile.
Desktop	Double-click the application's desktop icon.
Taskbar	Click the application's taskbar button.
Windows 7 Start menu	Click Start, and look in the pinned or recently used programs. Or click All Programs, and locate the Office application or the Microsoft Office 2013 folder.
All locations	Press ⊞, type the application's name, and then press [Enter].

Figure 1

Figure 2

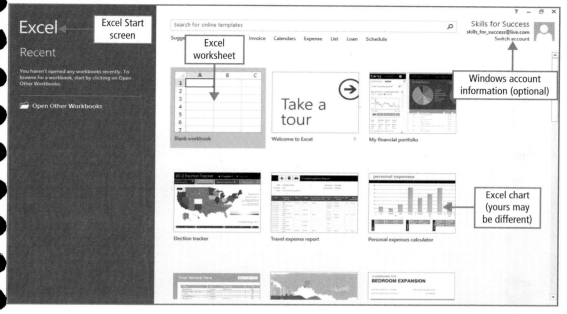

Figure 3

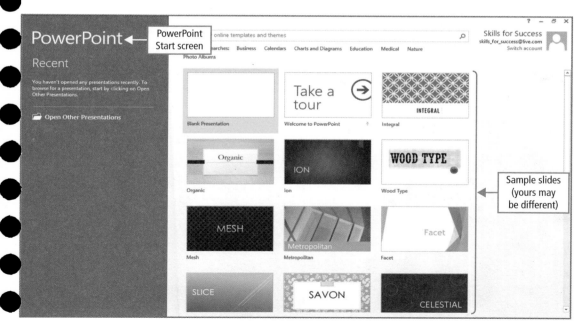

Figure 4

3. If desired, click **Sign in to get the most out of Office**, and then follow the onscreen directions to sign in using your Microsoft account.

   Logging in enables you to access Microsoft Cloud services such as opening and saving files stored on your SkyDrive. Unless otherwise directed, signing in to your Microsoft account is always optional in this book. To protect your privacy, you should sign in only if you are already signed in to Windows using a unique username, not a shared account. For example, many public computers share an account for guests.

4. Using the technique just practiced, start **Excel 2013**, and then compare your screen with Figure 3.

   Worksheets are divided into *cells*—boxes formed by the intersection of a row and column into which text, objects, and data can be inserted. In Excel, cells can contain text, formulas, and functions. Worksheets can also display charts based on the values in the cells.

   When you are logged in to your Microsoft account, your name and picture will display in the upper right corner of the window.

5. Start **PowerPoint 2013**, and then compare your screen with Figure 4.

   PowerPoint presentations consist of *slides*—individual pages in a presentation that can contain text, pictures, or other objects. PowerPoint slides are designed to be projected as you talk in front of a group of people. The PowerPoint Start screen has thumbnails of several slides formatted in different ways.

■ **You have completed Skill 1 of 10**

- ► Office provides access to hundreds of **templates**—pre-built documents into which you insert text using the layout and formatting provided in the documents.
- ► Templates for Word documents, Excel workbooks, PowerPoint presentations, and Access databases can be opened from the start screen or the New page on each application's File tab.

1. On the taskbar, click the **Word** button 🄌 to make it the active window.

2. If the Word Start screen no longer displays, on the File tab, click New.

3. Click in the **Search for online templates** box, and then type memo Click the **Start searching** button 🔍, and then compare your screen with **Figure 1**.

   The New page displays templates that are available online. These online templates are provided by Microsoft and others who submit them to microsoft.com. These online templates must be downloaded before you can work with them. Because the template list is dynamic, your search results may be different.

   On the New page, the right pane can be used to filter your search by category. You can also pin a template so that it always displays on the start screen and New page.

4. Scroll down the list of memos, and then click the **Memo (Professional design)** thumbnail. Compare your screen with **Figure 2**.

   The preview screen provides information about the template so that you can evaluate it before deciding to download it to your computer. You should download templates only from sources that you trust.

■ **Continue to the next page to complete the skill**

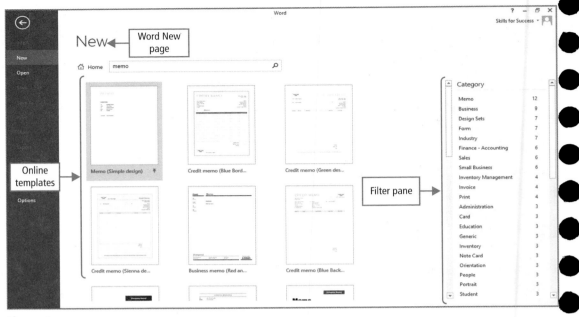

Figure 1

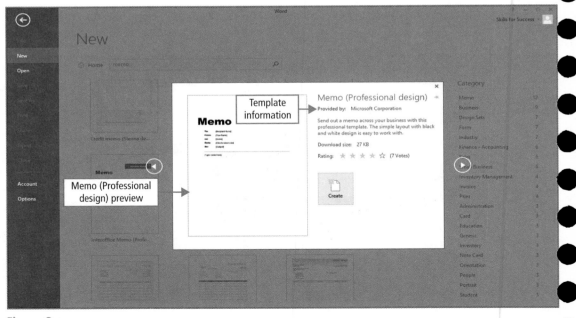

Figure 2

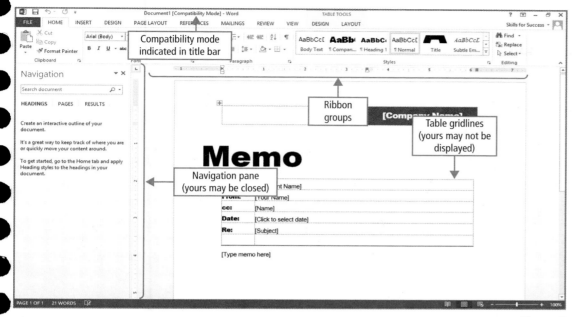

Figure 3

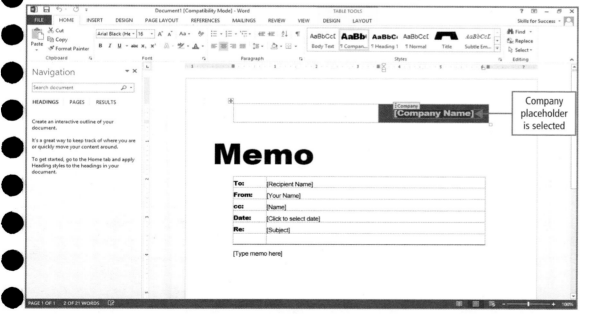

Figure 4

5. In the **Memo (Professional design)** preview, click the **Create** button. Wait a few moments for the memo to download and open. Compare your screen with Figure 3.

   Templates create new, unsaved documents. Here, the title bar displays the text *Document1* and ***Compatibility Mode***—a mode that limits formatting and features to ones that are supported in earlier versions of Office.

   Above the memo, the Quick Access Toolbar and Ribbon display. The Office Ribbon organizes commands into groups. Because the Ribbon adapts to the size of the document window, you may need to adjust the size of your window if you want your Ribbon to display exactly as shown in the figures in this book.

   To the left of the document, the Navigation pane is used to move through the document. Below the word *Memo*, the table gridlines may or may not display depending on your settings. These gridlines do not print, and you can work with documents with them displayed or turned off.

6. In the upper-right corner of the memo, click—or tap—the **Company** placeholder—*[Company Name]*—to select it, and then compare your screen with Figure 4.

   Templates often contain ***placeholders***— reserved, formatted spaces into which you enter your own text or objects. If no text is entered, the placeholder text will not print.

7. With the **Company** placeholder selected, type Aspen Falls City Hall

8. Leave the memo open for the next skill.

■ **You have completed Skill 2 of 10**

▶ To *edit* is to insert, delete, or replace text in an Office document, workbook, or presentation.

▶ To edit text, you need to position the *insertion point*—a flashing vertical line that indicates where text will be inserted—at the desired location, or select the text you want to replace.

1. Click the first **Name** placeholder—*[Recipient Name]*—and then type Janet Neal

2. Click the second **Name** placeholder—*[Your Name]*—and then type your own first and last name.

3. In the third **Name** placeholder—*[Name]*—type Maria Martinez

4. Click the **Date** placeholder—*[Click to select date]*— and then type the current date.

5. In the **Subject** placeholder, type Sales Tax Revenue Compare your screen with **Figure 1**.

6. Click *[Type memo here]*, and then type the following: As per your request, the Retail Sales slides will be ready by the end of today. I will send them to you so you can insert them into your presentation. Let me know if you have any questions. Compare your screen with **Figure 2**.

As you type, the insertion point moves to the right. To improve clarity, the figures in this book typically will not display the insertion point.

At the right margin, Word determines whether the word you are typing will fit within the established margin. If it does not fit, Word moves the entire word to the beginning of the next line. This feature is called *word wrap*. Within a paragraph, you do not need to press Enter to create new lines.

■ **Continue to the next page to complete the skill** ➤

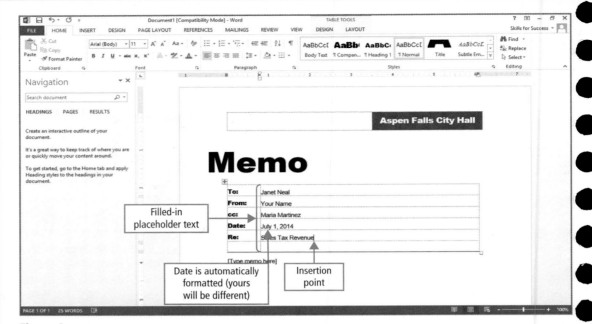

Figure 1

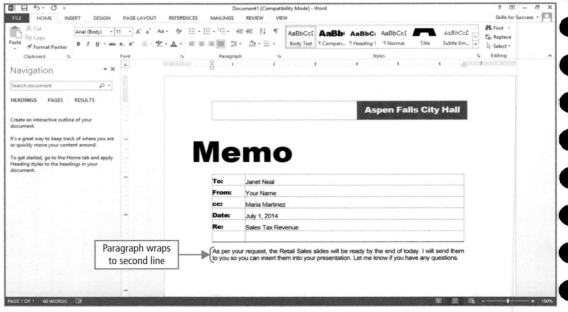

Figure 2

Mini toolbar

Selected text

Figure 3

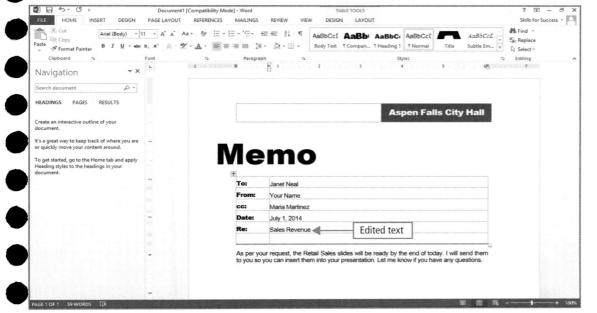

Edited text

Figure 4

7. In the **Re:** line, click to the left of *Sales* to place the insertion point at the beginning of the word. Press ⌨Delete six times to delete the word *Sales* and the space that follows it.

   The Delete key deletes one letter at a time moving from left to right. The name on your keyboard may vary—for example, DEL, Del, or Delete.

8. In the **Re:** line, click to the right of *Revenue* to place the insertion point at the end of the word.

9. Press ⌨Backspace eight times to delete the word *Revenue* and the space that precedes it.

   The Backspace key deletes one letter at a time moving from right to left. The name on your keyboard may vary—for example, BACK, Backspace, or simply a left-facing arrow.

10. In the **Re:** line, double-click—or double-tap—the word *Tax* to select it, and then compare your screen with **Figure 3**.

    To **double-click** is to click the left mouse button two times quickly without moving the mouse. To **double-tap**, tap the screen in the same place two times quickly.

    After selecting text, the **Mini toolbar**—a toolbar with common formatting commands—displays near the selection.

11. Type Sales Revenue to replace the selected word, and then compare your screen with **Figure 4**.

    When a word or paragraph is selected, it is replaced by whatever you type next, and the Mini toolbar no longer displays.

■ **You have completed Skill 3 of 10**

▶ New documents are stored in **RAM**—the computer's temporary memory—until you save them to more permanent storage such as your hard drive, USB flash drive, or online storage.

1. If you are saving your work on a USB flash drive, insert the drive into the computer. If a notice to choose what happens with removable drives displays, ignore it.

   This book assumes that your work will be saved to SkyDrive or a USB flash drive. If you are saving your work to a different location, you will need to adapt these steps as necessary.

2. On the Word **Quick Access Toolbar**, click the **Save** button 🔲, and then compare your screen with **Figure 1**.

   The Save As page is used to select the location where you want to save your work. You can choose to save to your SkyDrive or other locations on your computer. If you have favorite folders in which you like to save your files, you can add them to the Save As page so that you can then select them with a single click.

3. Under **Recent Folders**, click the location where you are saving your work. If your location is not displayed, click the **Browse** button, and then in the Save As dialog box, navigate to your location.

4. On the **Save As** dialog box toolbar, click the **New folder** button, and then type Common Features Chapter 1 Compare your screen with **Figure 2**.

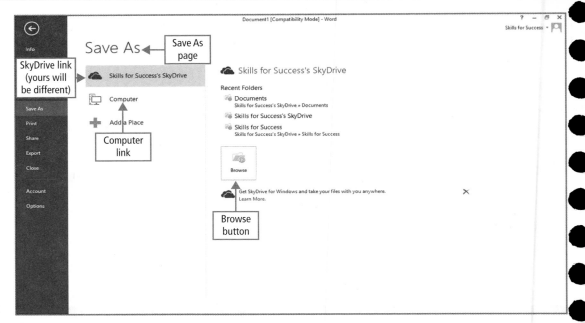

Figure 1

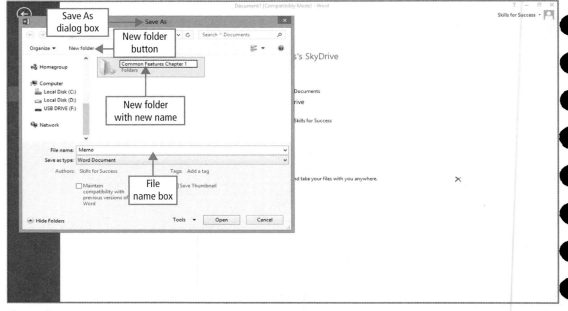

Figure 2

■ **Continue to the next page to complete the skill**

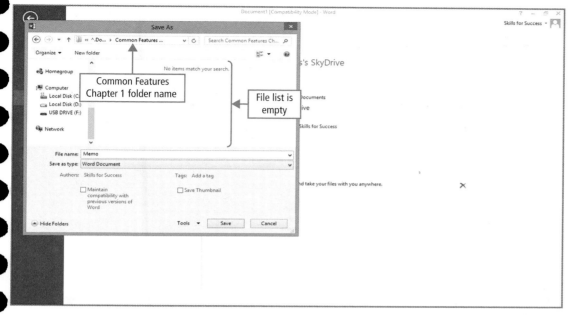

Figure 3

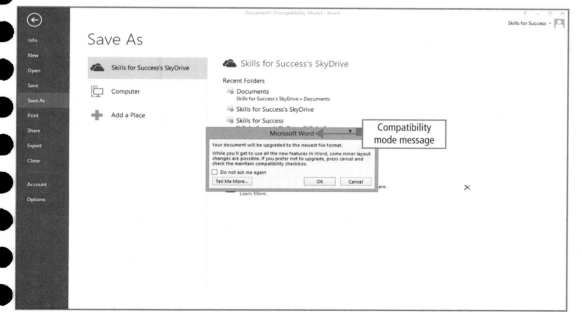

Figure 4

5. Press Enter to accept the folder name, and then press Enter again to open the new folder as shown in Figure 3.

> Before saving a new file, you should open the folder in which you want to store the file.

6. In the **Save As** dialog box, click in the **File name** box one time to highlight all of the existing text.

7. With the text in the **File name** box still highlighted, using your own name, type Last_First_cf01_RetailMemo

> In this book, you should substitute your first and last name whenever you see the text *Last_First* or *Your Name*.

8. Click **Save**, and then compare your screen with Figure 4.

> A message may display to inform you that the document will convert to the latest file format for Word documents.

9. Read the displayed message, and then click **OK**.

> After the document is saved, the name of the file displays on the title bar at the top of the window and the text *[Compatibility Mode]* no longer displays.

10. Leave the memo open for the next skill.

■ **You have completed Skill 4 of 10**

▶ To **format** is to change the appearance of the text—for example, changing the text color to red.

▶ Before formatting an Office document, it is a good idea to pick a **theme**—a pre-built set of unified formatting choices including colors and fonts.

1. Click the **Design tab**. In the **Themes group**, click the **Themes** button, and then compare your screen with **Figure 1**.

   Each theme displays as a thumbnail in a **gallery**—a visual display of selections from which you can choose.

2. In the **Themes** gallery, point to—but do not click—each thumbnail to preview its formatting with **Live Preview**—a feature that displays what the results of a formatting change will be if you select it.

3. In the **Themes** gallery, click the third theme in the second row—**Retrospect**.

   A **font** is a set of characters with the same design and shape. Each theme has two font categories—one for headings and one for body text.

4. Click anywhere in the text *Aspen Falls City Hall* to make it the active paragraph. With the insertion point in the paragraph, click the **Home tab**.

5. In the **Paragraph group**, click the **Shading arrow** 🖌▾. In the first row of the gallery under **Theme Colors**, click the sixth choice—**Orange, Accent 2**. Compare your screen with **Figure 2**.

   In all themes, the Accent 2 color is the sixth choice in the color gallery, but the color varies depending on the theme. Here, the Retrospect theme Accent 2 color is a shade of orange.

■ **Continue to the next page to complete the skill**

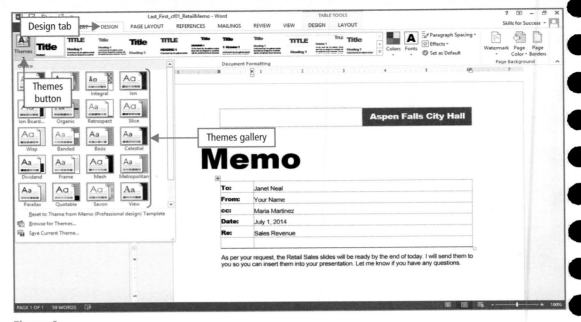

Figure 1

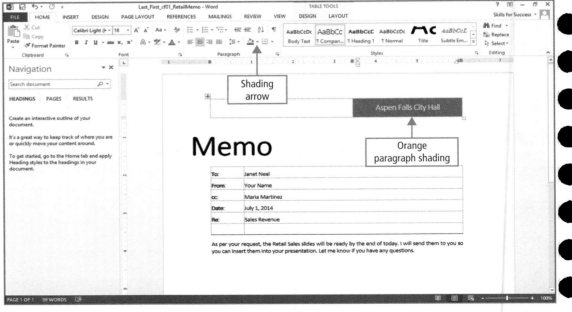

Figure 2

Figure 3

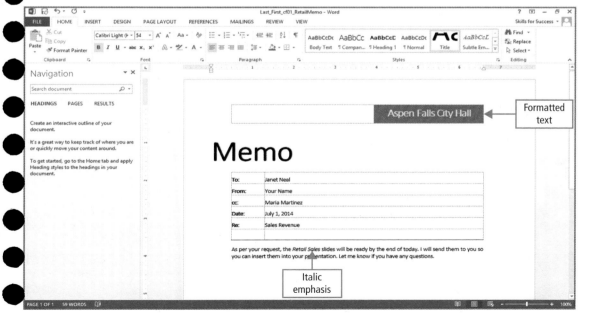

Figure 4

6. In the upper-right corner, ***drag***—press and hold the left mouse button while moving the mouse—to select the text *Aspen Falls City Hall,* and then compare your screen with **Figure 3**. To select by dragging with a touch display, tap in the text, and then drag the selection handle.

    Before formatting text, the text must be selected. If the Mini toolbar does not display, you can right-click or tap the selected text.

7. On the Mini toolbar, click the **Font Size arrow** 11, and then from the list, click **20** to increase the size of the selected text. On the Mini toolbar, click the **Bold** button B.

8. On the Mini toolbar, click the **Font Color arrow** A, and then under **Theme colors**, click the fifth color in the second row—**Orange**, **Accent 1**, **Lighter 80%**. Alternately, on the Home tab, in the Font group, click the **Font Color arrow** A.

9. In the paragraph that begins *As per your*, drag to select the text *Retail Sales*. From the Mini toolbar, click the **Italic** button I.

    Alternately, you can use a ***keyboard shortcut***—a combination of keys that performs a command. Here, you could press Ctrl + I.

10. Click a blank area of the document, and then compare your screen with **Figure 4**. Carefully check the memo for spelling errors. If spelling errors are found, use the techniques practiced previously to correct them.

11. Click the **Save** button.

■ **You have completed Skill 5 of 10**

▶ Before printing, it is a good idea to preview the document on the Print page.

▶ On the Print page, you can check that blank pages won't be printed by accident.

1. Click the **File tab**, and then compare your screen with **Figure 1**.

    Backstage view is a collection of pages on the File tab used to open, save, print, and perform other file management tasks. In Backstage view, you can return to the open document by clicking the Back button.

2. On the **File tab**, click **Print** to display the Print page. Click the **Printer** menu, and then compare your screen with **Figure 2**.

    The Printer list displays available printers for your computer along with their status. For example, a printer may be offline because it is not turned on. The ***default printer*** is indicated by a check mark, and is automatically selected when you do not choose a different printer.

    In a school lab or office, it is a good idea to check the list of available printers and verify that the correct printer is selected. It is also important that you know where the printer is located so that you can retrieve your printout.

3. Press ⎄Esc⎦—located in the upper-left corner of most keyboards—to close the Printer menu without selecting a different printer.

Figure 1

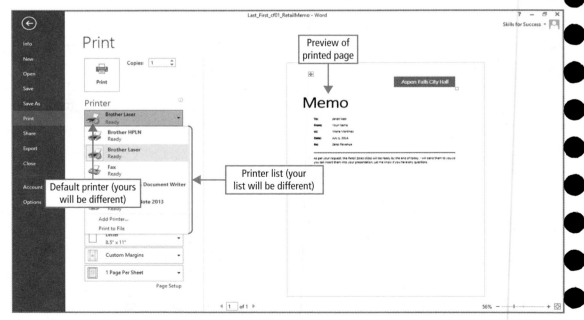

Figure 2

■ **Continue to the next page to complete the skill**

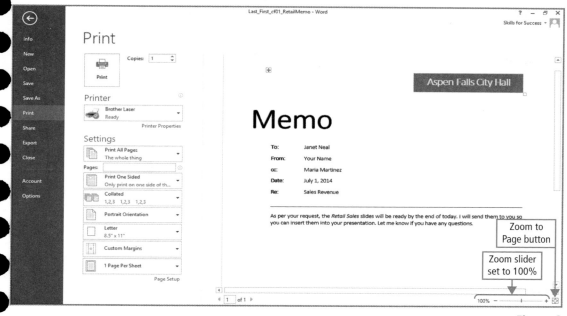

Figure 3

Common Touch Screen Gestures	
Gesture	**Description**
Tap	Touch one time with the finger.
Slide	Touch an object and then move the finger across the screen.
Swipe	Slide in from a screen edge to display app commands, charms, or other temporary areas.
Pinch	Slide two fingers closer together to shrink or zoom in.
Stretch	Slide two fingers apart to enlarge or zoom out.

Figure 4

4. In the lower-right corner of the **Print** page, click the **Zoom In** button until the zoom level displays **100%**. Compare your screen with **Figure 3**.

   The size of the print preview depends on the size of your monitor. When previewed on smaller monitors, some documents may not display accurately. If this happens, you can zoom in to see a more accurate view.

5. To the right of the **Zoom** slider, click the **Zoom to Page** button to return to your original zoom level.

   If you are working at a touch display, you can zoom in and out using gestures. The gestures are summarized in the table in **Figure 4**.

6. If you are printing your work for this project, note the location of the selected printer, click the **Print** button, and then retrieve your printouts from the printer.

   You should print your work only if your instructor has asked you to do so. Many instructors prefer to grade electronic versions that have been sent as e-mail attachments, copied to a network drive, or uploaded to a learning management system such as Blackboard.

7. In the upper-right corner of the window, click the **Close** button.

   If you have made changes to a document without saving them, you will be prompted to save those changes when you close the document.

■ **You have completed Skill 6 of 10**

▶ In this book, you will frequently open student data files.

1. Before beginning this skill, the student files folder for this chapter should be downloaded and unzipped or copied similar to the one described in Figure 1. Follow the instructions in the book or provided by your instructor.

2. On the taskbar, click the **Excel** button to return to the Excel 2013 Start screen. If necessary, start Excel.

3. On the **Excel 2013** Start screen, click **Open Other Workbooks** to display the Open page. If you already had a blank workbook open, click the File tab instead.

4. On the **Open** page, click **Computer**, and then click the **Browse** button.

5. In the **Open** dialog box Navigation pane, navigate to the student files for this chapter, and then compare your screen with Figure 2.

6. In the **Open** dialog box, select **cf01_ RetailChart**, and then click the **Open** button.

7. If the Protected View message displays, click the **Enable Editing** button.

> Documents downloaded from a website typically open in ***Protected View***—a view applied to documents downloaded from the Internet that allows you to decide if the content is safe before working with the document.

8. Click the **File tab**, and then click **Save As**. On the **Save As** page, click the location where you created your chapter folder, and then navigate as needed to open the **Common Features Chapter 1**. If necessary, click Browse and then navigate in the Save As dialog box.

■ **Continue to the next page to complete the skill**

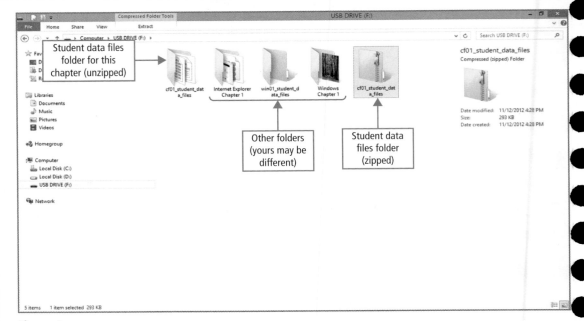

Figure 1

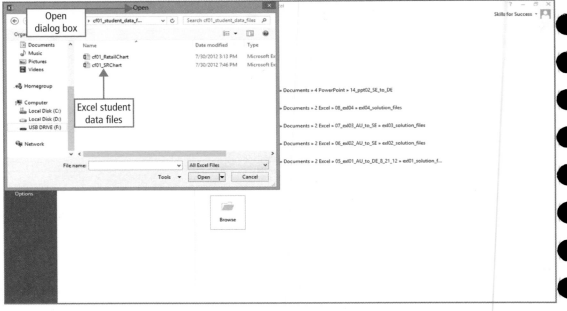

Figure 2

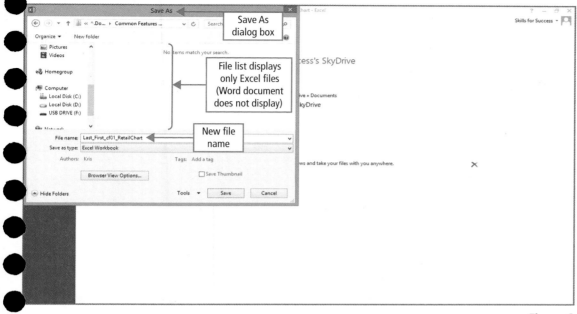

Figure 3

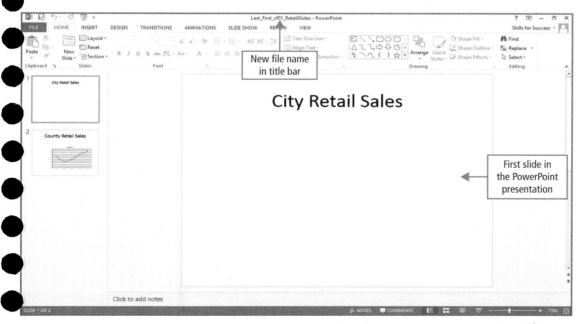

Figure 4

9. In the **File Name** box, change the existing text to Last_First_cf01_RetailChart using your own name.

10. Compare your screen with **Figure 3**, and then click the **Save** button.

   In this manner, you can use the Save As command to create a copy of a file with a new name. The original student data file will remain unchanged.

   By default, the Save As dialog box displays only those files saved in the current application file format. Here, the Excel file is listed, but the Word file you saved previously may not display.

11. On the taskbar, click the **PowerPoint** button 📷 to return to the PowerPoint Start screen. If necessary, start PowerPoint.

12. On the **PowerPoint 2013** Start screen, click **Open Other Presentations** to display the Open page. If you already had a blank presentation open, click the File tab instead.

13. On the **Open** page, click **Computer**, and then click the **Browse** button. In the **Open** dialog box, navigate to the student files for this chapter, and then open **cf01_RetailSlides**. If necessary, enable the content.

14. On the **File tab**, click **Save As**, and then use the Save As page to navigate as needed to open your **Common Features Chapter 1** folder in the Save As dialog box.

   On most computers, your Word and Excel files will not display because the PowerPoint Save As dialog box is set to display only presentation files.

15. Name the file Last_First_cf01_RetailSlides and then click **Save**. Compare your screen with **Figure 4**.

■ **You have completed Skill 7 of 10**

▶ To keep formatting consistent across all of your Office documents, the same themes are available in Word, Excel, PowerPoint, and Access.

▶ To format text in Excel, you typically select the cell that holds the text and then click the desired formatting command.

1. On the taskbar, click the **Excel** button to return to the workbook.

2. Click cell **B9**—the intersection of column **B** and row **9**—to select the cell. Compare your screen with Figure 1.

    A selected cell is indicated by a thick, dark-green border.

3. With cell **B9** selected, type 4.37 and then press Enter to accept the change and update the chart.

    The chart is based on the data in columns A and B. When the data is changed, the chart changes to reflect the new values.

4. On the **Page Layout tab**, in the **Themes group**, click the **Themes** button, and then click the **Restrospect** thumbnail. Compare your screen with Figure 2.

    The Retrospect theme applies the same colors, fonts, and effects as the Retrospect theme in other Office applications. Here, the font was changed to Calibri.

5. At the top of the worksheet, right-click the title *Aspen Falls* to display the Mini toolbar. Click the **Font Size arrow** [11 ▾], and then click **14** to increase the font size.

■ **Continue to the next page to complete the skill**

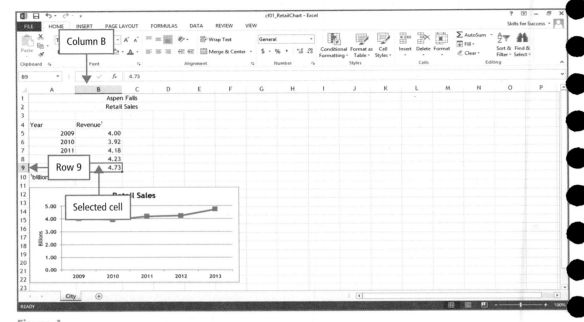

Figure 1

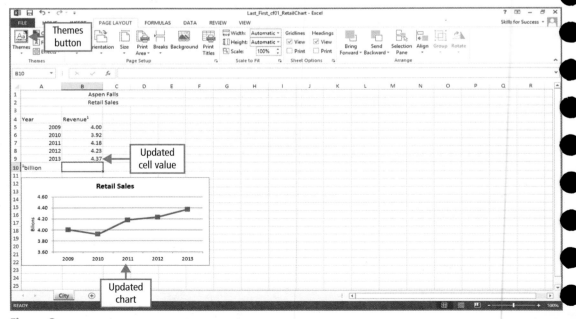

Figure 2

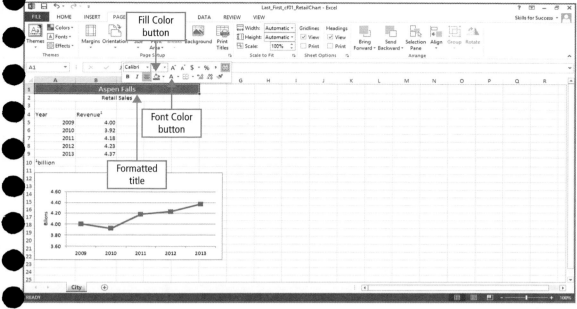

Figure 3

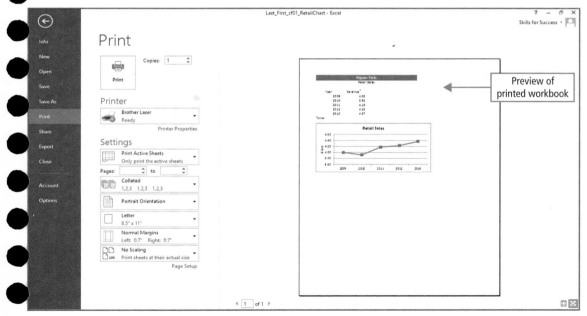

Figure 4

6. With the title cell still selected, on the Mini toolbar, click the **Fill Color arrow** , and then under **Theme Colors**, click the sixth choice—**Orange, Accent 2**.

7. In the **Font group**, click the **Font Color arrow** , and then under **Theme Colors**, click the first choice—**White, Background 1**. Compare your screen with **Figure 3**.

8. Click cell **A4**. On the **Home tab**, in the **Alignment group**, click the **Center** button ≡ to center the text. Repeat to center the text in cell **B4**.

9. Click cell **A10**, and then in the **Font group**, change the **Font Size** to **9**.

10. On the **File tab**, click **Print**, and then compare your screen with **Figure 4**.

   The Excel Print page is used in the same manner as the Word Print page. Here, you can preview the document, select your printer, and verify that the worksheet will print on a single page. By default, the gridlines do not print.

11. If you are printing your work for this project, print the worksheet. Otherwise, click the **Back** button ⊙ to return to Normal view.

12. On the **Quick Access Toolbar**, click **Save** 🖫.

■ **You have completed Skill 8 of 10**

▶ In Office, the **copy** command places a copy of the selected text or object in the **Office Clipboard**—a temporary storage area that holds text or an object that has been cut or copied.

▶ The **paste** command inserts a copy of the text or object from the Office Clipboard.

1. In the Excel window, click the chart's border to select the chart, and compare your screen with **Figure 1**.

   In Office, certain graphics such as charts and SmartArt display a thick border when they are selected.

2. On the **Home tab**, in the **Clipboard group**, click the **Copy** button 🗐 to place a copy of the chart into the Office Clipboard.

3. On the taskbar, click the **PowerPoint** button 🗐 to return to **Last_First_cf01_RetailSlides**, which you saved previously.

4. With **Slide 1** as the active slide, on the **Home tab**, in the **Clipboard group**, click the **Paste** button to insert the copied Excel chart. If you accidentally clicked the Paste arrow to display the Paste Options, click the Paste button that is above it. Compare your screen with **Figure 2**.

5. Click the **Design tab**, and then in the **Themes group**, click the **More** button ▼. Point to several thumbnails to preview their formatting, and then under **Office**, click the seventh choice—**Retrospect**.

   In PowerPoint, themes are sets of colors, fonts, and effects optimized for viewing in a large room with the presentation projected onto a screen in front of the audience.

■ **Continue to the next page to complete the skill** ⮞

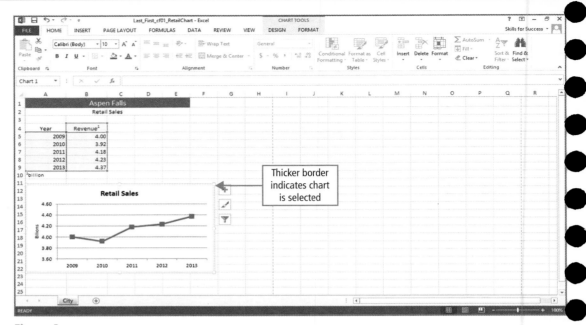

Figure 1

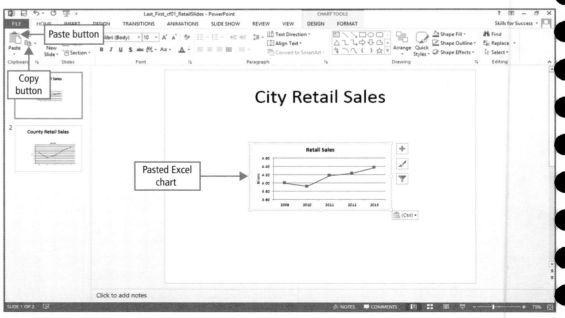

Figure 2

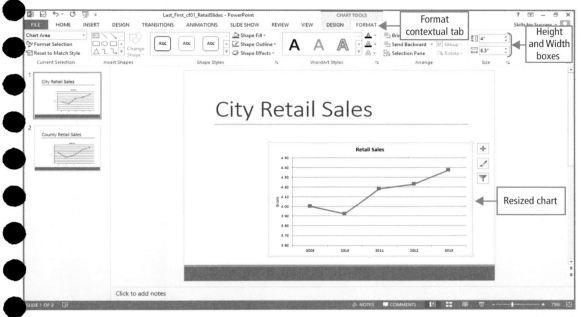

Figure 3

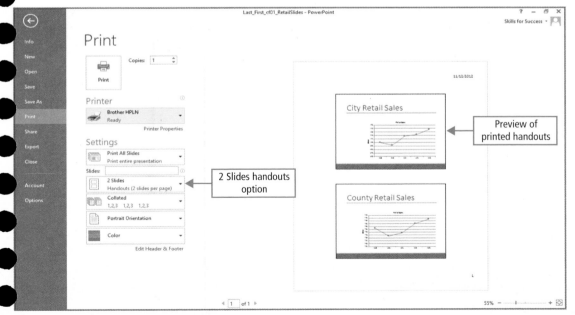

Figure 4

6. Drag through the slide title text *City Retail Sales* to select it. On the **Home tab**, in the **Font group**, click the **Font Size arrow**, and then click **60**. Alternately, right-click the selected text, and then use the Mini toolbar to change the font size.

7. Click any area in the chart, and then click the chart's border so that only the chart is selected.

8. Click the **Format tab**, and then in the **Size group**, click the **Height** spin box up arrow until the value is **4"**. Repeat this technique to change the **Width** value to **6.5"**, and then compare your screen with **Figure 3**.

> The Format tab is a *contextual tab*—a tab that displays on the Ribbon only when a related object such as a graphic or chart is selected.

9. On the **File tab**, click **Print**. On the **Print** page, under **Settings**, click the button with the text *Full Page Slides*. In the gallery that displays, under **Handouts**, click **2 Slides**. Compare your screen with **Figure 4**.

10. If you are printing your work, click **Print** to print the handout. Otherwise, click the **Back** button to return to Normal view.

11. Click **Save**, and then **Close** the presentation window.

12. On the taskbar, click the **Excel** button to make it the active window, and then **Close** the window. If a message displays asking you to save changes, click Save.

■ **You have completed Skill 9 of 10**

▶ CF 1-10
VIDEO

▶ Access reports present data in a way that is optimized for printing.

1. Start **Access 2013**, and then on the Start screen, click **Open Other Files**. On the **Open** page, click **Computer**, and then click **Browse**.

2. In the **Open** dialog box, navigate to the location where you are storing your student data files for this chapter. In the **Open** dialog box, select **cf01_RetailData**, and then click the **Open** button.

3. Take a few moments to familiarize yourself with the Access Window objects as described in Figure 1.

   Database files contain several different types of objects such as tables, queries, forms, and reports. Each object has a special purpose summarized in the table in Figure 2.

4. On the **File tab**, click **Save As**. With **Save Database As** selected, click the **Save As** button.

5. In the **Save As** dialog box, navigate to your **Common Features Chapter 1** folder. In the **File name** box, name the file Last_First_cf01_RetailData and then click **Save**. If a security message displays, click the Enable Content button.

   Malicious persons sometimes place objects in database files that could harm your computer. For this reason, the security message may display when you open a database that you did not create. You should click the Enable Content button only when you know the file is from a trusted source.

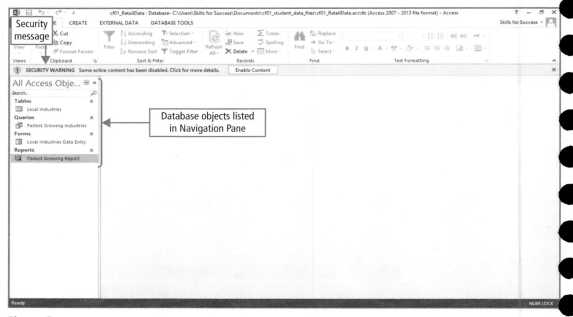

Figure 1

Common Database Objects

Object	Description
Table	Stores the database data so that records are in rows and fields are in columns.
Query	Displays a subset of data in response to a question.
Form	Used to find, update, and add table records.
Report	Presents tables or query results optimized for onscreen viewing or printing.

Figure 2

■ **Continue to the next page to complete the skill** ➤

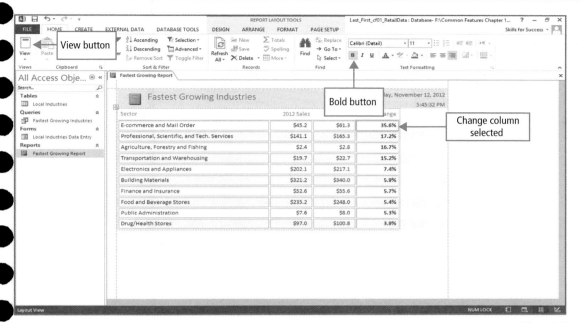

Figure 3

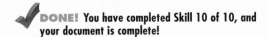

Figure 4

6. In the **Navigation pane**, under **Reports**, double-click **Fastest Growing Report**.

7. On the **Home tab**, in the **Views group**, click the **View** button one time to switch to Layout view.

8. On the **Design tab**, in the **Themes group**, click **Themes**, and then click the seventh thumbnail—**Retrospect**.

9. Near the top of the **Change** column, click the first value—*35.6%*—to select all the values in the column.

10. Click the **Home tab**, and then in the **Text Formatting group**, click the **Bold** button B. Compare your screen with **Figure 3**.

11. On the **Home tab**, click the **View arrow**, and then click **Print Preview**. Compare your screen with **Figure 4**. If necessary, in the Zoom group, click the One Page button to zoom to 100%.

12. If your instructor asked you to print your work, click the Print button and then print the report.

13. Click **Save** to save the formatting changes, and then **Close** the report.

Objects such as reports are opened and closed without closing the Access application itself.

14. **Close** the Access window, and then submit your printouts or files for this chapter as directed by your instructor.

✔ DONE! You have completed Skill 10 of 10, and your document is complete!

The following More Skills are located at **www.pearsonhighered.com/skills**

More Skills ⓫ Store Office Files on SkyDrive

You can sign in to your Microsoft account from Word, Excel, or PowerPoint, and then open and save files from online storage services such as SkyDrive. Storing files on SkyDrive enables you to access your files from any computer connected to the Internet. After signing in to your account, you can open and save files stored on SkyDrive using the same techniques used for files stored on local computer drives.

In More Skills 11, you will create a Microsoft account if you don't already have one. You will sign in to that account, connect your Office program to SkyDrive, and then save a Word, Excel, and PowerPoint file to SkyDrive. You will document your work by creating a snip of your SkyDrive folder.

To begin, open your web browser, navigate to www.pearsonhighered.com/skills, locate the name of your textbook, and then follow the instructions on the website.

More Skills ⓬ Use Office Help

Microsoft Office 2013 has a Help system in which you can search for articles that show you how to accomplish tasks.

In More Skills 12, you will use the Office 2013 Help system to learn how to find out which version of Office you are using. You will then paste a snip of that screen into a Word document.

To begin, open your web browser, navigate to www.pearsonhighered.com/skills, locate the name of your textbook, and then follow the instructions on the website.

More Skills ⓭ Send Files as E-mail Attachments

You can send a document, workbook, or presentation as a file attached to an e-mail message. On the Save & Send page, you can attach the file in its native format or change it to a format that can be opened in a different program. To complete this skill, you need to have a mail program such as Outlook installed and configured to send mail using your e-mail account.

In More Skills 13, you will send a Word document as an e-mail attachment. You will document your work by creating a snip, and then either send the e-mail message and attachment or cancel without sending.

To begin, open your web browser, navigate to www.pearsonhighered.com/skills, locate the name of your textbook, and then follow the instructions on the website.

More Skills ⓮ Optimize Office 2013 RT

Office 2013 RT is a version of Office designed for phones and tablets. Instead of the mouse and keyboard, you can use gestures and the Touch Keyboard to perform tasks.

In More Skills 14, you will work with Excel Office RT. You will switch between Full Screen and Standard views, use gestures instead of the mouse, and type via an onscreen keyboard.

To begin, open your Internet browser, navigate to www.pearsonhighered.com/skills, locate the name of your textbook, and then follow the instructions on the website.

Please note that there are no additional projects to accompany the More Skills Projects, and they are not covered in the End-of-Chapter projects.

The following table summarizes the **SKILLS AND PROCEDURES** covered in this chapter.

Skills Number	Task	Step	Icon	Keyboard Shortcut
1	Start Office applications	Display Start menu or screen, and then type application name		⊞
2	Open a template	Start the application; or if already started: File tab → New		
4	Create a new folder while saving	Save As dialog box toolbar → New folder		
4	Save	Quick Access toolbar → Save	🖫	Ctrl + S
5	Change a font	Home tab → Font group → Font arrow	Calibri (Body) ▾	Ctrl + Shift + F
5	Apply italic	Home tab → Font group → Italic	*I*	Ctrl + I
5, 8	Change font color	Home tab → Font group → Font Color arrow	A ▾	
5, 8	Change background color	Home tab → Font group → Fill Color arrow	◇ ▾	
5, 8, 9, 10	Apply a theme	Design tab → Themes		
5, 8, 9, 10	Change font size	Home tab → Font group → Font Size arrow	11 ▾	Ctrl + < Ctrl + >
5, 10	Apply bold	Home tab → Font group → Bold	**B**	Ctrl + B
6, 7, 9, 10	Preview the printed page	File tab → Print		Alt + Ctrl + I
7	Open a file	File tab → Open		Ctrl + O
7, 9, 10	Save a file with new name and location	File tab → Save As		F12
8	Center align text	Home tab → Paragraph group → Center	≡	Ctrl + E
9	Copy	Select text or object → Home tab → Clipboard group → Copy	📋	Ctrl + C
9	Paste	Home tab → Clipboard group → Paste	📋	Ctrl + V

Key Terms

Matching

Match each term in the second column with its correct definition in the first column by writing the letter of the term on the blank line in front of the correct definition.

____ **1.** An individual page in a presentation that can contain text, pictures, or other objects.

____ **2.** A pre-built document into which you insert text using the layout and formatting provided in that document.

____ **3.** A mode applied to documents that limits formatting and features to ones that are supported in earlier versions of Office.

____ **4.** To insert, delete, or replace text in an Office document, workbook, or presentation.

____ **5.** A pre-built set of unified formatting choices including colors, fonts, and effects.

____ **6.** To change the appearance of text.

____ **7.** A set of characters with the same design and shape.

____ **8.** A feature that displays the result of a formatting change if you select it.

____ **9.** A view applied to documents downloaded from the Internet that allows you to decide if the content is safe before working with the document.

____ **10.** A command that moves a copy of the selected text or object to the Office clipboard.

A Compatibility
B Copy
C Edit
D Font
E Format
F Live Preview
G Protected
H Slide
I Template
J Theme

Multiple Choice (MyITLab®)

Choose the correct answer.

1. The flashing vertical line that indicates where text will be inserted when you start typing.
   A. Cell reference
   B. Insertion point
   C. KeyTip

2. A reserved, formatted space into which you enter your own text or object.
   A. Gallery
   B. Placeholder
   C. Title

3. Until you save a document, the document is stored here.
   A. Office Clipboard
   B. Live Preview
   C. RAM

4. A collection of pages on the File tab used to open, save, print, and perform other file management tasks.
   A. Backstage view
   B. Page Layout view
   C. File gallery

5. A temporary storage area that holds text or an object that has been cut or copied.
   A. Office Clipboard
   B. Dialog box
   C. Live Preview

6. A toolbar with common formatting buttons that displays after you select text.
   A. Gallery toolbar
   B. Mini toolbar
   C. Taskbar toolbar

7. A command that inserts a copy of the text or object from the Office Clipboard.
   A. Copy
   B. Insert
   C. Paste

8. A visual display of choices—typically thumbnails—from which you can choose.
   A. Gallery
   B. Options menu
   C. Shortcut menu

9. A tab that displays on the Ribbon only when a related object such as a graphic or chart is selected.
   A. Contextual tab
   B. File tab
   C. Page Layout tab

10. A database object that presents tables or query results in a way that is optimized for onscreen viewing or printing.
    A. Form
    B. Report
    C. Table

Topics for Discussion

1. You have briefly worked with four Microsoft Office programs: Word, Excel, PowerPoint, and Access. Based on your experience, describe the overall purpose of each program.

2. Many believe that computers enable offices to go paperless—that is, to share files electronically instead of printing and then distributing them. What are the advantages of sharing files electronically, and in what situations is it best to print documents?

Skills Review

MyITLab®
Grader

To complete this project, you will need the following files:

- cf01_SRData (Access)
- cf01_SRChart (Excel)
- cf01_SRSlide (PowerPoint)

You will save your files as:

- Last_First_cf01_SRData (Access)
- Last_First_cf01_SRChart (Excel)
- Last_First_cf01_SRSlide (PowerPoint)
- Last_First_cf01_SRMemo (Word)

1. Start **Access 2013**, and then click **Open Other Files**. Click **Computer**, and then click **Browse**. In the **Open** dialog box, navigate to the student data files for this chapter, click **cf01_SRData**, and then click **Open**.

2. On the **File tab**, click **Save As**, and then click the **Save As** button. In the **Save As** dialog box, navigate to your chapter folder. Name the file Last_First_cf01_SRData, and then click **Save**. If necessary, enable the content.

3. In the **Navigation** pane, double-click **Budget Report**, and then click the **View** button to switch to Layout view. On the **Design tab**, click **Themes**, and then click **Retrospect**.

4. Click the **View arrow**, click **Print Preview**, and then compare your screen with **Figure 1**. If you are printing this project, print the report.

5. Click **Save**, **Close** the report, and then **Close** Access.

6. Start **Excel 2013**, and then click **Open Other Workbooks**. Use the **Open** page to locate and open the student data file **cf01_SRChart**.

7. On the **File tab**, click **Save As**. Click **Browse**, and then navigate to your chapter folder. Name the file Last_First_cf01_SRChart and then click **Save**.

8. With the worksheet title selected, on the **Home tab**, in the **Font group**, click the **Font Size arrow**, and then click **24**.

9. Click cell **B7**, type 84.3 Press ⏎ Enter , and then click **Save**.

10. Click the border of the chart, and then compare your screen with **Figure 2**.

Figure 1

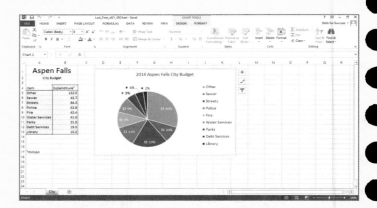

Figure 2

■ **Continue to the next page to complete this Skills Review** ➤

11. On the **Home tab**, in the **Clipboard group**, click the **Copy** button.

12. Close the **Excel** window, and then start **PowerPoint 2013**. Click **Open Other Presentations**, and then open the student data file **cf01_SRSlide**.

13. On the **File tab**, click **Save As**. Click **Browse**, and then navigate to your chapter folder. Name the file Last_First_cf01_SRSlide and then click **Save**.

14. On the **Home tab**, in the **Clipboard group**, click **Paste** to insert the chart.

15. On the **Design tab**, in the **Themes group**, click the seventh choice—**Retrospect**. Compare your screen with Figure 3.

16. If you are printing this project, on the File tab, click Print, change the Settings to Handouts, 1 Slide, and then print the handout.

17. Click **Save**, and then **Close** PowerPoint.

18. Start **Word 2013**. On the Start screen, in the **Search for online templates** box, type memo and then click the **Start searching** button. Locate the **Memo (Elegant design)**, click its thumbnail, and then click the **Create** button to open it.

19. Click *[RECIPIENT NAME]*, and then type Janet Neal

20. Change *[YOUR NAME]* to your own name, and then change *[SUBJECT]* to City Budget

21. Change *[CLICK TO SELECT DATE]* to the current date, and then change *[NAME]* to Maria Martinez

22. Change *[Type your memo text here]* to the following: I am pleased to tell you that the city budget items that you requested are ready. I will send you the Access report and PowerPoint slide today.

23. Click to the left of *INTEROFFICE* and then press Delete several times to delete the word and the space following it.

24. On the **Design tab**, click the **Themes** button, and then click **Retrospect**.

25. Double-click the word *MEMORANDUM* to select it. On the Mini toolbar, click the **Font Color arrow**, and then click the fifth color—**Orange, Accent 1**.

26. With *MEMORANDUM* still selected, on the Mini toolbar, click the **Bold** button one time to remove the bold formatting from the selection, and then change the **Font Size** to **24**.

27. Click **Save**, click **Browse**, and then navigate to your chapter folder. Name the file Last_First_cf01_SRMemo and then click **Save**. In the compatibility message, click **OK**. Click a blank area of the document, and then compare your screen with Figure 4.

28. If you are printing your work, print the memo.

Figure 3

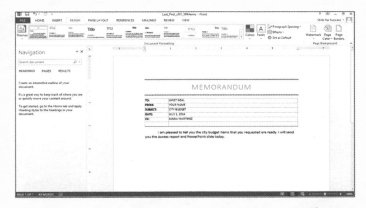

Figure 4

29. Click **Save**, and then **Close** the memo. Submit your printouts or files as directed by your instructor.

 **DONE! You have completed this Skills Review**

Create Workbooks with Excel 2013

▶ Microsoft Office Excel 2013 is used worldwide to create workbooks and to analyze data that is organized into columns and rows.

▶ After data is entered into Excel, you can perform calculations on the numerical data and analyze the data to make informed decisions.

▶ When you make changes to one or more number values, you can immediately see the effect of those changes in totals and charts that rely on those values.

▶ An Excel workbook can contain a large amount of data—up to 16,384 columns and 1,048,576 rows.

▶ The basic skills you need to work efficiently with Excel include entering and formatting data and navigating within Excel.

▶ When planning your worksheet, think about what information will form the rows and what information will form the columns. Generally, rows are used to list the items and columns to group or describe the items in the list.

© Elenathewise / Fotolia

Aspen Falls Outdoor Recreation

In this chapter, you will create a workbook for Amado Pettinelli, the Outdoor Recreation Supervisor. Mr. Pettinelli wants to know the attendance at each city attraction and the revenue each venue generates for the city. He plans to recommend to the Aspen Falls City Council that the busiest attractions receive more city funding in the next fiscal year.

A business spreadsheet can be used for many purposes including tracking budgets, manufacture measurements, or employees. The spreadsheet data can be manipulated using arithmetic and mathematical formulas commonly used in the modern-day business world. If you are asked to create a spreadsheet, you need to know if the results of the data manipulation will be presented in numerical or in graphical format.

In this project, you will create a new Excel workbook and enter data which displays the total number of visitors at the various city attractions in Aspen Falls. You will format the data, construct formulas, and insert functions. You will calculate the percent of weekday visitors at each of the locations and insert a footer. Finally, you will check the spelling in the workbook.

Time to complete all 10 skills – 60 to 90 minutes

Student data file needed for this chapter:

Blank Excel workbook

You will save your workbook as:

Last_First_exl01_Visitors

Outcome

Using the skills in this chapter, you will be able to work with Excel worksheets like this:

Aspen Falls Outdoor Recreation						
Visitors to City Attractions						
Location	Weekends	Weekdays	All Visitors	Difference	Entrance Fee	Total Fees
Zoo	3,169	1,739	4,908	1,430	$ 10	$ 49,080
Pool	5,338	3,352	8,690	1,986	$ 10	$ 86,900
Aquarium	9,027	3,868	12,895	5,159	$ 12	$ 154,740
Garden	4,738	2,788	7,526	1,950	$ 4	$ 30,104
Museum	3,876	913	4,789	2,963	$ 11	$ 52,679
Total	26,148	12,660	38,808			$ 373,503
Percent of Weekday Visitors						
Zoo	35.4%					
Pool	38.6%					
Aquarium	30.0%					
Garden	37.0%					
Museum	19.1%					

SKILLS

Skills 1–10 Training

At the end of this chapter you will be able to:

Skill 1 Create and Save Workbooks
Skill 2 Enter Data and Merge and Center Titles
Skill 3 Construct Addition and Subtraction Formulas
Skill 4 Construct Multiplication and Division Formulas
Skill 5 Adjust Column Widths and Apply Cell Styles
Skill 6 Insert the SUM Function
Skill 7 AutoFill Formulas and Data
Skill 8 Format, Edit, and Check Spelling
Skill 9 Insert Footers and Adjust Page Settings
Skill 10 Display Formulas and Print Worksheets

MORE SKILLS

Skill 11 Create Workbooks from Templates
Skill 12 Insert Names into Formulas
Skill 13 Create Templates
Skill 14 Manage Document Properties

▶ An Excel **workbook** is a file that you can use to organize various kinds of related information. A workbook contains **worksheets**, also called **spreadsheets**—the primary documents that you use in Excel to store and work with data.

▶ The worksheet forms a grid of vertical columns and horizontal rows. The small box where one column and one row meet is a cell.

1. Start **Excel 2013**, and then click **Blank workbook**. In the lower right, notice the zoom—magnification level.

   Your zoom level should be 100%, but most figures in this chapter are zoomed to 120%.

2. Verify the cell in the upper left corner is the **active cell**—the cell outlined in green in which data is entered when you begin typing—as shown in Figure 1.

   In a worksheet, columns have alphabetical headings across the top, and rows have numerical headings down the left side. When a cell is active, the headings for the column and row in which the cell is located are shaded. The column letter and row number that identify a cell is the **cell address**, also called the **cell reference**.

3. In cell **A1**, type Aspen Falls Outdoor Recreation and then press Enter to accept the entry.

4. In cell **A2**, type Visitors and then press Enter two times. Compare your screen with Figure 2.

5. In cell **A4**, type Location and press Tab to make the cell to the right—**B4**—active.

■ Continue to the next page to complete the skill

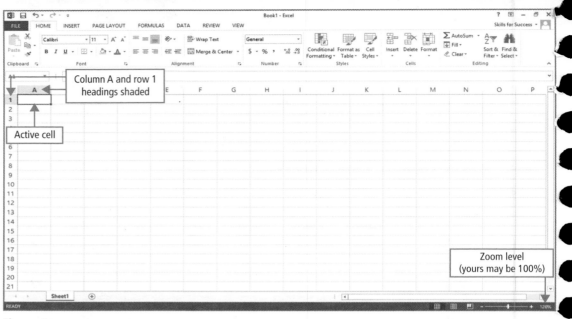

Figure 1

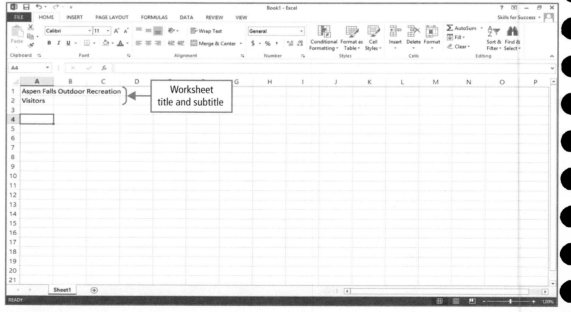

Figure 2

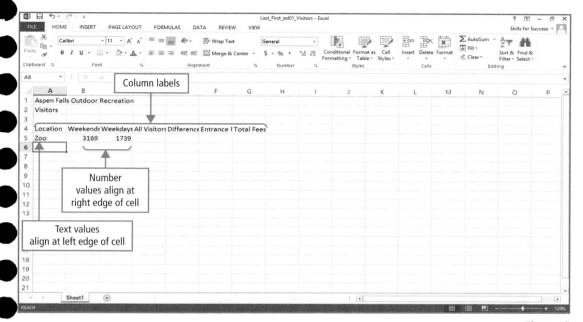

Figure 3

Common Ways to Move or Scroll Through a Worksheet	
Key	**Description**
Enter	Move down one row.
Tab	Move one column to the right.
Shift + Tab	Move one column to the left.
↓ ↑ → ←	Move one cell in the direction of the arrow.
Ctrl + Home	Move to cell A1.
Ctrl + End	Move to the lowest row and the column farthest to the right that contains data.

Figure 4

6. With cell **B4** the active cell, type the following labels, pressing [Tab] between each label:
   Weekends
   Weekdays
   All Visitors
   Difference
   Entrance Fee
   Total Fees

   Labels at the beginning of columns or rows help readers understand the data.

   To correct typing errors, click a cell and retype the data. The new typing will replace the existing data.

7. Click cell **A5**, type Zoo and then press [Tab]. Type 3169 and press [Tab]. Type 1739 and then press [Enter]. Compare your screen with **Figure 3**.

   Data in a cell is called a ***value***. You can have a ***text value***—character data in a cell that labels number values, or a ***number value***—numeric data in a cell. A text value is also referred to as a ***label***. Text values align at the left cell edge, and number values align at the right cell edge.

8. Click **Save** 🔲. On the **Save As** page, click **Computer**, and then click the **Browse** button. In the **Save As** dialog box, navigate to the location where you are saving your files. Click **New folder**, type Excel Chapter 1 and then press [Enter] two times. In the **File name** box, name the workbook Last_First_exl01_Visitors and then press [Enter].

9. Take a few moments to familiarize yourself with common methods to move between cells as summarized in the table in **Figure 4**.

■ **You have completed Skill 1 of 10**

▶ To create an effective worksheet, you enter titles and subtitles and add labels for each row and column of data. It is a good idea to have the worksheet title and subtitle span across all the columns containing data.

----

1. In cell **A6**, type Aquarium and press `Tab`.

2. In cell **B6**, type 9027 and press `Tab`. In cell **C6**, type 3868 and press `Enter`.

3. In row **7** and row **8**, type the following data:

Garden	5738	2877
Museum	3876	913

4. In cell **A9**, type Total and press `Enter`. Compare your screen with **Figure 1**.

5. Click cell **B1**, type Worksheet and press `Enter`. Click cell **A1**, and then compare your screen with **Figure 2**.

> When text is too long to fit in a cell and the cell to the right of it contains data, the text will be ***truncated***—cut off. Here, the text in cell A1 is truncated.

> The ***formula bar***—a bar below the Ribbon that displays the value contained in the active cell and is used to enter or edit values or formulas.

> Data displayed in a cell is the ***displayed value***. Data displayed in the formula bar is the ***underlying value***. Displayed values often do not match their underlying values.

6. On the Quick Access Toolbar, click the **Undo** button ↺ to remove the text in cell **B1**.

> Long text in cells overlaps into other columns only when those cells are empty. Here, A1 text now overlaps B1 because that cell is empty.

■ **Continue to the next page to complete the skill** ▶

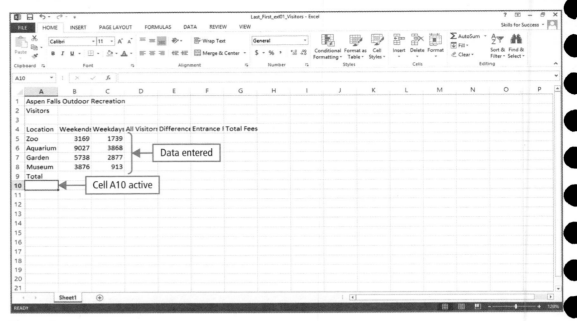

Figure 1

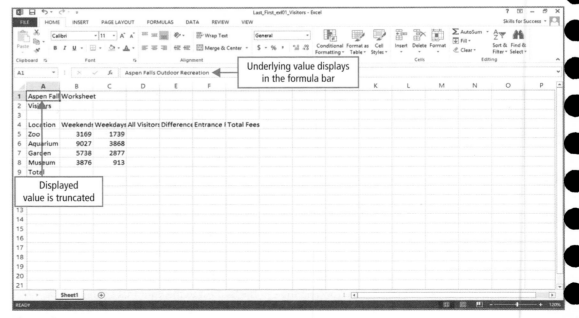

Figure 2

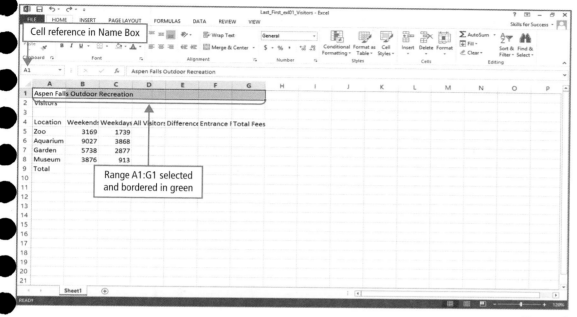

Cell reference in Name Box

Range A1:G1 selected and bordered in green

Figure 3

7. Point to the middle of cell **A1** to display the ✛ pointer. Hold down the left mouse button, and then drag to the right to select cells **A1** through **G1**. Compare your screen with Figure 3. To select a range on a touch screen, tap the cell, and then drag the selection handle.

   The selected range is referred to as *A1:G1* (A1 through G1) A ***range*** is two or more cells in a worksheet that are adjacent (next to each other). A colon (:) between two cell references indicates that the range includes the two cell references and all the cells between them.

   When you select a range, a thick green line surrounds the range, and all but the first cell in the range are shaded. The first cell reference will be displayed in the ***Name Box***—an area by the formula bar that displays the active cell reference.

8. On the **Home tab**, in the **Alignment group**, click the **Merge & Center** button.

   The selected range, A1:G1, merges into one larger cell, and the data is centered in the new cell. The cells in B1 through G1 can no longer be selected individually because they are merged into cell A1.

9. Using the technique just practiced, merge and center the range **A2:G2**.

10. **Save** 🖫 the workbook, and then compare your screen with Figure 4.

■ **You have completed Skill 2 of 10**

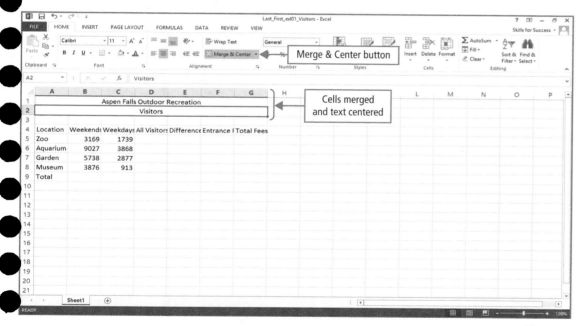

Merge & Center button

Cells merged and text centered

Figure 4

EXL 1-3
VIDEO

▶ A cell's underlying value can be a text value, a number value, or a *formula*—an equation that performs mathematical calculations on number values in the worksheet.

▶ Formulas begin with an equal sign and often include an *arithmetic operator*—a symbol that specifies a mathematical operation such as addition or subtraction.

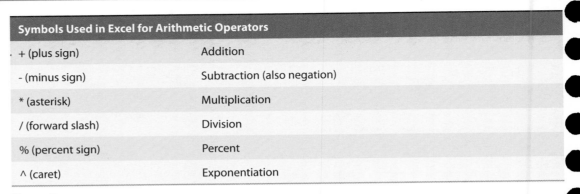

Symbols Used in Excel for Arithmetic Operators	
+ (plus sign)	Addition
- (minus sign)	Subtraction (also negation)
* (asterisk)	Multiplication
/ (forward slash)	Division
% (percent sign)	Percent
^ (caret)	Exponentiation

Figure 1

1. Study the symbols that Excel uses to perform mathematical operations, as summarized in the table in **Figure 1**.

2. In cell **D5**, type =B5+C5 and then press [Enter].

> When you include cell references in formulas, the values in those cells are inserted. Here, the total number of visitors for the Zoo location equals the sum of the values in cells B5 and C5 (3169+ 1739 = 4908).

> When you type a formula, you might see a brief display of function names that match the first letter you type. This Excel feature, called *Formula AutoComplete*, suggests values as you type a function.

3. In cell **D6**, type the formula to add cells **B6** and **C6**, =B6+C6 and then press [Enter].

4. In cell **D7**, type = and then click cell **B7** to automatically insert *B7* into the formula. Compare your screen with **Figure 2**.

> Cell **B7** is surrounded by a moving border indicating that it is part of an active formula.

5. Type + Click cell **C7**, and then press [Enter] to display the result *8615*.

> You can either type formulas or construct them by pointing and clicking in this manner.

■ **Continue to the next page to complete the skill**

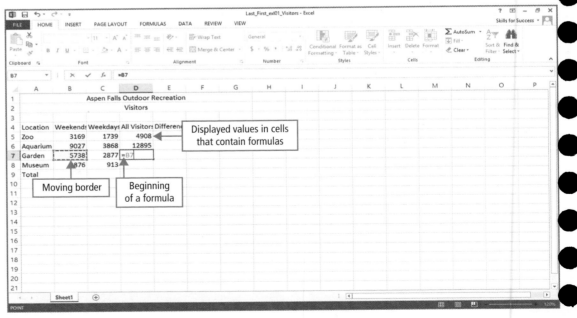

Figure 2

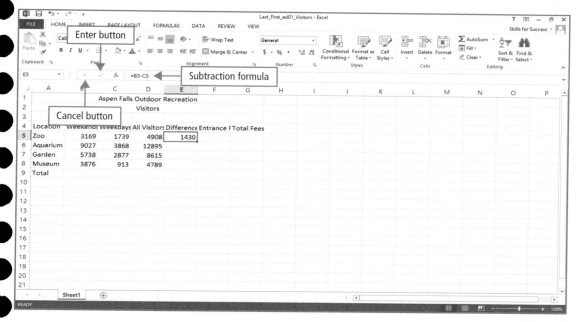

Figure 3

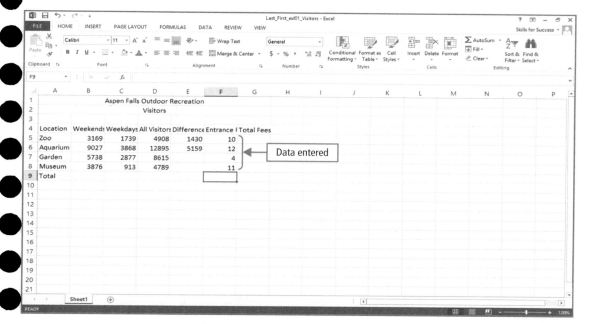

Figure 4

6. In cell **D8**, use point and click to construct a formula that adds cells **B8** and **C8**.

7. In cell **E5**, type =B5-C5 On the formula bar, click the **Enter** button ☑ to confirm the entry while keeping cell *E5* the active cell, and then compare your screen with **Figure 3**.

    Here, the underlying value for cell E5 displays as a formula in the formula bar and the displayed value, *1430*, displays in the cell as a result of the formula.

    If you make an error entering a formula, you can click the Cancel button and then start over. Alternately, you can press the Esc key.

8. In cell **E6**, use point and click to enter the formula =B6-C6 to display the difference for the Aquarium weekend and weekday visitors. (You will complete the column E formulas in Skill 7.)

9. Type the following data using the ↓ to move to the next row, and then compare your screen with **Figure 4**.

Cell	Value
F5	10
F6	12
F7	4
F8	11

10. **Save** 🖫 the workbook.

■ **You have completed Skill 3 of 10**

► **EXL 1-4 VIDEO**

► The four most common operators for addition (+), subtraction (-), multiplication (*), and division (/) can be found on the number keypad at the right side of a standard keyboard, or on the number keys at the top of a keyboard.

1. In cell **G5**, type =D5*F5—the formula that multiplies the total Zoo visitors by its entrance fee. On the formula bar, click the **Enter** button ✓, and then compare your screen with **Figure 1**.

   The *underlying formula*—the formula as displayed in the formula bar—multiplies the value in cell D5 (*4908*)—by the value in cell F5 (*10*) and displays the result in cell G5 (*49080*).

2. In the range **G6:G8**, enter the following formulas:

Cell	Formula
G6	=D6*F6
G7	=D7*F7
G8	=D8*F8

3. In cell **A11**, type Percent of Weekday Visitors and then press Enter. Compare your screen with **Figure 2**.

■ **Continue to the next page to complete the skill** ►

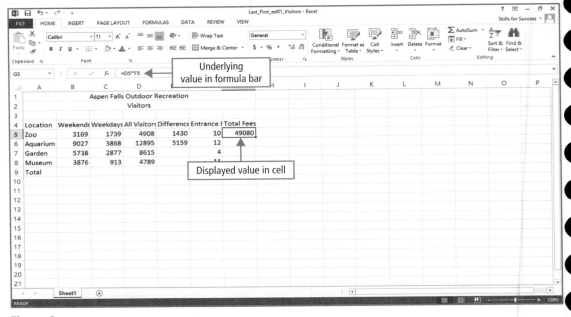

Figure 1

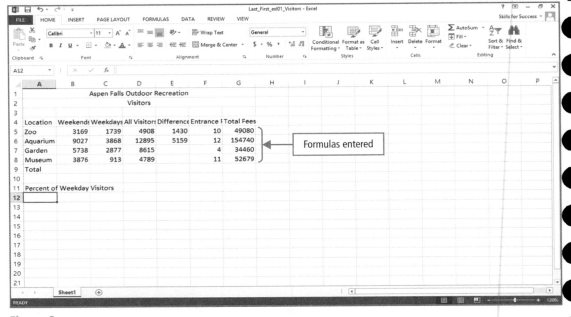

Figure 2

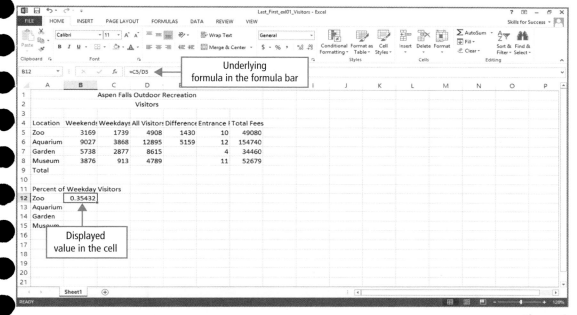

Underlying formula in the formula bar

Displayed value in the cell

Figure 3

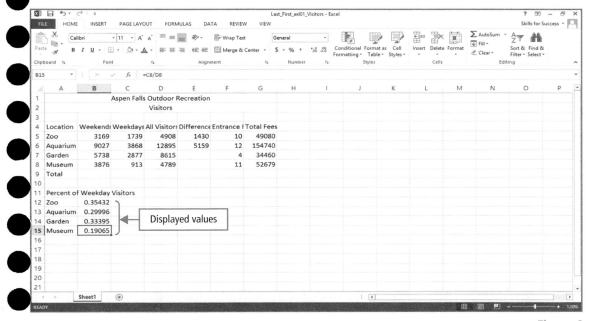

Displayed values

Figure 4

4. Select the range **A5:A8**, and then on the **Home tab**, in the **Clipboard group**, click the **Copy** button. Click cell **A12**, and then in the **Clipboard group**, click the **Paste** button.

   The four location labels are copied to the range A12:A15.

5. Press Esc to remove the moving border around the copied cells.

6. In cell **B12**, construct the formula to divide the number of Weekday Zoo visitors by the Total Zoo visitors, =C5/D5 and then click the **Enter** button ✓. Compare your screen with Figure 3.

   Percentages are calculated by taking the amount divided by the total and will be displayed in decimal format. Here, the underlying formula in B12 (=C5/D5) divides the weekday Zoo visitors (*1739*) by the total Zoo visitors (*4908*).

7. Construct the formulas to calculate the percent of weekday visitors for each location, and then compare your screen with Figure 4.

Cell	Formula
B13	=C6/D6
B14	=C7/D7
B15	=C8/D8

8. **Save** the workbook.

■ **You have completed Skill 4 of 10**

EXL 1-5 VIDEO

▶ The letter that displays at the top of a column is the **column heading**. The number that displays at the left of a row is the **row heading**.

▶ **Formatting** is the process of specifying the appearance of cells or the overall layout of a worksheet.

1. Click cell **A4**. On the **Home tab**, in the **Cells group**, click the **Format** button, and then click **Column Width**. In the **Column Width** dialog box, type 13

2. Compare your screen with **Figure 1**, and then click **OK**.

   The default column width will display 8.43 characters when formatted in the standard font. Here, the width is increased to display more characters.

3. Select the range **B4:G4**. In the **Cells group**, click the **Format** button, and then click **Column Width**. In the **Column Width** dialog box, type 12 and then click **OK**.

4. Select cells **A11:B11**. On the **Home tab**, in the **Alignment group**, click the **Merge & Center arrow** 🔲 Merge & Center ▾ , and then on the displayed list, click **Merge Across**. Compare your screen with **Figure 2**.

   Merge Across merges the selected cells without centering them.

5. Click cell **A1** to select the merged and centered range A1:G1. In the **Cells group**, click the **Format** button, and then click **Row Height**. In the **Row Height** dialog box, type 22.5 and then click **OK**.

■ **Continue to the next page to complete the skill** ▶

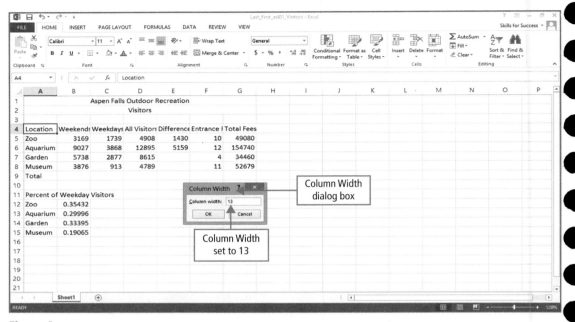

Figure 1

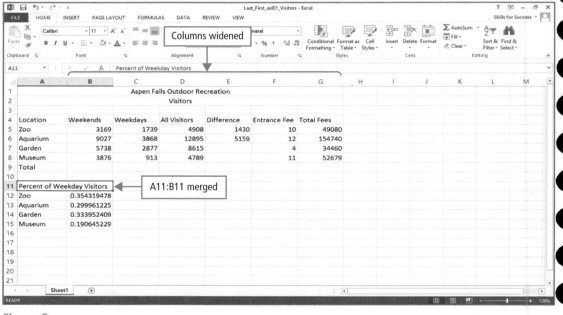

Figure 2

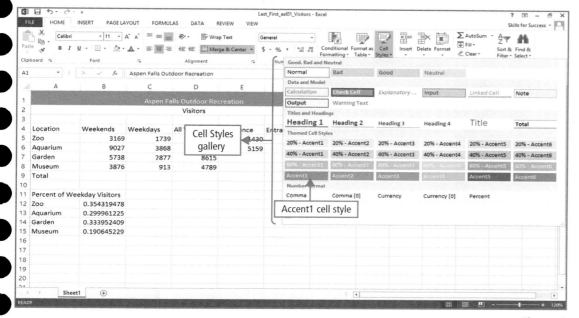

Figure 3

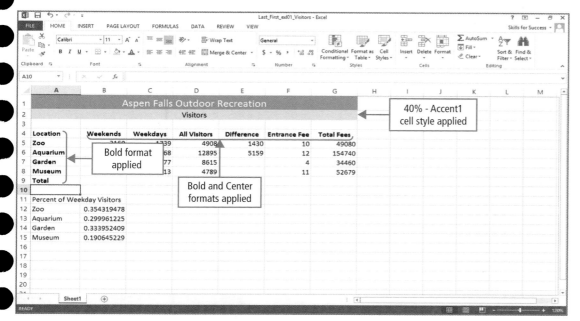

Figure 4

6. With **A1:G1** still selected, in the **Styles group**, click the **Cell Styles** button. In the **Cell Styles** gallery, under **Titles and Headings**, use Live Preview to view the title as you point to **Heading 1** and then **Heading 2**.

    A *cell style* is a prebuilt set of formatting characteristics, such as font, font size, font color, cell borders, and cell shading.

7. Under **Themed Cell Styles**, point to the **Accent1** style. Compare your screen with **Figure 3**, and then click **Accent1**.

8. In the **Font group**, click the **Font Size arrow** ⟨11 ▾⟩ and then click **16**.

9. Click cell **A2**, and then using the technique you just practiced, apply the **40% - Accent1** cell style. In the **Font group**, click the **Increase Font Size** button ⟨A⟩ one time to change the font size to **12**.

10. Select the range **B4:G4**. Right-click the selected range to display a shortcut menu and the Mini toolbar. On the Mini toolbar, click the **Bold** button ⟨B⟩ and then click the **Center** button ⟨≡⟩ to apply bold and to center the text within each of the selected cells.

11. Select the range **A4:A9**. Display the Mini toolbar, and then apply **Bold** to the selected range. Click cell **A10**, and then compare your screen with **Figure 4**.

12. **Save** ⟨💾⟩ the workbook.

■ **You have completed Skill 5 of 10**

▶ EXL 1-6
VIDEO

▶ You can create your own formulas, or you can use a *function*—a prewritten Excel formula that takes a value or values, performs an operation, and returns a value or values.

▶ The AutoSum button is used to insert common summary functions into a worksheet.

▶ When cell references are used in a formula or function, the results are automatically recalculated whenever those cells are edited.

1. Click cell **B9**. On the **Home tab**, in the **Editing group**, click the **AutoSum** button, and then compare your screen with **Figure 1**.

   SUM is an Excel function that adds all the numbers in a range of cells. The range in parentheses, *(B5:B8)*, indicates the range of cells on which the SUM function will be performed.

   When the AutoSum button is used, Excel first looks *above* the selected cell for a suitable range of cells to sum. When no suitable data is detected, Excel then looks to the *left* and proposes a range of cells to sum. Here, the range B5:B8 is surrounded by a moving border, and *=SUM(B5:B8)* displays in cell B9.

2. Press Enter to display the function result—*21810*.

3. Select the range **C9:D9**. In the **Editing group**, click the **AutoSum** button, and then compare your screen with **Figure 2**.

■ **Continue to the next page to complete the skill**

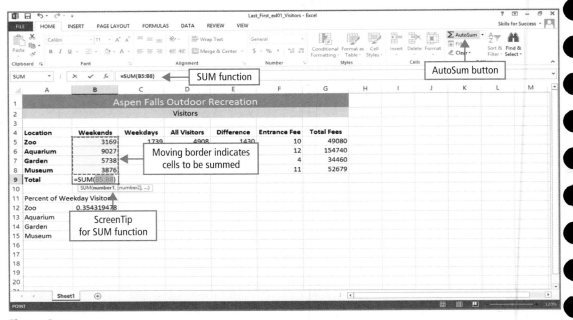

Figure 1

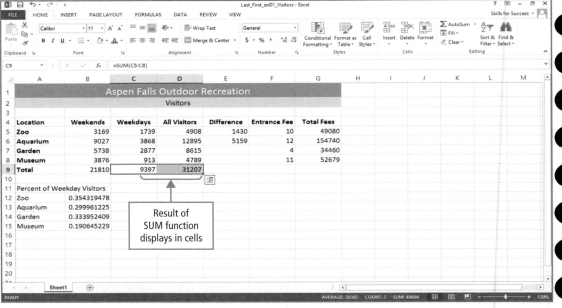

Figure 2

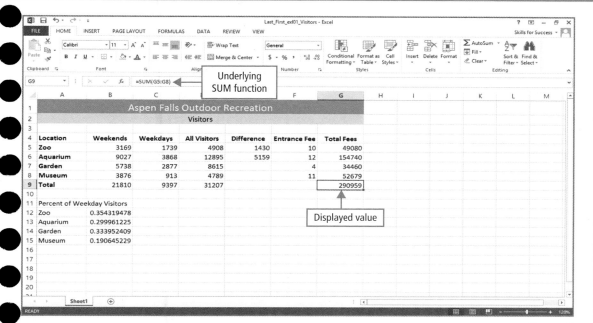

Figure 3

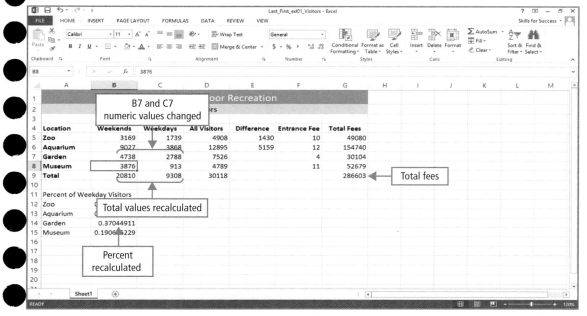

Figure 4

4. Click cell **C9**, and then in the formula bar, verify that the SUM function adds the values in the range *C5:C8*.

5. Click cell **D9**, and verify that the SUM function adds the values in the range *D5:D8*.

6. Using the technique just practiced, in cell **G9**, insert the SUM function to add the values in the range **G5:G8**. Verify cell **G9** is the active cell, and then compare your screen with **Figure 3**.

7. In cell **B7**, type 4738 Watch the total in cell **B9** update as you press Tab .

    In cell B9, the displayed value changed to 20810, but the underlying formula remained the same.

8. In cell **C7**, type 2788 and then press Enter to update the values in cells that contain formulas referring to cell C7. Compare your screen with **Figure 4**.

9. **Save** 🖫 the workbook.

■ **You have completed Skill 6 of 10**

▶ EXL 1-7
VIDEO

► Text, numbers, formulas, and functions can be copied down rows and also across columns to insert formulas and functions quickly.

► When a formula is copied to another cell, Excel adjusts the cell references relative to the new location of the formula.

1. Click cell **E6**. With cell **E6** selected, point to the ***fill handle***—the small green square in the lower right corner of the selection—until the ⊞ pointer displays as shown in **Figure 1**.

   To use the fill handle, first select the cell that contains the content you want to copy—here the formula *=B6-C6*.

2. Drag the ⊞ pointer down to cell **E8**, and then release the mouse button.

3. Click cell **E7**, and verify on the formula bar that the formula copied from E6 changed to *=B7-C7*. Click cell **E8**, and then compare your screen with **Figure 2**.

   In each row, the cell references in the formula adjusted *relative to* the row number—B6 changed to B7 and then to B8. This adjustment is called a ***relative cell reference*** because it refers to cells based on their position *in relation to* (relative to) the cell that contains the formula.

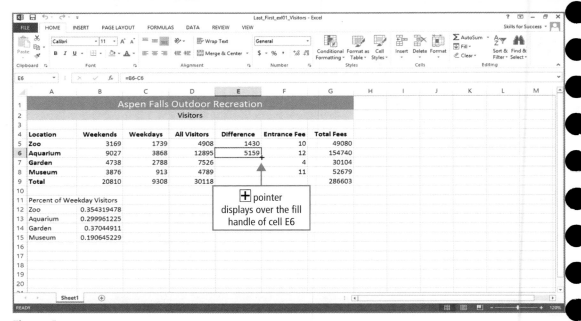

Figure 1

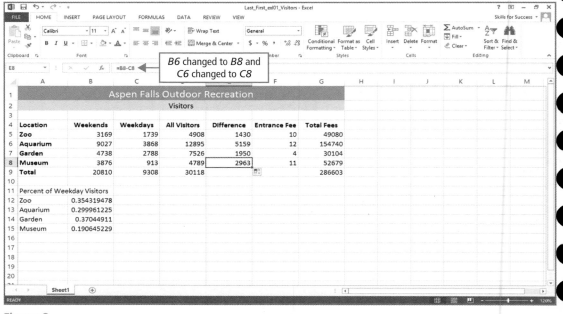

Figure 2

■ **Continue to the next page to complete the skill** ▶

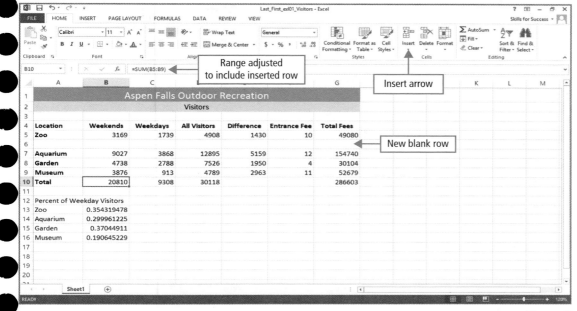

Figure 3

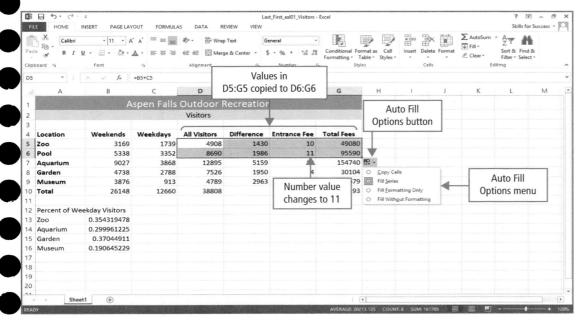

Figure 4

4. Click cell **A6**. In the **Cells group**, click the **Insert arrow**, and then click **Insert Sheet Rows**. Click cell **B10**, and then compare your screen with **Figure 3**.

   When you insert a new row or column, the cell references and the ranges in formulas or in functions adjust to include the new row or column. Here, in cell B10, the range in the function automatically updated to include the new row in the range.

5. In cell **A6**, type Pool and then press Tab.

   By default, formatting (bold) from the row above is applied to an inserted row.

6. In cell **B6**, type 5338 and then press Tab to enter the value and update the column total in cell *B10* to *26148*.

7. In cell **C6**, type 3352 and press Tab.

8. Select cells **D5:G5**. Point to the fill handle so that the ⊞ pointer displays, and then drag the ⊞ pointer down one row. Release the mouse button, and then click the **Auto Fill Options** button ⊞₊. Compare your screen with **Figure 4**.

   When you copy number values using the fill handle, the numbers automatically increment for each row or column. Here, the number value in cell F5 increased by one when it was copied to cell F6.

9. In the **Auto Fill Options** menu, click **Copy Cells**.

   With the Copy Cells option, number values are literally copied and do not increment. Here, the number value in cell F6 changes to *10*.

10. **Save** 🖫 the workbook.

■ **You have completed Skill 7 of 10**

▶ Always check spelling after you have finished formatting and editing your worksheet data.

1. Click cell **A14**, and repeat the technique used previously to insert a new row. In cell **A14**, type Pool and then press ⌷Enter⌷.

2. Click cell **B13**, and then use the fill handle to copy the formula down to cell **B14**.

3. Double-click cell **A2** to edit the cell contents. Use the arrow keys to move to the right of the word *Visitors*. Add a space, type to City Attractions and then press ⌷Enter⌷.

   Alternately, double-tap cell A2 to edit the cell.

4. Select the range **F5:G10**. In the **Styles group**, click the **Cell Styles** button, and then under **Number Format**, click **Currency [0]**. Take a few moments to familiarize yourself with the Number Formats as summarized in the table in **Figure 1**.

5. Select the range **B5:E10**. Click the **Cell Styles** button, and then under **Number Format**, click **Comma [0]**.

6. Select the range **B13:B17**. In the **Number group**, click the **Percent Style** button %, and then click the **Increase Decimal** button one time. Compare your screen with **Figure 2**.

   The Increase Decimal and Decrease Decimal buttons do not actually add or remove decimals, but they change how the underlying decimal values display in the cells.

▪ **Continue to the next page to complete the skill** ▶

Number Formats	
Format	**Description**
Comma	Adds commas where appropriate and displays two decimals.
Comma [0]	Adds commas where appropriate and displays no decimals.
Currency	Adds the dollar sign, commas where appropriate, and displays two decimals.
Currency [0]	Adds the dollar sign, commas where appropriate, and displays no decimals.
Percent	Adds the percent sign and multiplies the number by 100.

Figure 1

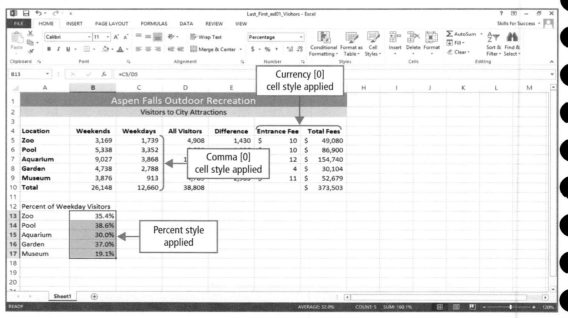

Figure 2

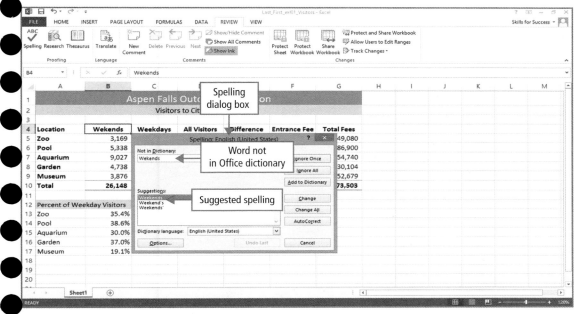

Figure 3

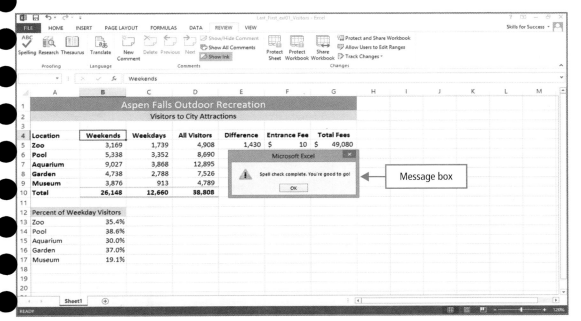

Figure 4

7. Select the range **B10:D10**. Hold down Ctrl, and then click cell **G10**. Click the **Cell Styles** button. Under **Titles and Headings**, click the **Total** style.

8. Select cell **A12**, and then click the **Cell Styles** button. Under **Themed Cell Styles**, click **40% - Accent1**.

9. Press Ctrl + Home to make cell **A1** active. On the **Review tab**, in the **Proofing group**, click the **Spelling** button.

   The spelling checker starts with the active cell and moves to the right and down, so making cell A1 the active cell before beginning is useful.

10. In the **Spelling** dialog box, under **Not in Dictionary**, a misspelled word displays as shown in **Figure 3**.

   This word is not in the Office dictionary; however, words not in the dictionary are not necessarily misspelled. Many proper nouns or less commonly used words are not in the Office dictionary.

   To correct a misspelled word and to move to the next word not in the Office dictionary, under Suggestions, verify that the correct spelling is selected, and then click the Change button.

11. Continue to use the spelling checker to correct any remaining errors you may have made. When the message **Spell check complete. You're good to go!** displays, as shown in **Figure 4**, click **OK**.

   When words you use often are not in the Office dictionary, you can click *Add to Dictionary* to add them.

12. **Save** 🖫 the workbook.

■ **You have completed Skill 8 of 10**

▶ In Excel, **Page Layout view** is used to adjust how a worksheet will look when it is printed.

1. Click the **Insert tab**, and then in the **Text group**, click the **Header & Footer** button to switch to **Page Layout view** and to display the **Header & Footer Tools Design** contextual tab.

2. On the **Design tab**, in the **Navigation group**, click the **Go to Footer** button to move to the Footer area. Click just above the word **Footer** to place the insertion point in the left section of the Footer area.

3. In the **Header & Footer Elements group**, click the **File Name** button. Compare your screen with **Figure 1**.

   Predefined headers and footers insert placeholders with instructions for printing. Here, the *& [File]* placeholder instructs Excel to insert the file name when the worksheet is printed.

4. In the **Header & Footer Elements group**, click in the middle section of the Footer area, and then click the **Current Date** button. Click the right section of the Footer area, and type City Attractions Click in a cell just above the footer to exit the Footer area.

5. Click the **Page Layout tab**. In the **Sheet Options group**, under **Gridlines**, select the **Print** check box.

6. In the **Page Setup group**, click the **Margins** button. Below the **Margins** gallery, click **Custom Margins**. In the **Page Setup** dialog box, under **Center on page**, select the **Horizontally** check box, and then compare your screen with **Figure 2**.

■ **Continue to the next page to complete the skill**

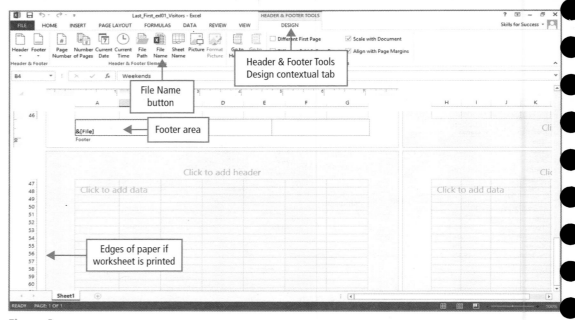

Figure 1

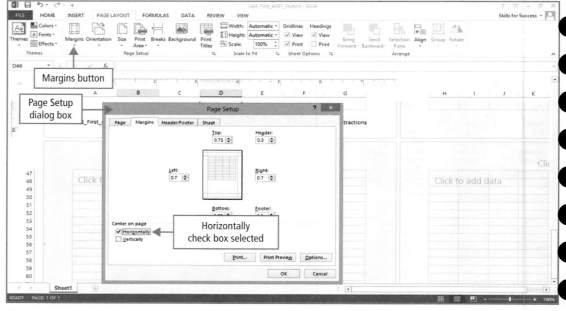

Figure 2

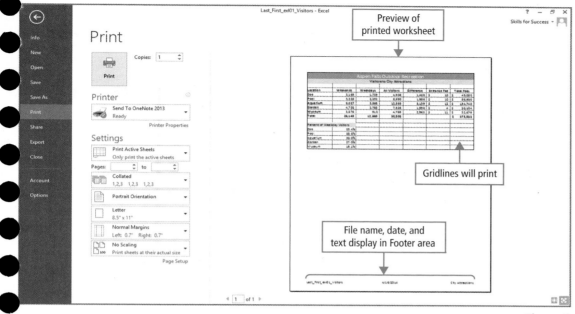

Figure 3

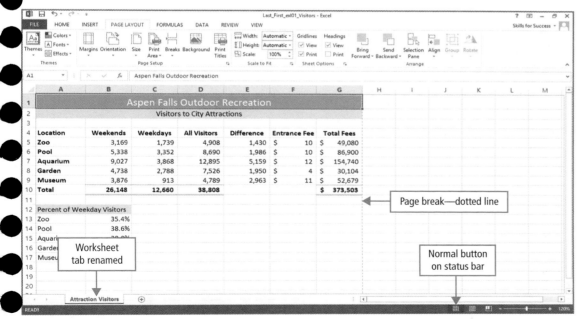

Figure 4

7. In the **Page Setup** dialog box, click **Print Preview**, and then compare your screen with Figure 3.

8. Click the **Back** button ⊙. On the lower right side of the status bar, click the **Normal** button ▦ to return to Normal view, and then press Ctrl + Home to make cell **A1** active.

   Normal view maximizes the number of cells visible on the screen. The page break—the dotted line between columns G and H—indicates where one page ends and a new page begins.

9. At the bottom of your worksheet, right-click the **Sheet1** worksheet tab, and then from the shortcut menu, click **Rename**. Type Attraction Visitors and then press Enter to change the worksheet tab name. Compare your screen with Figure 4.

10. **Save** ▤ the workbook.

■ **You have completed Skill 9 of 10**

▶ Underlying formulas and functions can be displayed and printed.

▶ When formulas are displayed in cells, the orientation and worksheet scale may need to be changed so that the worksheet prints on a single page.

1. Click the **Formulas tab**. In the **Formula Auditing group**, click the **Show Formulas** button to display the underlying formulas in the cells. Compare your screen with **Figure 1**.

   Columns often become wider when formulas are displayed. Here, the printed worksheet extends to a second page.

2. Click the **File tab**, and then click **Print**.

   Below the preview of the printed page, *1 of 3* indicates that the worksheet will print on three pages.

3. In **Backstage** view, on the bottom of the **Print** page, click the **Next Page** button ▶ two times to view the second and the third pages, and then compare your screen with **Figure 2**.

4. Click the **Back** button ⊙. On the **Page Layout tab**, in the **Page Setup group**, click the **Orientation** button, and then click **Landscape** so that the page orientation will be wider than it is tall.

■ **Continue to the next page to complete the skill**

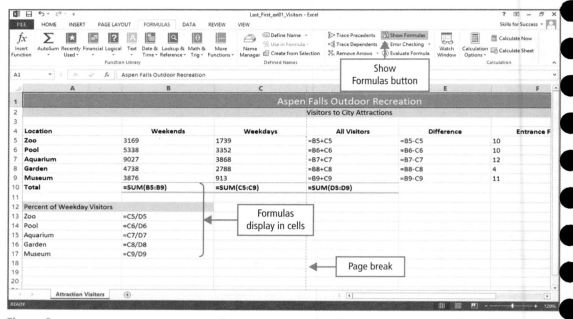

Figure 1

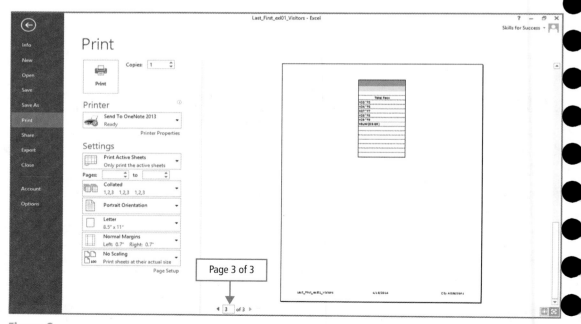

Figure 2

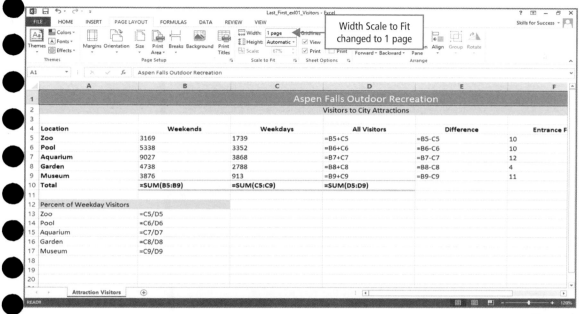

Figure 3

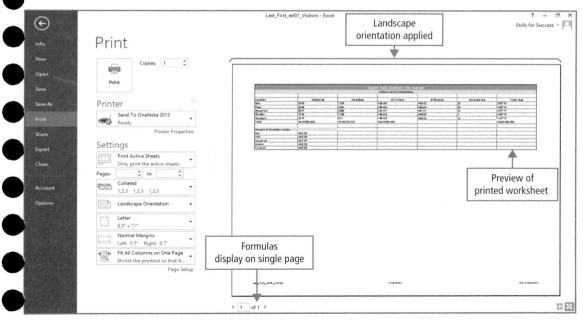

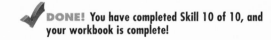

Figure 4

5. In the **Scale to Fit group**, click the **Width arrow**, and then click **1 page**. Compare your screen with **Figure 3**.

> Scaling adjusts the size of the printed worksheet to fit on the number of pages that you specify.

6. Click the **File tab**, and then click **Print**. Compare your screen with **Figure 4**.

> *1 of 1* displays at the bottom of the Print page to notify you that the worksheet will now print on one page.

7. If you are directed by your instructor to submit a printout with your formulas displayed, click the Print button.

8. Click the **Back** button ⊙. On the **Formulas tab** in the **Formula Auditing group**, click the **Show Formulas** button to hide the formulas.

9. If you are printing your work, print the worksheet with the values displayed and formulas hidden.

10. **Save** 🖫 the workbook, and then **Close** ☒ Excel. Submit the workbook file or printouts as directed by your instructor.

✔ **DONE! You have completed Skill 10 of 10, and your workbook is complete!**

More Skills

The following More Skills are located at **www.pearsonhighered.com/skills**

More Skills Create Workbooks from Templates

Templates are used to build workbooks without having to start from scratch. You can save time by using one of many predefined templates from Microsoft Office Online.

In More Skills 11, you will use a Calendar template downloaded from Microsoft Office Online to create a schedule.

To begin, open your web browser, navigate to www.pearsonhighered.com/skills, locate the name of your textbook, and then follow the instructions on the website.

More Skills Insert Names into Formulas

Instead of using cell references in formulas and functions, you can assign names that refer to the same cell or range. Names can be easier to remember than cell references, and they can add meaning to formulas, making them easier for you and others to understand.

In More Skills 12, you will open a workbook and practice various ways to name cell ranges. You will then use the names in formulas.

To begin, open your web browser, navigate to www.pearsonhighered.com/skills, locate the name of your textbook, and then follow the instructions on the website.

More Skills Create Templates

You can save one of your own workbooks as a template to use again, or you can download a template from Microsoft Office Online and then customize the template.

In More Skills 13, you will modify a Time Card template downloaded from Microsoft Office Online and then use the template to create a new weekly time card.

To begin, open your web browser, navigate to www.pearsonhighered.com/skills, locate the name of your textbook, and then follow the instructions on the website.

More Skills Manage Document Properties

Document properties are the detailed information about your workbook that can help you identify or organize your files, including the name of the author, the title, and keywords. Some workbook properties are added to the workbook when you create it. You can add others as necessary.

In More Skills 14, you will open a workbook, open the Document Information Panel, and add document properties.

To begin, open your web browser, navigate to www.pearsonhighered.com/skills, locate the name of your textbook, and then follow the instructions on the website.

Please note that there are no additional projects to accompany the More Skills Projects, and they are not covered in the End-of-Chapter projects.

The following table summarizes the **SKILLS AND PROCEDURES** covered in this chapter.

Skill Number	Task	Step	Icon	Keyboard Shortcut
2	Merge cells	Home tab → Alignment group → Merge & Center	Merge & Center ▾	
3	Accept a cell entry	Formula bar → Enter	✓	Enter
5	Adjust Column Width	Home tab → Cells group → Format → Column Width		
5	Adjust Row Height	Home tab → Cells group → Format → Row Height		
5	Apply Cell Styles	Home tab → Styles group → Cell Styles		
6	Insert SUM function	Home tab → Editing group → AutoSum	Σ AutoSum ▾	
7	Insert a row	Home tab → Cells group → Insert → Insert Sheet Rows		
8	Check spelling	Review tab → Proofing group → Spelling		F7
8	Edit inside cells	Double-click		F2
8	Increase Decimals	Home tab → Number group → Increase Decimal	.00→.0	
8	Decrease Decimals	Home tab → Number group → Decrease Decimal	.00→.0	
9	Display workbook in Normal View	Status bar → Normal	▦	
9	Move to cell A1			Ctrl + Home
9	Insert text and fields into footers	Insert tab → Text group → Header & Footer		
9	Rename a worksheet tab	Right-click worksheet tab → Rename		
10	Display formulas	Formulas tab → Formula Auditing group → Show Formulas		Ctrl + [']
10	Scale to Print on one page	Page Layout tab → Scale to Fit group → Width		
10	Change Page Orientation	Page Layout tab → Page Setup group → Orientation		

Key Terms

Online Help Skills

1. Start **Excel 2013**, and then in the upper right corner of the start page, click the **Help** button [?].

2. In the **Excel Help** window **Search help** box, type Broken formula and then press [Enter].

3. In the search result list, click **Why is my formula broken**, and then compare your screen with **Figure 1**.

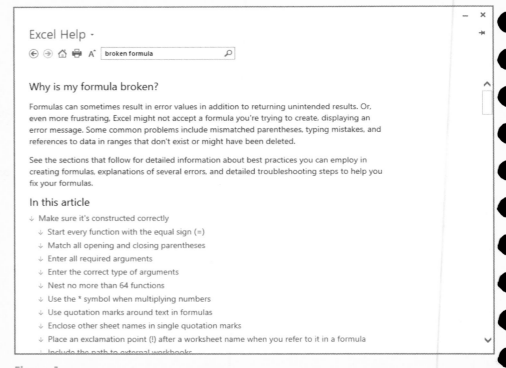

Figure 1

4. Read the article to answer the following questions: What results in a #DIV/0 error? What function can you nest with your division operation to avoid this error?

Matching

Match each term in the second column with its correct definition in the first column by writing the letter of the term on the blank line in front of the correct definition.

____ **1.** An Excel file that contains one or more worksheets.

____ **2.** The primary document that you use in Excel to store and work with data.

____ **3.** The cell, surrounded by a green border, ready to receive data or be affected by the next Excel command.

____ **4.** The identification of a specific cell by its intersecting column letter and row number.

____ **5.** Data in a cell—text or numbers.

____ **6.** Data in a cell made up of text only.

____ **7.** Data in a cell made up of numbers only.

____ **8.** Two or more cells on a worksheet.

____ **9.** The Excel window area that displays the address of a selected cell.

____ **10.** An Excel feature that suggests values as you type a function.

A Active cell

B Cell reference

C Formula AutoComplete

D Name Box

E Number value

F Range

G Text value

H Value

I Workbook

J Worksheet

BizSkills Video

1. What are the best ways to network online?

2. What are some of the biggest pitfalls in using social media to communicate a personal brand?

Multiple Choice

Choose the correct answer.

1. An Excel window area that displays the value contained in the active cell.
   - A. Formula bar
   - B. Workbook
   - C. Name Box

2. The column letter and row number that identify a cell.
   - A. Cell window
   - B. Cell address
   - C. Cell file name

3. The data displayed in a cell.
   - A. Viewed value
   - B. Inspected value
   - C. Displayed value

4. An equation that performs mathematical calculations on number values.
   - A. Method
   - B. Formula
   - C. System

5. Page headers and footers can be changed in this view.
   - A. Print preview
   - B. Page Layout view
   - C. Normal view

6. Symbols that specify mathematical operations such as addition or subtraction.
   - A. Hyperlinks
   - B. Bookmarks
   - C. Arithmetic operators

7. The number that displays at the left of a row.
   - A. Row heading
   - B. Row name
   - C. Row border

8. A prewritten Excel formula.
   - A. Method
   - B. Function
   - C. Exponent

9. The small green square in the lowerright corner of the active cell.
   - A. Border
   - B. Fill handle
   - C. Edge

10. A view that maximizes the number of cells visible on the screen.
    - A. Page Layout view
    - B. Standard view
    - C. Normal view

Topics for Discussion

1. What is the advantage of using cell references instead of actual number values in formulas and functions?

2. What are some things you can do to make your worksheet easier for others to read and understand?

3. According to the Introduction to this chapter, how do you decide which information to put in columns and which to put in rows?

Skills Review

To complete this project, you will need the following file:

- Blank Excel document

You will save your file as:

- Last_First_exl01_SRFitness

1. Start **Excel 2013**. In cell **A1**, type Aspen Falls Fitness Events and then in cell **A2**, type Number of Participants In cell **A4**, type Department and then pressing Tab after each label, type Spring, Fall, Total Participants and Difference

2. In rows **5** through **9**, enter the following data starting in cell **A5**:

City Hall	185	140	Engineering	169	147
Finance	147	136	City Council	195	152
IT Services	130	117			

3. In cell **D5**, type =B5+C5 and then in cell **E5**, type =B5-C5 Select the range **D5:E5**. Point to the fill handle, and then drag down through row **9**. Compare your screen with **Figure 1**.

4. **Save** the workbook in your chapter folder with the name Last_First_exl01_SRFitness

5. On the **Insert tab**, in the **Text group**, click the **Header & Footer** button. In the **Navigation group**, click the **Go to Footer** button, and then click in the left footer. In the **Header & Footer Elements group**, click the **File Name** button. Click in a cell just above the footer. On the lower right side of the status bar, click the **Normal** button, and then press Ctrl + Home.

6. In cell **A10**, type Total and then select the range **B10:D10**. On the **Home tab**, in the **Editing group**, click the **AutoSum** button.

7. Click cell **A7**. In the **Cells group**, click the **Insert arrow**, and then click **Insert Sheet Rows**. In the new row **7**, type the following data: Public Works and 95 and 87

8. Select the range **D6:E6**, and then use the fill handle to copy the formulas down one row.

9. In cell **A13**, type Fall Participants as a Percent of Total

10. Select the range **A5:A10**, and then on the **Home tab**, in the **Clipboard group**, click the **Copy** button. Click cell **A14**, and then in the **Clipboard group**, click the **Paste** button. Press Esc and then compare your screen with **Figure 2**.

- Continue to the next page to complete this Skills Review

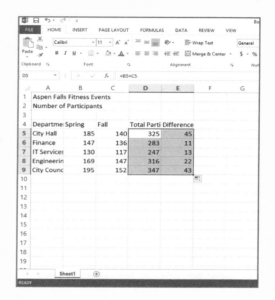

Figure 1

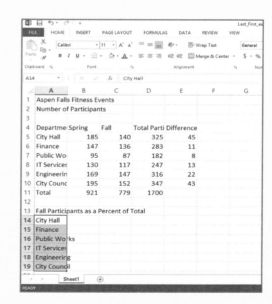

Figure 2

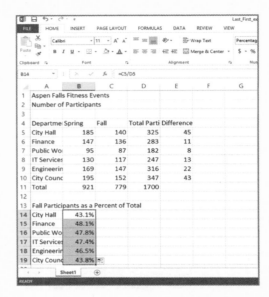

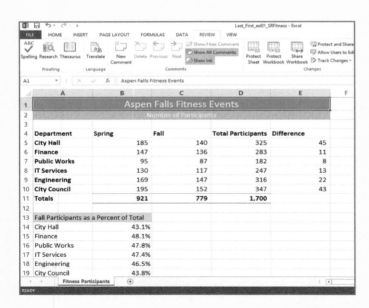

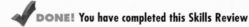

Figure 3

Figure 4

11. In cell **B14**, type =C5/D5 and then on the formula bar, click the **Enter** button. In the **Number group**, click the **Percent Style** button, and then click the **Increase Decimal** button one time. With cell **B14** still the active cell, use the fill handle to copy the formula down through row **19**. Compare your screen with **Figure 3**.

12. Select the range **A1:E1**, and then on the **Home tab**, in the **Alignment group**, click the **Merge & Center** button. In the **Styles group**, click the **Cell Styles** button, and then click **Accent 6**. In the **Font group**, click the **Font Size arrow**, and then click **16**. Select the range **A2:E2**, and then click the **Merge & Center** button. Click the **Cell Styles** button, and then click **60% - Accent 6**.

13. Select the range **A4:E4**. On the **Home tab**, in the **Cells group**, click the **Format** button, and then click **Column Width**. In the **Column Width** dialog box, type 16 and the click **OK**.

14. With the range **A4:E4** still selected, hold down Ctrl, and then select the range **A5:A11**. In the **Font group**, click the **Bold** button.

15. Select range **B5:E11**. In the **Styles group**, click the **Cell Styles** button, and then click **Comma [0]**. Select the range **B11:D11**. Click the **Cell Styles** button, and then click the **Total** style.

16. Select the range **A13:B13**. In the **Alignment group**, click the **Merge & Center arrow**, and then click **Merge Across**. Click the **Cell Styles** button, and then click **40% - Accent6**.

17. Press Ctrl + Home. On the **Review tab**, in the **Proofing group**, click the **Spelling** button, and then correct any spelling errors.

18. Right-click the **Sheet1** worksheet tab, and from the shortcut menu, click **Rename**. Type Fitness Participants and then press Enter. **Save**, and then compare your screen with **Figure 4**. If directed by your instructor, display and format the worksheet formulas as described in Skill 10, and then print the worksheet.

19. Submit the printouts or workbook as directed by your instructor.

✔ **DONE! You have completed this Skills Review**

Skills Assessment 1

MyITLab®
Grader

To complete this project, you will need the following file:

- exl01_SA1Path

You will save your workbook as:

- Last_First_exl01_SA1Path

1. Start **Excel 2013**. From your student data files, open **exl01_SA1Path**. Save the workbook in your chapter folder as Last_First_exl01_SA1Path Add the file name to the worksheet's left footer, add the current date to the center footer, and then type Bike Path Costs in the right footer. Return to **Normal** view.

2. For the range **A1:E1**, merge and center and apply the **Accent5** cell style. Increase the font size to **18** points. For the range **A2:E2**, merge and center and apply the **40% - Accent 5** cell style. Widen column **A** to _20_. For all column and row labels, apply **Bold**.

3. For the range **E5:E13**, insert the **SUM** function to add the three costs for each row. In the range **B14:E14**, insert the **SUM** function to provide totals for each column.

4. Select the nonadjacent ranges **B5:E5** and **B14:E14**. Apply the **Currency [0]** cell style.

5. Select the range **B6:E13**, and then apply the **Comma [0]** cell style. Select the range **B14:E14**, and then apply the **Total** cell style.

6. Insert a new row above row **7**. In cell **A7**, type Aspen Lakes and as the costs for the new location, type 4763 and 18846 and 1498 Use the fill handle to copy the formula in cell **E6** to cell **E7**.

7. **Copy** the location names from the range **A5:A14** to the range **A20:A29**.

8. Making sure to type the decimals, in cells **B20** and **B21**, type .03 In cells **B22** and **B23**, type .05 and in cell **B24**, type .06 Use the fill handle to copy the value in cell **B24** down through cell **B29**. Select the range **B20:B29**, and then apply the **Percent Style** number format.

9. In cell **C20**, enter a formula that calculates the cost by multiplying cell **E5** by cell **B20**. AutoFill the formula in cell **C20** down through cell **C29**.

10. Rename the **Sheet 1** worksheet tab as Path Costs

Aspen Falls				
Bike Path Construction Costs				
Location	Brush Clearing	Paving	Landscaping	Total Cost
Cornish Forest	$ 5,883	$ 15,580	$ 3,271	$ 24,734
Haack Center	6,234	18,916	1,697	26,847
Aspen Lakes	4,763	18,846	1,498	25,107
Hamilton Hills Park	4,981	17,169	1,805	23,955
Hansen Hills	4,209	14,062	2,437	20,708
Plasek Park	3,247	12,691	3,971	19,909
Price Lakes	3,648	19,387	2,927	25,962
Rodman Creek	4,515	13,120	1,934	19,569
Schroder Brook	3,862	19,166	2,036	25,064
Terry Park	2,569	17,506	1,756	21,831
Total	$ 43,911	$ 166,443	$ 23,332	$ 233,686

Location	Increase	Cost Increase
Cornish Forest	3%	$ 742.02
Haack Center	3%	$ 805.41
Aspen Lakes	5%	$ 1,255.35
Hamilton Hills Park	5%	$ 1,197.75
Hansen Hills	6%	$ 1,242.48
Plasek Park	6%	$ 1,194.54
Price Lakes	6%	$ 1,557.72
Rodman Creek	6%	$ 1,174.14
Schroder Brook	6%	$ 1,503.84
Terry Park	6%	$ 1,309.86

Figure 1

11. Use **Page Setup** to center the worksheet **Horizontally**. Set the **Gridlines** to print.

12. Check and correct any spelling errors, ignoring the proper names.

13. **Save** the workbook. Submit the workbook as directed by your instructor. If you are instructed to do so, display the worksheet formulas, scale the worksheet to print on one page.

14. Compare your completed worksheet with Figure 1.

DONE! You have completed Skills Assessment 1

Skills Assessment 2

To c̶o̶m̶p̶l̶e̶t̶e̶ ̶t̶h̶i̶s̶ ̶p̶r̶o̶j̶e̶c̶t̶,̶ ̶y̶o̶u̶ ̶w̶i̶l̶l̶ ̶n̶e̶e̶d̶ ̶t̶h̶e̶ following file:

You

(handwritten note overlay:)
(+) addition
(–) subtraction
(*) multiplication
(/) division

1. Sta... 01_SA2Guests.
   Sa... st_exl01_
   SA... ooter, and then
   ad... rmal view.

2. In c... 2nd Qtr. guests
   wh... ate the increase
   of g... are *Over 70*.

3. In c... ivide *2nd Qtr.*
   gue...

4. AutoFill the formulas in the range **D5:F5** down through row **17**.

5. In cell **A18**, type Total and then in row **18**, insert the functions to total columns **B:D**.

6. Insert a new row above row **15**, and then in the new cell, **A15**, type 20 to 25 In cell **B15**, type 17196 and in cell **C15** type 19133

7. For the range **B5:E19** apply the **Comma [0]** cell style, and for the range **F5:F18** apply the **Percent** number style and display one decimal.

8. Merge and center the range **A1:F1**, and then apply the **Accent6** cell style. Increase the font size to **18**. Merge and center the range **A2:F2**, and then apply the **40% - Accent 6** cell style. Increase the font size to **14**.

9. Widen columns **A:C** to **11.00**, and then widen columns **D:F** to **14.00**.

10. For the column and row labels, apply **Bold**. In the range **B19:D19**, apply the **Total** cell style.

11. For the range **A22:C22**, apply the **Merge Across** alignment and the **40% - Accent 6** cell style.

12. In cell **C24**, construct a formula to multiply *1st Half Total Guests* in the *Over 70* row by the *Projected Percent Increase* in cell **B24**. Apply the **Comma [0]** cell style. AutoFill the formula down through row **37**.

13. Rename the worksheet tab Aspen Lakes Guests

14. Check and correct any spelling errors.

15. Use Page Setup to center the page **Horizontally**. Set the **Gridlines** to print, and then **Save** the workbook.

16. If you are instructed to do so, display the worksheet formulas, scale the worksheet to print on one page, and then print with the formulas displayed.

17. Switch to **Normal** view, and then compare your completed worksheet with Figure 1. **Close** Excel, and then submit the workbook as directed by your instructor.

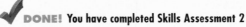 **DONE!** You have completed Skills Assessment 2

| Aspen Lakes Recreation Area | | | | | |
| Number of Guests | | | | | |
Ages	1st Qtr.	2nd Qtr.	1st Half Total Guests	2nd Qtr. Increase Over 1st Qtr.	2nd Qtr. as Percent of Total
Over 70	14,102	15,216	29,318	1,114	51.9%
65 to 70	15,125	17,854	32,979	2,729	54.1%
60 to 65	11,175	18,273	29,448	7,098	62.1%
55 to 60	15,110	16,572	31,682	1,462	52.3%
50 to 55	19,114	19,841	38,955	727	50.9%
45 to 50	18,475	21,418	39,893	2,943	53.7%
40 to 45	12,064	13,242	25,306	1,178	52.3%
35 to 40	14,628	16,232	30,860	1,604	52.6%
30 to 35	14,543	19,975	34,518	5,432	57.9%
25 to 30	17,933	19,724	37,657	1,791	52.4%
20 to 25	17,196	19,133	36,329	1,937	52.7%
15 to 20	30,516	32,597	63,113	2,081	51.6%
10 to 15	13,469	17,439	30,908	3,970	56.4%
Under 10	17,876	19,599	37,475	1,723	52.3%
Total	231,326	267,115	498,441		

| Projected 2nd Half Guests | | |
Ages	Projected Percentage Increase	Projected Increase in Guests
Over 70	2%	586
65 to 70	8%	2,638
60 to 65	4%	1,178
55 to 60	1%	317
50 to 55	5%	1,948
45 to 50	6%	2,394
40 to 45	9%	2,278
35 to 40	3%	926
30 to 35	6%	2,071
25 to 30	15%	5,649
20 to 25	14%	5,086
15 to 20	18%	11,360
10 to 15	21%	6,491
Under 10	23%	8,619

Figure 1

Visual Skills Check

To complete this project, you will need the following file:

- Blank Excel workbook

You will save your workbook as:

- Last_First_exl01_VSWorkers

Start **Excel 2013**. Open a new blank workbook, and then **Save** the workbook in your chapter folder as Last_First_exl01_VSWorkers Create the worksheet shown in **Figure 1**. The width of column **A** is 20 and the width of columns **B:F** is 13. Construct formulas that display the results shown in columns **D** and **F**, row **13**, and the range **B18:B25**. The title uses the **Accent4** cell style, and the font size is **20**. The subtitle uses the **40% - Accent 4** cell style, and the font size is **16**. The title and subtitle should be merged and centered. Using **Figure 1** as your guide, apply the **Currency [0]** cell style, the **Comma [0]** cell style, the **Total** cell style, the **Percent** number style, and the **Bold** format. On the range **A17:B17**, use Merge Across and apply the **40%-Accent2** cell style. Rename the *Sheet1* sheet tab as Park Workers Check and correct any spelling errors. Add the file name to the left footer. **Save** the workbook, and then submit the workbook as directed by your instructor.

✔️ **DONE! You have completed Visual Skills Check**

					Aspen Falls		
					Park Workers		
	Price Park	**Silkwood Park**	**Total Workers**	**Wage**		**Total Wages**	
Ticket Sellers	75	52	127	$	15	$	1,905
Security	92	79	171		25		4,275
Landscapers	19	11	30		20		600
Life Guards	23	23	46		15		690
Cashiers	73	58	131		15		1,965
Parking Attendants	15	11	26		15		390
Maintenance	21	28	49		20		980
Cleaning	29	17	46		18		828
Total	**347**	**279**	**626**			$	**11,633**

Price Park as Percent of Total Workers	
Ticket Sellers	59.1%
Security	53.8%
Landscapers	63.3%
Life Guards	50.0%
Cashiers	55.7%
Parking Attendants	57.7%
Maintenance	42.9%
Cleaning	63.0%

Figure 1

My College Enrollment

Course Name	Fall	Spring	Summer	Course Total
Algebra	1,173	938	415	2,526
Intro to Computers	1,043	857	497	2,397
Biology	578	311	253	1,142
World History	688	549	372	1,609
American History	824	598	397	1,819
Management	367	228	103	698
English	1,292	1,125	573	2,990
Semester Total	5,965	4,606	2,610	13,181

Summer as a Percent of Total	
Algebra	16.4%
Intro to Computers	20.7%
Biology	22.2%
World History	23.1%
American History	21.8%
Management	14.8%
English	19.2%

Figure 1

My Skills

To complete this project, you will need the following file:

- exl01_MYCollege

You will save your workbook as:

- Last_First_exl01_MYCollege

1. Start **Excel 2013**. From the student data files, open **exl01_MYCollege**. Save the workbook in your chapter folder as Last_First_exl01_MYCollege Add the file name to the worksheet's left footer, and then return to **Normal** view.

2. For the range **A1:E1**, merge and center and apply the **Accent3** cell style.

3. Widen column **A** to 20, and then widen columns **B:E** to 12

4. For the range **B3:E3**, center the labels. For all column and row labels, apply **Bold**.

5. In cell **E4**, insert the **SUM** function to provide the total for the row. AutoFill the formula in cell **E4** down through cell **E9**.

6. For the range **B10:E10**, insert the **SUM** function to provide totals for each column. With the range **B10:E10** still selected, apply the **Total** cell style.

7. For the range **B4:E10**, apply the **Comma [0]** cell style.

8. Insert a new row above row **7**. In cell **A7**, type World History and as the enrollment for the new course, type 688 and 549 and 372 AutoFill the formula in cell **E6** to cell **E7**.

9. **Copy** the course names from the range **A4:A10** to the range **A15:A21**.

10. In cell **B15**, create a formula that calculates the summer semester as a percent of the total course enrollment by dividing cell **D4** by cell **E4**. Apply the **Percent Style** number format, and display one decimal. AutoFill the formula in cell **B15** down through cell **B21**.

11. For the range **A14:B14**, merge across and apply the **40% - Accent3** cell style.

12. Rename the **Sheet 1** worksheet tab as Enrollment

13. Use **Page Setup** to center the worksheet **Horizontally**.

14. Check and correct any spelling errors.

15. **Save** the workbook. Submit the workbook as directed by your instructor. If you are instructed to do so, display the worksheet formulas, scale the worksheet to print on one page.

16. Compare your completed worksheet with Figure 1.

✓ DONE! You have completed My Skills

Skills Challenge 1

To complete this project, you will need the following file:

- exl01_SC1Employees

You will save your workbook as:

- Last_First_exl01_SC1Employees

Start **Excel 2013**, and then open the workbook **exl01_SC1Employees**. Save the workbook in your chapter folder as Last_First_exl01_SC1Employees Duncan Chueng, the Park Operations Manager for Aspen Falls, wants to total and compare the number of employees at the city recreation areas. Using the skills you practiced in this chapter, correct the SUM function for each row and column. Format the worksheet using cell styles and number formats as practiced in this chapter. Merge and center the title across the correct columns.

Correct the number formats. No decimals should display in rows 5:11. Adjust column widths as necessary to display all data. Set the gridlines to print, and center the data horizontally on the page. Add the file name in the worksheet's left footer, and check for spelling errors. Save the workbook, and then submit the workbook as directed by your instructor.

✔ **DONE! You have completed Skills Challenge 1**

Skills Challenge 2

To complete this project, you will need the following file:

- exl01_SC2Painting

You will save your workbook as:

- Last_First_exl01_SC2Painting

Start **Excel 2013**, and then open the workbook **exl01_SC2Painting**. Save the workbook in your chapter folder as Last_First_exl01_SC2Painting The Art Center wants to total and compare the number of students enrolled in the painting classes in the different neighborhoods. Using the skills you practiced in this chapter, insert appropriate formulas and functions. Adjust column widths and row heights as necessary

to display all data. Format the worksheet as appropriate. Add the file name in the worksheet's left footer, and check for spelling errors. Save the workbook, and then submit the workbook as directed by your instructor.

✔ **DONE! You have completed Skills Challenge 2**

CHAPTER 2

Insert Summary Functions and Create Charts

- ▶ Functions are prewritten formulas that have two parts—the name of the function and the arguments that specify the values or cells to be used by the function.

- ▶ Functions analyze data to answer financial, statistical, or logical questions. Summary functions are used to recap information.

- ▶ Excel provides various types of charts that can make your data easier to understand.

- ▶ Column charts show data changes over a period of time or illustrate comparisons among items.

- ▶ Pie charts illustrate how each part relates to the whole. Pie charts display the relative sizes of items in a single data series.

- ▶ Charts can be enhanced with effects such as 3-D and soft shadows to create compelling graphical summaries.

Fotolia: Zwei Frauen im Büro © Jeanette Dietl

Aspen Falls City Hall

In this chapter, you will finish a workbook for Thelma Perkins, a Risk Management Specialist in the Finance Department. The workbook displays the department expenditures for Aspen Falls. The City Council requires that the Finance Department present departmental information annually for review and approval.

Companies use formulas and statistical functions to manipulate and summarize data to make better decisions. Summary results can include the data totals or averages. Results can be displayed graphically as charts, providing a visual representation of data. Commonly used chart types include line charts to illustrate trends over time or bar charts to illustrate comparisons among individual items. Based on the type of data selected, the Quick Analysis tools provide chart type options.

In this project, you will open an existing workbook, construct formulas containing absolute cell references, and AutoFill the formulas to other cells. You will insert the statistical functions AVERAGE, MAX, and MIN. You will create and format column charts and pie charts, and insert WordArt. Finally, you will prepare the chart sheet and the worksheet to meet printing requirements.

Time to complete all 10
skills – 60 to 90 minutes

Student data file needed for this chapter:

exl02_Expenditures

You will save your workbook as:

Last_First_exl02_Expenditures

Outcome

Using the skills in this chapter, you will be able to
work with Excel worksheets like this:

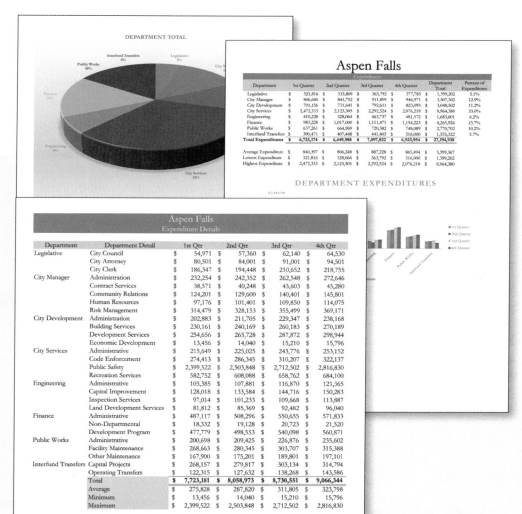

SKILLS MyITLab®
Skills 1-10 Training

At the end of this chapter you will be able to:

Skill 1 Align and Wrap Text
Skill 2 Apply Absolute Cell References
Skill 3 Format Numbers
Skill 4 Insert the AVERAGE Function
Skill 5 Insert the MIN and MAX Functions
Skill 6 Create Column Charts
Skill 7 Format Column Charts
Skill 8 Create and Format Pie Charts
Skill 9 Update Charts and Insert WordArt
Skill 10 Preview and Print Multiple Worksheets

MORE SKILLS

Skill 11 Insert, Edit, and Delete Comments
Skill 12 Change Chart Types
Skill 13 Copy Excel Data to Word Documents
Skill 14 Fill Data with Flash Fill

▶ The **_Text wrap_** format displays text on multiple lines within a cell.

1. Start **Excel 2013**, open the student data file **exl02_Expenditures**, and then compare your screen with **Figure 1**.

2. On the **File tab**, click **Save As**. On the **Save As** page, click the **Browse** button. Navigate to the location where you are saving your files. Click **New folder**, type Excel Chapter 2 and then press `Enter` two times. In the **File name** box, name the workbook Last_First_exl02_Expenditures and then press `Enter`.

3. Verify *Expenditures* is the active worksheet. On the **Insert tab**, in the **Text group**, click the **Header & Footer** button. In the **Navigation group**, click the **Go to Footer** button. Click just above the word **Footer**, and then in the **Header & Footer Elements group**, click the **File Name** button. Click a cell above the footer. On the status bar, click the **Normal** button ⊞, and then press `Ctrl` + `Home`.

4. Click cell **B2**. Point at the fill handle to display the ⊞ pointer, and drag right through cell **E2** to AutoFill the labels. Compare your screen with **Figure 2**.

   Excel's AutoFill feature can generate a series of values into adjacent cells. A **_series_** is a group of numbers, text, dates, or time periods that come one after another in succession. For example, the months *January, February, March* are a series. Likewise, *1st Quarter, 2nd Quarter, 3rd Quarter*, and *4th Quarter* form a series.

■ **Continue to the next page to complete the skill** ▶

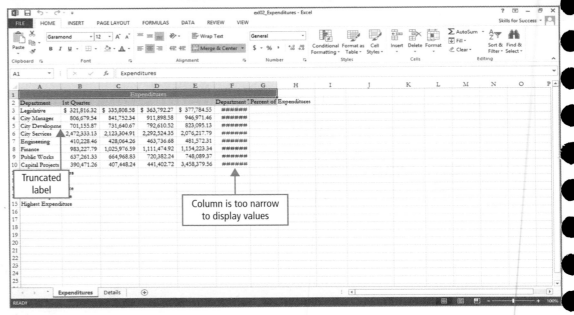

Figure 1

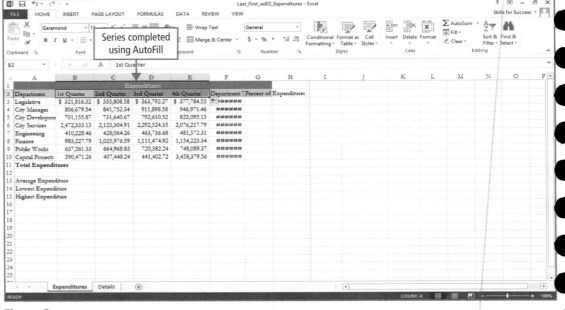

Figure 2

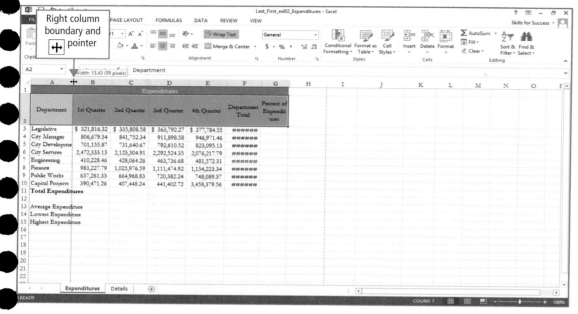

Figure 3

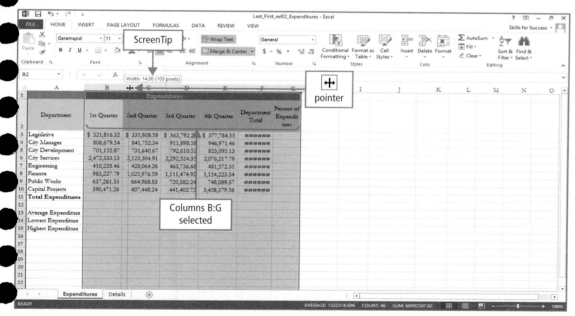

Figure 4

5. Select the range **A2:G2**. On the **Home tab**, in the **Alignment group**, click the **Wrap Text** button, the **Middle Align** button ≡, and the **Center** button ≡.

6. In the column heading area, point to the right boundary of column **A** to display the ⊞ pointer, as shown in **Figure 3**.

7. With the ⊞ pointer displayed, double-click to **AutoFit** the column—automatically change the column width to accommodate the longest entry.

8. In the column heading area, click the column **B** heading, and then drag right through column **G** to select columns **B:G**. Click the right boundary of column **B** to display the ⊞ pointer, and then drag to the right until the ScreenTip indicates *Width: 14:00 (103 pixels)* as shown in **Figure 4**. Release the mouse button.

9. Select the range **A3:A10**, and then in the **Alignment group**, click the **Increase Indent** button ⧉.

10. Save ⊟ the workbook.

■ **You have completed Skill 1 of 10**

▶ The Quick Analysis Lens button is used to apply conditional formatting or to insert charts and totals.

▶ Excel uses rules to check for formula errors. When a formula breaks a rule, the cell displays an **error indicator**—a green triangle that indicates a possible error in a formula.

▶ An **absolute cell reference** is a cell reference that remains the same when it is copied or filled to other cells. To make a cell reference absolute, insert a dollar sign ($) before the row and column references.

1. Select **B3:F10**, click the **Quick Analysis Lens** button 📋, and then compare your screen with **Figure 1**.

2. In the **Quick Analysis** gallery, click **Totals**, and then click the first option—**SUM**—to insert column totals.

3. Click **G3**, and then type =F3/F11 On the formula bar, click the **Enter** button ✓. Double-click **G3** to display the range finder, and then compare your screen with **Figure 2**.

   The **range finder** outlines all of the cells referenced in a formula. It is useful for verifying which cells are used in a formula and for editing formulas.

4. Press Esc to close the range finder. Point to the **G3** fill handle, and then AutoFill the formula down through **G10** to display **error values**—messages that display whenever a formula cannot perform the calculations in a formula. The *#DIV/0!* error value displays in a cell whenever the underlying formula attempts to divide by zero.

■ Continue to the next page to complete the skill ▶

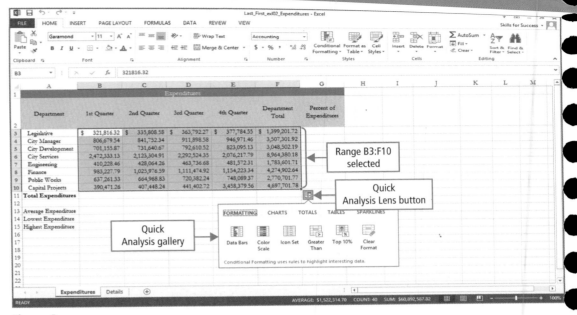

Figure 1

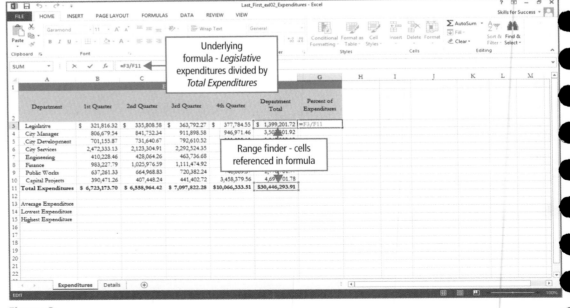

Figure 2

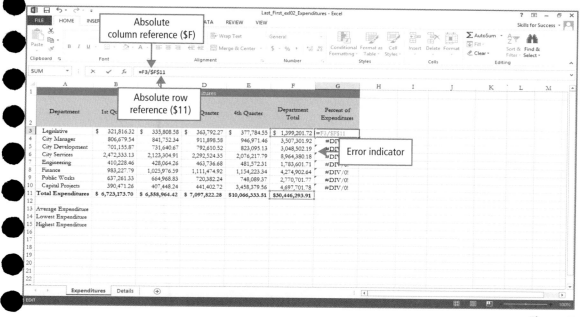

Figure 3

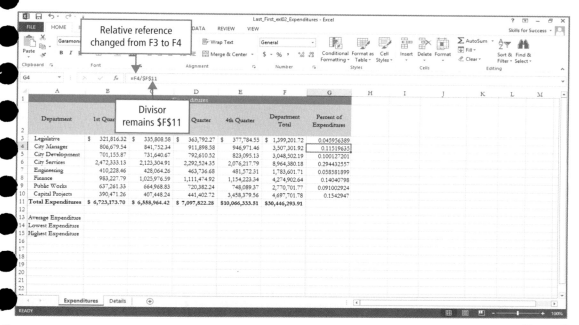

Figure 4

5. Click cell **G4**. To the left of the cell, point to the **Error Message** button [▼] to display the ScreenTip—*The formula or function used is dividing by zero or empty cells.*

6. Double-click cell **G4** to display the range finder.

   The formula was copied with a relative cell reference. In the copied formula, the cell reference to cell F4 is correct, but the formula is dividing by the value in cell F12, an empty cell. In this calculation, the divisor must be cell F11.

7. Press [Esc] and then double-click cell **G3**. In the formula, click the reference to cell **F11**, and then press [F4] to insert a dollar sign ($) before the column reference *F* and the row reference *11* as shown in **Figure 3**.

   The dollar signs are used to indicate an absolute cell reference.

8. On the **formula bar**, click the **Enter** button [✓] and then AutoFill the formula in cell **G3** down through cell **G10**.

9. Click cell **G4**, and verify that the divisor refers to cell *$F$11*, as shown in **Figure 4**.

   The cell reference for the row *City Manager Department Total* changed relative to its row; however, the value used as the divisor—*Total Expenditures* in cell F11—remains absolute.

10. Press the [↓] two times and verify that the divisor remains constant—$F$11—while the dividend changes relative to the row.

11. **Save** [💾] the workbook.

▪ **You have completed Skill 2 of 10**

▶ A *number format* is a specific way that Excel displays numbers. For example, the number of decimals, or whether commas and special symbols such as dollar signs display.

▶ By default, Excel displays the *General format*—a number format that does not display commas or trailing zeros to the right of a decimal point.

1. Click cell **B2**, and then on the **Home tab**, in the **Number group**, notice that *General* displays. Compare your screen with **Figure 1**.

2. Select the range **B3:F11**. In the **Number group**, click the **Decrease Decimal** button 🔢 two times to round the number and hide the decimals. Click cell **B6**, and then compare your screen with **Figure 2**.

   The Decrease Decimal button hides the displayed value decimals. The underlying value shows the decimals.

3. Select the range **G3:G10**. In the **Number group**, click the **Percent Style** button 🔢 and then click the **Increase Decimal** button 🔢 one time to add one decimal to the applied Percent Style. In the **Alignment group**, click the **Center** button ▤.

■ Continue to the next page to complete the skill ➤

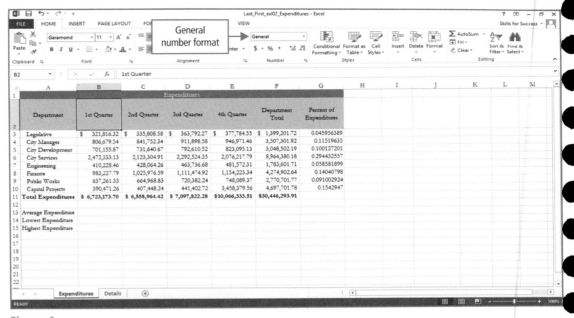

Figure 1

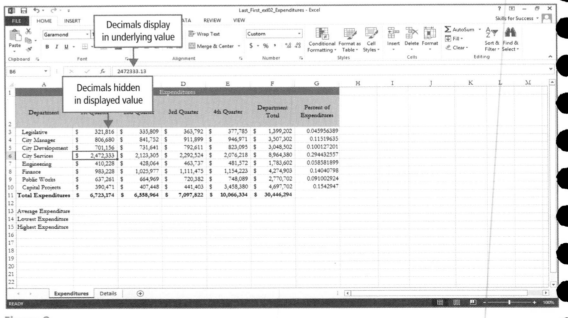

Figure 2

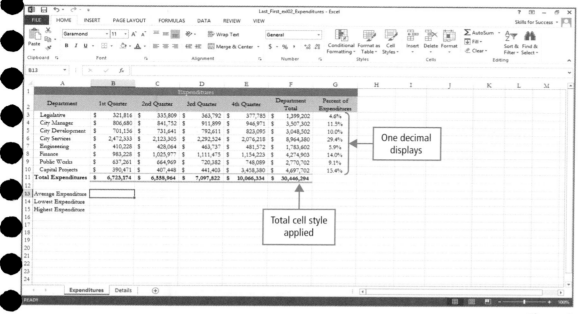

Figure 3

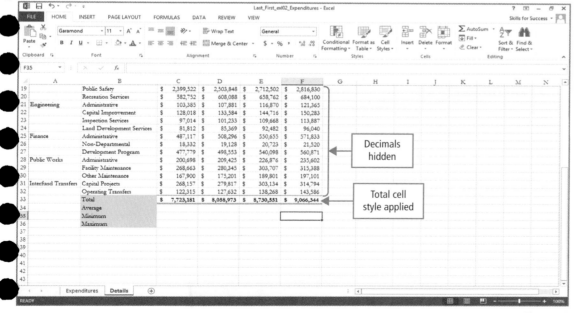

Figure 4

4. Select the range **B11:F11**. In the **Styles group**, click the **Cell Styles** button, and then under **Titles and Headings**, click **Total**. Click cell **B13**, and then compare your screen with Figure 3.

5. Along the bottom of the Excel window, notice the **worksheet tabs**, the labels along the lower border of the workbook window that identify each worksheet. Click the **Details** worksheet tab to make it the active worksheet.

6. Click cell **C5**. Hold down the Ctrl + Shift keys. With both keys held down, press the ↓ one time and the → one time to select the range **C5:F32**.

7. With the range **C5:F32** selected, click the **Quick Analysis Lens** button. In the **Quick Analysis** gallery, click **Totals**, and then click the first option—**SUM**.

8. With the range **C5:F32** still selected, hold down the Shift key and press the ↓ one time to include row **33**—the range *C5:F33* is selected. In the **Number group**, click the **Decrease Decimal** button two times.

9. Select the range **C33:F33**, and then apply the **Total** cell style. Click cell **F35**, and then compare your screen with Figure 4.

10. **Save** the workbook.

■ **You have completed Skill 3 of 10**

► **Statistical functions** are predefined formulas that describe a collection of data—for example, averages, maximums, and minimums.

► The **AVERAGE function** adds a group of values and then divides the result by the number of values in the group.

1. Click the **Expenditures** worksheet tab, and then click cell **B13**. On the **Home tab**, in the **Editing group**, click the **AutoSum arrow**, and then in the list of functions, click **Average**. Look in the formula bar and in cell B13 to verify that the range *B3:B12* is the suggested range of cells that will be averaged as shown in Figure 1.

   The range in parentheses is the function **argument**—the values that a function uses to perform operations or calculations. The arguments each function uses are specific to that function. Common arguments include numbers, text, cell references, and range names.

   When data is above or to the left of a selected cell, the function argument will automatically be entered. Often, you will need to edit the argument range.

2. With the insertion point in the function argument, click cell **B3**. On the range finder, click a sizing handle, and then drag down to select the argument range **B3:B10**, to exclude the *Total Expenditures* value in cell B11. On the formula bar, click the **Enter** button ✓ to display the result *$840,397*. Compare your screen with Figure 2.

■ **Continue to the next page to complete the skill** ▶

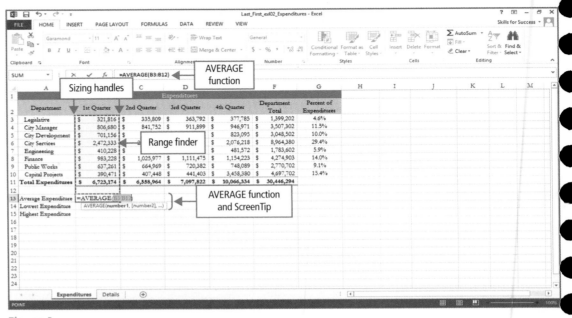

Figure 1

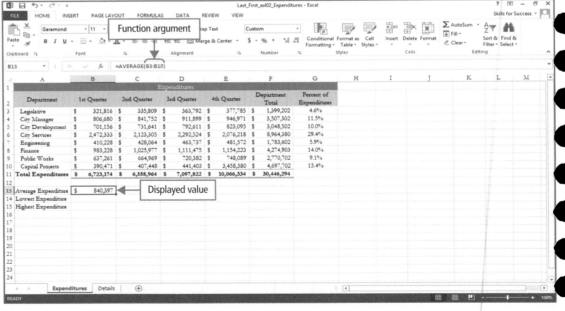

Figure 2

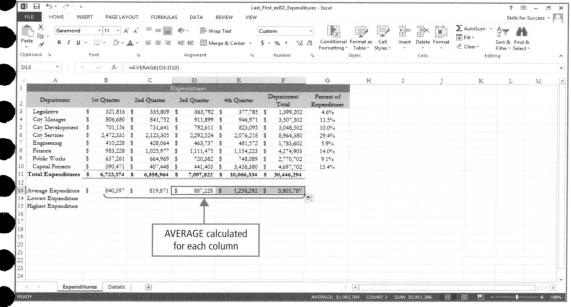

AVERAGE calculated for each column

Figure 3

3. Click cell **C13**. In the **Editing group**, click the **AutoSum arrow**, and then in the list of functions, click **Average**. In the formula bar and in the cell, notice that Excel proposes to average the value in cell *B13*, not the values in column C.

4. With cell reference B13 highlighted in the function argument, click cell **C3**, and then use the range finder sizing handle to select the range **C3:C10**. On the formula bar, click the **Enter** button ✔ to display the result *$819,871*.

5. Click cell **D13**. Using the techniques just practiced, enter the **AVERAGE** function using the argument range **D3:D10**, and then on the formula bar, click the **Enter** button ✔.

6. Verify that cell **D13** is the active cell, and then AutoFill the function to the right through cell **F13**. Compare your sheet to Figure 3.

7. Click the **Details** worksheet tab, and then click cell **C34**. Enter the **AVERAGE** function using the argument range **C5:C32**. Do not include the *Total* value in cell *C33* in the function argument. Compare your sheet to Figure 4.

8. Display the worksheet footers, click in the left footer, and then click the **File Name** button. Click in the right footer, and then click the **Sheet Name** button. Return to Normal view.

9. **Save** 🖫 the workbook.

■ **You have completed Skill 4 of 10**

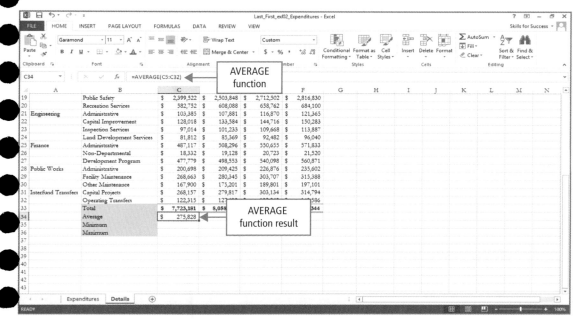

AVERAGE function

AVERAGE function result

Figure 4

▶ The **MIN function** returns the smallest value in a range of cells.

▶ The **MAX function** returns the largest value in a range of cells.

1. Click cell **C35**. Type =Mi and then in the Formula AutoComplete list, double-click **MIN**. With the insertion point blinking in the function argument, click cell **C32**, and then use the range finder sizing handles to drag up and select the range **C5:C32**. Press Enter to display the result *$13,456*.

   The MIN function evaluates the range provided in the function argument—C5:C32—and then returns the lowest value—*$13,456*. Here, the *Total* and *Average* values in cells *C33* and *C34* should not be included in the argument range.

2. Verify that **C36** is the active cell. Type =Ma and then in the Formula AutoComplete list, double-click **MAX**. Using the technique just practiced, select the range **C5:C32**, and then on the formula bar, click the **Enter** button ✔ to display the result *$2,399,522*. Compare your screen with Figure 1.

   The MAX function evaluates all of the values in the range C5:C32 and then returns the highest value found in the range.

3. Select the range **C34:C36**. AutoFill the formulas to the right through column **F**, and then compare your screen with Figure 2.

   In this manner, you can AutoFill several different functions or formulas at the same time. Here, the different functions at the beginning of each row are filled across the columns.

■ **Continue to the next page to complete the skill**

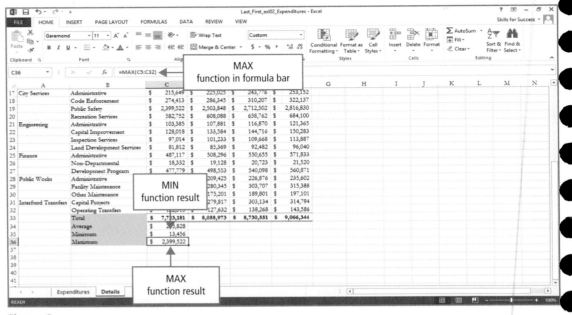

Figure 1

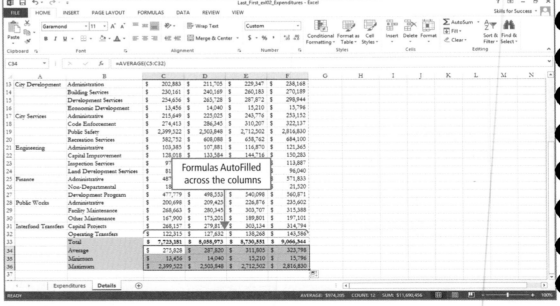

Figure 2

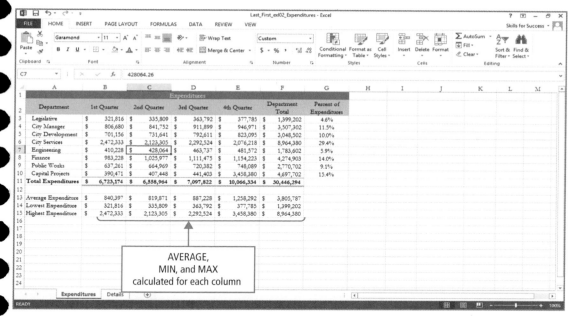

AVERAGE,
MIN, and MAX
calculated for each column

Figure 3

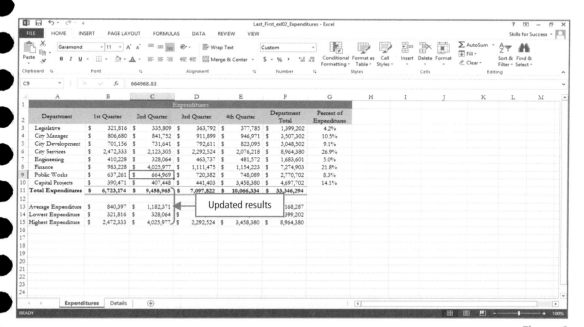

Updated results

Figure 4

4. Click the **Expenditures** worksheet tab. In cell **B14**, repeat the technique just practiced to insert the **MIN** function, using the range **B3:B10** as the function argument in the parentheses. Verify that the result is *$321,816*.

5. In cell **B15**, insert the **MAX** function using the range **B3:B10** as the function argument. Verify that the result is *$2,472,333*. Take care that the argument range does not include the cells with the total expenditures or average expenditures.

6. AutoFill the formulas in **B14:B15** to the right through column **F**. Review the functions, and verify that the lowest and highest values in each column were selected from each of the ranges for the MIN and MAX functions. Click cell **C7**, and then compare your screen with Figure 3.

7. With cell **C7** as the active cell, type 328,064 and then press Enter. In cell **C8**, type 4,025,977 and then press Enter. Verify that the MIN and MAX values in cells **C14** and **C15**, and the SUM and AVERAGE functions were automatically updated. Compare your screen with Figure 4.

8. **Save** 🖫 the workbook.

■ **You have completed Skill 5 of 10**

▶ A *chart* is a graphical representation of data used to show comparisons, patterns, and trends.

▶ A *column chart* is useful for illustrating comparisons among related numbers.

1. Verify *Expenditures* is the active worksheet. Select the range **A2:E10**—do *not* include the *Department Total* column or the *Total Expenditures* row in your selection. Click the **Quick Analysis Lens** button , and then in the **Quick Analysis** gallery, click **Charts**. Compare your screen with **Figure 1**.

2. In the **Quick Analysis** gallery, click the third chart—**Clustered Column**—to insert the chart and display the *Chart Tools* contextual tabs. Compare your screen with **Figure 2**.

When you insert a chart in this manner, an *embedded chart*—a chart that is placed on the worksheet containing the data—is created. Embedded charts are beneficial when you want to view or print a chart with its source data.

An *axis* is a line bordering the chart plot area that is used as a frame of reference for measurement. The *category axis* is the axis that displays the category labels. A *category label* is nonnumeric text that identifies the categories of data. Here, the worksheet's row labels—the department names in A2:A10—are used for the category labels.

The *value axis* is the axis that displays the worksheet's numeric data.

The *y-axis* is the vertical axis of a chart, and the *x-axis* is the horizontal axis of a chart.

■ **Continue to the next page to complete the skill** ▶

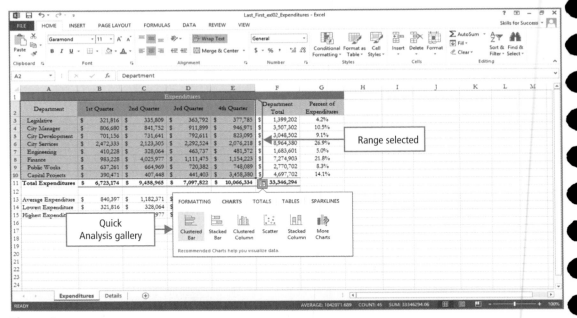

Figure 1

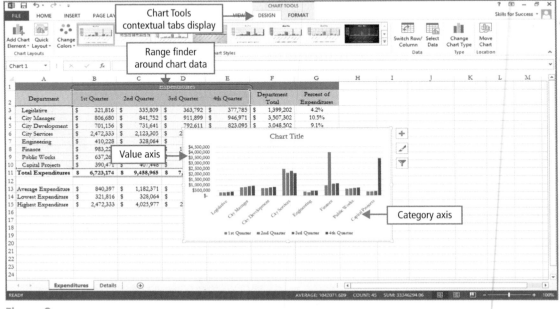

Figure 2

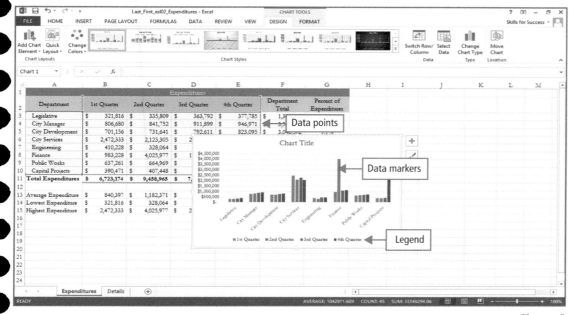

Figure 3

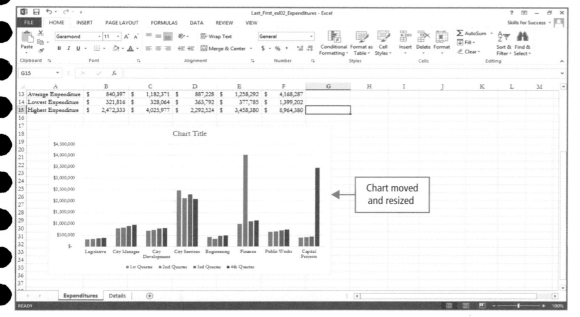

Figure 4

3. On the left side of the chart, locate the numerical scale, and then on the bottom, locate the quarters displayed in the legend. Compare your screen with Figure 3.

In the worksheet, each cell in the blue range finder is referred to as a ***data point***—a chart value that originates in a worksheet cell. Each data point is represented in a chart by a ***data marker***—a column, a bar, an area, a dot, a pie slice, or another symbol that represents a single data point.

Data points that are related to one another form a ***data series***, and each data series has a unique color or pattern represented in the chart ***legend***—a box that identifies the patterns or colors that are assigned to the data series or categories in the chart. Here, each quarter is a different data series, and the legend shows the color assigned to each quarter.

4. Point to the upper border of the chart to display the ⟲ pointer, and then move the chart to position its upper left corner in the middle of cell **A17**. If you are working with a touch screen, you can touch the chart and slide it to the correct position.

5. Scroll down to display row **36**. Point to the lower right corner of the chart to display the ⤡ pointer, and then drag to resize the chart to display the lower right chart corner in the middle of cell **G36**. Click cell **G15** and then compare your screen with Figure 4.

6. Save 🖫 the workbook.

■ **You have completed Skill 6 of 10**

▶ You can modify the overall look of a chart by applying a ***chart layout***—a pre-built set of chart elements that can include a title, a legend, or labels.

▶ You can modify the overall look of a chart by applying a ***chart style***—a pre-built chart format that applies an overall visual look to a chart by modifying its graphic effects, colors, and backgrounds.

1. Click the border of the chart to select the chart and display the chart buttons.

2. To the right of the chart, click the **Chart Styles** button, and then click **Style 3**. At the top of the **Chart Styles** gallery, click the **Color tab**, and then under **Colorful**, click **Color 3**. Compare your screen with **Figure 1**.

3. Click the **Chart Styles** button to close the gallery.

4. On the **Design tab**, in the **Chart Layouts group**, click the **Quick Layout** button. Point at the different layouts to preview the layouts on the chart. Point at **Layout 9**, and then compare your screen with **Figure 2**.

5. In the **Quick Layout** gallery, click **Layout 9** to add the axes titles and to move the legend to the right side of the chart.

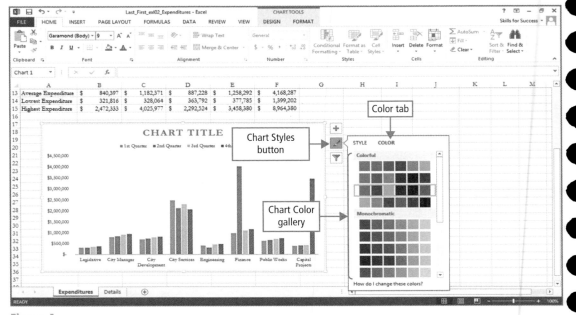

Figure 1

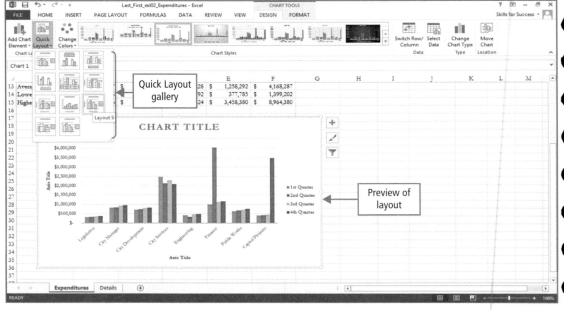

Figure 2

■ Continue to the next page to complete the skill ▶

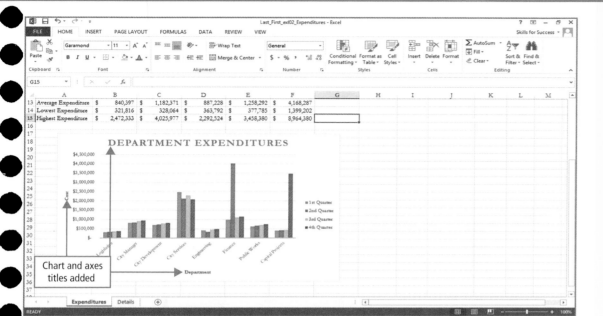

Figure 3

6. At the top of the chart, click the text *Chart Title*, and then type Department Expenditures to insert the text into the formula bar. Press Enter to accept the text. Verify that your text replaced any text in the chart title.

7. Below the horizontal axis, click the text *Axis Title*, type Department and then press Enter.

8. To the left of the vertical axis, click the text *Axis Title*, type Cost and then press Enter.

9. Click cell **G15** to deselect the chart. **Save** 🖫 the workbook, and then compare your screen with **Figure 3**.

10. Take a moment to examine the various types of charts available in Excel, as summarized in **Figure 4**.

■ **You have completed Skill 7 of 10**

Chart Types Commonly Used in Excel	
Chart type	**Used to**
Column	Illustrate data changes over a period of time or illustrate comparisons among items.
Line	Illustrate trends over time, with time displayed along the horizontal axis and the data point values connected by a line.
Pie	Illustrate the relationship of parts to a whole.
Bar	Illustrate comparisons among individual items.
Area	Emphasize the magnitude of change over time.

Figure 4

▸ A *pie chart* displays the relationship of parts to a whole.

▸ A *chart sheet* is a workbook sheet that contains only a chart and is useful when you want to view a chart separately from the worksheet data.

1. Verify *Expenditures* is the active sheet. Select the range **A2:A10**. Hold down Ctrl, and then select the nonadjacent range **F2:F10**.

2. On the **Insert tab**, in the **Charts group**, click the **Recommended Charts** button, and then compare your screen with **Figure 1**.

3. In the **Insert Chart** dialog box, click the **Pie** thumbnail, and then click **OK**.

> Here, the row labels identify the slices of the pie chart, and the department totals are the data series that determine the size of each pie slice.

4. On the **Design tab**, in the **Location group**, click the **Move Chart** button. In the **Move Chart** dialog box, select the **New sheet** option button. In the **New sheet** box, replace the highlighted text *Chart1* with Expenditure Chart as shown in **Figure 2**.

5. In the **Move Chart** dialog box, click **OK** to move the pie chart to a chart sheet.

6. On the **Design tab**, in the **Type group**, click the **Change Chart Type** button. In the **Change Chart Type** dialog box, click the **3-D Pie** thumbnail and then click **OK**.

> The chart is changed from a two-dimensional chart to a three-dimensional chart. **3-D**, which is short for *three-dimensional*, refers to an image that appears to have all three spatial dimensions—length, width, and depth.

■ **Continue to the next page to complete the skill**

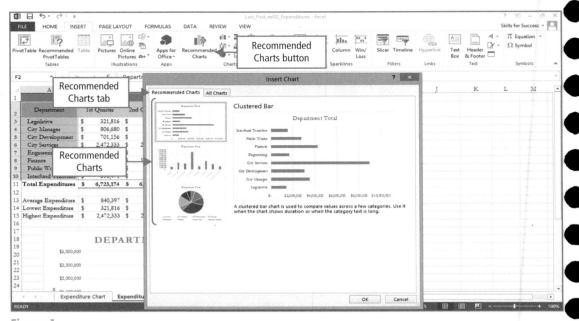

Figure 1

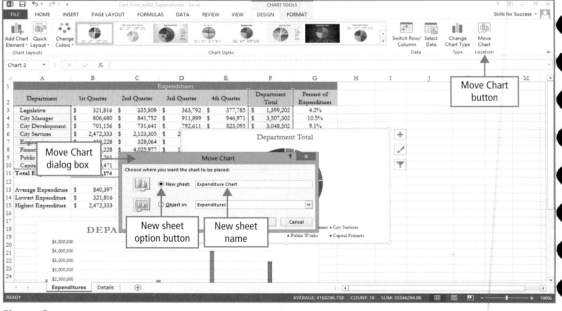

Figure 2

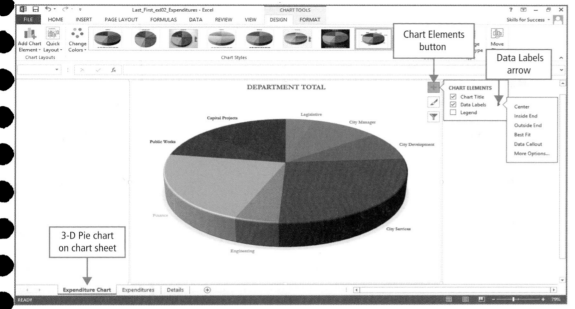

Figure 3

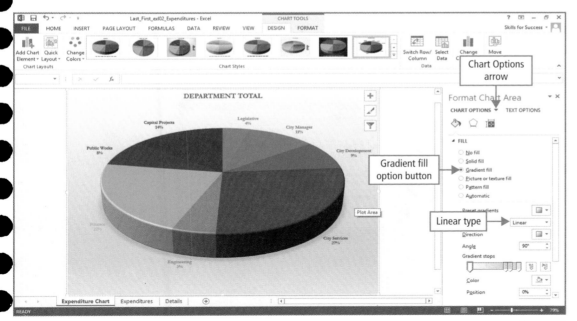

Figure 4

7. To the right of the chart, click the **Chart Styles** button. In the **Chart Styles** gallery, scroll down, and then click **Style 8**.

8. To the right of the chart, click the **Chart Elements** button. Under **Chart Elements**, point at **Data Labels**, and then click the **Data Labels arrow**. Compare your screen with **Figure 3**.

9. In the **Data Labels** list, click **More Options** to open the Format Data Labels pane.

10. In the **Format Data Labels** pane, under **Label Contains**, select the **Percentage** check box. Verify that the **Category Name** check box is selected, and then clear any other check boxes.

11. At the top of the pane, click the **Label Options arrow** and then click **Chart Area**, to open the Format Chart Area pane. In the **Format Chart Area** pane, click the **Fill & Line** button, and then click **Fill**. Click the **Gradient fill** option button, and verify that the Type is *Linear*. Compare your screen with **Figure 4**.

12. **Close** the **Format Chart Area** pane.

13. On the **Insert tab**, in the **Text group**, click the **Header & Footer** button. In the **Page Setup** dialog box, click the **Custom Footer** button. Verify that the insertion point is in the **Left section** box, and then click the **Insert File Name** button. Click in the **Right section** box, and then click the **Insert Sheet Name** button. Click **OK** two times.

14. **Save** the workbook.

■ **You have completed Skill 8 of 10**

▶ A chart's data series and labels are linked to the source data in the worksheet. When worksheet values are changed, the chart is automatically updated.

1. Click the **Expenditures** worksheet tab to display the worksheet. Scroll as necessary to display row **8** at the top of the window and the chart at the bottom of the window. In the column chart, note the height of the *Finance* data marker for the 2nd Quarter and the *Capital Projects* data marker for the 4th Quarter.

2. Click cell **C8**. Type 1,017,000 and then press Enter to accept the new value. Notice the animation in the chart when changes are made to its source data. Compare your screen with **Figure 1**.

3. Click cell **E10**, type 316,000 and then press Enter.

   In cell G10, the *Capital Projects* expenditure now represents 5.7% of the projected total.

4. Click the **Expenditure Chart** worksheet tab to display the pie chart. Verify that in the pie chart, the slice for *Capital Projects* displays 6%.

   When underlying data is changed, the pie chart percentages and pie slices are automatically recalculated and resized. On the chart, 5.7% is rounded up to 6%.

5. Right-click the **Capital Projects** data label to select all of the data labels, and in the shortcut menu click **Font**. In the **Size** box, type 11 Compare your screen with **Figure 2**, and then click **OK**.

■ **Continue to the next page to complete the skill** ▶

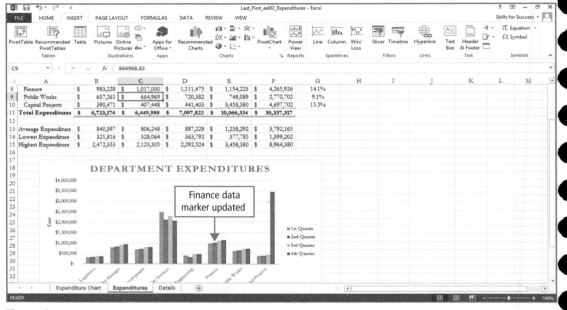

Figure 1

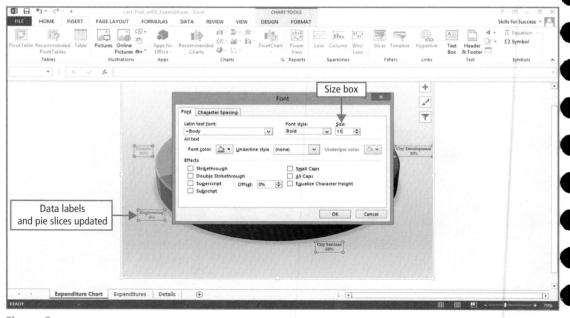

Figure 2

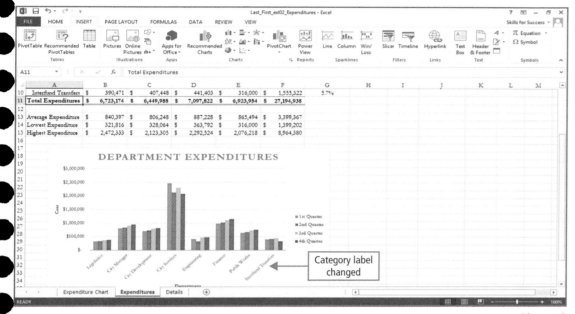

Category label
changed

Figure 3

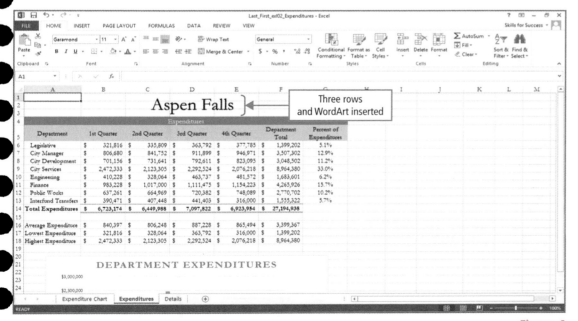

Three rows
and WordArt inserted

Figure 4

6. Click the **Expenditures** worksheet tab, and then in cell **A10**, change *Capital Projects* to Interfund Transfers Press [Enter] and then scroll down to verify that the column chart category label changed. Compare your screen with Figure 3.

7. Click the **Expenditure Chart** worksheet tab, and verify that the data label on the pie chart displays as *Interfund Transfers*.

8. Click the **Expenditures** worksheet tab. Scroll up, and then select the range **A1:G3**. On the **Home tab**, in the **Cells group**, click the **Insert arrow**, and then click **Insert Sheet Rows** to insert three blank rows.

9. On the **Insert tab**, in the **Text group**, click the **Insert WordArt** button [A ▾]. In the **WordArt** gallery, click the first style in the first row—**Fill - Black**, **Text 1**, **Shadow**. Immediately type Aspen Falls

10. Select the WordArt text. In the mini toolbar, click the **Font Size** button [11 ▾] and then click **32**.

11. Point to the bottom border of the WordArt box, and then with the [✥] pointer, drag to position the WordArt object to approximately the range **C1:E3**. Click cell **A1** to deselect the WordArt, and then compare your screen with Figure 4.

12. **Save** [💾] the workbook.

■ **You have completed Skill 9 of 10**

▶ Before you print an Excel worksheet, you can use Page Layout view to preview and adjust the printed document.

1. Verify *Expenditures* is the active worksheet. Scroll down, and then click the column chart to select the chart. Click the **File tab**, and then click **Print**. Compare your screen with **Figure 1**.

    When an embedded chart is selected, only the chart will print.

2. Click the **Back** button ⊙. Click cell **A19** to deselect the chart.

3. On the **View tab**, in the **Workbook Views group**, click the **Page Layout** button. On the left side of the status bar, notice that *Page: 1 of 2* displays, informing you that the data and the column chart would print on two pages.

4. On the **Page Layout tab**, in the **Scale to Fit group**, click the **Width arrow**, and then click **1 page**. Click the **File tab**, and then click **Print**. Compare your screen with **Figure 2**.

    1 of 1 displays at the bottom of the screen, indicating that the WordArt, the data, and the column chart will all print on one page.

5. Click the **Back** button ⊙. On the status bar, click the **Normal** button ▦ and then press Ctrl + Home to make cell **A1** the active cell.

■ **Continue to the next page to complete the skill** ▶

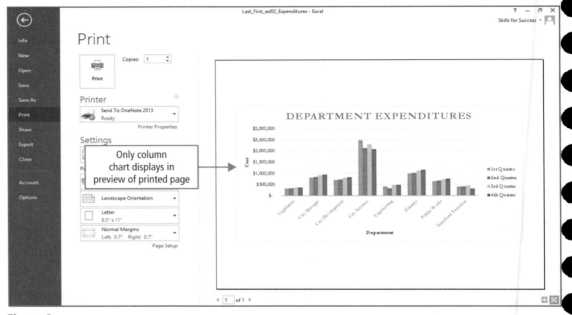

Figure 1

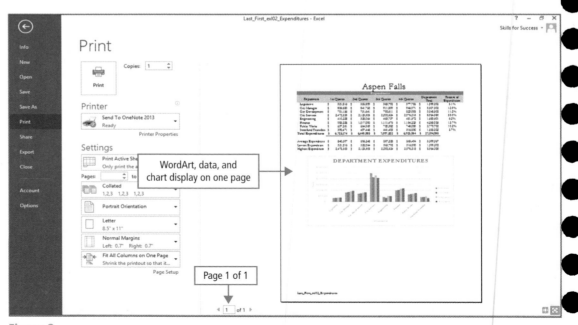

Figure 2

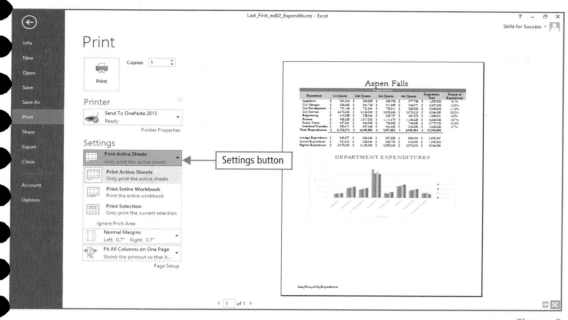

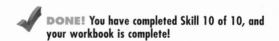

Figure 3

6. On the **Review tab**, in the **Proofing group**, click the **Spelling** button, and then check the spelling of the worksheet. When the message *Spell check complete. You're good to go!* displays, click **OK**.

7. **Save** 🖫 the workbook.

8. Click the **File tab**, and then click **Print**. Under **Settings**, click the first button. Compare your screen with Figure 3.

9. On the displayed list, click **Print Entire Workbook**. Notice at the bottom of the screen, *1 of 3* displays, and the chart sheet with the pie chart is the first page. Compare your screen with Figure 4.

10. At the bottom of the screen, click the **Next Page** button ▶ to preview the worksheet containing your WordArt, the data, and the column chart. Save 🖫 the workbook. Submit the workbook as directed by your instructor. If you are printing your work for this project, print the workbook. Otherwise, click the **Back** button ⊙.

11. If your instructor asked you to print formulas, display the worksheet formulas, AutoFit the column widths, and then print the formulas.

12. **Close** ⊠ Excel. Submit the file or printouts as directed by your instructor.

✔ **DONE! You have completed Skill 10 of 10, and your workbook is complete!**

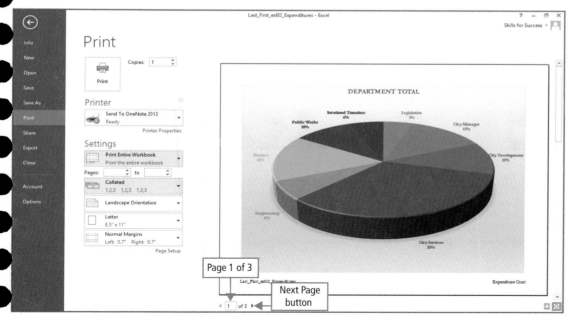

Figure 4

The following More Skills are located at **www.pearsonhighered.com/skills**

More Skills Insert, Edit, and Delete Comments

You can add comments to cells in a worksheet to provide reminders, to display clarifying information about data within the cells, or to document your work. When you point to a cell that contains a comment, the comment and the name of the person who created the comment display.

In More Skills 11, you will insert, edit, and delete comments.

To begin, open your web browser, navigate to www.pearsonhighered.com/skills, locate the name of your textbook, and then follow the instructions on the website.

More Skills Change Chart Types

After you create a chart, you may determine that a different chart type might be easier for the readers of your chart to understand. For example, you can change a bar chart to a column chart. The column chart and a bar chart are good choices to illustrate comparisons among items.

In More Skills 12, you will create a bar chart and then change the chart type to a column chart.

To begin, open your web browser, navigate to www.pearsonhighered.com/skills, locate the name of your textbook, and then follow the instructions on the website.

More Skills Copy Excel Data to Word Documents

You can copy the data and objects created in one application to another application, saving time and ensuring accuracy because data is entered only one time.

In More Skills 13, you will create a chart in Excel and then copy the chart and paste it into a Word document.

To begin, open your web browser, navigate to www.pearsonhighered.com/skills, locate the name of your textbook, and then follow the instructions on the website.

More Skills Fill Data with Flash Fill

Instead of entering data manually, you can use Flash Fill to recognize a pattern in your data and automatically enter the rest of your data. You can use the fill handle or the fill command to AutoFill data that follow a pattern or series—for example, hours, days of the week, or numeric sequences such as even numbers.

In More Skills 14, you will use Flash Fill to enter data in cells.

To begin, open your web browser, navigate to www.pearsonhighered.com/skills, locate the name of your textbook, and then follow the instructions on the website.

Please note that there are no additional projects to accompany the More Skills Projects, and they are not covered in the End-of-Chapter projects.

The following table summarizes the **SKILLS AND PROCEDURES** covered in this chapter.

Skill Number	Task	Step	Icon	Keyboard Shortcut
1	Wrap text	Home tab → Alignment group → Wrap Text		
1	Middle align text	Home tab → Alignment group → Middle Align	☰	
1	Center text	Home tab → Alignment group → Center	☰	
1	Increase indent	Home tab → Alignment group → Increase Indent	🔲	
2	Insert the SUM function	Quick Analysis Lens button → Totals → SUM	🔲	
2	Create an absolute cell reference	Select cell reference → Type $		F4
3	Apply the Percent style	Home tab → Number group → Percent Style	%	
3	Increase the number of display decimals	Home tab → Number group → Increase Decimal	.00	
4	Calculate an average	Home tab → Editing group → Sum arrow → Average		
5	Calculate a minimum	Home tab → Editing group → Sum arrow → Min		
5	Calculate a maximum	Home tab → Editing group → Sum arrow → Max		
6	Insert a chart using the Quick Analysis Lens	Quick Analysis Lens button → Charts → select desired chart	🔲	
7	Apply a chart style	Chart Style → Style		
7	Apply a chart layout	Design tab → Chart Layouts group → Quick Layout → Layout		
8	Insert a recommended chart	Insert tab → Charts group → Recommended Charts → select desired chart		
8	Move a chart to its own worksheet	Design tab → Locations group → Move Chart → New sheet		
8	Change the chart type	Design tab → Type group → Change Chart Type → Type		
8	Change chart data labels	Chart Elements → Data labels arrow → More Options → Format Data labels pane		
9	Insert WordArt	Insert tab → Text group → WordArt	A ▾	
10	Adjust scale	Page Layout tab → Scale to Fit group → Width arrow → Page		
10	Print an entire workbook	File tab → Print → Settings → Print Entire Workbook		

Key Terms

Online Help Skills

1. Start **Excel 2013**, and then in the upper right corner of the start page, click the **Help** button ⬚?⬚ .

2. In the **Excel Help** window **Search help** box, type Keyboard shortcuts and then press ⬚Enter⬚ .

3. In the search result list, click **Keyboard shortcuts in Excel**, and then compare your screen with Figure 1.

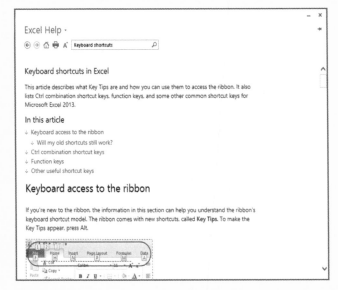

Figure 1

4. Read the article to answer the following question: How can you use Key Tips to access the ribbon?

Matching

Match each term in the second column with its correct definition in the first column by writing the letter of the term on the blank line in front of the correct definition.

____ **1.** A command with which you can display text on multiple lines within a cell.

____ **2.** A cell reference that refers to a cell by its fixed position in a worksheet and does not change when the formula is copied.

____ **3.** Rules that specify the way numbers should display.

____ **4.** The default format applied to numbers.

____ **5.** The value(s) that determine how a function should be used.

____ **6.** A graphical representation of data in a worksheet that shows comparisons, patterns, and trends.

____ **7.** A chart line that contains words as labels.

____ **8.** A chart line that contains numeric data.

____ **9.** The function that adds a group of values and then divides the result by the number of values in the group.

____ **10.** The Excel feature that outlines all of the cells referenced in a formula.

A Absolute cell reference

B Argument

C AVERAGE

D Category axis

E Chart

F General format

G Number format

H Range finder

I Text wrap

J Value axis

BizSkills Video

1. Why should you practice for an interview?

2. How should you answer a question about a missing reference?

Multiple Choice

Choose the correct answer.

1. Automatically changing the column width to accommodate the longest column entry.
    A. Drag and drop
    B. AutoFit
    C. Auto adjust

2. A green triangle that indicates a possible error in a formula.
    A. Error indicator
    B. Message
    C. Dialog Box Launcher

3. A chart type useful for illustrating comparisons among related numbers.
    A. Pie chart
    B. Area chart
    C. Column chart

4. A chart placed on a worksheet with the source data.
    A. Chart sheet
    B. Column chart
    C. Embedded chart

5. The related data points in a chart.
    A. Column
    B. Data series
    C. Chart point

6. The box that identifies the patterns or colors assigned to the data series.
    A. Legend
    B. Dialog box
    C. Message box

7. A predesigned combination of chart elements.
    A. 3-D chart
    B. Chart layout
    C. Chart

8. A pre-built chart format that applies an overall visual look to a chart.
    A. Data marker
    B. Chart finder
    C. Chart style

9. The chart type that best displays the relationship of parts to a whole.
    A. Pie chart
    B. Area chart
    C. Column chart

10. A worksheet that contains only a chart.
    A. Worksheet
    B. Chart area
    C. Chart sheet

Topics for Discussion

1. Search current newspapers and magazines for examples of charts. Which charts catch your eye and why? Do the charts appeal to you because of their color or format? Is something intriguing revealed to you in the chart that you have never considered before? What are some formatting changes that you think make a chart interesting and valuable to a reader?

2. Do you think 3-D pie charts distort the data in a way that is misleading? Why or why not?

Skills Review

To complete this project, you will need the following file:

- exl02_SRRevenue

You will save your file as:

- Last_First_exl02_SRRevenue

1. Start **Excel 2013**, and open the file **exl02_SRRevenue**. **Save** the file in your chapter folder as Last_First_exl02_SRRevenue Add the file name in the worksheet's left footer, and the sheet name in the right footer. Return to Normal view.

2. In the column heading area, point to the right boundary of column **A** and double-click to AutoFit the column width. Click the column **B** heading, and then drag right to select columns **B:F**. Click the right boundary of column **B**, and then drag to the right until the ScreenTip indicates *Width:13:00 (109 pixels)*.

3. Select the range **A1:F1**. On the **Home tab**, in the **Alignment group**, click the **Wrap Text**, **Middle Align**, and **Center** buttons.

4. Select the range **B2:E13**. Click the **Quick Analysis** button, click **Totals**, and then click the first option—**SUM**.

5. Select the range **B2:E14**. In the **Number group**, click the **Decrease Decimal** button two times. Select the range **B14:E14**. In the **Styles group**, click the **Cell Styles** button, and then click **Total**.

6. In cell **F2**, type =E2/$E$14 and then on the formula bar, click the **Enter** button. With cell F2 the active cell, in the **Number group**, click the **Percent Style** button, and the **Increase Decimal** button. In the **Alignment group**, click the **Center** button. AutoFill the formula in cell **F2** down through cell **F13**. Click cell **A15**, and then compare your screen with **Figure 1**.

7. Click cell **B16**. Type =Av and then in the formula AutoComplete list, double-click **AVERAGE**. For the function argument, select the range **B2:B13**, and then press Enter. Using the same function argument range, in cell **B17**, enter the **MAX** function. Select the range **B16:B17**, and then AutoFill the formulas to the right through column **D**. Compare your screen with **Figure 2**.

■ Continue to the next page to complete this Skills Review

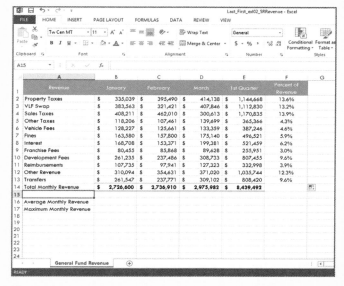

Figure 1

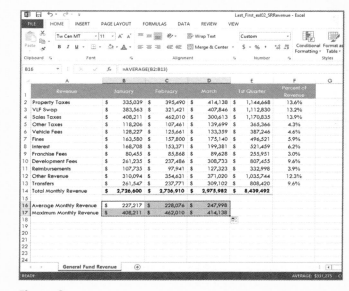

Figure 2

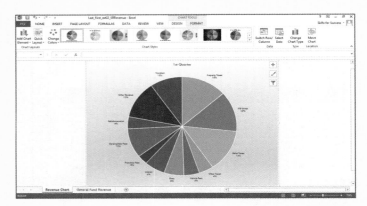

Figure 3

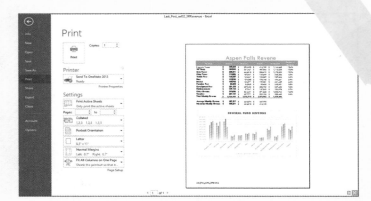

Figure 4

8. Select the range **A1:D13**. Click the **Quick Analysis Lens** button, click **Charts**, and then click the **Clustered Column** thumbnail. Move and resize the chart to display in approximately the range **A20:F40**. At the top right corner of the chart, click the **Chart Styles** button, and then click the **Style 9** thumbnail. Click the **Chart Title**, type General Fund Revenue and then press Enter.

9. Select the nonadjacent ranges **A1:A13** and **E1:E13**. On the **Insert tab**, in the **Charts group**, click the **Recommended Charts** button. On the **All Charts tab**, click **Pie**, and then click **OK**.

10. On the **Design tab**, in the **Location group**, click the **Move Chart** button. In the **Move Chart** dialog box, select the **New sheet** option button, type the sheet name Revenue Chart and then click **OK**.

11. On the **Design tab**, in the **Chart Layouts group**, click the **Quick Layout** button, and then click **Layout 1**.

12. Click the **Chart Elements** button, click the **Data Labels arrow**, and then click **More Options**. In the **Format Data Labels** pane, under **Label Position**, click **Outside End**.

13. Click the **Label Options arrow**, and then click **Chart Area**. In the **Format Chart Area** pane, click the **Fill & Line** button, and then click **Fill**. Select the **Gradient fill** option button, and then **Close** the Format Chart Area pane. Compare your screen with Figure 3.

14. On the **Insert tab**, in the **Text group**, click the **Header & Footer** button. In the **Page Setup** dialog box, click the **Custom Footer** button. Insert the **File Name** in the left section, and insert the **Sheet Name** in the right section.

15. Click the **General Fund Revenue** worksheet tab. Select the range **A1:A3**. On the **Home tab**, in the **Cells group**, click the **Insert arrow**, and then click **Insert Sheet Rows**. On the **Insert tab**, in the **Text group**, click the **Insert WordArt** button, and then in the first row, click the second thumbnail—**Fill - Turquoise, Accent 1 Shadow**. Immediately type Aspen Falls Revenue Select the text in the WordArt. On the mini toolbar, change the **Font Size** to **36**. Point to the bottom border of the WordArt, and then move the WordArt to approximately the range **B1:E3**.

16. Click cell **A1**. Click the **Page Layout tab**. In the **Scale to Fit group**, click the **Width** arrow, and then click **1 page** button.

17. Click the **File tab**, and then click **Print**. Compare your screen with Figure 4.

18. **Save** the workbook, and then submit the workbook as directed by your instructor.

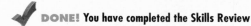 **DONE! You have completed the Skills Review**

Skills Assessment 1

To complete this project, you will need the following file:

- exl02_SA1Debt

You will save your workbook as:

- Last_First_exl02_SA1Debt

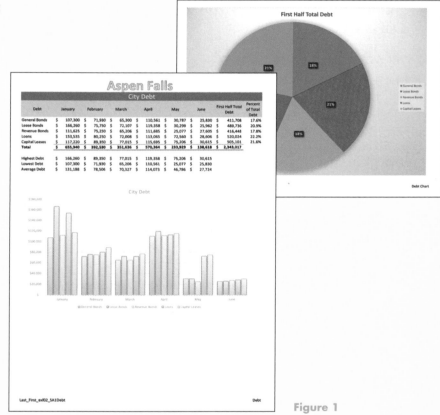

1. Start **Excel 2013**, and open the file **exl02_SA1Debt. Save** the workbook in your chapter folder as Last_First_exl02_SA1Debt Add the file name in the worksheet's left footer and the sheet name in the right footer. Return to Normal view.

2. Select the range **A2:I2**, and then apply the alignment **Wrap Text** and **Middle Align**.

3. Select the column headings **B:I**, and then AutoFit the column widths.

4. In the range **B8:H8**, insert the column totals, and apply the **Total** cell style.

5. Select the range **B3:H8**, and then display no decimals.

6. In cell **I3**, calculate the *Percent of Total Debt*. In the formula, use an absolute cell reference when referring to cell **H8**. AutoFill the formula down through cell **I7**, and then format the results as percentages with one decimal place.

7. In the range **B10:G10**, insert a function to calculate the highest monthly debt. In the range **B11:G11**, insert a function to calculate the lowest monthly debt. In the range **B12:G12**, insert a function to calculate the average monthly debt.

8. Insert a **Pie** chart based on the nonadjacent ranges **A2:A7** and **H2:H7**. Move the pie chart to a chart sheet with the sheet name Debt Chart

9. For the pie chart, apply **Layout 6**, and then apply the **Chart Style 3**. Change the data label **Font Size** to **12**. Add the file name in the chart sheet's left footer and the sheet name in the right footer.

10. On the **Debt** worksheet, insert a **Clustered Column** chart based on the range **A2:G7**. Move the chart below the data, and then resize the chart to approximately the range **A15:I38**. Apply the chart **Style 5**. Change the chart title to City Debt

Figure 1

11. Insert three sheet rows at the top of the worksheet. Insert **WordArt**, using the style **Gradient Fill – Purple, Accent 4, Outline - Accent 4**. Change the WordArt text to Aspen Falls and then change the **Font Size** to **36**. Move the WordArt to the top of the worksheet, centering it above the data.

12. Adjust the **Scale to Fit** to fit the WordArt, data, and column chart on one page.

13. **Save** the workbook, and then compare your completed workbook with Figure 1.

14. **Close** Excel, and then submit the workbook as directed by your instructor.

 **DONE! You have completed Skills Assessment 1**

Skills Assessment 2

To complete this project, you will need the following file:

- exl02_SA2Cost

You will save your workbook as:

- Last_First_exl02_SA2Cost

1. Start **Excel 2013**, and open the file **exl02_SA2Cost**. **Save** the workbook in your chapter folder as Last_First_exl02_SA2Cost Add the file name in the worksheet's left footer, and the sheet name in the right footer. Return to Normal view.

2. For column **A**, AutoFit the column width. For columns **B:K**, change the column width to **11.00 (93 pixels)**.

3. In the range **B3:K3**, apply the **Center** alignment. In the range **A4:A20**, apply the **Increase Indent** alignment.

4. In the range **I4:I20**, insert a function to calculate the average monthly cost. In the range **J4:J20**, insert a function to calculate the minimum monthly cost. In the range **K4:K20**, insert a function to calculate the maximum monthly cost.

5. In row **21**, insert totals for columns **B:H**, and then apply the **Total** cell style.

6. In cell **B22**, calculate the *Percent of First Half Costs*. In the formula, use an absolute cell reference when referring to cell **H21**. Format the result as a percent and display two decimals. AutoFill the formula to the right through column **G**.

7. Insert a **Stacked Bar** chart based on the range **A3:G20**. Move the stacked bar chart to a chart sheet named Projected Costs Chart Apply the chart **Style 11**. Change the Chart Title to Projected Monthly Costs Add the file name in the chart sheet's left footer and the sheet name in the right footer.

8. Click the **Cost** worksheet tab. Insert a **Pie** chart based on the nonadjacent ranges **A3:G3** and **A21:G21**. Move the pie chart to a chart sheet named Total Monthly Cost Apply the chart **Layout 1**. Change the data label position to **Data Callout**, and change the data label **Font Size** to **12**. Add the file name in the chart sheet's left footer and the sheet name in the right footer.

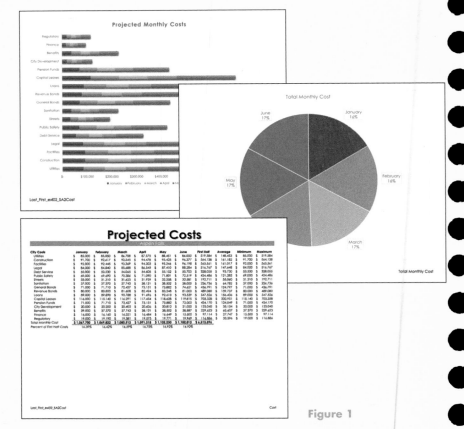

Figure 1

9. On the **Cost** worksheet, insert four blank lines at the top of the worksheet. Insert a WordArt with the **Fill - Black**, **Text 1**, **Outline - Background 1**, **Hard Shadow - Background 1** style. In the WordArt, type the text Projected Costs and then change the **Font Size** to **44**. Move the WordArt to the top of the worksheet, centering it above the data.

10. Scale the **Cost** worksheet to print on **1 page**.

11. **Save** the workbook, and then compare your completed workbook with Figure 1.

12. **Close** Excel, and then submit the workbook as directed by your instructor.

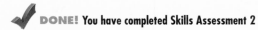 **DONE! You have completed Skills Assessment 2**

Visual Skills Check

To complete this project, you will need the following file:

- exl02_VSNetAssets

You will save your workbook as:

- Last_First_exl02_VSNetAssets

Start **Excel 2013**, and open the file **exl02_VSNetAssets**. **Save** the workbook in your chapter folder as Last_First_exl02_VSNetAssets Create the worksheet as shown in **Figure 1**. Calculate the *Percent of Total Net Assets* using an absolute cell reference. In rows **13:15**, insert the statistical functions that correspond with the row labels. Format the values and text as shown. Create the pie chart, and then move and resize the chart as shown in the figure. The chart uses the **Layout 4** chart layout, data label font size **11**, and in the chart area the **Linear Down** gradient fill. Insert the file name in the worksheet's left footer. **Save** the workbook, and then submit the workbook as directed by your instructor.

✔ **DONE! You have completed Visual Skills Check**

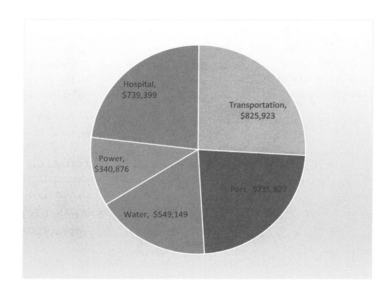

Aspen Falls
Net Assets
Business-type Activities

Asset	July	August	September	Total	Percent of Total Net Assets
Transportation	$ 268,755	$ 275,082	$ 282,086	$ 825,923	25.9%
Port	$ 242,886	$ 245,688	$ 247,253	$ 735,827	23.1%
Water	$ 175,885	$ 180,256	$ 193,008	$ 549,149	17.2%
Power	$ 117,006	$ 108,832	$ 115,038	$ 340,876	10.7%
Hospital	$ 213,468	$ 250,865	$ 275,066	$ 739,399	23.2%
Total Net Assets	$ 1,018,000	$ 1,060,723	$ 1,112,451	$ 3,191,174	
Minimum Asset	$ 117,006	$ 108,832	$ 115,038		
Maximum Asset	$ 268,755	$ 275,082	$ 282,086		
Average Asset	$ 203,600	$ 212,145	$ 222,490		

Hospital, $739,399

Transportation, $825,923

Power, $340,876

Port, $735,827

Water, $549,149

Last_First_exl02_VSNetAssets

Figure 1

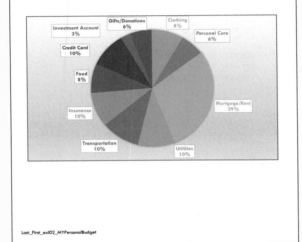

Figure 1

My Skills

To complete this project, you will need the following file:

- exl02_MYPersonalBudget

You will save your workbook as:

- Last_First_exl02_MYPersonalBudget

1. Start **Excel 2013**, and open the file **exl02_MYPersonalBudget**. **Save** the workbook in your chapter folder as Last_First_exl02_MYPersonalBudget Add the file name in the worksheet's left footer, and then return to Normal view.

2. Change the alignments of the row **3** labels, and indent the column **A** expense labels. In the range **B14:E14**, insert the column totals.

3. In the range **B15:D15**, insert a function to calculate the average monthly expense. In the range **B16:D16**, insert a function to calculate the maximum monthly expense.

4. In cell **F4**, calculate the *Expense as a Percent of Total*. In the formula, use an absolute cell reference when referring to the total. Format the results as percentages with one decimal, and then AutoFill the formula down through cell **F13**.

5. Apply the **Total** cell style where appropriate.

6. Insert a **Pie** chart based on the nonadjacent ranges **A3:A13** and **E3:E13**.

7. Move the pie chart to an appropriate location below your data, and then resize the chart.

8. Format the pie chart with any of the chart options of your choice including layout, style, or color.

9. At the top of the worksheet, insert three blank rows. Insert a WordArt using your first and last names as the WordArt text. Move the WordArt above the data and resize to fit in the blank rows.

10. Adjust the scaling to fit the data and the pie chart on one page when printed.

11. **Save** the workbook, and then submit the workbook as directed by your instructor. Compare your completed workbook with Figure 1.

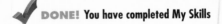 **DONE! You have completed My Skills**

Skills Challenge 1

To complete this project, you will need the following file:

- exl02_SC1Budget

You will save your workbook as:

- Last_First_exl02_SC1Budget

Start **Excel 2013.** Open the file **exl02_SC1Budget**, and then save the workbook in your chapter folder as Last_First_exl02_SC1Budget During the fourth quarter of this year, the Accounting Department developed a summary of the proposed Aspen Falls budget. Correct the errors in the statistical functions—you may want to display the formulas. Use an absolute cell reference when correcting the percent. Correct the number formats, and format the labels appropriately. Modify the WordArt and the column chart. Verify that the WordArt, data, and column chart will print on one page. Add the file name in the worksheet's left footer. Save the workbook, and then submit the workbook as directed by your instructor.

 DONE! You have completed Skills Challenge 1

Skills Challenge 2

To complete this project, you will need the following file:

- exl02_SC2Classes

You will save your workbook as:

- Last_First_exl02_SC2Classes

Start **Excel 2013**, and then open the workbook **exl02_SC2Classes**. Save the workbook in your chapter folder as Last_First_exl02_SC2Classes Carter Horikoshi, the Art Center Supervisor, created a workbook to track how many students attended Community Center classes last summer. He wants to determine if he should offer more classes this summer based on the number of students from last summer. He wants to know the total enrollment and the average enrollment for each month and for each class. He would like to view a chart that summarized the enrollment data. Using the skills you learned in this chapter, provide Mr. Horikoshi a workbook to assist him in his decision. Add the file name in the worksheet's left footer. Save the workbook, and then submit the workbook as directed by your instructor.

 DONE! You have completed Skills Challenge 2

CHAPTER 3

Manage Multiple Worksheets

- ► Organizations typically create workbooks that contain multiple worksheets. In such a workbook, the first worksheet often summarizes the detailed information in the other worksheets.

- ► In an Excel workbook, you can insert and move worksheets to create the detailed worksheets and summary worksheet that you need.

- ► By grouping worksheets, you can edit and format the data in multiple worksheets at the same time. The changes you make on the active sheet are reflected in all of the sheets included in the group.

- ► You can create multiple worksheets quickly by copying and pasting information from one worksheet to other worksheets.

- ► You can color code each worksheet tab so that detailed information can be quickly located.

- ► When you use multiple math operators in a single formula, you must take care to ensure the operations are carried out in the intended order.

- ► When building a summary worksheet, you will typically use formulas that refer to cells in the other worksheets.

© Jas

Aspen Falls City Hall

In this chapter, you will work with a spreadsheet for Diane Payne, the Public Works Director in Aspen Falls. She wants to know the revenue generated from parking meters and parking tickets in different locations throughout the city. Understanding how much revenue is generated from the meters and tickets and the costs associated with park maintenance and upgrades will help Diane decide if more meters should be added and if more personnel should be hired to enforce parking regulations.

A workbook, composed of multiple worksheets, allows Diane to collect data from different worksheets but analyze those worksheets grouped together as a whole. When you have a large amount of data to organize in a workbook, dividing the data into logical elements, such as locations or time periods, and then placing each element in a separate worksheet often makes sense. In other words, it is often better to design a system of worksheets instead of trying to fit all of the information on a single worksheet. You can then collect and input the data on an individual basis and see the summarized results with minimal effort.

In this project, you will work with grouped worksheets to enter formulas and apply formatting on all selected worksheets at the same time. You will create formulas that use multiple math operators, construct formulas that refer to cells in other worksheets, and create and format a clustered bar chart.

Time to complete all 10
skills – 60 to 90 minutes

Student data file needed for this chapter:

exl03_Parking

You will save your workbook as:

Last_First_exl03_Parking

Outcome

Using the skills in this chapter, you will be able to
work with Excel worksheets like this:

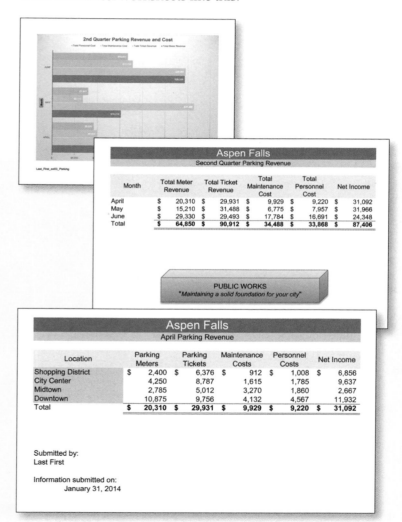

SKILLS

Skills 1-10 Training

At the end of this chapter you will be able to:

Skill 1   Organize Worksheet Tabs

Skill 2   Enter and Format Dates

Skill 3   Clear Cell Contents and Formats

Skill 4   Move Cell Contents and Use Paste Options

Skill 5   Enter Data in Grouped Worksheets

Skill 6   Insert Multiple Math Operators in Formulas

Skill 7   Format Grouped Worksheets

Skill 8   Insert, Hide, Delete, and Move Worksheets

Skill 9   Create Summary Worksheets

Skill 10   Create Clustered Bar Charts

MORE SKILLS

Skill 11   Create Organization Charts

Skill 12   Create Line Charts

Skill 13   Set and Clear Print Areas

Skill 14   Create, Edit, and Delete Hyperlinks

▶ EXL 3-1
VIDEO

▶ When a workbook contains more than one worksheet, you can move among worksheets by clicking the worksheet tabs.

▶ *Tab scrolling buttons* are buttons to the left of worksheet tabs used to display worksheet tabs that are not in view.

1. Start **Excel 2013**, and then open the student data file **exl03_Parking**. Click the **File tab**, and then click **Save As**. Click the **Browse** button, and then navigate to the location where you are saving your files. Click **New folder**, type Excel Chapter 3 and then press Enter two times. In the **File name** box, using your own name, name the workbook Last_First_exl03_ Parking and then press Enter.

2. At the bottom of the Excel window, click the **Sheet2** worksheet tab to make it the active worksheet, and then compare your screen with **Figure 1**.

3. Click the **Sheet1** worksheet tab to make it the active worksheet.

4. On the **Home tab**, in the **Cells group**, click the **Format** button, and then click **Rename Sheet**. Compare your screen with **Figure 2**.

5. Verify the **Sheet1** worksheet tab name is selected, type April and then press Enter to accept the name change.

> You can use up to 31 characters in a worksheet tab name.

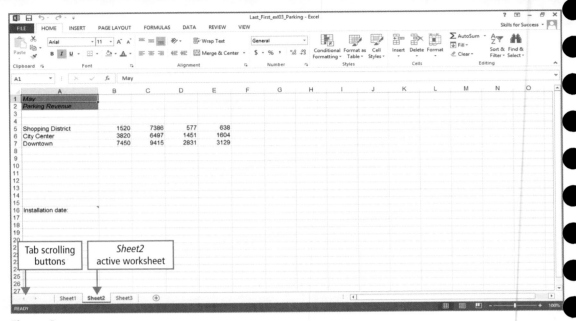

Figure 1

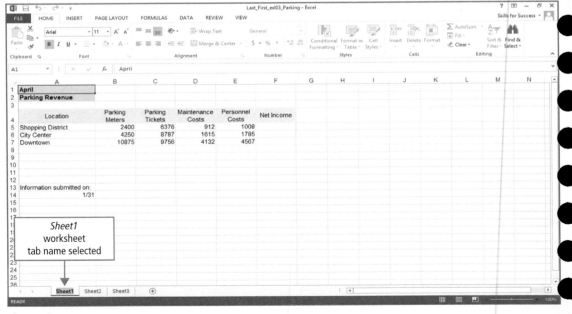

Figure 2

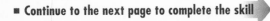
■ **Continue to the next page to complete the skill**

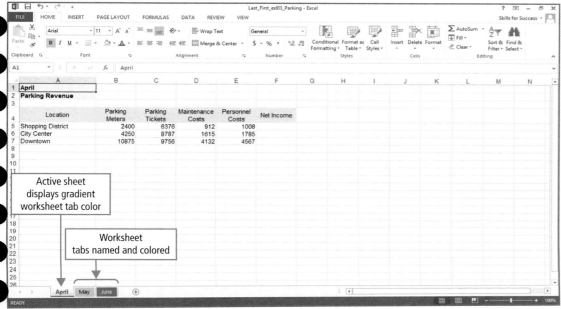

Figure 3

Figure 4

6. Double-click the **Sheet2** worksheet tab to make it the active sheet and to select the sheet name. Compare your screen with **Figure 3**.

7. With the **Sheet2** worksheet tab name selected, type May and then press [Enter].

8. Using either of the two methods just practiced, rename the **Sheet3** worksheet tab as June and then press [Enter].

9. Verify that the **June** sheet is the active worksheet. On the **Page Layout tab**, in the **Themes group**, click the **Colors** button. Scroll down, and then click **Slipstream** to change the theme colors for this workbook.

10. On the **Home tab**, in the **Cells group**, click the **Format** button, and then point to **Tab Color** to display the colors associated with the *Slipstream* theme colors. Click the fifth color in the first row—**Blue, Accent 1**. Alternately, right-click the worksheet tab, and then click Tab Color.

   A gradient color on a worksheet tab indicates that the worksheet is active. When a worksheet is not active, the entire worksheet tab is filled with the selected color.

11. Use the technique just practiced to change the worksheet tab color of the **May** worksheet tab to the sixth color in the first row—**Turquoise, Accent 2**.

12. Change the worksheet tab color of the **April** worksheet tab to the seventh color in the first row—**Green, Accent 3**. Compare your screen with **Figure 4**.

13. **Save** 🖫 the workbook.

■ **You have completed Skill 1 of 10**

EXL 3-2
VIDEO

▶ When you enter a date, it is assigned a *serial number*—a sequential number.

▶ Dates are stored as sequential serial numbers so they can be used in calculations. By default, January 1, 1900, is serial number 1. January 1, 2014, is serial number 41640 because it is 41,640 days after January 1, 1900. Serial numbers make it possible to perform calculations on dates, for example, to find the number of days between two dates by subtracting the older date from the more recent date.

▶ When you type any of the following values into cells, Excel interprets them as dates: *7/4/10, 4-Jul, 4-Jul-10, Jul-10*. When typing in these date formats, the ⟨-⟩ (hyphen) key and the ⟨/⟩ (forward slash) key function identically.

▶ You can enter months using the entire name or first three characters. Years can be entered as two or four digits. When the year is left off, the current year will be inserted.

1. On the **April** sheet, click cell **A14** to display the underlying value *1/31/2014* in the formula bar. On the **Formulas tab**, in the **Formula Auditing group**, click the **Show Formulas** button. Compare your screen with Figure 1.

   The date, *January 31, 2014*, displays as 41670—the number of days since the reference date of January 1, 1900.

2. On the **Formulas tab**, in the **Formula Auditing group**, click the **Show Formulas** button to display the date.

3. On the **Home tab**, in the **Number group**, click the **Number Format arrow** (Figure 2).

   In the Number Format list, you can select common date, time, and number formats, or click *More Number Formats* to display additional built-in number formats.

▪ **Continue to the next page to complete the skill**

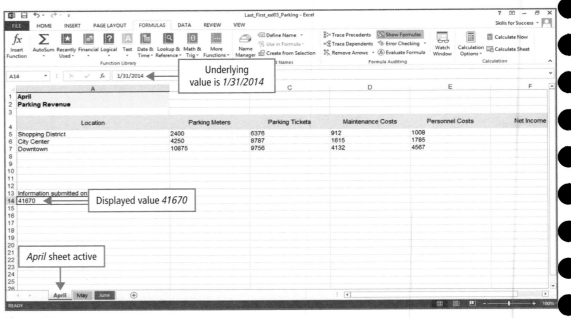

Figure 1

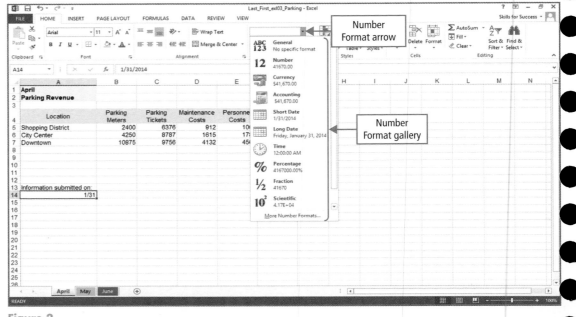

Figure 2

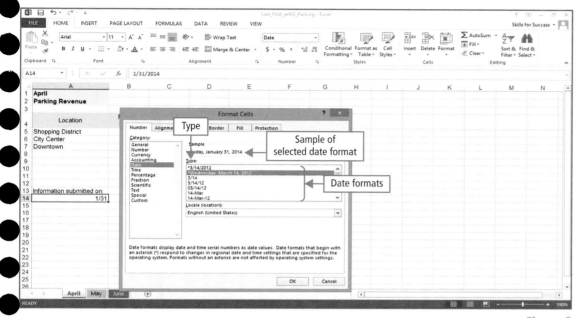

Figure 3

4. At the bottom of the **Number Format** list, click **More Number Formats**. On the **Number tab** of the **Format Cells** dialog box, notice Date is selected at the left. Under **Type**, click ***Wednesday, March 14, 2012**, to show a sample of the selected date format. Compare your screen with **Figure 3**.

   The date *Wednesday, March 14, 2012*, will not display in your worksheet. This is a sample of a format that can be applied to your current date.

5. Under **Type**, scroll down, click **March 14, 2012**, and then click **OK** to display the date in cell A14 as *January 31, 2014*.

6. Click the **May** worksheet tab to make it the active worksheet, and then click cell **A17**. Type 8/11/98 and then on the **formula bar**, click the **Enter** button ✓ to accept the entry and change the year from *98* to *1998*.

   When a two-digit year between 30 and 99 is entered, a twentieth-century date is applied to the date format—*8/11/1998*.

7. Click the **June** worksheet tab, and then click cell **A17**. Hold down Ctrl and press ⁏—the semicolon key. Press Enter to confirm the entry and to enter the current date.

   The Ctrl + ⁏ shortcut enters the current date, obtained from your computer, into the selected cell using the default date format. The table in **Figure 4** summarizes how Excel interprets various date formats.

8. **Save** 🖫 the workbook.

- **You have completed Skill 2 of 10**

Date Format AutoComplete	
Date Typed As	**Completed by Excel As**
7/4/14	7/4/2014
7-4-98	7/4/1998
7/4 or 7-4	4-Jul (current year assumed)
July 4 or Jul 4	4-Jul (current year assumed)
Jul/4 or Jul-4	4-Jul (current year assumed)
July 4, 1998	4-Jul-98
July 2014	Jul-14
July 1998	Jul-98

Figure 4

► Cells can contain formatting, comments, hyperlinks, and *content*—underlying formulas and data.

► You can clear the formatting, comments, hyperlinks, or the contents of a cell.

1. Click the **April** worksheet tab, and then click cell **A1**. On the **Home tab**, in the **Editing group**, click the **Clear** button, and then compare your screen with **Figure 1**.

2. On the menu, click **Clear Contents**. Look at cell **A1**, and verify that the text has been cleared but that the fill color applied to the cell still displays.

   Alternately, to delete the contents of a cell, you can press Delete , or you can tap a cell and then on Mini toolbar, click Clear.

3. In cell **A1**, type Parking Revenue and then on the **formula bar**, click the **Enter** button ✓.

4. With cell **A1** still selected, in the **Editing group**, click the **Clear** button, and then click **Clear Formats** to clear the formatting from the cell. Compare your screen with **Figure 2**.

5. Select cell **A2**. On the **Home tab**, in the **Editing group**, click the **Clear** button, and then click **Clear All** to clear both the cell contents and the cell formatting.

■ **Continue to the next page to complete the skill**

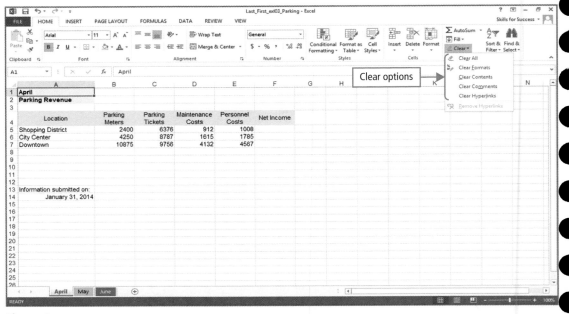

Figure 1

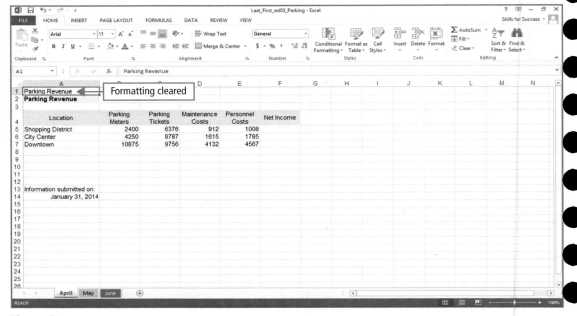

Figure 2

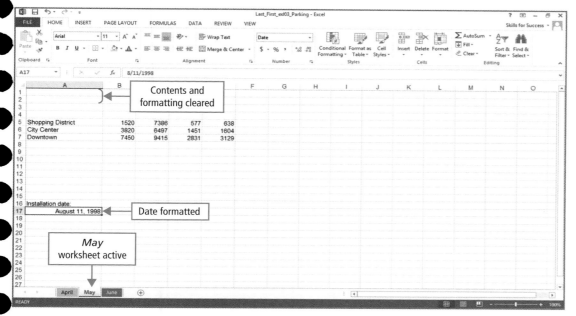

Figure 3

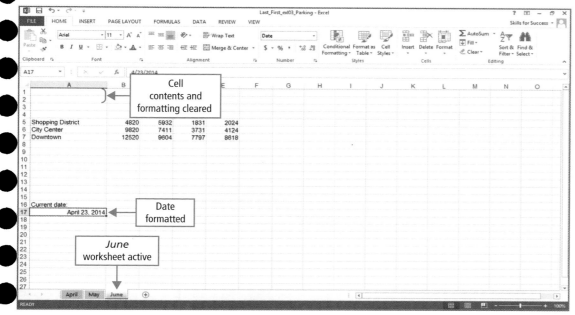

Figure 4

6. Display the **May** worksheet, and then select the range **A1:A2**. In the **Editing group**, click the **Clear** button, and then click **Clear All**.

7. Click cell **A16** to display the comment. On the **Home tab**, in the **Editing group**, click the **Clear** button, and then click **Clear Comments** to clear the comment from the cell.

8. Click cell **A17**. On the **Home tab**, in the **Number group**, click the **Number Format arrow**. At the bottom of the **Number Format** list, click **More Number Formats**. In the **Format Cells** dialog box, under **Type**, scroll down, click **March 14, 2012**, and then click **OK** to display the date in cell **A17** as *August 11, 1998*. Compare your screen with **Figure 3**.

9. Display the **June** worksheet. Select the range **A1:A2**, and then use the technique just practiced to clear the contents and formatting from the selected range.

10. Click cell **A17**, and then use the technique just practiced to apply the date format *March 14, 2012*, to the current date. Compare your screen with **Figure 4**.

11. Make **April** the active sheet, and then **Save** 🖫 the workbook.

■ **You have completed Skill 3 of 10**

EXL 3-4
VIDEO

▶ Data from cells and ranges can be copied and then pasted to other cells in the same worksheet, to other worksheets, or to worksheets in another workbook.

▶ The **Clipboard** is a temporary storage area for text and graphics. When you use either the Copy command or the Cut command, the selected data is placed in the Clipboard, from which the data is available to paste.

1. On the **April** sheet, select the range **A13:A14**. Point to the lower edge of the green border surrounding the selected range until the pointer displays. Drag downward until the ScreenTip displays *A16:A17*, as shown in Figure 1, and then release the left mouse button to complete the move.

   Drag and drop is a method of moving objects in which you point to the selection and then drag it to a new location.

2. Select the range **A4:F4**. In the **Clipboard group**, click the **Copy** button.

   A moving border surrounds the selected range, and a message on the status bar indicates *Select destination and press ENTER or choose Paste,* confirming that your selected range has been copied to the Clipboard.

3. Display the **May** sheet, and then click cell **A4**. In the **Clipboard group**, click the **Paste arrow** to display the **Paste Options** gallery. Point at the second option in the second row—**Keep Source Column Widths**, and then compare your screen with Figure 2.

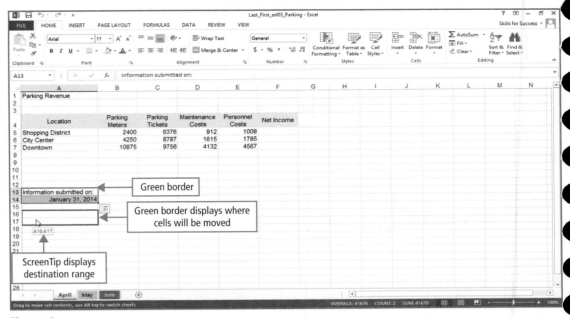

Figure 1

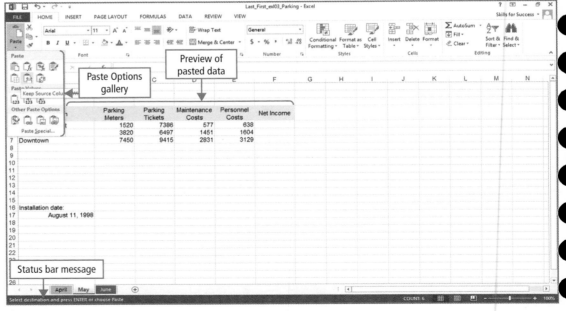

Figure 2

■ Continue to the next page to complete the skill

Paste Options

Option	Icon	Content and format pasted
Paste		Both the contents and cell formatting
Formulas		Only the formula
Formulas & Number Formatting		Both the formula and the number formatting
Keep Source Formatting		All content and cell formatting from original cells
No Borders		All content and cell formatting except borders
Keep Source Column Widths		All content and formatting including the column width format
Transpose		Orientation of pasted entries change—data in rows are pasted as columns
Formatting		Only the formatting

Figure 3

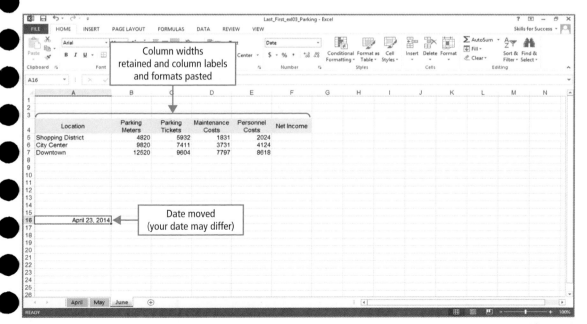

Column widths retained and column labels and formats pasted

Date moved (your date may differ)

Figure 4

4. In the **Paste Options** gallery, click the option **Keep Source Column Widths** to paste the column labels and to retain the column widths from the source worksheet. The table in Figure 3 summarizes the Paste Options.

   When pasting a range of cells, you need to select only the cell in the upper left corner of the *paste area*—the target destination for data that has been cut or copied. When an item is pasted, it is not removed from the Clipboard, as indicated by the status bar message.

5. Display the **June** sheet, and then click cell **A4**. Using the technique just practiced, paste the column labels using the Paste Option **Keep Source Column Widths**.

6. Click cell **A17**, and then point to the upper green border surrounding the cell to display the pointer. Drag up to move the cell contents to cell **A16**. In the message box *There's already data here. Do you want to replace it?* click **OK** to replace the contents. Compare your screen with Figure 4.

7. Click the **April** worksheet tab. **Save** workbook.

■ **You have completed Skill 4 of 10**

EXL 3-5
VIDEO

▶ You can group any number of worksheets in a workbook. After the worksheets are grouped, you can edit data or format cells in all of the grouped worksheets at the same time.

▶ Grouping worksheets is useful when you are creating or modifying a set of worksheets that are similar in purpose and structure.

1. Right-click the **April** worksheet tab, and then from the shortcut menu, click **Select All Sheets**.

2. At the top of the screen, on the title bar, verify that *[Group]* displays as shown in **Figure 1**.

    Here, all three worksheet tabs are shaded with a gradient color and *[Group]* displays on the title bar to indicate that the three worksheets are active as a group.

3. Select the range **A5:A7**, and then apply the **40% - Accent1** cell style.

4. Display the **May** worksheet to ungroup the sheets and to verify that the cell style you selected in the previous step displays as shown in **Figure 2**.

    In the worksheet tab area, both the *April* worksheet tab and the *June* worksheet tab display a solid color, indicating that they are no longer active in the group. At the top of your screen, *[Group]* no longer displays on the title bar.

    Selecting a single worksheet cancels a grouping. Because the worksheets were grouped, formatting was applied to all of the selected worksheets. In this manner, you can make the same changes to all selected worksheets at the same time.

■ Continue to the next page to complete the skill ▶

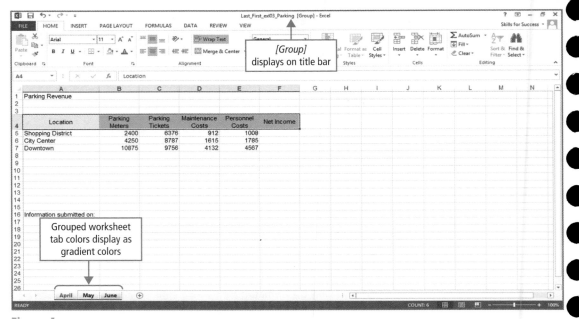

Figure 1

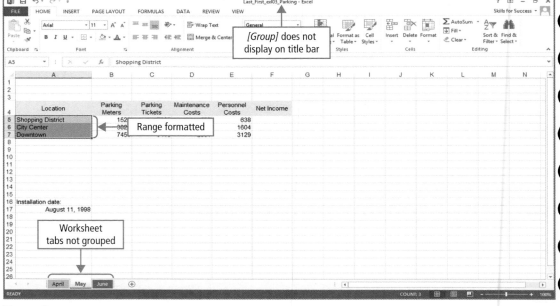

Figure 2

Figure 3

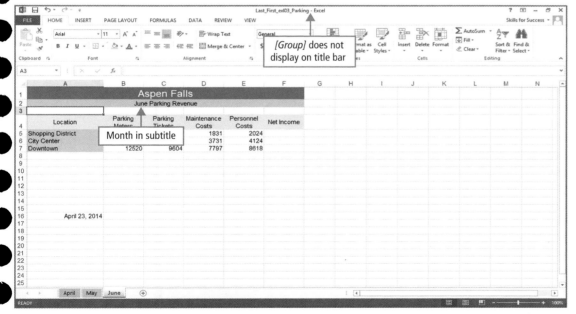

Figure 4

5. Right-click the **April** worksheet tab, and then from the shortcut menu, click **Select All Sheets**.

6. In cell **A1**, press Delete , type Aspen Falls and then press Enter . Select the range **A1:F1**, and then in the **Alignment group**, click the **Merge & Center** button. Apply the **Accent1** cell style. Click the **Font Size** button 11 ▾ , and then click **18**.

7. In cell **A2**, type Parking Revenue and then press Enter . Select the range **A2:F2**, and then click the **Merge & Center** button. Apply the **40% - Accent1** cell style, and then compare your screen with **Figure 3**.

8. Right-click the **April** worksheet tab, and then from the shortcut menu, click **Ungroup Sheets**. Verify that *[Group]* no longer displays on the title bar.

9. Double-click cell **A2** to edit the cell contents. Use the arrow keys to move to the left of the word *Parking*. Type April and add a space, and then press Enter . Display the **May** worksheet. Using the same technique, edit cell **A2** to May Parking Revenue Display the **June** worksheet, and then edit cell **A2** to June Parking Revenue Compare your screen with **Figure 4**.

10. **Save** 💾 the workbook.

■ **You have completed Skill 5 of 10**

▶ When you combine several math operators in a single formula, ***operator precedence***—a set of mathematical rules for performing calculations within a formula—are followed. Expressions within parentheses are calculated first. Then, multiplication and division are performed before addition and subtraction.

▶ When a formula contains operators with the same precedence level, Excel evaluates the operators from left to right. Multiplication and division are considered to be on the same level of precedence. Addition and subtraction are considered to be on the same level of precedence.

1. Right-click the **June** worksheet tab, and then click **Select All Sheets**. Verify that *[Group]* displays on the title bar.

2. Click cell **F5**, enter the formula =(B5+C5)-(D5+E5) and then compare your screen with **Figure 1**.

   The formula *Net Income = Total Revenue – Total Cost* is represented by *(Parking Meters + Parking Tickets) – (Maintenance Cost + Personnel Cost)*. By placing parentheses in the formula, the revenue is first added together, the costs are added together, and then the total costs are subtracted from the total revenues. Without the parentheses, the formula would give an incorrect result.

3. On the **formula bar**, click the **Enter** button. AutoFill the formula down through cell **F7**. Compare your screen with **Figure 2**.

■ **Continue to the next page to complete the skill**

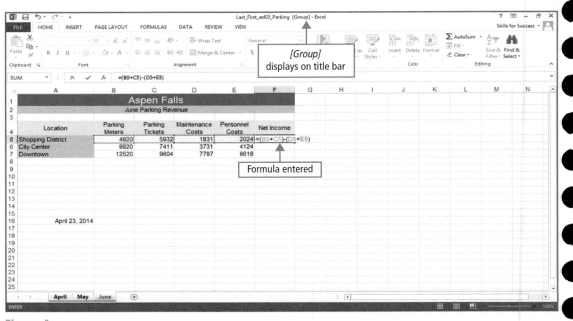

Figure 1

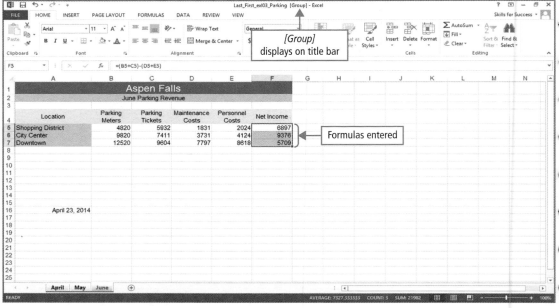

Figure 2

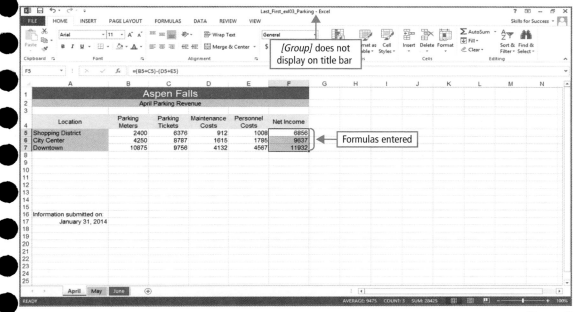

[Group] does not display on title bar

Formulas entered

Figure 3

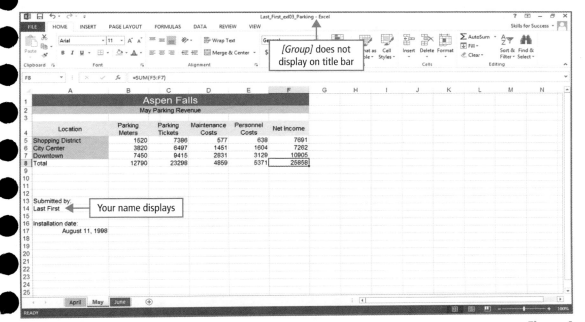

[Group] does not display on title bar

Your name displays

Figure 4

4. Display the **April** worksheet to ungroup the sheets and to verify that the formula results display in the worksheet. Compare your screen with **Figure 3**.

   Because the worksheets were grouped, the formulas have been entered on all selected worksheets.

5. Right-click the **April** worksheet tab, and then click **Select All Sheets**. Verify that [Group] displays on the title bar.

6. In cell **A8**, type Total and then press [Enter]. Select the range **B8:F8**, and then on the **Home tab**, in the **Editing group**, click the **AutoSum** button to insert the column totals.

7. Click cell **A13**, type Submitted by: and then press [Enter]. In cell **A14**, using your name, type Last First and then press [Enter].

8. Click the **May** worksheet tab. Click cell **F8**, and then compare your screen with **Figure 4**.

   On the *May* worksheet, the formula in cell F8 displays as the value *25858*.

9. **Save** 🖫 the workbook.

■ **You have completed Skill 6 of 10**

EXL 3-7
VIDEO

▶ When worksheets are grouped, any changes made to a single worksheet are made to each worksheet in the group. For example, if you change the width of a column or add a row, all the worksheets in the group are changed in the same manner.

1. Right-click the **May** worksheet tab, and then click **Select All Sheets**.

2. In the row heading area, point to row 7 to display the → pointer. Right-click, and then compare your screen with **Figure 1**.

3. From the shortcut menu, click **Insert** to insert a new blank row above the *Downtown* row in all of the grouped worksheets. In cell **A7**, type Midtown and press Tab.

4. Click the **April** worksheet tab to make it the active worksheet and to ungroup the worksheets. Beginning in cell **B7**, enter the following *Midtown* data for April:

   2785   5012   3270   1860

5. Click the **May** worksheet tab, and then beginning in cell **B7**, enter the following *Midtown* data for May:

   2420   8190   1916   2586

6. Click the **June** worksheet tab, and then beginning in cell **B7**, enter the following *Midtown* data for June:

   2170   6546   4425   1925

7. Click each of the worksheet tabs, and then verify that you entered the values correctly. Click the **June** worksheet tab, and then compare your screen with **Figure 2**.

■ Continue to the next page to complete the skill

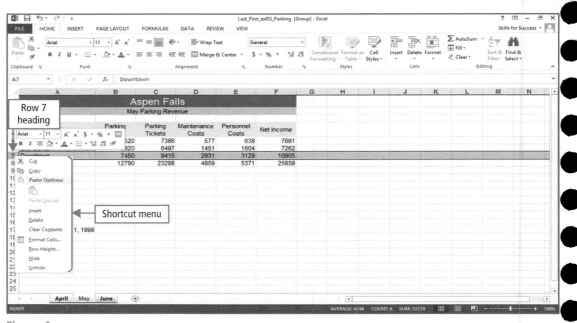

Figure 1

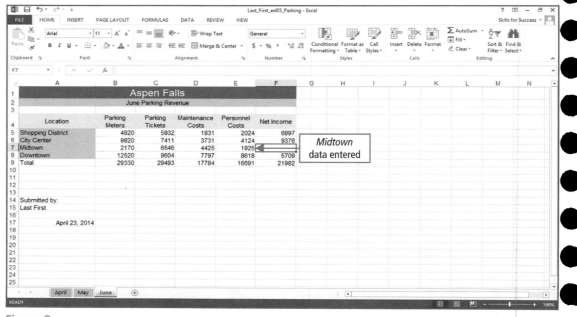

Figure 2

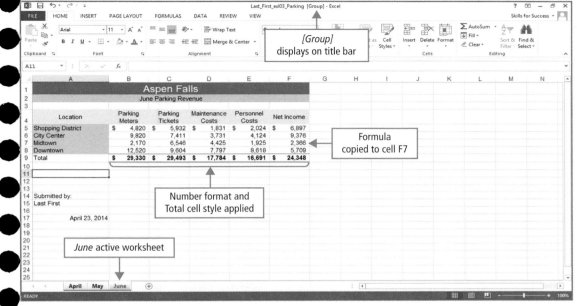

Figure 3

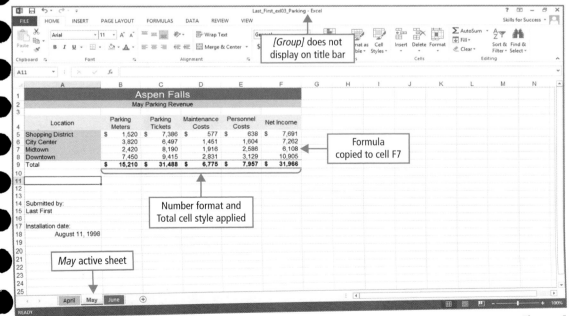

Figure 4

8. Right-click the **June** worksheet tab, and then click **Select All Sheets**. Click cell **F6**, and then AutoFill the formula down to cell **F7**.

> On the *June* worksheet, the formula in cell *F9* displays as the value *$24,348*.

9. Select the range **B5:F5**, hold down `Ctrl`, and then select the range **B9:F9**. With the nonadjacent ranges selected, in the **Styles group**, click the **Cell Styles** button, and then click **Currency [0]**.

10. Select the range **B6:F8**, and then apply the **Comma [0]** cell style.

11. Select the range **B9:F9**, and then apply the **Total** cell style. Click cell **A11**, and then compare your screen with **Figure 3**.

12. Display the **April** sheet, and then verify that the same formatting was applied.

13. Click the **May** worksheet tab to make it the active worksheet, and verify that the formulas and formatting changes were made. Compare your screen with **Figure 4**.

> On the *May* sheet, the formula in cell *F9* displays as the value *$31,966*.

14. Save 🖫 the workbook.

■ **You have completed Skill 7 of 10**

▶ EXL 3-8 VIDEO

▶ To organize a workbook, you can position worksheet tabs in any order you desire.

▶ You can add new worksheets to accommodate new information.

1. Right-click the **April** worksheet tab, and then from the shortcut menu, click **Unhide**. Compare your screen with **Figure 1**.

2. In the **Unhide** dialog box, verify *1st Qtr* is selected and then click **OK**. Use the same technique to **Unhide** the **2010** and the **2011** worksheets.

3. Right-click the **2010** worksheet tab, and then click **Delete**. Read the message that displays, and then click **Delete**. Use the same technique to **Delete** the **2011** worksheet.

> Because you can't undo a worksheet deletion, it is a good idea to verify that you selected the correct worksheet before you click Delete.

4. To the right of the **June** worksheet tab, click the **New Sheet** button ⊕ to create a new worksheet. Rename the new worksheet tab as Summary

5. In cell **A2**, type Second Quarter Parking Revenue and press [Enter]. In cell **A4**, type Month and then press [Tab]. Type the following labels in row **4**, pressing [Tab] after each label: Total Meter Revenue, Total Ticket Revenue, Total Maintenance Cost, Total Personnel Cost, Net Income

6. In cell **A5**, type April and then AutoFill the months down through cell **A7**.

7. Change the **Column Width** of columns **A:F** to 12 Click cell **A9**, and then compare your screen with **Figure 2**.

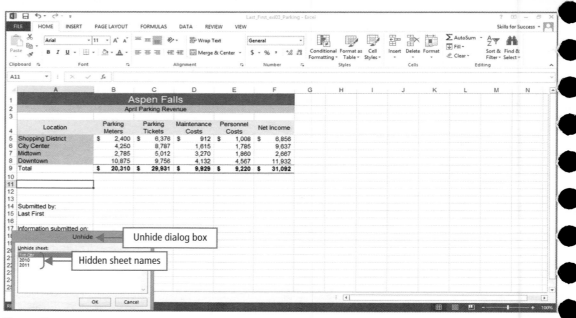

Figure 1

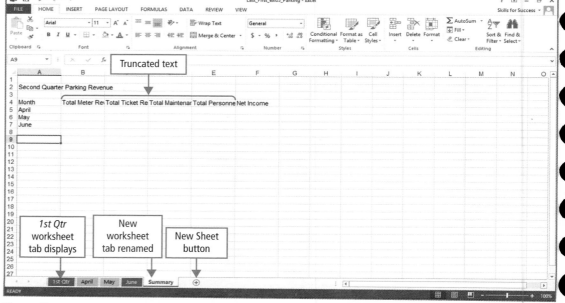

Figure 2

■ **Continue to the next page to complete the skill** ➡

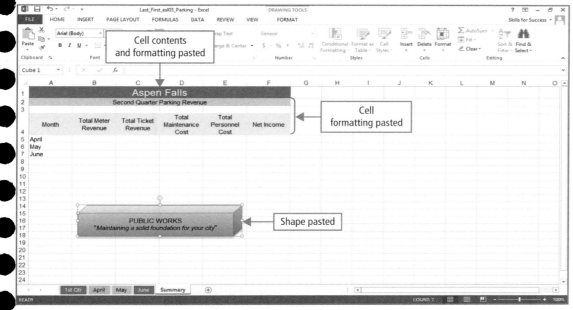

Cell contents and formatting pasted

Cell formatting pasted

Shape pasted

Figure 3

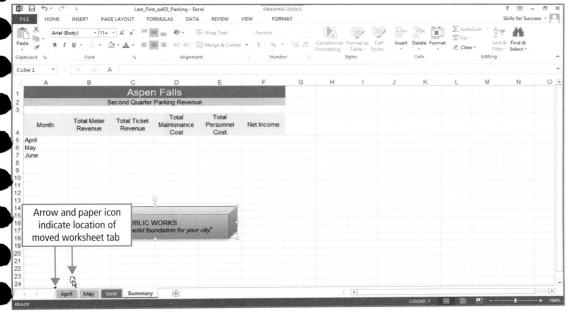

Arrow and paper icon indicate location of moved worksheet tab

Figure 4

8. Display the **June** sheet. Click cell **A1**, and then in the **Clipboard group**, click the **Copy** button. Display the **Summary** sheet. Click cell **A1**, and then click the **Paste** button to paste the cell content and format.

9. Display the **June** sheet, and then press [Esc] to remove the moving border. Select the range **A2:F4**, and then click the **Copy** button. Display the **Summary** sheet, and then click cell **A2**. In the **Clipboard group**, click the **Paste arrow**. In the **Paste Options** gallery, under **Other Paste Options**, click the first option—**Formatting** to paste only the format.

10. Display the **1st Qtr** sheet. Click the shape, and then click the **Copy** button. Display the **Summary** sheet. In the **Clipboard group**, click the **Paste** button. Move the shape to approximately the range **B14:E18**. Compare your screen with **Figure 3**.

11. Right-click the **1st Qtr** worksheet tab, and then click **Hide**.

12. Click the **Summary** worksheet tab. Hold down the left mouse button and drag to the left to display an arrow and the pointer. Drag to the left until the arrow is to the left of the **April** worksheet tab, as shown in **Figure 4**.

13. Release the left mouse button to complete the worksheet move. **Save** the workbook.

■ **You have completed Skill 8 of 10**

EXL 3-9
VIDEO

▶ A *summary sheet* is a worksheet that displays and summarizes totals from other worksheets. A *detail sheet* is a worksheet with cells referred to by summary sheet formulas.

▶ Changes made to the detail sheets that affect totals will automatically recalculate and display on the summary sheet.

1. On the **Summary** sheet, click cell **B5**. Type = and then click the **April** worksheet tab. On the **April** sheet, click cell **B9**, and then press Enter to display the April sheet *B9* value in the Summary sheet *B5* cell.

2. In the **Summary** sheet, click cell **B5**. In the formula bar, notice that the cell reference in the underlying formula includes both a worksheet reference and a cell reference as shown in **Figure 1**.

> By using a formula that refers to another worksheet, changes made to the Total in cell *B9* of the *April* sheet will be automatically updated in this *Summary* sheet.

3. Click cell **B6**, type = and then click the **May** worksheet tab. On the **May** sheet, click cell **B9**, and then press Enter.

4. On the **Summary** sheet, repeat the technique just practiced to display the **June** sheet **B9** value in the **Summary** sheet **B7** cell.

5. On the **Summary** sheet, select the range **B5:B7**, and then AutoFill to the right through column **F**. Click cell **F7**, and then compare your screen with **Figure 2**.

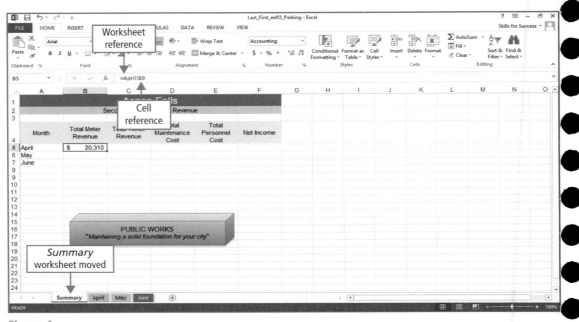

Figure 1

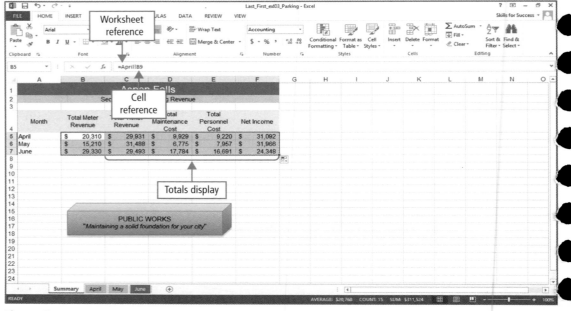

Figure 2

■ Continue to the next page to complete the skill

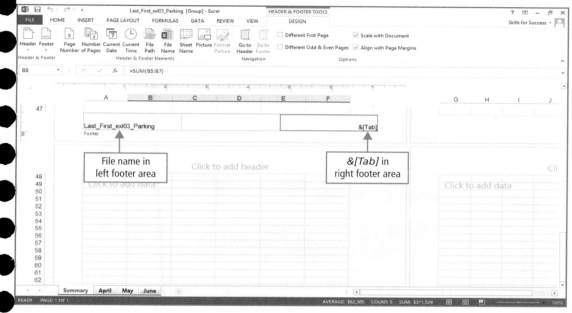

Figure 3

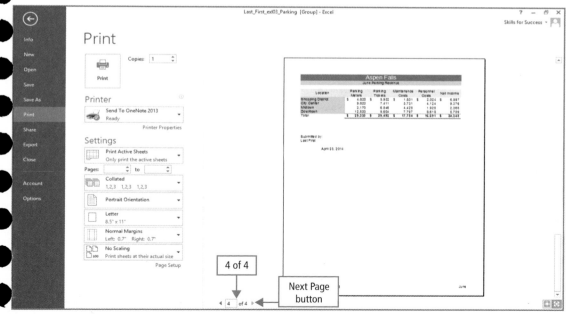

Figure 4

6. On the **Summary** sheet, click cell **A8**, type Total and then select the range **B8:F8**. In the **Editing group**, click the **AutoSum** button, and then apply the **Total** cell style.

7. Right-click the **Summary** worksheet tab, and then click **Select All Sheets**.

8. Insert the file name in the worksheet's left footer. Click the right section of the footer, and then in the **Header & Footer Elements group**, click the **Sheet Name** button, and then compare your screen with **Figure 3**.

   By grouping worksheets, you can insert headers and footers into each worksheet quickly and consistently.

9. Click in a cell just above the footer to exit the **Footer area**. On the lower right side of the status bar, click the **Normal** button. Hold down Ctrl, and press Home to make cell **A1** the active cell on all selected worksheets.

10. With the sheets still grouped, click the **File tab**, and then click **Print**. At the bottom of the screen, click the **Next Page** button three times to view each of the four worksheets, and then compare your screen with **Figure 4**.

    Because the worksheets are grouped, all four worksheets are included in the preview.

11. **Save** the workbook.

- **You have completed Skill 9 of 10**

EXL 3-10
VIDEO

▶ A *clustered bar chart* is useful when you want to compare values across categories; bar charts organize categories along the vertical axis and values along the horizontal axis.

1. Click the **Back** button ⊙. Right-click the **Summary** worksheet tab, and then click **Ungroup Sheets**. On the **Summary** sheet, select the range **A4:E7**. On the **Insert tab**, in the **Charts group**, click the **Recommended Charts** button. In the **Insert Chart** dialog box, verify the first choice is selected—**Clustered Bar**, and then click **OK**.

2. On the **Design tab**, in the **Location group**, click the **Move Chart** button. In the **Move Chart** dialog box, select the **New sheet** option button, type 2nd Qtr Chart and then click **OK**.

3. On the **Design tab**, in the **Data group**, click the **Switch Row/Column** button to display the months on the vertical axis. Compare your screen with **Figure 1**.

   Because you want to look at revenue and costs by month, displaying the months on the vertical axis is useful.

4. In the **Chart Layouts group**, click the **Quick Layout** button, and then click **Layout 3**.

5. To the right of the chart, click the **Chart Styles** button 🖌, and then click **Style 3**.

6. Edit the **Chart Title** to 2nd Quarter Parking Revenue and Cost and then compare your screen with **Figure 2**.

■ **Continue to the next page to complete the skill** ➤

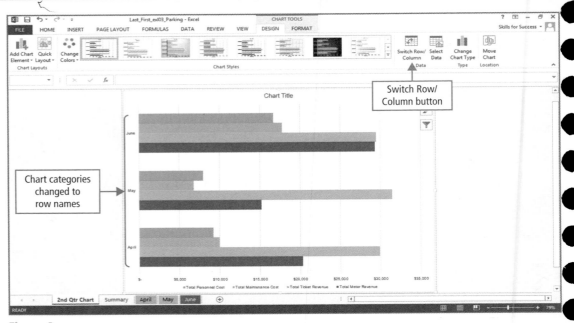
Figure 1

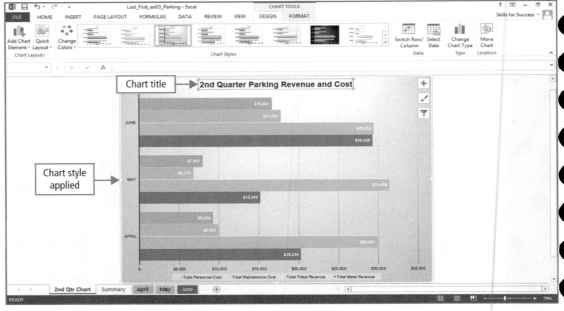
Figure 2

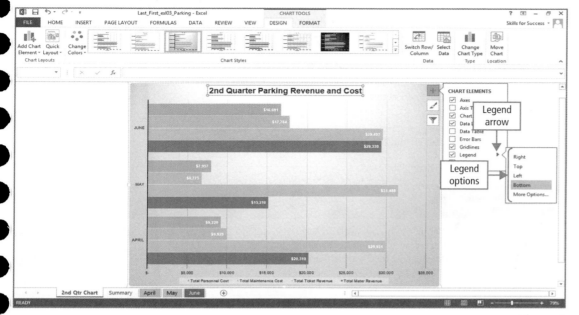

Figure 3

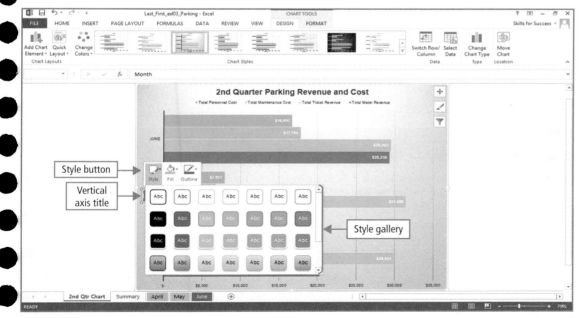

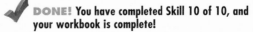

Figure 4

7. At the top right corner of the chart, click the **Chart Elements** button ➕. Point to **Legend**, and then click the **Legend arrow**. Compare your screen with Figure 3.

8. In the list, click **Top** to move the legend to the top of the chart sheet.

9. In the **Chart Elements** gallery, point to **Axis Titles**, and then click the **Axis Titles arrow**. Select the **Primary Vertical** check box to add the vertical axis title. Click the **Chart Elements** button ➕ to close the gallery.

10. On the left side of the chart, change the vertical **Axis Title** text to Month Right-click the *Month* title, and then on the Mini toolbar, click the **Style** button and compare your screen with Figure 4.

11. In the **Style** gallery, click the second thumbnail in the fourth row—**Subtle Effect - Blue, Accent 1**.

12. On the **Insert tab**, in the **Text group**, click the **Header & Footer** button. In the **Page Setup** dialog box, click the **Custom Footer** button. In the **Footer** dialog box, verify the insertion point is in the **Left section** and then click the **Insert File Name** button 🔲. Click the **Right section** of the footer, and then click the **Insert Sheet Name** button 🔲. Click **OK** two times.

13. **Save** 🔲 the workbook, and then **Close** ✖ Excel. Submit the project as directed by your instructor.

✔ **DONE! You have completed Skill 10 of 10, and your workbook is complete!**

The following More Skills are located at **www.pearsonhighered.com/skills**

More Skills Create Organization Charts

You can add SmartArt graphics to a worksheet to create timelines, illustrate processes, or show relationships. When you click the SmartArt button on the Ribbon, you can select from among a broad array of graphics, including an organization chart. An organization chart graphically represents the relationships between individuals and groups in an organization.

In More Skills 11, you will insert and modify a SmartArt graphic to create an organization chart.

To begin, open your web browser, navigate to www.pearsonhighered.com/skills, locate the name of your textbook, and then follow the instructions on the website.

More Skills Create Line Charts

Use a line chart when you want to compare more than one set of values over time. Time is displayed along the bottom axis and the data point values are connected with a line. The curves and directions of the lines make trends obvious to the reader.

In More Skills 12, you will create a line chart comparing three sets of values.

To begin, open your web browser, navigate to www.pearsonhighered.com/skills, locate the name of your textbook, and then follow the instructions on the website.

More Skills Set and Clear Print Areas

If you are likely to print the same portion of a particular worksheet over and over again, you can save time by setting a print area.

In More Skills 13, you will set and then clear print areas in a worksheet.

To begin, open your web browser, navigate to www.pearsonhighered.com/skills, locate the name of your textbook, and then follow the instructions on the website.

More Skills Create, Edit, and Delete Hyperlinks

You can insert a hyperlink in a worksheet that can link to a file, a location in a file, a web page on the World Wide Web, or a web page on an organization's intranet. Creating a hyperlink in a workbook is a convenient way to provide quick access to related information. You can edit or delete hyperlinks.

In More Skills 14, you will create hyperlinks to related information on the web and to other worksheets in the workbook.

To begin, open your web browser, navigate to www.pearsonhighered.com/skills, locate the name of your textbook, and then follow the instructions on the website.

Please note that there are no additional projects to accompany the More Skills Projects, and they are not covered in the End-of-Chapter projects.

The following table summarizes the **SKILLS AND PROCEDURES** covered in this chapter.

Skills Number	Task	Step	Keyboard Shortcut
1	Rename worksheet tabs	Right-click worksheet tab → Rename → Type new name → Enter	
1	Rename worksheet tabs	Double-click worksheet tab → Type new name → Enter	
1	Format worksheet tabs	Home tab → Cells group → Format → Tab Color	
1	Format worksheet tabs	Right-click worksheet tab → Tab Color	
2	Format dates	Home tab → Number group → Number Format arrow → More Number Formats	
2	Enter the current date		Ctrl + :
3	Clear cell contents	Home tab → Editing group → Clear → Clear Contents	Delete
3	Clear cell formatting	Home tab → Editing group → Clear → Clear Formats	
3	Clear cell contents and formatting	Home tab → Editing group → Clear → Clear All	
4	Paste with options	Home tab → Clipboard group → Paste Arrow → Select desired option	
5	Group worksheets	Right-click worksheet tab → Select All Sheets	
5	Ungroup worksheets	Right-click worksheet tab → Ungroup Sheets or click a single worksheet tab	
8	Insert worksheets	Home tab → Cells group → Insert arrow → Insert Sheet	
8	Delete worksheet	Home tab → Cells group → Delete arrow → Delete Sheet	
8	Hide worksheet	Right-click worksheet tab → Hide	
8	Unhide worksheet	Right-click worksheet tab → Unhide → Worksheet name	
8	Move worksheet tab	Drag worksheet tab to new location	

Key Terms

Online Help Skills

1. Start **Excel 2013**, and then in the upper right corner of the start page, click the **Help** button ?.

2. In the **Excel Help** window **Search help** box, type numbers to dates and then press Enter.

3. In the search result list, click **Stop automatically changing numbers to dates**, and then compare your screen with Figure 1.

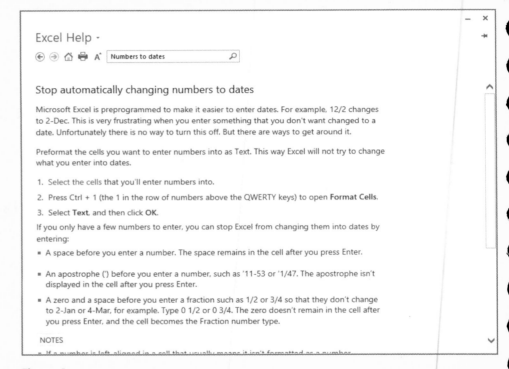

Figure 1

4. Read the article to answer the following question: What cell format can be applied to stop changing numbers into dates?

Matching

Match each term in the second column with its correct definition in the first column by writing the letter of the term on the blank line in front of the correct definition.

____ **1.** The labels along the lower edge of the workbook window that identify each worksheet.

____ **2.** Controls to the left of the worksheet tabs used to display worksheet tabs that are not in view.

____ **3.** A sequential number assigned to a date.

____ **4.** A temporary storage area for text and graphics.

____ **5.** A method of moving or copying the content of selected cells in which you point to the selection and then drag it to a new location.

____ **6.** The target destination for data that has been cut or copied using the Clipboard.

____ **7.** The mathematical rules that specify the order in which calculations are performed.

____ **8.** A worksheet that displays and recaps totals from other worksheets.

____ **9.** A worksheet that contains the detailed information in a workbook.

____ **10.** A chart type that is useful when you want to compare values across categories.

A Clipboard

B Clustered bar chart

C Detail sheet

D Drag and drop

E Operator precedence

F Paste area

G Serial number

H Summary sheet

I Tab scrolling buttons

J Worksheet tabs

BizSkills Video

1. Why should you arrive early for an interview?

2. What should you do at the end of an interview?

Multiple Choice MyITLab®

Choose the correct answer.

1. An active worksheet tab will display in this way.
   A. With a solid tab color
   B. With a gradient tab color
   C. Always as the first worksheet

2. Worksheets can be grouped in this way.
   A. Right-clicking a worksheet tab and then clicking Select All Sheets
   B. Double-clicking a worksheet tab
   C. Clicking the New Sheet button

3. Clearing the contents of a cell deletes this.
   A. Only the contents
   B. Only the formatting
   C. Both contents and formatting

4. When pasting a range of cells, this cell needs to be selected in the paste area.
   A. Bottom right cell
   B. Center cell
   C. Top left cell

5. Worksheets can be hidden in this way.
   A. Move the worksheet as the last sheet
   B. Right-click a worksheet tab and then click Hide
   C. Double-click a worksheet tab

6. If a workbook contains grouped worksheets, this word will display on the title bar.
   A. [Collection]
   B. [Set]
   C. [Group]

7. When a formula contains operators with the same precedence level, the operators are evaluated in this order.
   A. Left to right
   B. Right to left
   C. From the center out

8. Addition and this mathematical operator are considered to be on the same precedence level.
   A. Multiplication
   B. Division
   C. Subtraction

9. Changes made in a detail worksheet will automatically recalculate and display on this sheet.
   A. Summary
   B. Final
   C. Outline

10. The paste option Keep Source Column Widths will paste this.
    A. The cell formatting
    B. Only the column width formatting
    C. All content and cell formatting including the column width format

Topics for Discussion

1. Some people in an organization will only view the summary worksheet without examining the detail worksheets. When might this practice be acceptable and when might it cause mistakes?

2. Illustrate some examples of how a formula's results will be incorrect if parentheses are not used to group calculations in the order they should be performed. Think of a class where you have three exam grades and a final exam grade. If the three tests together count as 50 percent of your course grade, and the final exam counts as 50 percent of your course grade, how would you write the formula to get a correct result?

Skills Review

MyITLab®
Grader

To complete this project, you will need the following file:

- exl03_SRPayroll

You will save your file as:

- Last_First_exl03_SRPayroll

1. Start **Excel 2013**. From your student data files, open **exl03_SRPayroll**. Save the workbook in your chapter folder as Last_First_exl03_SRPayroll

2. Right-click the worksheet tab, and then click **Select All Sheets**. Click cell **A19**. On the **Home tab**, in the **Editing group**, click the **Clear** button, and then click **Clear All**. Select the range **A4:F4**, and then apply the **40% - Accent3** cell style. In the **Alignment group**, click the **Wrap Text** and the **Center** buttons.

3. In cell **F5**, type =B5-(C5+D5+E5) and then press [Enter] to construct the formula to compute the Net Pay as *Total Gross Pay – (Income Tax + Social Security (FICA) Tax + Health Insurance)*. AutoFill the formula in cell **F5** down through cell **F12**. Compare your screen with Figure 1.

4. Verify that the worksheets are still grouped. Select the range **B6:F12**, and then apply the **Comma [0]** cell style. Select the range **B13:F13**, and then apply the **Total** cell style. Click the **Courthouse** worksheet tab.

5. To the right of the **Courthouse** worksheet tab, click the **New Sheet** button. Rename the new worksheet tab Summary and then change the **Tab Color** to **Orange, Accent 6**. Click the **Summary** worksheet tab, and drag it to the left of the *Community Center* worksheet tab. Compare your screen with Figure 2.

6. Right-click the worksheet tab, and then click **Select All Sheets**. Add the file name in the worksheet's left footer. Click the right footer section, and then in the **Header & Footer Elements group**, click the **Sheet Name** button. Return to Normal view, and then press [Ctrl] + [Home].

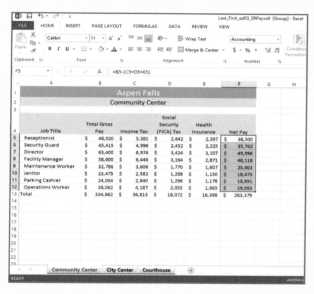

Figure 1

Figure 2

■ Continue to the next page to complete this Skills Review ▶

Figure 3

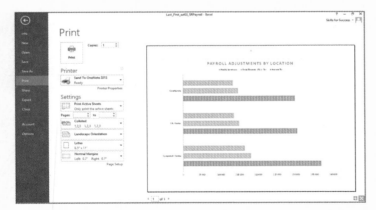

Figure 4

7. Display the **Community Center** sheet, select the range **A1:F4**, and then click **Copy**. Display the **Summary** sheet and then click cell **A1**. Click the **Paste arrow** and then click **Keep Source Column Widths**. In cell **A2**, replace the text with City Payroll in cell **A4**, replace the text with Location and then press [Enter]. Type the following labels in column **A**, pressing [Enter] after each label: Community Center, City Center, Courthouse, and Total

8. On the **Summary** sheet, click **B5**, type = and then click the **Community Center** worksheet tab. On the **Community Center** sheet, click cell **B13**, and then press [Enter]. Use the same technique in cells **B6** and **B7** to place the *Total Gross Pay* amounts from the *City Center* and the *Courthouse* sheets on the *Summary* sheet.

9. On the **Summary** sheet, select the range **B5:B7**. Click the **Quick Analysis Lens** button, click **Totals**, and then click the first option **Sum**. Select the range **B5:B8**, and then AutoFill the formulas to the right through column **F**. Select the range **B8:F8**, and then apply the **Total** cell style. Click cell **A10**, and then compare your screen with Figure 3.

10. On the **Summary** sheet, select the nonadjacent ranges **A4:A7** and **C4:E7**. On the **Insert tab**, in the **Charts group**, click the **Recommended Charts** button. In the **Insert Chart** dialog box, click **Clustered Bar**, and then click **OK**. On the **Design tab**, in the **Location group**, click the **Move Chart** button. In the **Move Chart** dialog box, select the **New sheet** option button, type Payroll Adjustments and then click **OK**.

11. On the **Design tab**, in the **Data group**, click the **Switch Row/Column** button. Click the **Chart Styles** button, and then click **Style 2**. Change the **Chart Title** to Payroll Adjustments by Location

12. On the **Summary** sheet, click cell **A12**, type Date Created and then click [Enter]. In cell **A13**, press [Ctrl] + ; (the semicolon), and then press [Enter].

13. Right-click the **Summary** worksheet tab, and then click **Unhide**. In the **Unhide** dialog box, click **OK**. Right-click the **Art Center** worksheet tab, and then click **Delete**. In the message box, click **Delete**.

14. **Group** the worksheets, and then check the spelling.

15. Click the **File tab**, and then click **Print**. Compare your workbook with Figure 4.

16. **Save** the workbook, and then submit the workbook as directed by your instructor.

✔ **DONE! You have completed this Skills Review**

Skills Assessment 1

MyITLab®
Grader

To complete this workbook, you will need the following file:

- exl03_SA1Center

You will save your workbook as:

- Last_First_exl03_SA1Center

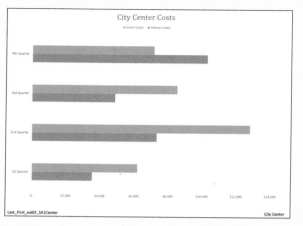

1. Start **Excel 2013**, and open the file **exl03_SA1Center**. **Save** the workbook in your chapter folder as Last_First_exl03_SA1Center

2. Group the worksheets. In cell **E5**, construct a formula to compute *Net Income = Income – (Indirect Costs + Direct Costs)*. AutoFill the formula down through cell **E7**.

3. In the nonadjacent ranges **B5:E5** and **B8:E8**, apply the **Currency [0]** cell style.

4. Insert a new worksheet. Rename the new worksheet tab Summary and apply the worksheet tab color **Brown**, **Accent 5**. Move the new worksheet tab to make it the first worksheet in the workbook.

5. Copy the range **A1:E4** from any of the detail worksheets, and then on the **Summary** sheet, click cell **A1**. Paste the range using the **Keep Source Column Widths** paste option. Change the subtitle of cell **A2** to City Center Annual Revenue and then change the label in cell **A4** to Quarter

6. In cell **A5**, type 1st Quarter and then AutoFill the labels in the range **A6:A8**. In cell **A9**, type Total

7. In the *Summary* worksheet, enter a formula in cell **B5** setting the cell to equal cell **B8** in the *1st Quarter* worksheet. Enter the *Income* total from the *2nd Quarter,* the *3rd Quarter,* and the *4th Quarter* worksheets in the range **B6:B8**.

8. Select the range **B5:B8**, and then use the **Quick Analysis Lens** button to insert the column total.

9. AutoFill the range **B5:B9** to the right through **column E**. In **row 9**, apply the **Total** cell style.

10. Insert a **Clustered Bar** chart using the nonadjacent ranges **A4:A8** and **C4:D8** as the source data. Move the chart to a chart sheet with the sheet name City Center

Aspen Falls
City Center Annual Revenue

Quarter	Income	Indirect Costs	Direct Costs	Net Income
1st Quarter	$ 17,700	$ 3,540	$ 6,195	$ 7,965
2nd Quarter	$ 36,590	$ 7,318	$ 12,806	$ 16,466
3rd Quarter	$ 24,320	$ 4,864	$ 8,511	$ 10,945
4th Quarter	$ 25,604	$ 10,270	$ 7,126	$ 8,208
Total	$ 104,214	$ 25,992	$ 34,638	$ 43,584

Aspen Falls
City Center Rental Revenue: 1st Quarter

Rental Item	Income	Indirect Costs	Direct Costs	Net Income
City Center Rental	$ 9,200	$ 1,840	$ 3,220	$ 4,140
AV Equipment	4,800	960	1,680	2,160
Display Equipment	3,700	740	1,295	1,665
Total	$ 17,700	$ 3,540	$ 6,195	$ 7,965

Figure 1

11. Apply the **Style 10** chart style. Change the **Chart Title** to City Center Costs

12. Group the worksheets. Add the file name in the left footer and the sheet name in the right footer. Return to Normal view, and then press Ctrl + Home.

13. Check the spelling of the workbook, and then ungroup the sheets.

14. **Save** the workbook. Compare your completed workbook with Figure 1. Submit the workbook as directed by your instructor.

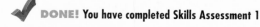 **DONE! You have completed Skills Assessment 1**

Skills Assessment 2

To complete this workbook, you will need the following file:

- exl03_SA2Taxes

You will save your workbook as:

- Last_First_exl03_SA2Taxes

---

1. Start **Excel 2013**, and open the file **exl03_SA2Taxes**. **Save** the workbook in your chapter folder as Last_First_exl03_SA2Taxes

2. Group the sheets. In cell **F5**, construct a formula to compute *Net Revenue = (Taxes Paid + Late Fees) – (Office Costs + Personnel Costs)*. AutoFill the formula down through **row 10**.

3. Select the nonadjacent ranges **B5:F5** and **B11:F11**, and then apply the **Currency [0]** cell style.

4. Ungroup the worksheets, and then hide the **April** worksheet. Compare the *January* worksheet with **Figure 1**.

5. Insert a new sheet, rename the worksheet tab 1st Qtr Summary and then change the worksheet tab color to **Brown, Text 2**. Move the worksheet to the first position in the workbook. Copy the range **A1:F4** from another sheet, and then paste the range at the top of the *1st Qtr Summary* sheet using the **Keep Source Column Widths** paste option.

6. On the **1st Qtr Summary** sheet, change the subtitle in cell **A2** to 1st Quarter Tax Revenue and then change the label in cell **A4** to Month In the range **A5:A7**, enter the months January, February, and March and in cell **A8**, type Total

7. In cell **B5**, enter a formula setting the cell to equal the total *Taxes Paid* in the *January* worksheet. In cells **B6** and **B7** of the **1st Qtr Summary** sheet, enter the total *Taxes Paid* from the *February* and the *March* worksheets.

8. Total column **B** and then AutoFill the range **B5:B8** to the right through column **F**. In the range **B8:F8**, apply the **Total** cell style.

9. Select the range **A4:C7**, and then insert a **Stacked Bar** chart. Move the chart to approximately the range **A10:F26**.

10. Apply the **Layout 9** chart layout and the **Style 2** chart style. Change the chart title to 1st Quarter

11. Group the worksheets and then check the spelling of the workbook. Add the file name in the left footer and the sheet name in the right footer. Return to Normal view, and then press Ctrl + Home.

12. **Save** the workbook. Compare your *1st Qtr Summary* sheet with **Figure 1**. Submit the workbook as directed by your instructor.

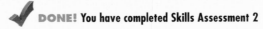 **DONE!** You have completed Skills Assessment 2

Aspen Falls
1st Quarter Tax Revenue

Month	Taxes Paid	Late Fees	Office Costs	Personnel Costs	Net Revenue
January	$ 630,090	$ 274,527	$ 23,357	$ 284,629	$ 596,631
February	$ 654,466	$ 338,305	$ 22,029	$ 263,466	$ 707,276
March	$ 771,693	$ 407,095	$ 22,915	$ 320,350	$ 835,523
Total	$ 2,056,249	$ 1,019,927	$ 68,301	$ 868,445	$ 2,139,430

1ST QUARTER

■ January ■ February ■ March

LATE FEES
$407,095
$338,305
$274,527

TAXES PAID
$771,693
$654,466
$630,090

Aspen Falls
January Tax Revenue

Tax	Taxes Paid	Late Fees	Office Costs	Personnel Costs	Net Revenue
Motor Vehicle	$ 82,831	$ 58,255	$ 2,879	$ 49,255	$ 88,952
Sales	154,520	47,280	3,796	51,529	146,475
Franchise	72,956	46,998	4,915	60,061	54,978
Utilities	98,750	35,107	5,688	38,378	89,791
Property	120,000	40,762	3,200	24,320	133,242
Other	101,033	46,125	2,879	61,086	83,193
Totals	$ 630,090	$ 274,527	$ 23,357	$ 284,629	$ 596,631

Figure 1

Visual Skills Check

To complete this workbook, you will need the following file:

- exl03_VSWater

You will save your workbook as:

- Last_First_exl03_VSWater

Start **Excel 2013**, and open the file **exl03_VSWater**. Save the workbook in your chapter folder as Last_First_exl03_VSWater Complete the **Summary** sheet as shown in Figure 1. Create a summary sheet for the 4th Quarter with the totals from each month and the titles as shown in the figure. Name the worksheet tab 4th Qtr Summary and apply the worksheet tab color **Orange, Accent 1**. Move the **Summary** sheet to be the first worksheet. Insert a **Clustered Bar** chart based on the range **A4:D7**, and then move the chart below the data. Apply the **Style 12** chart style. On all sheets, add a footer with the file name in the left section and the sheet name in the right section. **Save** the workbook, and then submit the workbook as directed by your instructor.

 DONE! You have completed Visual Skills Check

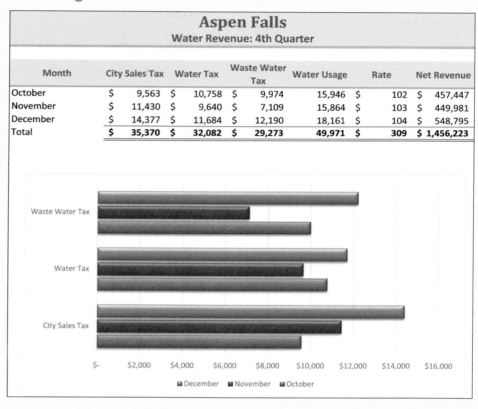

Aspen Falls
Water Revenue: 4th Quarter

Month	City Sales Tax	Water Tax	Waste Water Tax	Water Usage	Rate	Net Revenue
October	$ 9,563	$ 10,758	$ 9,974	15,946	$ 102	$ 457,447
November	$ 11,430	$ 9,640	$ 7,109	15,864	$ 103	$ 449,981
December	$ 14,377	$ 11,684	$ 12,190	18,161	$ 104	$ 548,795
Total	$ 35,370	$ 32,082	$ 29,273	49,971	$ 309	$ 1,456,223

Aspen Falls
Water Revenue: October

Building Type	City Sales Tax	Water Tax	Waste Water Tax	Water Usage	Rate	Net Revenue
Residential	$ 1,575	$ 1,890	$ 1,507	3,181	$ 19	$ 65,411
Commercial	4,233	5,762	5,671	5,440	27	162,546
Industrial	3,170	2,404	2,191	6,118	31	197,423
Apartments	585	702	605	1,207	25	32,067
Total	$ 9,563	$ 10,758	$ 9,974	15,946	$ 102	$ 457,447

Figure 1

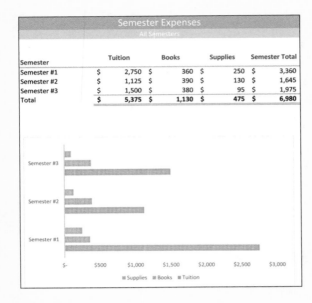

Semester Expenses
All Semesters

Semester	Tuition	Books	Supplies	Semester Total
Semester #1	$ 2,750	$ 360	$ 250	$ 3,360
Semester #2	$ 1,125	$ 390	$ 130	$ 1,645
Semester #3	$ 1,500	$ 380	$ 95	$ 1,975
Total	$ 5,375	$ 1,130	$ 475	$ 6,980

Semester Expenses
Semester #1

Class	Tuition	Books	Supplies	Class Total
Class 1	$ 500	$ 125	$ 50	$ 675
Class 2	250	50	55	$ 355
Class 3	500	50	50	$ 600
Class 4	750	75	45	$ 870
Class 5	750	60	50	$ 860
Total	$ 2,750	$ 360	$ 250	$ 3,360

Figure 1

My Skills

To complete this workbook, you will need the following file:

- exl03_MYClasses

You will save your workbook as:

- Last_First_exl03_MYClasses

1. Start **Excel 2013**, and open the file **exl03_MyClasses**. **Save** the workbook in your chapter folder as Last_First_exl03_MYClasses

2. Group the worksheets. In cell **E5**, use the SUM function to total the row and then AutoFill the formula down through cell **E9**. In **row 10**, use the SUM function to total the columns.

3. Select cell **A2**, and then apply the **60% - Accent3** cell style.

4. Insert a new worksheet. Rename the new worksheet tab Semester Costs and apply the worksheet tab color **Blue, Accent 5**. Move the new worksheet tab to make it the first worksheet in the workbook.

5. Copy the range **A1:E4** from any of the detail worksheets, and then on the **Semester Costs** worksheet, click cell **A1**. Paste the range using the **Keep Source Column Widths** paste option. Change the subtitle of cell **A2** to All Semesters then change the label in cell **A4** to Semester and then change the label in cell **E4** to Semester Total

6. In cell **A5**, type Semester #1 and then AutoFill the label down through A7. In cell **A8**, type Total

7. In cell **B5** insert a formula to equal the value in cell **B10** in the *Semester #[?]1* worksheet. In the cells **B6** and **B7**, insert

formulas that equal the *Tuition* total from the *Semester #2* and *Semester #3* worksheets.

8. Use the **Quick Analysis Lens** button to insert the **column B** total, and then AutoFill the formulas in **column B** to the right through **column E**. Select the range **B8:E8**, and then apply the **Total** cell style.

9. Insert a **Clustered Bar** chart using the range **A4:D7** as the source data. Move and resize the chart to display below the data in approximately the range **A12:E28**.

10. Apply the **Style 2** chart style, and then delete the **Chart Title**. Move the legend to the bottom of the chart.

11. On the **Semester Costs** sheet, in cell **A36**, enter the current date, and then apply the **March 14, 2012**, date format.

12. Group the worksheets. Add the file name in the left footer and the sheet name in the right footer. Return to Normal view, and then press Ctrl + Home.

13. Check the spelling of the workbook, and then ungroup the sheets.

14. **Save** the workbook. Compare your completed workbook with Figure 1. Submit the workbook as directed by your instructor.

 DONE! You have completed My Skills

Skills Challenge 1

To complete this workbook, you will need the following file:

- exl03_SC1Visitors

You will save your workbook as:

- Last_First_exl03_SC1Visitors

During each quarter, Carter Horikoshi, the Art Center Supervisor, tracked the revenue and costs at the Art Center. Open the file **exl03_SC1Visitors**, and then save the workbook in your chapter folder as Last_First_exl03_SC1Visitors Hide the Convention Center worksheet, and then move the remaining worksheets into the correct order. Assign a tab color to each worksheet tab. Group the worksheets, and then adjust the column widths to display all values. Format the labels in rows 1 through 4 consistently across all the worksheets. In cell F5, insert parentheses so that the sum of *Marketing Costs* and *Operating Costs* is subtracted from the sum of *Entrance Fees* and *Food Revenue*. Copy the corrected formula down. Format

the numbers appropriately. Unhide the Annual Summary worksheet, and move it as the first worksheet. Move and resize the bar chart to display below the data. On the Annual Summary sheet, format the values and the chart appropriately. Verify the formulas on the Summary sheet are correct. On all sheets, insert the file name in the left footer and the sheet name in the right footer. Check the spelling of the workbook and then verify that each sheet will print on one page. Save the workbook, and then submit the workbook as directed by your instructor.

 DONE! You have completed Skills Challenge 1

Skills Challenge 2

To complete this workbook, you will need the following file:

- exl03_SC2Durango

You will save your workbook as:

- Last_First_exl03_SC2Durango

During each month of the summer season, Duncan Chueng, the Park Operations Manager, tracked the revenue and cost at the various locations in the Durango County Recreation Area. Open the file **exl03_SC2Durango**, and then save the workbook in your chapter folder as Last_First_exl03_SC2Durango Using the skills you learned in the chapter, create a new summary worksheet with an appropriate sheet name. On the summary sheet, insert a clustered bar chart that displays the revenue for

each month. Format the chart appropriately. Move the summary sheet to the first position in the workbook. On all sheets, insert the file name in the left footer and the sheet name in the right footer. Adjust the page settings to print each worksheet on one page. Save the workbook, and then submit the workbook as directed by your instructor.

 DONE! You have completed Skills Challenge 2

CHAPTER 4

More Functions and Excel Tables

▶ The Excel Function Library contains hundreds of special functions that perform complex calculations quickly.

▶ Function Library categories include statistical, financial, logical, date and time, and math and trigonometry.

▶ Conditional formatting helps you see important trends and exceptions in your data by applying various formats such as colored gradients, data bars, or icons.

▶ You can convert data that is organized in rows and columns into an Excel table that adds formatting, filtering, and AutoComplete features.

▶ An Excel table helps you manage information by providing ways to sort and filter the data and to analyze the data using summary rows and calculated columns.

© alisonhancock

Aspen Falls City Hall

In this chapter, you will revise a spreadsheet for Jack Ruiz, the Aspen Falls Community Services Director. He has received permission from the City Council to create community gardens in open space areas in Aspen Falls. In order to promote the gardens, the city will provide materials to community members. He has a workbook with a list of materials and wants to know if any items need to be reordered and if new suppliers should be contacted for quotes when replacing the items. He is also tracking the donations received from local retail stores.

Using workbooks to track information is a primary function of a spreadsheet application. Because spreadsheets can be set up to globally update when underlying data is changed, managers often use Excel to help them make decisions in real time. An effective workbook uses functions, conditional formatting, summary statistics, and charts in ways that describe past trends and help decision makers accurately forecast future needs.

In this project, you will use the functions TODAY, NOW, COUNT, and IF to generate useful information for the director. You will apply conditional formatting to highlight outlying data and create sparklines to display trends. To update the underlying data, you will use the Find and Replace tool. Finally, you will create and format Excel tables, and then search the tables for data.

Student data file needed for this chapter:

exl04_Garden

You will save your workbook as:

Last_First_exl04_Garden

Outcome

Using the skills in this chapter, you will be able to work with Excel worksheets like this:

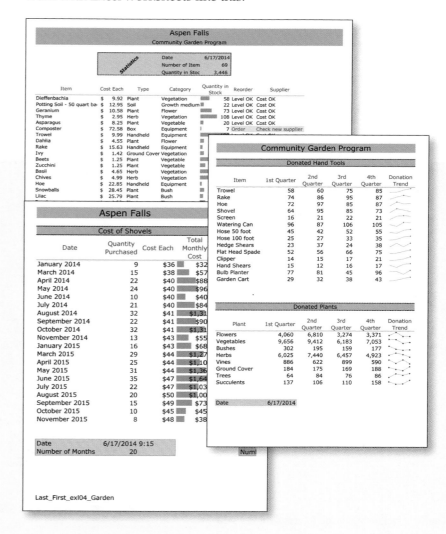

SKILLS

Skills 1-10 Training

At the end of this chapter you will be able to:

Skill 1   Insert the TODAY, NOW, and COUNT Functions

Skill 2   Insert the IF Function

Skill 3   Move Functions, Add Borders, and Rotate Text

Skill 4   Apply Conditional Formatting

Skill 5   Insert Sparklines

Skill 6   Use Find and Replace

Skill 7   Freeze and Unfreeze Panes

Skill 8   Create, Sort, and Filter Excel Tables

Skill 9   Filter Data

Skill 10 Convert Tables to Ranges, Hide Rows and Columns, and Format Large Worksheets

MORE SKILLS

Skill 11 Apply Conditional Color Scales with Top and Bottom Rules and Clear Rules

Skill 12 Insert the Payment (PMT) Function

Skill 13 Create PivotTable Reports

Skill 14 Use Goal Seek

▶ The **TODAY function** returns the serial number of the current date.

▶ The **NOW function** returns the serial number of the current date and time.

▶ The **COUNT function** counts the number of cells that contain numbers.

1. Start **Excel 2013**, and then open the student data file **exl04_Garden**. Click the **File tab**, and then click **Save As**. Click the **Browse** button, and then navigate to the location where you are saving your files. Click **New folder**, type Excel Chapter 4 and then press Enter two times. In the **File name** box, using your own name, name the workbook Last_First_exl04_ Garden and then press Enter.

2. On the **Inventory** sheet, click cell **E4**. On the **Formulas tab**, in the **Function Library group**, click the **Date & Time** button, and then click **TODAY**. Read the message that displays, compare your screen with **Figure 1**, and then click **OK** to enter the function.

   The TODAY function takes no arguments, and the result is **volatile**—the date will not remain as entered but rather will be updated each time this workbook is opened.

3. Click the **Donations** worksheet tab, scroll down, and then click cell **B36**. Use the technique just practiced to enter the **TODAY** function. Compare your screen with **Figure 2**.

■ **Continue to the next page to complete the skill**

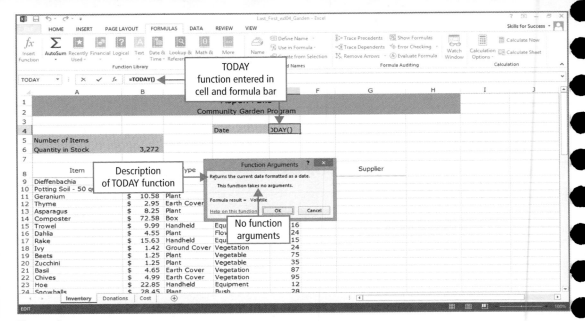

Figure 1

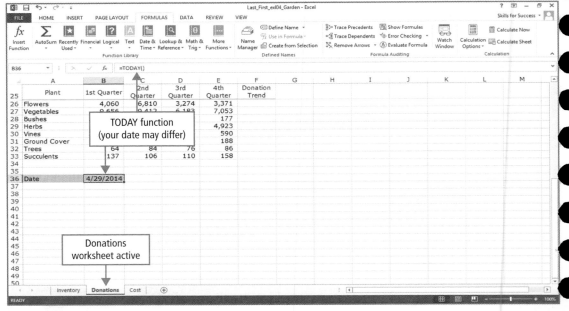

Figure 2

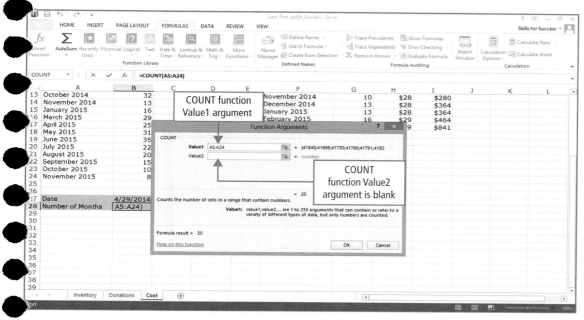

Figure 3

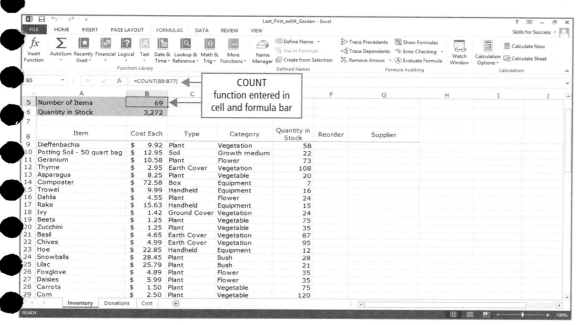

Figure 4

4. Click the **Cost** worksheet tab, scroll down and then click the merged cell **B27**. In the **Function Library group**, click the **Date & Time** button, and then click **NOW**. Read the message that displays, and then click **OK** to insert the function.

5. Click cell **B28**. In the **Function Library group**, click the **More Functions** button. Point to **Statistical**, and then click **COUNT**.

6. In the **Function Arguments** dialog box, in the **Value1** box, type A5:A24 and then compare your screen with **Figure 3**.

7. In the **Function Arguments** dialog box, click **OK**.

> The number of cells in the range A5:A24 that contain values is *20*.

8. Click cell **G28**. Use the technique just practiced to enter a **COUNT** function with the range F5:F17 as the **Value1** argument. The result should be *13*.

9. Click the **Inventory** worksheet tab, and then click cell **B5**. In the **Function Library group**, click the **More Functions** button, point to **Statistical**, and then click **COUNT**. If necessary, move the Function Arguments dialog box to the right to view column **B**. In the **Function Arguments** dialog box, with the insertion point in the **Value1** box, click cell **B9**. Press Ctrl + Shift + ↓ to select the range **B9:B77**. Click **OK** to display the result *69*. Compare your screen with **Figure 4**.

10. **Save** 🖫 the workbook.

■ **You have completed Skill 1 of 10**

▶ A *logical function* applies a logical test to determine whether a specific condition is met.

▶ A *logical test* is any value or expression that can be evaluated as TRUE or FALSE and *Criteria* are the conditions specified in the logical test.

▶ The *IF function* is a logical function that checks whether criteria are met and then returns one value when the condition is TRUE and another value when the condition is FALSE.

1. On the **Inventory** worksheet, click cell **F9**. In the **Function Library group**, click the **Logical** button, and then on the list, point to **IF**. Read the ScreenTip, and then click **IF**.

2. In the **Function Arguments** dialog box, with the insertion point in the **Logical_test** box, type E9<10

   A *comparison operator* compares two values and returns either TRUE or FALSE. Here, the logical test *E9<10* uses the less than comparison operator, and will return TRUE only when the value in E9 is less than 10. The table in Figure 1 lists commonly used comparison operators.

3. Press Tab to move the insertion point to the **Value_if_true** box, and then type Order

4. Press Tab to move the insertion point to the **Value_if_false** box, type Level OK and then compare your screen with Figure 2.

   In function arguments, text values are surrounded by quotation marks. Here, quotation marks display around *Order* and will automatically be inserted around *Level OK* after you click OK.

▪ **Continue to the next page to complete the skill**

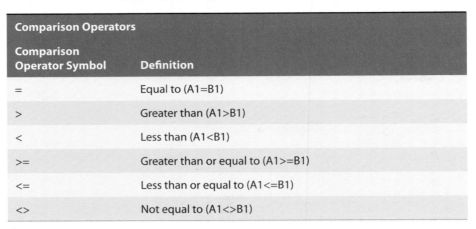

Comparison Operators	
Comparison Operator Symbol	**Definition**
=	Equal to (A1=B1)
>	Greater than (A1>B1)
<	Less than (A1<B1)
>=	Greater than or equal to (A1>=B1)
<=	Less than or equal to (A1<=B1)
<>	Not equal to (A1<>B1)

Figure 1

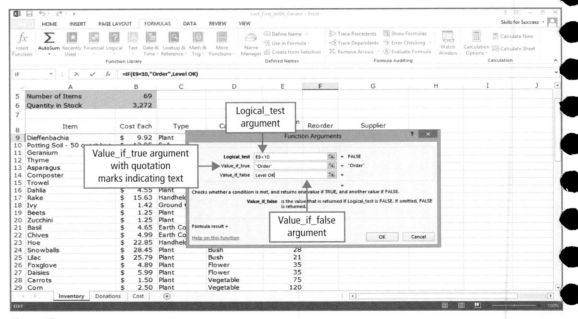

Figure 2

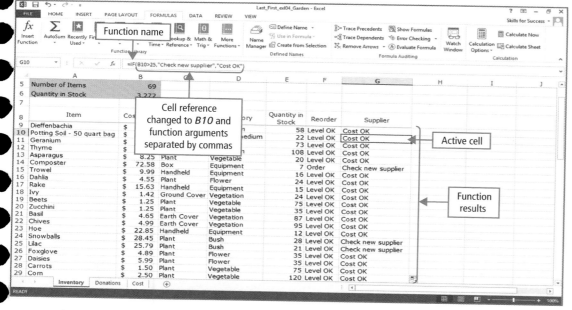

Figure 3

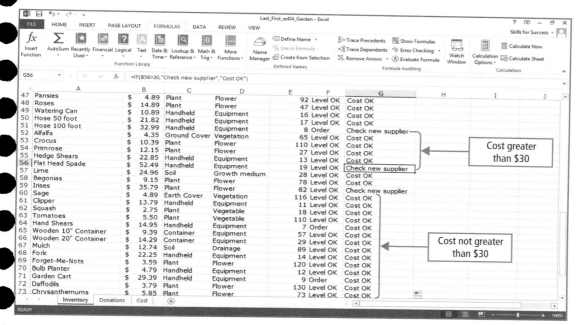

Figure 4

5. Click **OK** to display the result *Level OK*.

   The IF function tests whether E9 is less than 10. When this condition is TRUE, *Order* will display. Because E9 contains the value *58*, the condition is FALSE, and *Level OK* displays.

6. Click cell **G9**. In the **Function Library group**, click the **Logical** button, and then click **IF**. In the **Logical_test** box, type B9>25 and then in the **Value_if_true** box, type Check new supplier In the **Value_if_false** box, type Cost OK and then click the **OK** button to display *Cost OK*.

7. Select the range **F9:G9**. Point to the fill handle to display the ⊞ pointer, and then double-click to AutoFill the functions down through row **77**. Click **G10**, and then compare your screen with **Figure 3**.

   In each row of column G, the function evaluates the value in column B. When the value in column B is greater than $25, the text *Check new supplier* displays. Otherwise, the text *Cost OK* displays.

   When a function has multiple arguments, each argument is separated by a comma.

   When the function was copied down to G10, the cell reference changed from B9 to B10.

8. Scroll down and verify that nine items meet the condition and display the text *Check new supplier*. Click cell **G9**. In the formula bar, change the number *25* to *30* and then, click the **Enter** button ✓. AutoFill the function down through cell **G77**. Scroll down to verify that five items meet the changed condition. Click cell **G56**, and then compare your screen with **Figure 4**.

9. Save 🖫 the workbook.

▪ **You have completed Skill 2 of 10**

▶ When you move cells containing formulas or functions by dragging them, the cell references in the formulas or functions do not change.

▶ Borders and shading emphasize a cell or a range of cells, and rotated or angled text draws attention to text on a worksheet.

1. On the **Inventory** worksheet, press Ctrl + Home. Select the range **A5:B6**. Point to the top edge of the selected range to display the ⤢ pointer. Drag the selected range to the right until the ScreenTip displays the range **D5:E6**, as shown in Figure 1, and then release the mouse button to complete the move.

2. Click cell **E5**. Notice that the cell references in the function did not change.

3. Click the **Donations** worksheet tab. Select the merged cell **A3**. On the **Home** tab, in the **Font group**, click the **Border arrow** ⬚ ▾, and then click **Top and Bottom Border**.

4. Click the merged cell **A23**. In the **Font group**, click the **Border** button ⬚ ▾ to apply a top and bottom border. Click cell **A5**, and then compare your screen with Figure 2.

5. Click the **Cost** worksheet tab. Click the merged cell **A3**. Hold down Ctrl and then click the merged cell **F3**. Use the technique just practiced to apply a top and bottom border.

■ Continue to the next page to complete the skill ▶

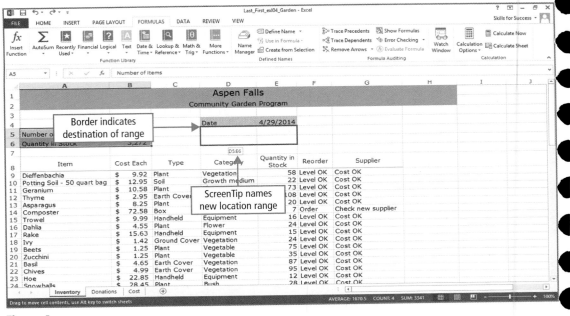

Figure 1

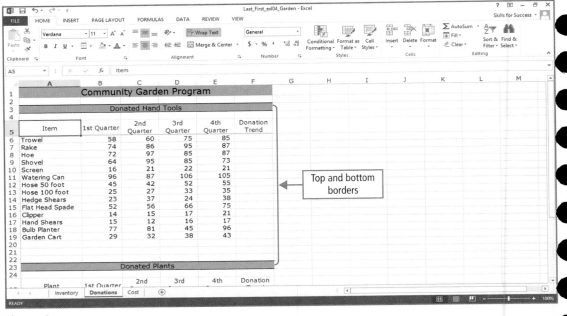

Figure 2

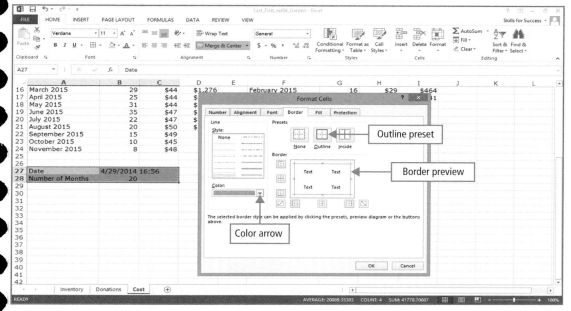

Figure 3

6. Scroll down, and then select the range **A27:C28**. In the **Font group**, click the **Border arrow**. At the bottom of the **Border** gallery, click **More Borders**.

7. In the **Format Cells** dialog box, click the **Color arrow**, and then click the fifth color in the first row—**Orange, Accent 1**. Under **Presets**, click **Outline**. Compare your screen with **Figure 3**, and then click **OK**.

8. Select the range **F28:G28**. Press F4 to repeat the last command, and then click cell **F30**.

    Pressing F4 will repeat the last command. In this instance it will apply an orange border to the selected range.

9. Click the **Inventory** worksheet tab. Click cell **B4**, type Statistics and then press Enter.

10. Select the range **B4:C6**. On the **Home tab**, in the **Alignment group**, click the **Merge & Center** button. Apply the **40% - Accent 4** cell style, and then click **Middle Align**, **Bold B**, and **Italic I**.

11. With the merged cell still selected, in the **Alignment group**, click the **Orientation** button, and then click **Angle Counterclockwise**.

12. Select the range **B4:E6**. In the **Font group**, click the **Border arrow**, and then click **Outside Borders**. Click cell **A8**, and then compare your screen with **Figure 4**.

13. **Save** the workbook.

■ **You have completed Skill 3 of 10**

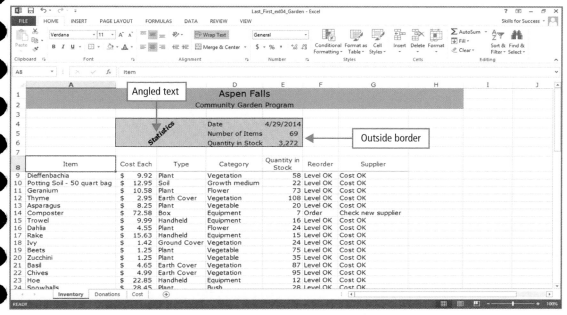

Figure 4

▶ **Conditional formatting** is a format, such as cell shading or font color, that is applied to cells when a specified condition is true.

▶ Conditional formatting makes analyzing data easier by emphasizing differences in cell values.

1. On the **Inventory** worksheet, click cell **F9**. Press Ctrl + Shift + ↓ to select the range **F9:F77**.

2. Click the **Quick Analysis Lens** button 📊, and then click **Text Contains**. In the **Text That Contains** dialog box, delete the text in the first box, and then type Order Compare your screen with **Figure 1**, and then click **OK**.

Within the range F9:F77, cells that contain the text *Order* display with light red fill and dark red text formatting.

3. Using the technique just practiced, select the range **G9:G77**, and then open the **Text That Contains** dialog box. In the first box, type Check new supplier To the right of the format box, click the **arrow**, and then compare your screen with **Figure 2**.

You can use the Text That Contains dialog box to specify the formatting that should be applied when a condition is true. If the formatting choice you need is not listed, you can open the Format Cells dialog box by clicking the Custom Format command.

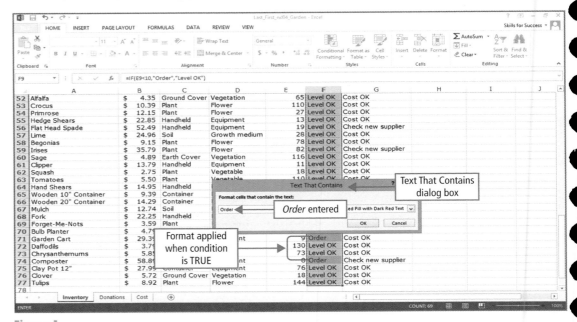

Figure 1

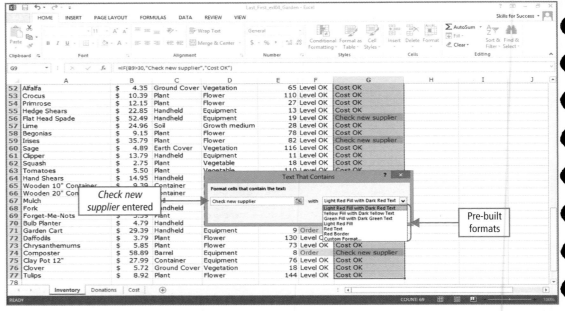

Figure 2

■ **Continue to the next page to complete the skill**

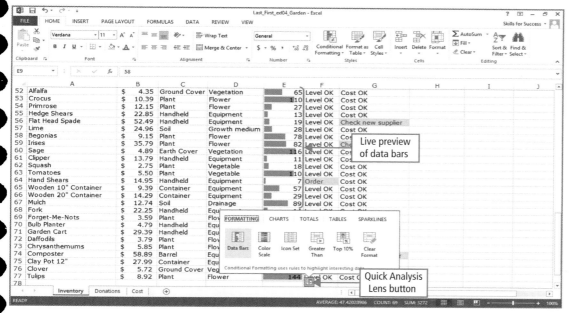

Figure 3

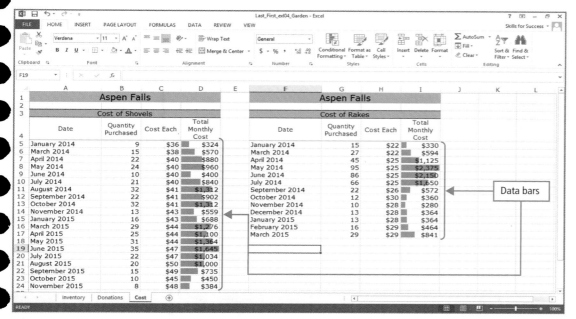

Figure 4

4. In the list of conditional formats, click **Green Fill with Dark Green Text**, and then click **OK**.

5. Select the range **E9:E77**. Click the **Quick Analysis Lens** button 📊, and then point to **Data Bars**. Compare your screen with **Figure 3**.

A ***data bar*** is a format that provides a visual cue about the value of a cell relative to other cells in a range. Data bars are useful to quickly identify higher and lower numbers within a large group of data, such as very high or very low levels of inventory.

6. In the **Quick Analysis** gallery, click **Data Bars** to apply the conditional formatting.

7. Scroll up, and then click cell **E15**. Type 190 and then press Enter to adjust all data bars to the new value.

Data bars are sized relative to the maximum value within a range. Here, when a new maximum value of 190 was entered, all the data bars adjusted.

8. Click the **Cost** worksheet tab. Select the range **D5:D24**, and then use the technique just practiced to apply the default data bar conditional format.

9. Select the range **I5:I17**, and then apply the default data bar conditional format. Click cell **F19**, and then compare your screen with **Figure 4**.

10. Save 💾 the workbook.

■ **You have completed Skill 4 of 10**

EXL 4-5
VIDEO

▶ A **sparkline** is a chart contained in a single cell that is used to show data trends.

1. Click the **Donations** worksheet tab to make it the active sheet, and then select the range **B6:E19**.

2. Click the **Quick Analysis Lens** button 📧, and then click **Sparklines**. In the **Sparklines** gallery, point to **Line** to display sparklines in **column F**. Compare your screen with **Figure 1**, and then click **Line**.

3. With the range **F6:F19** selected, on the **Design tab**, in the **Show group**, select the **High Point** check box to mark the highest point of data on each sparkline.

4. In the **Style group**, click the **Sparkline Color** button, and then click the fifth color in the first row—**Orange, Accent 1**. Click cell **E20**, and then compare your screen with **Figure 2**.

> The sparklines in column F show that the donation levels of hand tools are generally increasing over time.

■ **Continue to the next page to complete the skill**

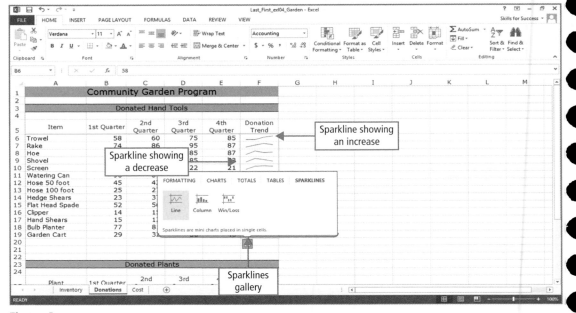

Figure 1

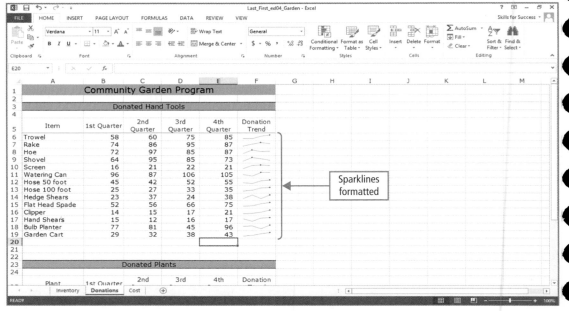

Figure 2

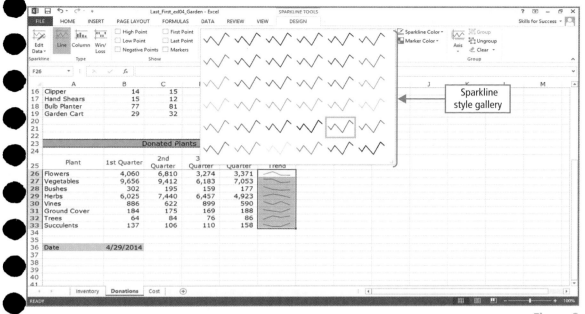

Figure 3

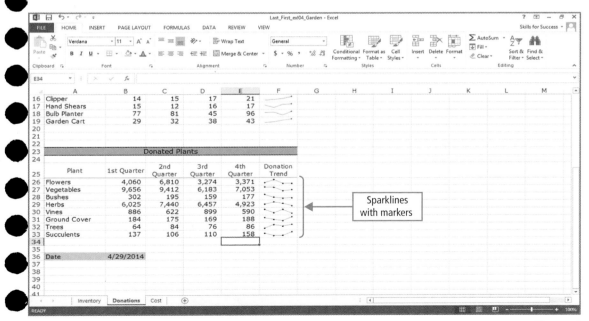

Figure 4

5. Scroll down and then select the range **B26:E33**. Use the techniques just practiced to insert the default **Line** sparklines.

6. With the range **F26:F33** selected, on the **Design tab**, in the **Style group**, click the **More** button ⊡, and then compare your screen with **Figure 3**.

7. In the **Style** gallery, click the first color in the third row—**Sparkline Style Accent 1, (no dark or light)**.

8. In the **Style group**, click the **Marker Color** button. In the displayed list, point to **Markers**, and then click the second color in the first row—**Black, Text 1** to mark each data point on the sparklines. Click cell **E34**, and then compare your screen with **Figure 4**.

9. Right-click the **Donations** worksheet tab, and then click **Select All Sheets**. Add the file name to the worksheet's left footer and the sheet name to the right footer. Return to **Normal** view and then press Ctrl + Home to make cell **A1** the active cell on each of the grouped worksheets.

10. Right-click the **Donations** worksheet tab, and then click **Ungroup Sheets**. **Save** 🖫 the workbook.

▪ **You have completed Skill 5 of 10**

EXL 4-6
VIDEO

▶ The **_Replace_** feature finds and then replaces a character or string of characters in a worksheet or in a selected range.

1. Click the **Inventory** worksheet tab, and then verify that cell **A1** is the active cell. On the **Home tab**, in the **Editing group**, click the **Find & Select** button, and then click **Replace**.

2. In the **Find and Replace** dialog box, in the **Find what** box, type Earth Cover and then press ⎀Tab⎀. In the **Replace with** box, type Herb and then compare your screen with **Figure 1**.

3. Click the **Find Next** button, and then verify that cell **C12** is the active cell. In the **Find and Replace** dialog box, click the **Replace** button to replace the value in cell **C12** with *Herb* and to select the next occurrence of *Earth Cover* in cell *C21*.

4. In the **Find and Replace** dialog box, click the **Replace All** button. Read the message that displays. Compare your screen with **Figure 2**, and then click **OK**.

   The Replace All option replaces all matches of an occurrence of a character or string of characters with the replacement value. Here, six values were replaced. Only use the Replace All option when the search string is unique.

■ **Continue to the next page to complete the skill**

Figure 1

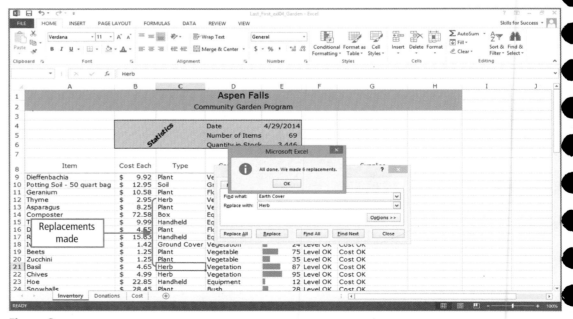

Figure 2

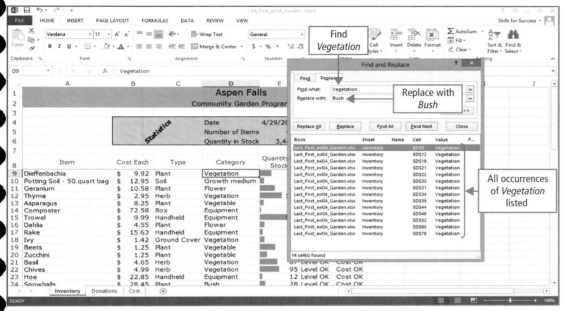

Figure 3

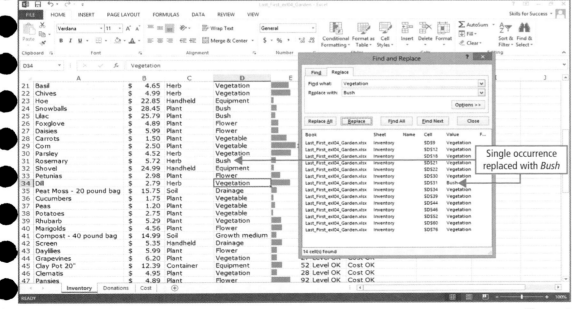

Figure 4

5. In the **Find and Replace** dialog box, in the **Find what** box, replace the text *Earth Cover* with Vegetation and then press Tab. In the **Replace with** box, replace the text *Herb* with Bush and then click the **Find All** button.

6. In the **Find and Replace** dialog box, point to the bottom border, and then with the ⬍ pointer, drag down to resize the dialog box until each listed occurrence displays as shown in Figure 3. If necessary, move the dialog box to display all occurrences.

    The Find All option finds all occurrences of the search criteria.

7. In the lower portion of the **Find and Replace** dialog box, in the **Cell** column, click **$D$31** to make cell **D31** the active cell, and then click the **Replace** button. Compare your screen with Figure 4.

    In this manner you can find all occurrences of cell text and use the list to replace only the occurrences you desire.

8. Use the technique just practiced to replace the two occurrences of the word Clay with the word Terracotta and then close all message and dialog boxes.

9. **Save** 🖫 the workbook.

■ **You have completed Skill 6 of 10**

▶ The **Freeze Panes** command keeps rows or columns visible when you are scrolling in a worksheet. The frozen rows and columns become separate panes so that you can always identify rows and columns when working with large worksheets.

1. On the **Inventory** sheet, scroll until **row 50** displays at the bottom of your window and the column labels are out of view. Compare your screen with **Figure 1**.

   When you scroll in large worksheets, the column and row labels may not be visible, which can make identifying the purpose of each row or column difficult.

2. Press Ctrl + Home , and then click cell **C15**. On the **View tab**, in the **Window group**, click the **Freeze Panes** button, and then click **Freeze Panes** to freeze the rows above and the columns to the left of C15—the active cell.

   A line displays along the upper border of row 15 and on the left border of column C to show where the panes are frozen.

3. Click the **Scroll Down** ⌄ and **Scroll Right** > arrows to display cell **M80**, and then notice that the top and left panes remain frozen. Compare your screen with **Figure 2**.

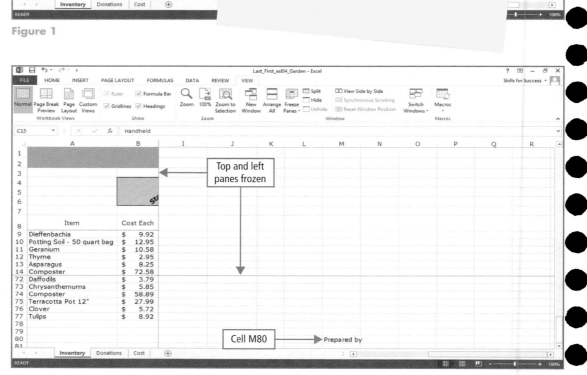

Figure 1

Figure 2

■ **Continue to the next page to complete the skill** ▶

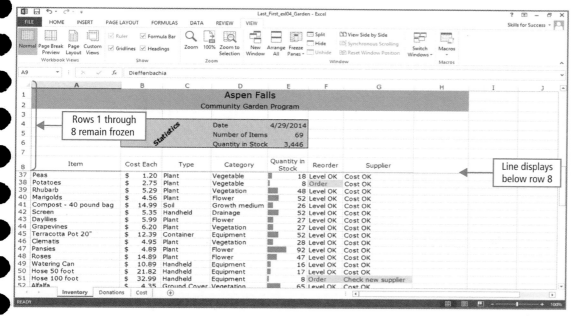

Figure 3

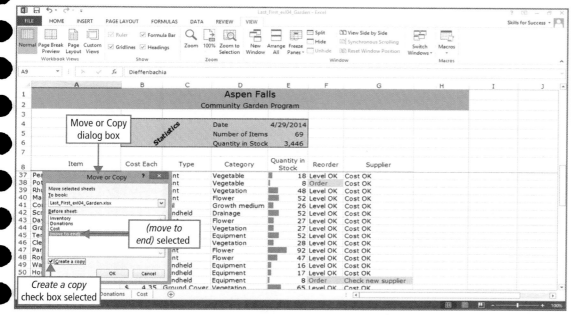

Figure 4

4. Click cell **M80** and then press [Delete].

5. In the **Window group**, click the **Freeze Panes** button, and then click **Unfreeze Panes**.

   The rows and columns are no longer frozen, and the border no longer displays on row 15 and on column C.

6. Click cell **A9**. In the **Window group**, click the **Freeze Panes** button, and then click **Freeze Panes** to freeze the rows above **row 9**.

7. Watch the row numbers below **row 8** as you scroll down to **row 50**. Compare your screen with Figure 3.

   The labels in row 1 through row 8 stay frozen while the remaining rows of data continue to scroll.

8. Right-click the **Inventory** worksheet tab, and then from the list, click **Move or Copy**. In the **Move or Copy** dialog box, click **(move to end)**, and then select the **Create a copy** check box. Compare your screen with Figure 4.

9. In the **Move or Copy** dialog box, click **OK** to create a copy of the worksheet named *Inventory (2)*.

   A *(2)* displays in the name since two sheets in a workbook cannot have the same name.

10. Right-click the **Inventory (2)** worksheet tab, click **Rename**, type Sort by Cost and then press [Enter].

11. In the **Window group**, click the **Freeze Panes** button, and then click **Unfreeze Panes** to unfreeze the panes.

12. Click the **Inventory** worksheet tab, and verify that on this worksheet, the panes are still frozen.

13. **Save** 🖫 the workbook.

■ **You have completed Skill 7 of 10**

EXL 4-8
VIDEO

▶ To analyze a group of related data, you can convert a range into an *Excel table*—a series of rows and columns that contain related data that has been formatted as a table. Data in an Excel table are managed independently from the data in other rows and columns in the worksheet.

▶ Data in Excel tables can be sorted in a variety of ways—for example, in ascending order or by color.

1. Click the **Sort by Cost** worksheet tab, and then click cell **A11**. On the **Home tab**, in the **Styles group**, click the **Format as Table** button. In the gallery, under **Light**, click the fifth choice—**Table Style Light 5**.

2. In the **Format as Table** dialog box, under **Where is the data for your table?** verify that the range =$A$8:$G$77 displays. Verify that the **My table has headers** check box is selected. Compare your screen with **Figure 1**, and then click **OK** to convert the range to an Excel table.

When creating an Excel table, you only need to click in the data. The layout of column and row headings determines the default range provided in the Format As Table dialog box.

3. Click cell **H8**, type Total Cost and then press Enter to automatically add the formatted column to the Excel table.

4. In cell **H9**, type =B9*E9 and then press Enter to create a *calculated column*—a column in an Excel table that uses a single formula which adjusts for each row. Compare your screen with **Figure 2**.

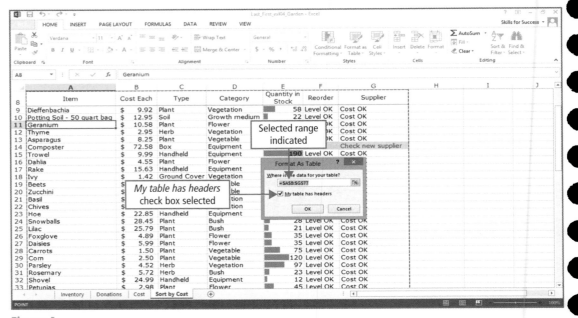
Figure 1

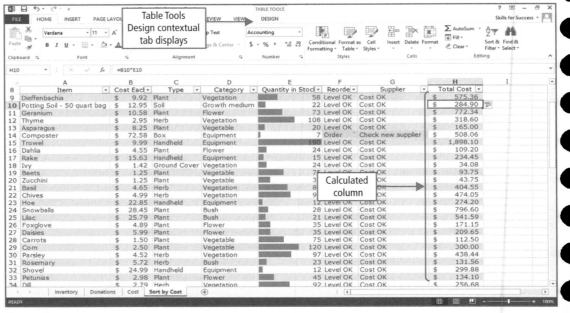
Figure 2

■ **Continue to the next page to complete the skill** ▶

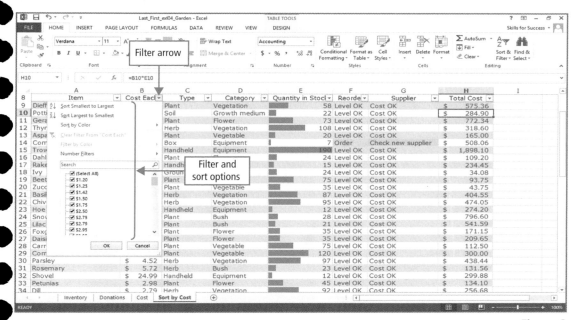

Figure 3

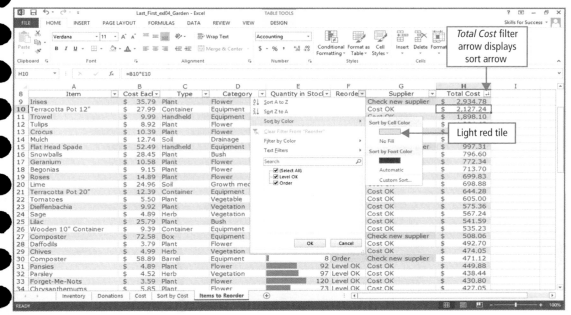

Figure 4

5. In the header row of the Excel table, click the **Cost Each filter arrow**, and then compare your screen with **Figure 3**.

6. In the **Filter** gallery, click **Sort Smallest to Largest**.

   The rows in the table are sorted by the *Cost Each* values, from the lowest to the highest, as indicated by the up arrow on the column's filter button.

7. In the header row, click the **Total Cost filter arrow**, and then click **Sort Largest to Smallest**.

   The rows in the table are now sorted from the highest to lowest *Total Cost* value, and the small arrow in the Total Cost filter arrow points down, indicating a descending sort. The previous sort on the *Cost Each* column no longer displays.

8. Right-click the **Sort by Cost** worksheet tab, and then click **Move or Copy**. In the **Move or Copy** dialog box, click **(move to end)**, select the **Create a copy** check box, and then click **OK**.

9. Rename the **Sort by Cost (2)** worksheet tab, as Items to Reorder.

10. In the **Items to Reorder** worksheet, click the **Reorder filter arrow**, and then point to **Sort by Color**. Notice that the color formats in **column F** display in the list. Compare your screen with **Figure 4**.

    If you have applied manual or conditional formatting to a range of cells, you can sort by these colors.

11. In the list, under **Sort by Cell Color**, click the **light red tile** to place the six items that need to be ordered at the top of the Excel table.

12. **Save** 🖫 the workbook.

■ **You have completed Skill 8 of 10**

► You can *filter* data to display only the rows of a table that meet specified criteria. Filtering temporarily hides rows that do not meet the criteria.

1. On the **Items to Reorder** worksheet, click the **Category filter arrow**. From the menu, clear the **(Select All)** check box to clear all the check boxes. Select the **Equipment** check box, as shown in **Figure 1**, and then click **OK** to display only the rows containing *Equipment*.

   The rows not meeting this criteria are hidden from view.

2. On the **Design tab**, in the **Table Style Options group**, select the **Total Row** check box to display the column total in cell **H78**.

   The *Total row* provides summary functions in drop-down lists for each column. Here, *Total* displays in cell A78. In cell H78, the number *$10,400.26* indicates the SUM of the Total Cost column for the filtered *Equipment* rows.

3. In the **Total** row, click cell **D78**, and then click the **arrow** that displays to the right of the selected cell. Compare your screen with **Figure 2**.

4. In the list of summary functions, click **Count** to count only the visible rows in column **D**—*20*.

5. In the header row, click the **Type filter arrow**. From the menu, clear the **Handheld** check box, and then click **OK**.

   Filters can be applied to more than one column. Here, both the Type and Category columns are filtered.

■ Continue to the next page to complete the skill ►

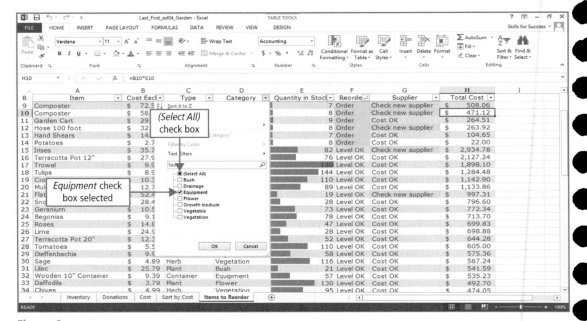

Figure 1

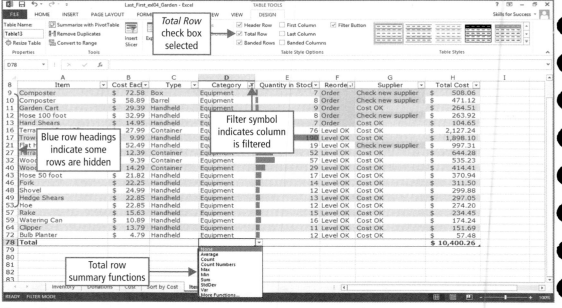

Figure 2

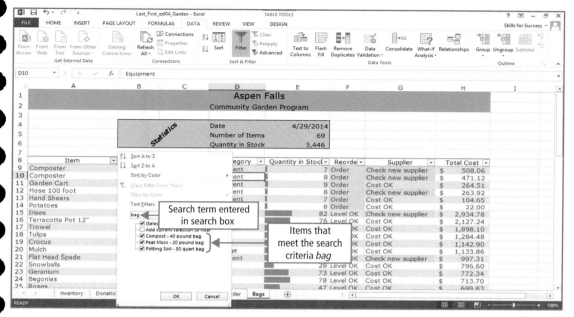

Figure 3

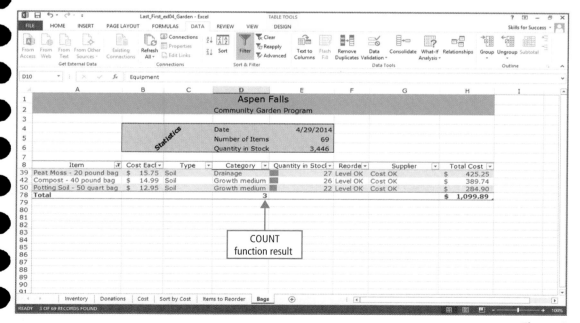

Figure 4

6. Right-click the **Items to Reorder** worksheet tab, and then using the techniques you just practiced, create a copy of the worksheet and move the sheet to the end. Rename the **Items to Reorder (2)** worksheet tab as Bags

7. With the **Bags** worksheet active, click any cell in the Excel table to make the Excel table active. On the **Data tab**, in the **Sort & Filter group**, click the **Clear** button to clear all the filters and to display all the rows in the Excel table.

8. In the header row, click the **Item filter arrow**. In the **Filter** list, click in the **Search** box, type bag and then compare your screen with **Figure 3**.

9. Click **OK** to display the three rows containing the text bag in the **Item** column. Compare your screen with **Figure 4**.

   In the Total row, the Category count in cell D78 and the Total Cost in cell H78 display the results of the filtered rows.

10. Save 🖫 the workbook.

■ **You have completed Skill 9 of 10**

▶ An Excel table can be converted into a range retaining the table format.

▶ When a large worksheet is too wide or too long to print on a single page, row and column headings can be printed on each page.

1. Right-click the **Bags** worksheet tab, create a copy of the sheet, and move it to the end of the workbook. Rename the **Bags (2)** worksheet tab as All Items

2. In the **All Items** sheet, click cell **A8**. On the **Design tab**, in the **Tools group**, click the **Convert to Range** button. Read the message box, as shown in **Figure 1**, and then click **Yes**.

   When converting an Excel table into a range, all filters are removed and the heading row no longer displays filter buttons. Any existing sorts and formatting remain.

3. Click the **File tab**, and then click **Print**. Click the **Next Page** button ▶ three times to view the four pages.

4. Click the **Back** button ◉. On the **Page Layout tab**, in the **Scale to Fit group**, click the **Width arrow**, and then click **1 page**. Click the **Height arrow**, and then click **1 page**.

5. Click the **Inventory** worksheet tab. In the **Scale to Fit group**, click the **Width** arrow, and then click **1 page**.

6. In the **Page Setup group**, click the **Print Titles** button, and then in the **Page Setup** dialog box, under **Print titles**, click in the **Rows to repeat at top** box. In the worksheet, click **row 8**, and then compare your screen with **Figure 2**.

■ Continue to the next page to complete the skill ▶

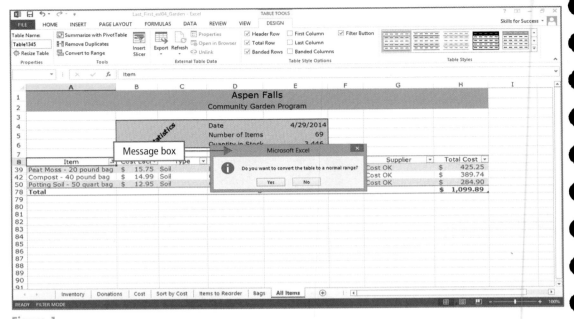

Figure 1

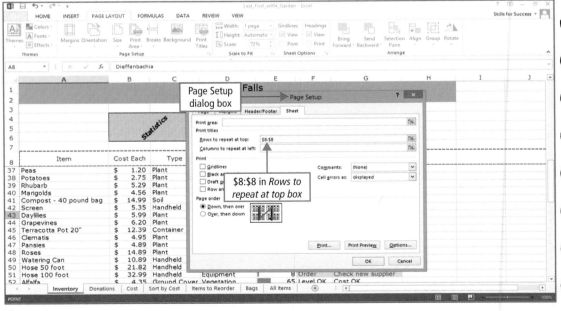

Figure 2

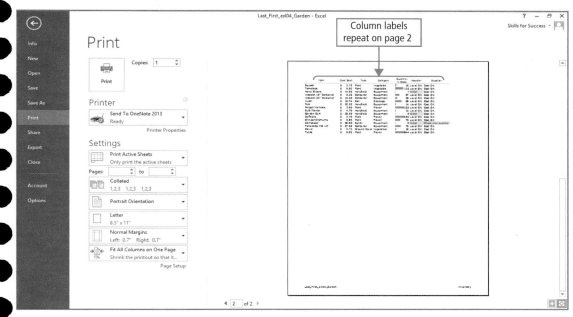

Column labels repeat on page 2

Figure 3

7. In the **Page Setup** dialog box, click the **Print Preview** button. Click the **Next Page** button ▶ to verify that the column labels from **row 8** display at the top of page 2. Compare your screen with **Figure 3**.

8. Click the **Back** button ⊙.

9. Click the **Cost** worksheet tab. Hold down Ctrl, and then click the **Items to Reorder** and the **Bags** worksheet tabs to group the three worksheets. In the **Page Setup group**, click the **Orientation** button, and then click **Landscape**. In the **Scale to Fit group**, click the **Width** arrow, and then click **1 page**.

   With the worksheets grouped, the orientation and scaling are applied to all three worksheets.

10. Click the **Sort by Cost** worksheet tab to select the worksheet and ungroup the three worksheets. Click cell **B13**. On the **Home tab**, in the **Cells group**, click the **Format** button, point to **Hide & Unhide**, and then click **Hide Columns**. Use the same technique to hide **column G**.

11. Select **rows 15:65**. In the **Cells group**, click the **Format** button, point to **Hide & Unhide**, and then click **Hide Rows**.

12. On the **Page Layout tab**, in the **Page Setup group**, click the **Orientation** button, and then click **Landscape**. Compare your screen with **Figure 4**.

13. **Save** 🖫 the workbook, and then **Close** ✕ Excel. Submit the workbook as directed by your instructor.

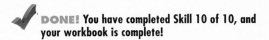
DONE! You have completed Skill 10 of 10, and your workbook is complete!

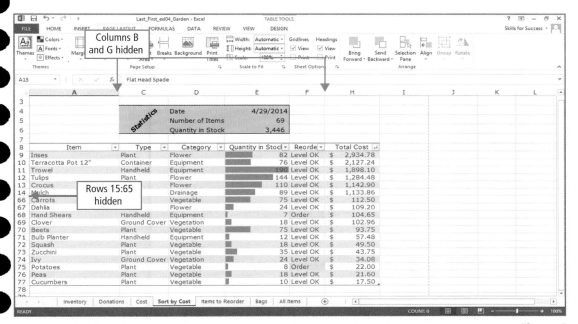

Columns B and G hidden

Rows 15:65 hidden

Figure 4

The following More Skills are located at **www.pearsonhighered.com/skills**

More Skills Apply Conditional Color Scales with Top and Bottom Rules and Clear Rules

You can apply color scales, which apply different colors to the cells, and top/bottom rules, which format the highest or lowest values. Conditional formatting rules can be cleared when no longer needed.

In More Skills 11, you will apply these additional types of conditional formats.

To begin, open your web browser, navigate to www.pearsonhighered.com/skills, locate the name of your textbook, and then follow the instructions on the website.

More Skills Insert the Payment (PMT) Function

The PMT function calculates the periodic payment for loans based on the loan amount, interest rate, and length of the loan. When you borrow money from a bank, the amount charged for your use of the borrowed money is called interest, and the interest amount is included in the PMT function.

In More Skills 12, you will use the PMT function to calculate various loan payments.

To begin, open your web browser, navigate to www.pearsonhighered.com/skills, locate the name of your textbook, and then follow the instructions on the website.

More Skills Create PivotTable Reports

A PivotTable report is an interactive way to summarize large amounts of data quickly, to analyze numerical data in depth, and to answer unanticipated questions about your data.

In More Skills 13, you will create a PivotTable report, pivot the data, and then filter the data.

To begin, open your web browser, navigate to www.pearsonhighered.com/skills, locate the name of your textbook, and then follow the instructions on the website.

More Skills Use Goal Seek

Goal Seek is a method to find a specific value for a cell by adjusting the value of another cell. With Goal Seek, you work backward from the desired outcome to find the necessary input to achieve your goal.

In More Skills 14, you will use Goal Seek to determine how much money can be borrowed to achieve a specific monthly payment.

To begin, open your web browser, navigate to www.pearsonhighered.com/skills, locate the name of your textbook, and then follow the instructions on the website.

Please note that there are no additional projects to accompany the More Skills Projects, and they are not covered in the End-of-Chapter projects.

The following table summarizes the **SKILLS AND PROCEDURES** covered in this chapter.

Skills Number	Task	Step	Icon	Keyboard Shortcut
1	Insert TODAY functions	Formula tab → Function Library group → Date & Time → TODAY		
1	Insert NOW functions	Formula tab → Function Library group → Date & Time → NOW		
1	Insert COUNT functions	Formula tab → Function Library group → More Functions → Statistical → COUNT		
2	Insert IF functions	Formula tab → Function Library group → Logical → IF		
3	Add borders	Home tab → Font group → Border arrow → Border		
3	Angle text	Home tab → Alignment group → Orientation		
4	Apply conditional formatting to text	Quick Analysis Lens button → Text Contains		
4	Apply conditional formatting to data bars	Quick Analysis Lens button → Data Bars		
5	Insert sparklines	Quick Analysis Lens button → Sparklines		
5	Add sparkline high points	Design tab → Show group → High Point		
6	Use Find and Replace	Home tab → Editing group → Find & Select → Replace		Ctrl + H
7	Freeze panes	View tab → Window group → Freeze Panes		
7	Unfreeze panes	View tab → Window group → Unfreeze Panes		
8	Create Excel tables	Home tab → Styles group → Format as Table		
8	Filter Excel tables	Click the column filter arrow		
8	Sort Excel tables	Column filter arrow		
9	Search Excel tables	Column filter arrow → Search criteria		
9	Insert Total rows	Design tab → Table Style Options group → Total Row		
10	Convert Excel tables to ranges	Design tab → Tools group → Convert to Range		
10	Repeat rows at the top of each printed page	Page Layout tab → Page Setup group → Print Titles		
10	Hide columns	Home tab → Cells group → Format → Hide & Unhide → Hide Columns		
10	Hide rows	Home tab → Cells group → Format → Hide & Unhide → Hide Rows		

Key Terms

Online Help Skills

1. Start **Excel 2013**, and then in the upper right corner of the start page, click the **Help** button [?].

2. In the **Excel Help** window **Search help** box, type use formulas in Excel tables and then press [Enter].

3. In the search result list, click **Using formulas in Excel tables**, and then compare your screen with **Figure 1**.

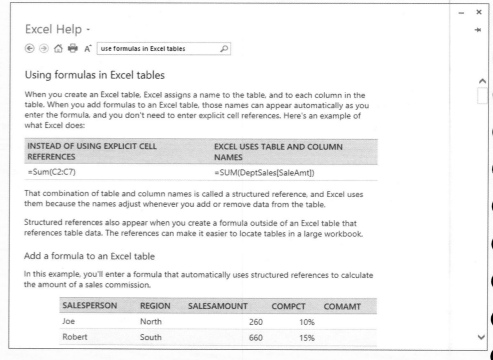

Figure 1

4. Read the article to answer the following question: What are structured references and why would you use them?

Matching

Match each term in the second column with its correct definition in the first column by writing the letter of the term on the blank line in front of the correct definition.

___ **1.** An Excel function that returns the serial number of the current date.

___ **2.** The result of a function that will be updated each time the workbook is opened.

___ **3.** The type of function that tests for specific conditions and typically uses conditional tests to determine whether specified conditions are TRUE or FALSE.

___ **4.** Conditions that determine how conditional formatting is applied or what values are returned in logical functions.

___ **5.** A cell shading or font color that is applied to cells when a specified circumstance is met.

___ **6.** A chart inside a single cell used to show data trends.

___ **7.** A series of rows and columns that are formatted together.

___ **8.** A column in an Excel table that uses a single formula that adjusts for each row.

___ **9.** A command to display only the rows of a table that meet specified criteria.

___ **10.** A row in an Excel table that provides summary functions.

A Calculated column

B Conditional formatting

C Criteria

D Excel table

E Filter

F Logical function

G Sparkline

H TODAY function

I Total row

J Volatile

BizSkills Video

1. What are some of the positive behaviors of the second applicant?

2. If you were the interviewer, which applicant would you hire and why would you hire that person?

Multiple Choice

Choose the correct answer.

1. This function checks whether criteria are met and returns one value if TRUE and another value if FALSE.
   A. IF
   B. UNKNOWN
   C. NEW

2. These symbols are inserted into logical functions to determine whether a condition is true or false—(<) and (=), for example.
   A. Comparison operators
   B. Mathematical operators
   C. Logical symbols

3. Applying this format to text draws attention to the text on a worksheet.
   A. Angle
   B. Slope
   C. Slant

4. This word describes a format, such as cell shading, that is applied to cells when a specified condition is true.
   A. Filtered
   B. Conditional
   C. Calculated

5. This format provides a visual cue about the value of a cell relative to other cells.
   A. Cell style
   B. Quick style
   C. Data bar

6. This command ensures that header rows and columns remain visible when a worksheet is scrolled.
   A. Total Panes
   B. Excel Panes
   C. Freeze Panes

7. Data in an Excel table can be sorted in this way.
   A. Large to largest
   B. Smallest to largest
   C. Small to smallest

8. This command displays only the rows of a table that meet specified criteria.
   A. Filter
   B. Standard
   C. Chart

9. This row displays as the last row in an Excel table and provides summary statistics.
   A. Total
   B. Sorted
   C. Changeable

10. This word describes the result of a function that is updated each time a workbook is opened.
    A. Volatile
    B. Changeable
    C. Unstable

Topics for Discussion

1. Think about current news stories, including sports stories, and identify statistical data that is presented by the media. What are the advantages of using conditional formatting with this type of data?

2. Sorting and filtering are two of the most valuable ways to analyze data. If you were presented with an Excel table containing names and addresses, what are some of the ways you might sort or filter the data? If you were presented with an Excel table of a day's cash transactions at your college's cafeteria, what are some ways you could sort, filter, and total?

Skills Review

To complete this project, you will need the following file:

- exl04_SRAuction

You will save your file as:

- Last_First_exl04_SRAuction

1. Start **Excel 2013**, and then open the file **exl04_SRAuction**. Save the workbook in your chapter folder as Last_First_exl04_SRAuction

2. On the **Materials List** sheet, click cell **B4**. On the **Formulas tab**, in the **Function Library group**, click the **Date & Time** button, and then click **TODAY**. In the message box, click **OK**. Click cell **B5**. In the **Function Library group**, click the **More Functions** button. Point to **Statistical**, and then click **COUNT**. In the **Value1** box, enter the range B9:B48, and then press [Enter]. Compare your screen with **Figure 1**.

3. Select the range **A4:B6**. Point to the right border of the selected range, and then move the data to the range **D4:E6**.

4. In cell **B4**, type Surplus and then merge and center the title in the range **B4:C6**. On the **Home tab**, in the **Alignment group**, click the **Middle Align** button. Click the **Orientation** button, and then click **Angle Counterclockwise**. Select the range **B4:E6**. In the **Font group**, click the **Border arrow**, and then click **Outside Borders**.

5. Click cell **A1**. In the **Editing group**, click the **Find & Select** button, and then click **Replace**. In the **Find what** box, type Sedan In the **Replace with** box, type Car and then click **Replace All**. Click **OK**, and then **Close** the dialog box.

6. Click cell **G9**. On the **Formulas tab**, in the **Function Library group**, click **Logical**, and then click **IF**. In the **Logical_test** box, type E9="Yes" In the **Value_if_true** box, type B9*F9 In the **Value_if_false** box, type 0 and then click **OK**. AutoFill the function down through **G48**, and then compare your screen with **Figure 2**.

7. Click cell **A9**. On the **View tab**, in the **Window group**, click the **Freeze Panes** button, and then click **Freeze Panes**.

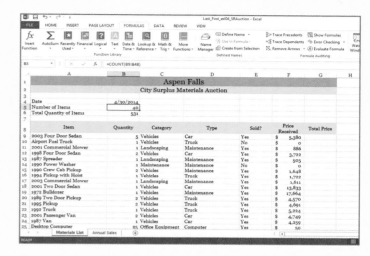

Figure 1

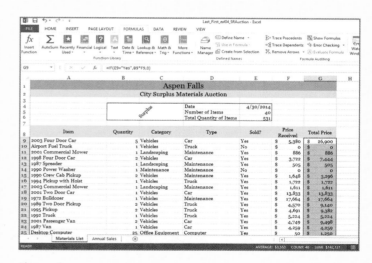

Figure 2

■ Continue to the next page to complete this Skills Review ▶

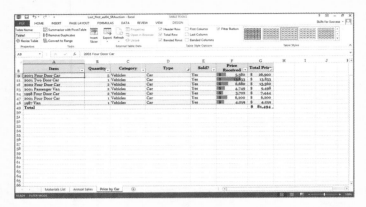

Figure 3

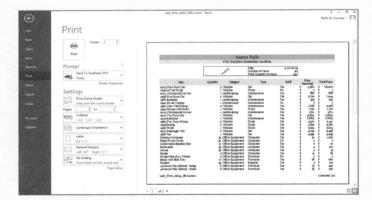

Figure 4

8. Right-click the **Materials List** worksheet tab, and then click **Move or Copy**. In the **Move or Copy** dialog box, click **(move to end)**, select the **Create a copy** check box, and then click **OK**. Rename the new worksheet tab as Price by Car

9. On the **Price by Car** sheet, in the **Window group**, click the **Freeze Panes** button, and then click **Unfreeze Panes**. On the **Home tab**, in the **Styles group**, click the **Format as Table** button, and then click **Table Style Light 17**. In the **Format As Table** dialog box, verify that the **My table has headers** check box is selected, and then click **OK**.

10. Click the **Type filter arrow**, and then clear the **(Select All)** check box. Select the **Car** check box, and then click **OK**. Click the **Total Price filter arrow**, and then click **Sort Largest to Smallest**. On the **Design tab**, in the **Table Style Options group**, select the **Total Row** check box.

11. Select the range **F9:F48**. Click the **Quick Analysis Lens** button, and then click **Data Bars**. Click cell **A9**, and then compare your screen with Figure 3.

12. Create a copy of the **Price by Car** sheet, move to the end, and then rename the new worksheet tab Pickups On the **Data tab**, in the **Sort & Filter group**, click the **Clear** button. Click the **Item filter arrow**. In the **Search** box, type Pickup and then click **OK**.

13. On the **Annual Sales** worksheet, select the range **B4:F9**. Click the **Quick Analysis Lens** button, click **Sparklines**, and then click the **Column** button.

14. Right-click the worksheet tab, and then click **Select All Sheets**. On the **Page Layout tab**, in the **Page Setup group**, click the **Orientation** button, and then click **Landscape**. In the **Scale to Fit group**, change the **Width** to **1 page**. Click the **Insert tab**, and add the file name in the left footer and the sheet name in the right footer. Return to **Normal** view, and then ungroup the worksheets.

15. Click the **Materials List** worksheet tab. On the **Page Layout tab**, in the **Page Setup group**, click the **Print Titles** button. In the **Page Setup** dialog box, click in the **Rows to repeat at top** box, click row **8**, and then click **OK**.

16. **Save** the workbook. Click the **File tab**, and then click the **Print tab**. Compare your workbook with Figure 4. Submit the workbook as directed by your instructor.

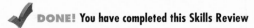 **DONE! You have completed this Skills Review**

Skills Assessment 1

MyITLab®
Grader

To complete this project, you will need the following file:

- exl04_SA1Recycling

You will save your workbook as:

- Last_First_exl04_SA1Recycling

---

1. Start **Excel 2013**, and open the file **exl04_SA1Recycling**. Save the file in your chapter folder as Last_First_exl04_SA1Recycling

2. In **E3**, insert the **NOW** function. Select **A5:G5**, and apply a **Bottom Border**.

3. In **F6:F27**, insert **Line Sparklines** using the data in **columns B:E**. Show the **Low Point**.

4. In **G6**, insert the **IF** function. For the logical test, check whether the **FY 2014** result is greater than the **FY 2013** value in the same row. If the logical test is TRUE, Yes should display, and if it is FALSE, Needs Work should display. **Center** the results, and then AutoFill **G6** down through **G27**.

5. Select **G6:G27**. Apply a **Text Contains** conditional format that will display any cells that contain *Needs Work* formatted with **Light Red Fill**.

6. Create a copy of the sheet, and move the copy to the end of the workbook. Rename the new worksheet tab Improvements

7. On the **Improvements** sheet, format **A5:G27** as an Excel table, using the **Table Style Light 16**. Filter **column G** to display only the rows that improved from the previous year.

8. Display the **Total** row, and then display the four FY sums. In **G28**, select **None**.

9. Sort the **FY 2014** column from the smallest to the largest value.

10. Hide **column B**.

11. Group the worksheets. Change the page orientation to **Landscape**. Add the file name in the left footer and the sheet name in the right footer. Return to **Normal** view, and ungroup the sheets.

12. On the **Recycling** sheet, change the Page Setup to repeat the titles in **row 5**. On the **Improvements** sheet, change the **Height** scale to fit on one page.

Recycling Volumes
Aspen Falls (in tons)

11/25/2012 16:32

Type	FY 2011	FY 2012	FY 2013	FY 2014	Trend	Improved from previous year?
Glass	$ 10,820	$ 8,857	$ 10,928	$ 11,036		Yes
Tin Cans	$ 825	$ 650	$ 833	$ 842		Yes
White goods	$ 11,010	$ 12,250	$ 11,120	$ 11,230		Yes
Other ferrous	$ 61,150	$ 63,000	$ 61,762	$ 62,373		Yes
Aluminum cans	$ 1,150	$ 1,320	$ 1,262	$ 1,173		Needs Work
Non-ferrous	$ 13,160	$ 13,270	$ 13,292	$ 13,423		Yes
High Grade Paper	$ 1,830	$ 2,490	$ 1,848	$ 1,867		Yes
Newsprint	$ 14,790	$ 13,370	$ 14,938	$ 15,086		Yes
Cardboard	$ 19,640	$ 16,350	$ 21,836	$ 20,033		Needs Work
Other paper	$ 4,340	$ 5,900	$ 4,383	$ 4,427		Yes
PETE	$ 703	$ 960	$ 710	$ 717		Yes
HDPE	$ 417	$ 710	$ 421	$ 425		Yes
Other plastics	$ 588	$ 920	$ 594	$ 600		Yes
Yard waste	$ 57,200	$ 55,829	$ 59,772	$ 58,344		Needs Work
Wood waste	$ 10,630	$ 11,825	$ 11,736	$ 10,843		Needs Work
Batteries	$ 2,900	$ 3,030	$ 2,929	$ 2,958		Yes
Oil	$ 8,840	$ 6,360	$ 8,928	$ 9,017		Yes

Recycling Volumes
Aspen Falls (in tons)

11/25/2012 16:32

Type	FY 2012	FY 2013	FY 2014	Trend	Improved from previous year?
Gypsum	$ 180	$ 227	$ 230		Yes
HDPE	$ 710	$ 421	$ 425		Yes
Other plastics	$ 920	$ 594	$ 600		Yes
PETE	$ 960	$ 710	$ 717		Yes
Tin Cans	$ 650	$ 833	$ 842		Yes
Tires	$ 806	$ 1,020	$ 1,030		Yes
High Grade Paper	$ 2,490	$ 1,848	$ 1,867		Yes
Electronics	$ 1,050	$ 1,869	$ 1,887		Yes
Other	$ 2,500	$ 2,010	$ 2,030		Yes
Batteries	$ 3,030	$ 2,929	$ 2,958		Yes
Other paper	$ 5,900	$ 4,383	$ 4,427		Yes
Textiles	$ 6,208	$ 6,474	$ 6,538		Yes
Oil	$ 6,360	$ 8,928	$ 9,017		Yes
Glass	$ 8,857	$ 10,928	$ 11,036		Yes
White goods	$ 12,250	$ 11,120	$ 11,230		Yes
Non-ferrous	$ 13,270	$ 13,292	$ 13,423		Yes
Newsprint	$ 13,370	$ 14,938	$ 15,086		Yes
Other ferrous	$ 63,000	$ 61,762	$ 62,373		Yes
Total	142,511	144,287	145,715		

Figure 1

13. **Save** the file. Click the **File tab**, click **Print**, and then compare your workbook with Figure 1. Submit the file as directed by your instructor.

 DONE! You have completed Skills Assessment 1

Skills Assessment 2

To complete this project, you will need the following file:

- exl04_SA2Equipment

You will save your workbook as:

- Last_First_exl04_SA2Equipment

---

1. Start **Excel 2013**, and open the file **exl04_SA2Equipment**. Save the workbook in your chapter folder as Last_First_exl04_SA2Equipment Insert the file name in the worksheet's left footer and the sheet name in the right footer. Return to **Normal** view.

2. In cell **A2**, insert the **TODAY** function.

3. Select the range **A4:G4**, and then apply **Outside Borders**.

4. In cell **F5**, insert the **IF** function. For the logical test, check whether the **Quantity in Stock** is less than **10**. If the logical test is TRUE, Order should display. If the logical test is FALSE, Level OK should display.

5. AutoFill the function in cell **F5** down through cell **F63**.

6. Select the range **F5:F63**, apply a **Text Contains** conditional format that will display any cells that indicate *Order* formatted with **Red Text**.

7. Find all occurrences of Removal and replace with Extrication

8. Format the range **A4:G63** as an Excel table, using the **Table Style Medium 10** table style.

9. Change the page orientation to **Landscape**, and then set the titles in **row 4** to repeat on each printed page.

10. Create a copy of the worksheet, and move the copied sheet to the end of the workbook. Rename the new worksheet tab Safety On the **Safety** worksheet, **Sort** the table in alphabetical order by **Category**. **Filter** the Excel table to display the **Safety** type.

11. Display the **Total** row, and then in cell **B64**, display the count for column B.

12. Hide **column D**.

13. **Save** your workbook, and then compare your workbook with Figure 1. Submit the workbook as directed by your instructor.

 **DONE!** You have completed Skills Assessment 2

Quantity in Stock	Item	Cost Each	Type	Category	Stock Level	Total Cost
11	Radio Chest Harness	$35	Safety	Safety Equipment	Level OK	$ 385
87	Rope Gloves	$32	Gloves	Outerwear	Level OK	$ 2,784
28	Safety Harness	$199	Safety	Safety Equipment	Level OK	$ 5,572
29	Chest Harness	$99	Safety	Safety Equipment	Level OK	$ 2,871
35	EMS Jacket	$399	Coat	Outerwear	Level OK	$ 13,965
47	EMS Pants	$289	Pants	Outerwear	Level OK	$ 13,583
89	Breakaway Vest	$29	Vest	Outerwear	Level OK	$ 2,581
15	Mesh Vest	$17	Vest	Outerwear	Level OK	$ 255
25	Mesh Traffic Vest	$29	Vest	Outerwear	Level OK	$ 725
89	Reflective Nylon Vest	$11	Vest	Outerwear	Level OK	$ 979
16	Handheld Remote Siren	$289	Siren	Traffic	Level OK	$ 4,624
19	Siren	$189	Siren	Traffic	Level OK	$ 3,591
27	Traffic Baton	$19	Baton	Traffic	Level OK	$ 513
37	Flare Beacon Kit	$305	Light	Traffic	Level OK	$ 11,285
90	Flares with Stands	$99	Light	Traffic	Level OK	$ 8,910
26	Traffic Flashlight	$18	Light	Traffic	Level OK	$ 468
56	Night Barrier Tape	$15	Tape	Traffic	Level OK	$ 840
17	Water Rescue Kit	$119	Safety	Water Rescue	Level OK	$ 2,023
38	Water Rescue Vest	$99	Safety	Water Rescue	Level OK	$ 3,762
4	Water Tether System	$59	Safety	Water Rescue	Order	$ 236
18	Wildfire Helmet	$59	Helmet	Outerwear	Level OK	$ 1,062
17	Full-Brim Helmet	$59	Helmet	Outerwear	Level OK	$ 1,003
58	Firefighting Goggles	$49	Helmet	Safety Equipment	Level OK	$ 2,842
31	Water Throw Bag	$59	Safety	Water Rescue	Level OK	$ 1,829
32	Dry Bag	$18	Safety	Water Rescue	Level OK	$ 576

Aspen Falls					
11/24/2012					
Quantity in Stock	Item	Type	Category	Stock Level	Total Cost
9	Gas Mask	Safety	Safety Equipment	Order	$ 2,331
9	Gas Mask Pouch	Safety	Safety Equipment	Order	$ 315
13	Respirator	Safety	Safety Equipment	Level OK	$ 4,797
45	Disaster Safe Bag	Safety	Safety Equipment	Level OK	$ 585
57	Disaster Kit	Safety	Safety Equipment	Level OK	$ 5,643
11	Radio Chest Harness	Safety	Safety Equipment	Level OK	$ 385
28	Safety Harness	Safety	Safety Equipment	Level OK	$ 5,572
29	Chest Harness	Safety	Safety Equipment	Level OK	$ 2,871
17	Water Rescue Kit	Safety	Water Rescue	Level OK	$ 2,023
38	Water Rescue Vest	Safety	Water Rescue	Level OK	$ 3,762
4	Water Tether System	Safety	Water Rescue	Order	$ 236
31	Water Throw Bag	Safety	Water Rescue	Level OK	$ 1,829
32	Dry Bag	Safety	Water Rescue	Level OK	$ 576
Total	13				$ 30,925

Figure 1

Visual Skills Check

To complete this project, you will need the following file:

- exl04_VSArt

You will save your workbook as:

- Last_First_exl04_VSArt

Start **Excel 2013**, and then open the file **exl04_VSArt**. Save the workbook in your chapter folder as Last_First_exl04_VSArt Add the file name in the worksheet's left footer. Insert the current date using a date function. Your date may be different than shown. In **column F**, use a logical function indicating *Insure* for art with a value greater than $50,000. The conditional formatting in the **Insurance** column is **Light Red Fill with Dark Red Text**. Display Data Bars in **column C**. The Excel table is formatted using the **Table Style Light 14** table style. Filter and sort the Excel table, and display the functions on the **Total** row as shown in Figure 1. **Save** the workbook, and then submit the workbook as directed by your instructor.

✔ **DONE!** You have completed Visual Skills Check

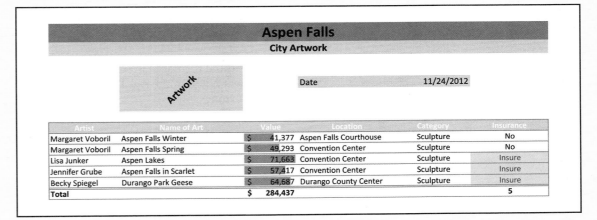

Artist	Name of Art	Value	Location	Category	Insurance
Margaret Voboril	Aspen Falls Winter	$ 41,377	Aspen Falls Courthouse	Sculpture	No
Margaret Voboril	Aspen Falls Spring	$ 49,293	Convention Center	Sculpture	No
Lisa Junker	Aspen Lakes	$ 71,663	Convention Center	Sculpture	Insure
Jennifer Grube	Aspen Falls in Scarlet	$ 57,417	Convention Center	Sculpture	Insure
Becky Spiegel	Durango Park Geese	$ 64,687	Durango County Center	Sculpture	Insure
Total		$ 284,437			5

Aspen Falls — City Artwork — Artwork — Date 11/24/2012

Figure 1

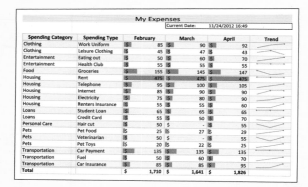

Figure 1

My Skills

To complete this project, you will need the following file:

- exl04_MYExpenses

You will save your workbook as:

- Last_First_exl04_MYExpenses

1. Start **Excel 2013**, and open the file **exl04_MYExpenses**. Save the workbook in your chapter folder as Last_First_exl04_MYExpenses

2. Add the file name in the left footer and the sheet name in the right footer. Return to **Normal** view.

3. Click the merged cell **E2**, and then insert the **NOW** function.

4. Select the range **D2:F2**, and then apply the **Outside Borders**.

5. Select the range **C5:E23**, and then insert **Data Bars**.

6. In the range **F5:F23**, insert **Line Sparklines** using the data in the **columns C:E**. On the sparklines, show the **High Point**.

7. Format the range **A4:F23** as an Excel table, using **Table Style Light 19**. Sort the

Spending Category column to display in alphabetical order.

8. Display the **Total** row, display the sums for **C24:E24**, and in the **Trend** column, select **None**.

9. Change the **Width** scale to fit on one page.

10. Create a copy of the worksheet, and move the copied sheet to the end of the workbook. Rename the new worksheet tab High Expenses

11. On the **High Expenses** worksheet, sort the **April** column from largest to smallest. Hide **rows 19:23**.

12. **Save** your workbook. Click the **File tab**, click **Print**, and then compare your workbook with Figure 1. Submit the workbook as directed by your instructor.

 DONE! You have completed My Skills

Skills Challenge 1

To complete this project, you will need the following file:

- exl04_SC1Classes

You will save your workbook as:

- Last_First_exl04_SC1Classes

Start **Excel 2013**, and then open the file **exl04_SC1Classes**. Save the workbook in your chapter folder as Last_First_exl04_SC1Classes Carter Horikoshi, the Art Center Supervisor, has started a workbook to track the art classes offered at different locations. He is concerned about large class sizes and wonders if he should hire an assistant for the instructors. Using the skills you practiced in this chapter, on the Classes worksheet, correct the date function. The panes no longer need to be frozen. In the Excel table, display all rows. In column D, the Data Bars should be applied to all cells. In column E, the logical function should calculate whether a class needs a Class Assistant—a class needs a Class Assistant if the class size is

greater than 30. The Excel table should be filtered to show the Computer Basics, Drawing, Painting, and Woodworking classes, and sorted from the largest to smallest class size. The titles in row 6 should repeat on each page. On the Enrollment sheet, the sparklines should be formatted to emphasize the high and low values in each row. The Enrollment sheet should print on one page. On both worksheets, add the file name in the left footer and the sheet name in the right footer. Save your workbook, and then submit the workbook as directed by your instructor.

 DONE! You have completed Skills Challenge 1

Skills Challenge 2

To complete this project, you will need the following file:

- exl04_SC2Water

You will save your workbook as:

- Last_First_exl04_SC2Water

Start **Excel 2013**, and then open the file **exl04_SC2Water**, and save the workbook in your chapter folder as Last_First_exl04_SC2Water Diane Payne, the Public Works Director, is responsible for testing the city water supply. She has started a workbook to track the water test results. Using the skills you practiced in this chapter, insert functions in the Water worksheet that provide the current date and count the number of samples. Insert a logical function to determine if the High Test amount is greater than the Farm Water Limit for each quarter. Display Yes if TRUE and No if FALSE. Format the

data as an Excel table using the table style of your choice, and then filter the Excel table to display violations. On the Test Results worksheet, insert sparklines to display trends. On both worksheets, add the file name in the left footer and the sheet name in the right footer. Each worksheet should print on one page. Save your workbook, and then submit the workbook as directed by your instructor.

 DONE! You have completed Skills Challenge 2

CAPSTONE PROJECT

To complete this workbook, you will need the following file:
exl_CAPBudget

You will save your workbook as:
Last_First_exl_CAPBudget

1. Start **Excel 2013**, and open the student data file **exl_CAPBudget**. **Save** the workbook in your chapter folder as Last_First_exl_CAPBudget

2. Group the worksheets. Widen **columns B:E** to *13.00*. Change the height of **row 4** to *15.00*. In cell **E5**, insert a function to total the row, and then AutoFill **E5** down through **E14**. In the range **E6:E14**, apply the **Comma [0]** cell style. In the range **B15:E15**, insert a function to total the columns, and then apply the **Total** cell style.

3. With the worksheets still grouped, in cell **B16**, insert a function to calculate the average *North* budget item. In cell **B17**, insert a function to calculate the highest *North* budget item.

4. In cell **B18**, insert a function to calculate the lowest *North* budget item.

5. AutoFill the range **B16:B18** to the right through **column D**, and then compare your screen with **Figure 1**.

6. Ungroup the worksheets. Insert a new worksheet. Rename the new worksheet tab Summary and apply the worksheet tab color **Orange**, **Accent 2**. Move the new worksheet tab to make it the first worksheet in the workbook.

7. Copy the range **A1:E4** from any of the quarter worksheets, and then on the **Summary** worksheet, paste the range into **A1:E4** using the **Keep Source Column Widths** paste option.

8. On the **Summary** worksheet, change the subtitle of cell **A2** to Annual Budget and then change the label in cell **A4** to Quarter

9. On the **Summary** worksheet, in cell **A5** type 1st Quarter and then AutoFill **A5** down through cell **A8**. In cell **A9**, type Annual Total

10. On the **Summary** worksheet, enter a formula in cell **B5** setting the cell equal to cell **B15** in the **First Quarter** worksheet. **Save** the workbook, and then compare your screen with **Figure 2**.

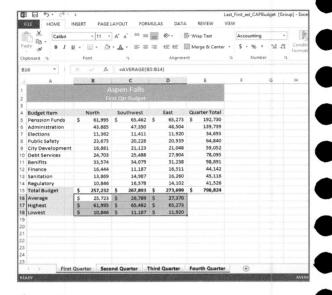

Figure 1

Figure 2

■ Continue to the next page to complete the skill

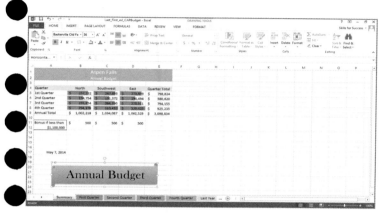

Figure 3

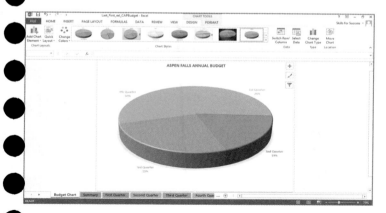

Figure 4

11. On the **Summary** worksheet, enter a formula for the *North* total from the **Second Quarter**, the **Third Quarter**, and the **Fourth Quarter** worksheets in the range **B6:B8**. AutoFill the range **B5:B8** to the right through **column E**.

12. On the **Summary** worksheet, in the range **B9:E9**, insert a function to calculate the column totals.

13. In cell **A11**, type Bonus if less than and then in cell **A12** type $1,100,000 Select the range **A11:A12**, and then apply the **Outside Borders**.

14. In cell **B11**, insert the **IF** function. For the logical test, check whether the *North* total is less than the value in cell **A12**. If the logical test is true, 500 should display, and if the logical test is false, 50 should display. In the function, use an absolute cell reference when referring to cell **A12**.

15. In cell **B11**, apply the **Currency [0]** cell style, and then AutoFill cell **B11** to the right through cell **D11**.

16. Select the range **B5:D8**, insert the default **Data Bars** conditional format.

17. In cell **A17**, insert the **TODAY** function. Format the date with the **March 14, 2012**, date format.

18. Unhide the **Last Year** worksheet. **Copy** the *Annual Budget* shape and then paste the shape in the **Summary** worksheet. Move the shape to approximately the range **A19:E24**, and then compare your screen with Figure 3.

19. **Hide** the **Last Year** worksheet.

20. Group the worksheets, and then press [Ctrl] + [Home]. Find and replace the four occurrences of Qtr with Quarter

21. With the worksheets still grouped, check and correct any spelling errors. Add the file name to the left footer and the sheet name to the right footer. Return to **Normal view**, and then make cell **A1** the active cell. Ungroup the worksheets.

22. Make the **Summary** worksheet the active worksheet. Insert a **3-D Pie** chart based on the nonadjacent ranges **A4:A8** and **E4:E8**. Move the pie chart to a chart sheet with the sheet name Budget Chart

23. For the pie chart, apply **Layout 1**, and then apply the **Chart Style 8**. Change the chart title to Aspen Falls Annual Budget and then for the data labels, change the font size to **12**. Add the file name in the chart sheet's left footer and the sheet name in the right footer. Compare your screen with Figure 4.

24. **Save**, and then **Close** the workbook. Submit the project as directed by your instructor.

 DONE! You have completed the Excel Capstone Project

Create Workbooks Using Excel Web App

▶ **Excel Web App** is a cloud-based application used to complete basic spreadsheet formulas using a web browser.

▶ Excel Web App can be used to create or edit workbooks using a web browser instead of the Excel program—Excel 2013 does not need to be installed on your computer.

▶ When you create a document using Excel Web App, it is saved on your SkyDrive so that you can work with it from any computer connected to the Internet.

▶ You can use Excel Web App to insert a chart and perform basic chart formatting tasks.

▶ If you need a feature not available in Excel Web App, you can edit the workbook in Microsoft Excel and save it on your SkyDrive.

© Maxim_Kazmin

Aspen Falls City Hall

In this project, you will assist Taylor and Robert Price, energy consultants for the city of Aspen Falls. They have asked you to use Excel Web App to create a spreadsheet that shows the energy consumption of a city building.

Excel Web App is used to create or open Excel workbooks from any computer or device connected to the Internet. When needed, you can edit text, enter formulas, or insert charts. You can save these workbooks on your SkyDrive, and continue working with them later when you are at a computer that has Excel 2013 available.

In this project, you will use Excel Web App to create a new workbook. You will enter data and then apply formats and number styles. You will insert formulas, functions, and a chart. Finally, you will open the workbook in Excel 2013 to format the chart and check the spelling in the worksheet.

Time to complete this project – 30 to 60 minutes

Student data file needed for this project:

New blank Excel Web App workbook

You will save your file as:

Last_First_exl_WAEnergy

SKILLS MyITLab®

At the end of this project you will be able to:

▶ Create new Excel workbooks from SkyDrive
▶ Enter data in Editing View
▶ Apply number styles
▶ Enter summary functions
▶ Enter formulas using absolute cell references
▶ Insert and format bar charts
▶ Edit workbooks created in Excel Web App in Excel 2013

Outcome

Using the skills in this project, you will be able to create and edit an Excel Web App workbook like this:

Aspen Falls
City Administrative Building

Total Square Footage	20,000
Energy Cost per Square Foot	$2.25
Annual Energy Cost	$45,000

Energy Consumption	Percent of Total Cost	Annual Cost
Building Heating	32%	$14,400
Water Heating	8%	$3,600
Lighting	15%	$6,750
Computers	18%	$8,100
Air Conditioning	27%	$12,150
		$45,000

Percent of Total Cost

- Building Heating
- Water Heating
- Lighting
- Computers
- Air Conditioning

1. Start **Internet Explorer**, navigate to live.com and log on to your Microsoft account. If you do not have an account, follow the links and directions on the page to create one.

2. After logging in, navigate as needed to display the **SkyDrive** page.

> SkyDrive and Web App technologies are accessed through web pages that may change and the formatting and layout of some pages may often be different from the figures in this book. When this happens, you may need to adapt the steps to complete the actions they describe.

3. On the toolbar, click **Create**, and then click **Excel workbook**.

4. In the **New Microsoft Excel workbook** dialog box, name the file Last_First_exl_WAEnergy and then compare your screen with **Figure 1**.

5. Click the **Create** button to save the workbook and start Excel Web App.

> The Excel Web App displays four tabs in Editing View: File, Home, Insert, and View.

6. In cell **A1** type Aspen Falls and then press [Enter].

7. In cell **A2** type City Administrative Building and then press [Enter].

8. Select the range **A1:F1**, and then on the **Home tab**, in the **Alignment group**, click the **Merge & Center** button [Merge & Center ▾]. Select the range **A2:F2**, and then click the **Merge & Center** button. Compare your screen with **Figure 2**.

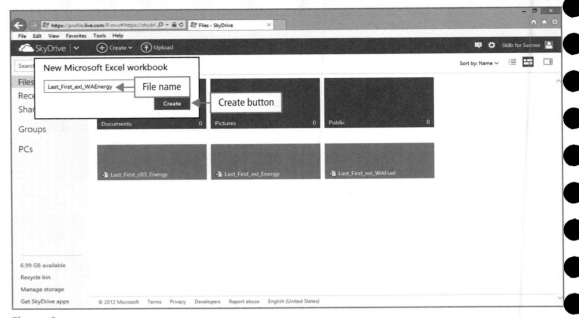

Figure 1

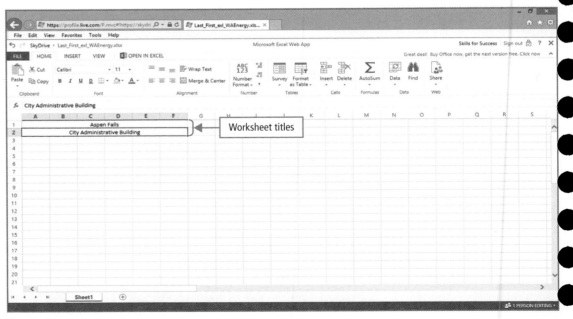

Figure 2

■ **Continue to the next page to complete the skill**

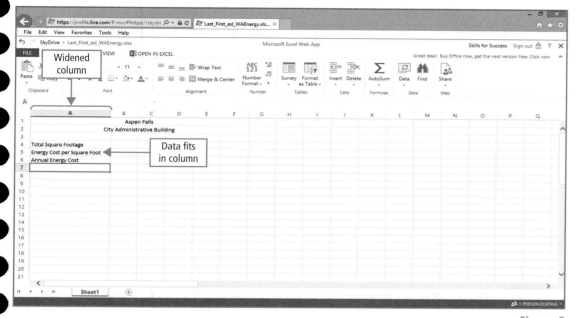

Figure 3

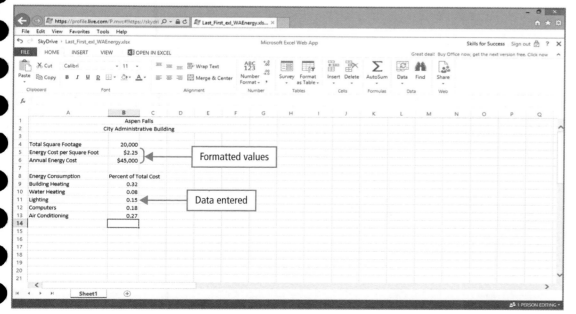

Figure 4

9. In cell **A4** type Total Square Footage and then press [Enter].

10. In cell **A5** type Energy Cost per Square Foot and then press [Enter].

11. In cell **A6** type Annual Energy Cost and then press [Enter].

12. In the column heading area, point to the right boundary of **column A** to display the ➕ pointer. Double-click between **columns A** and **B** to display all of the contents of cell **A5** in the column. Compare your screen with **Figure 3**.

13. Make cell **B4** the active cell. Type 20,000 and then press [Enter].

14. In cell **B5** type 2.25 and then press [Enter].

15. In cell **B6** type =B4*B5 and then press [Enter].

16. Click cell **B5**. On the **Home tab**, in the **Number group**, click the **Number Format** button, and then click **Currency**.

17. Click cell **B6**, and then apply the **Currency** number format. Click the **Decrease Decimal** button ▸.00 two times.

18. Click cell **A8**, type Energy Consumption and then press [Enter].

19. In the range **A9:A13**, pressing [Enter] after each entry, type Building Heating, Water Heating, Lighting, Computers and then Air Conditioning

20. Click cell **B8**, type Percent of Total Cost and then press [Enter].

21. In **B9:B13**, making sure you type the decimal in front of each number, type the following values: .32, .08, .15, .18 and then .27 Compare your screen with **Figure 4**.

■ **Continue to the next page to complete the skill**

22. Select the range **B9:B13**. In the **Number group**, click the **Number Format** button, and then click **Percentage**. Click the **Decrease Decimal** button 📉 two times.

23. Click **C8**, type Annual Cost and then press Enter.

24. Select the range **B8:C8**. In the **Alignment group**, click the **Wrap Text** button, click the **Middle Align** button ≡, and then click the **Center** button ≡.

25. Click **C9**, type =B9*$B$6 and then press Enter.

26. Click **C9**, point at the fill handle, and then compare your screen with **Figure 5**.

27. While still pointing at the fill handle, drag the fill handle to copy the formula down through cell **C13**.

> The absolute cell reference to $B$6 is copied to each of the other formulas.

28. Click **C14**. In the **Formulas group**, click the **AutoSum** button, and then press Enter.

29. Select the range **A8:B13**. On the **Insert tab**, in the **Charts group**, click the **Pie** button, and then point at the first chart— **2-D Pie**. Compare your screen with **Figure 6**, and then click the first chart.

> A contextual tab—the Chart Tools tab— displays on the Ribbon.

30. Move the chart to approximately the range **A16:F30**.

31. To the right of the tabs, click the **Open in Excel** button. If prompted, enter your ID and password.

32. If prompted, at the top of the screen, on the **Protected View** bar, click **Enable Editing**.

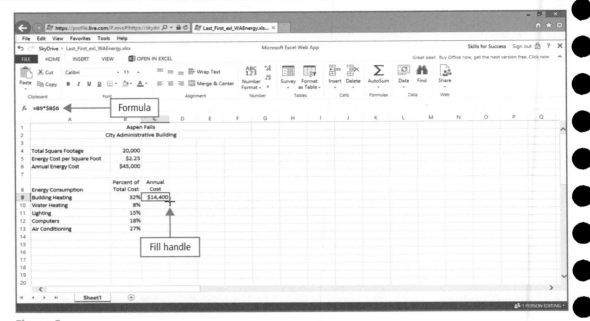

Figure 5

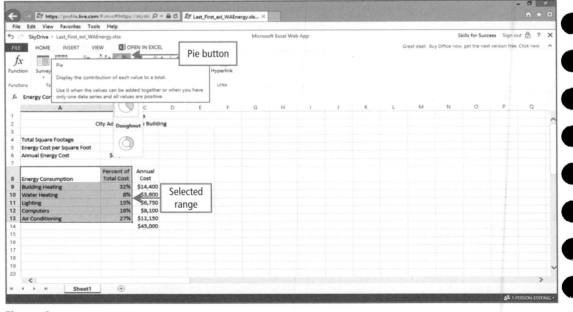

Figure 6

■ **Continue to the next page to complete the skill**

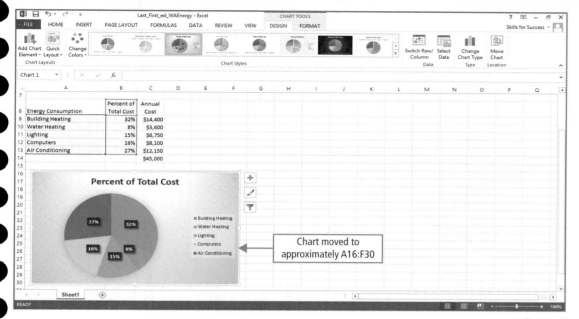

Figure 7

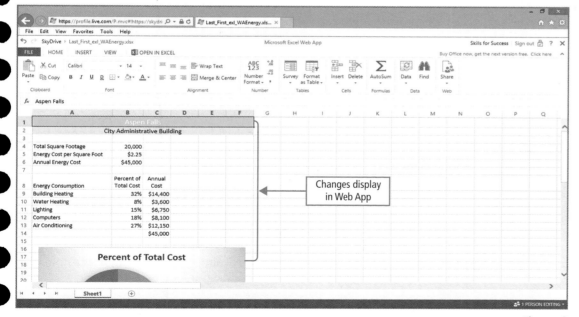

Figure 8

33. Click cell **A1**. On the **Home tab**, in the **Styles group**, click the **Cell Styles** button, and then click **Accent 4**. In the **Font group**, click the **Font Size** button 11, and then click **14**. In the **Cells group**, click the **Format** button, and then click **Row Height**. In the **Row Height** dialog box, type 20 and then click **OK**.

34. Click cell **A2**. In the **Styles group**, click the **Cell Styles** button, and then click **40% - Accent 4**. In the **Font group**, click the **Font Size** button 11, and then click **12**.

35. Click the chart to select the chart, and then on the **Design tab**, in the **Chart Styles group**, click the third style—**Style 3**. Compare your screen with **Figure 7**.

36. On the **Review tab**, in the **Proofing group**, click the **Spelling** button to check and correct any spelling errors. **Save** your workbook and then **Close** Excel 2013.

37. On the **SkyDrive** page, open the workbook in the Excel Web App. Compare your screen with **Figure 8**.

   The cell styles and the chart style 3 have been applied. Features not supported by Excel Web App, such as styles, cannot be changed in the Web App but they can be viewed.

38. Click the **View tab**, and then click **Reading View**. **Print** or **Share** the document as directed by your instructor.

39. In the top-left corner of the Internet Explorer window, click the **sign out** link, and then **Close** the browser window.

✓ **DONE! You have completed Excel Web App Project!**

CHAPTER 5

Format Cells and Worksheets

▶ In a worksheet, cells can be formatted to change the way data is displayed without changing the underlying values. Formatting the background and border of a cell often improves the appearance of the worksheet.

▶ Symbols are inserted to identify and format text.

▶ Cells can be formatted to provide a comparison or to emphasize cell values.

▶ You can copy and apply cell formatting more easily by using the Format Painter.

▶ Create and apply custom cell styles and document themes to maintain a consistent appearance for all worksheets.

▶ Spot trends and patterns in your data by using icons and colors to visually represent the data.

▶ Inserting background images as watermarks allows you to make spreadsheets unique.

Kwest / Fotolia

Aspen Falls City Hall

In this chapter, you will support Todd Austin, the Aspen Falls Tourism Director, by editing an existing workbook and using Excel formatting tools to enhance its appearance. One of Todd's responsibilities is to promote community events and gather and analyze Bureau of Tourism sales data. This data helps Todd plan future events and track trends.

Because Excel workbooks can contain multiple sheets where data can be updated, managers like Todd can combine worksheets to compare data. Businesses and organizations often use Excel workbooks to track and evaluate information using data analysis techniques that help them gain greater insight into organizational, industry, and customer trends.

In this project you will improve a worksheet's format by applying formatting to identify duplicate data, recognize data patterns, and identify fees collected from vendors and ticket sales from the City of Aspen Falls Annual Wine Festival. You also will use Excel formatting techniques, including copying formats, applying borders and shading, and creating custom formats and fonts, to improve the existing worksheet, making it easier to read, providing a professional appearance, and storing custom settings for future projects.

Time to complete all 10
skills – 60 to 90 minutes

Student data files needed for this chapter:

exl05_Festival
exl05_FestivalLogo

You will save your workbook as:

Last_First_exl05_Festival

Outcome

Using the skills in this chapter, you will be able to
create worksheets like this:

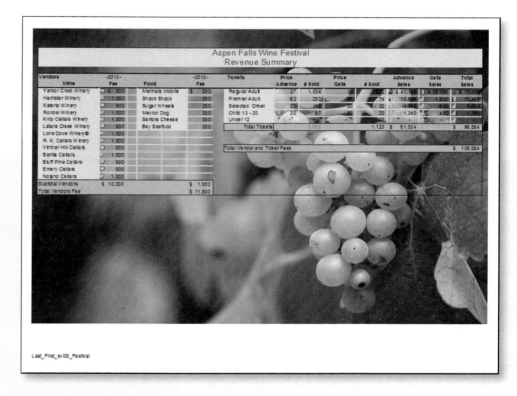

Last_First_exl05_Festival

SKILLS

Skills 1-10 Training

At the end of this chapter, you will be able to:

Skill 1 Insert Symbols and Create Custom Number Formats
Skill 2 Format Cells with the Format Painter
Skill 3 Apply Icon Sets as Conditional Formatting
Skill 4 Insert Formulas into Conditional Formatting Rules
Skill 5 Insert and Delete Rows, Columns, and Cells
Skill 6 Modify Cell Backgrounds and Borders
Skill 7 Create and Apply Custom Cell Styles
Skill 8 Customize, Save, and Apply Themes
Skill 9 Add Watermarks and Modify Background Colors
Skill 10 Hide Gridlines and Column and Row Headings

MORE SKILLS

Skill 11 Copy Styles Between Workbooks
Skill 12 Draw Borders
Skill 13 Convert Comma-Separated Text into Columns
Skill 14 Create Screen Shots

▶ A *symbol* is a character such as a font symbol or bullet character that is not found on common keyboards.

▶ Symbols are inserted to identify and format text.

▶ Once a symbol is inserted into a cell, the cell contents can be formatted as text.

1. Start **Excel 2013**. Open the file **exl05_Festival**. On the **File tab**, click **Save As**, and then click **Browse**. In the **Save As** dialog box, navigate to the location where you are saving your files. Click **New folder**, type Excel Chapter 5 and then press Enter two times. Name the workbook Last_First_exl05_Festival and then press Enter.

2. Select cell **A11**. On the formula bar, click to the right of *Winery*. On the Ribbon, click the **Insert tab**, and in the **Symbols group**, click the **Symbol** button.

3. In the **Symbol** dialog box, click the **Special Characters tab**. Compare your screen with **Figure 1**.

   Special characters are characters such as degree symbols and trademark symbols, and typically are not available on the standard keyboard. Special characters is a list of frequently used symbols that is shorter than the list on the Symbols tab, which includes fonts and other symbols.

4. Under **Character**, select the **Registered** (®) character. Click the **Insert** button to insert the character in cell **A11**, and then in the **Symbol** dialog box click the **Close** button. Press Enter, and then compare your screen with **Figure 2**.

■ **Continue to the next page to complete the skill**

Figure 1

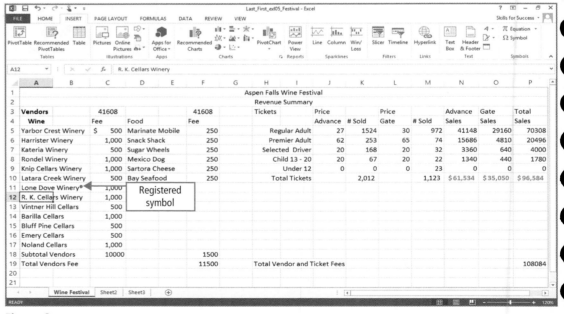

Figure 2

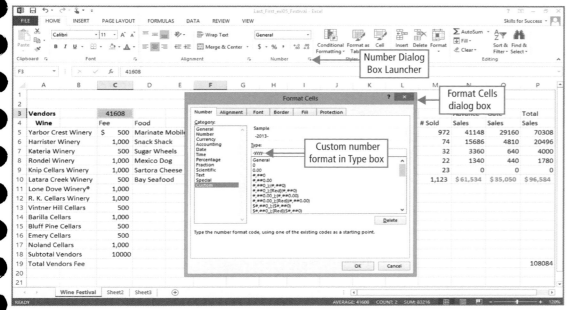

Figure 3

5. Select cell **C3**. Press and hold Ctrl, select cell **F3**, and then release Ctrl.

6. With the cells **C3** and **F3** selected, on the **Home tab**, in the **Number group**, click the **Number Dialog Box Launcher**.

7. In the **Format Cells** dialog box, on the **Number tab**, under **Category**, click **Custom**. In the **Type** box, replace the existing value by typing -yyyy- Be sure to include the hyphens (-), as shown in **Figure 3**.

   In this manner, you can create your own custom number formats. Here, the four characters indicate the numbers used to create a four-digit year, and the hyphens will be inserted before and after the number. Common formatting characters are summarized in the table shown in **Figure 4**.

8. Click **OK**. Notice the custom number format is applied to the two cells.

9. **Save** the workbook.

■ **You have completed Skill 1 of 10**

Common Custom Formatting Characters	
Character	**Description**
#	Specifies a placeholder for a digit.
0	Specifies a placeholder for any digit. When the value is less than zero, a 0 will be displayed.
.	Specifies the location of a decimal point.
,	Specifies the location where a comma will be displayed.
[color]	Specifies the color used to display negative numbers.
mm	Displays the month with a leading zero.
dd	Displays the day with a leading zero.
yyyy	Displays the year with four digits.

Figure 4

▶ In Excel, the *Format Painter* is used to copy text formats, number formats, borders, and cell shading.

1. Click on cell **A4**. On the **Home tab**, in the **Clipboard group**, click **Format Painter**. With the pointer, drag across the range **C4:F4**, and then release the left mouse button.

2. With the range **C4:F4** still selected, click **Format Painter**, drag across the range **H3:P4**, and then release the left mouse button.

3. Notice the format is applied, and the **Format Painter** button is no longer active, as shown in Figure 1.

> When Format Painter is clicked once, the formatting can be applied one time to a cell or a range of cells.

4. Drag to select the range **C6:C17**. On the **Home tab**, in the **Clipboard group**, click **Format Painter**, and then drag across the range **J5:P9**.

5. Click **Format Painter**, and apply the format to **F6:F10**. Compare your screen with Figure 2.

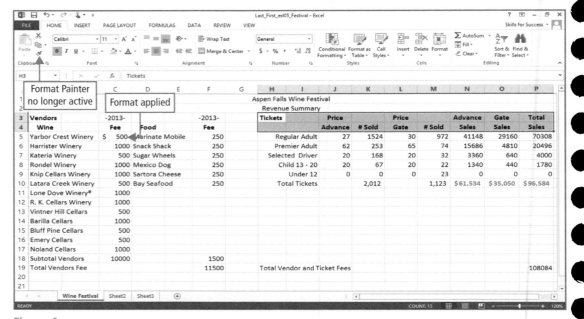

Figure 1

■ **Continue to the next page to complete the skill**

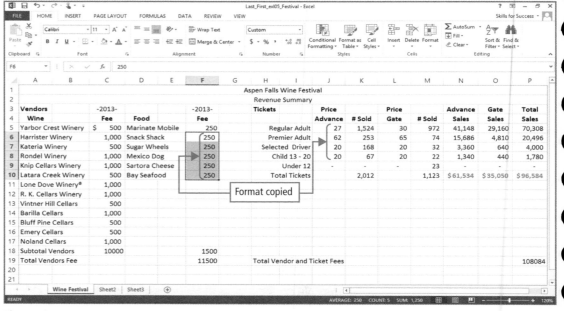

Figure 2

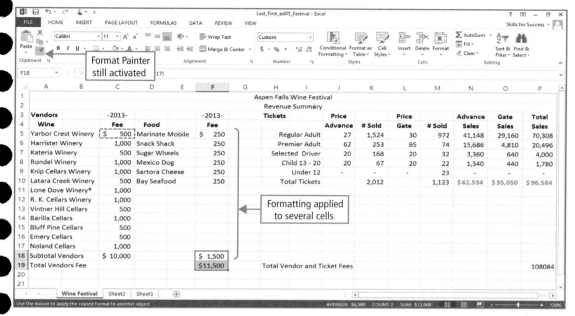

Figure 3

6. Select cell **C5**. Double-click **Format Painter** . With the pointer, select cells **F5** and **C18**, and then drag down the range **F18:F19**. Notice the **Format Painter** button is still activated, and compare your screen with **Figure 3**.

   When Format Painter is double-clicked, the formatting can be applied to multiple cells.

7. With **Format Painter** still activated, drag to select the range **N5:P5** and cell **P19**.

8. Click the **Format Painter** button to deactivate it. AutoFit **column P**. Compare your screen with **Figure 4**.

9. **Save** the workbook.

■ **You have completed Skill 2 of 10**

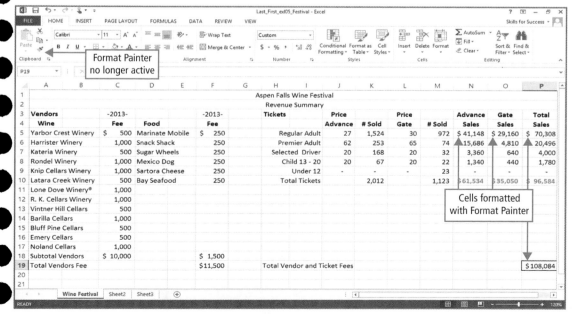

Figure 4

▶ **Conditional formatting** changes the appearance of a cell or range when one or more conditions are true.

▶ **Icon sets** classify a range of data into three to five categories and display small graphics in each cell, depending on that cell's value.

▶ In an icon set, styles or colors represent relative values of the cells in the range.

1. Select the range **C5:C17**. On the **Home tab**, in the **Styles group**, click the **Conditional Formatting** button. In the list, point to **Icon Sets**, and then compare your screen with **Figure 1**. Under **Indicators**, click the first choice—**3 Symbols (Circled)**.

    In this manner, you can add conditional formatting quickly by selecting a predefined icon set.

2. Select the range **N5:N9**, click the **Conditional Formatting** button, and then click **New Rule**. Compare your screen with **Figure 2**.

3. In the **New Formatting Rule** dialog box, under **Edit the Rule Description**, click the **Format Style** arrow, and then click **Icon Sets**.

    There are a number of predefined icon sets available.

4. Click the **Icon Style arrow**, scroll down the gallery, and then click the third from last option—**5 Ratings**.

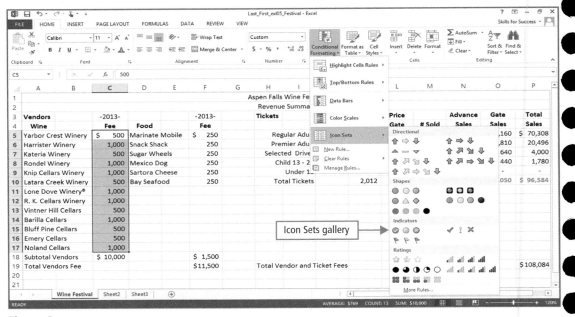

Figure 1

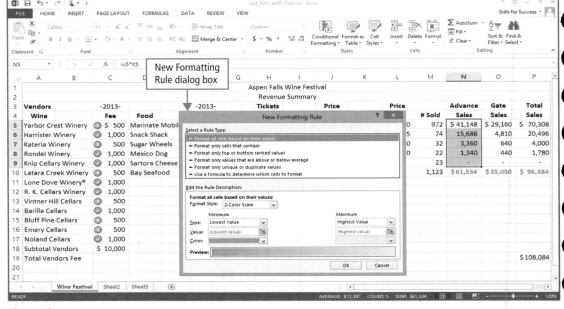

Figure 2

■ **Continue to the next page to complete the skill**

Figure 3

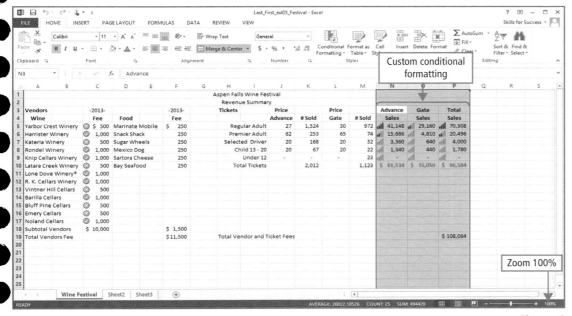

Figure 4

5. Under **Value**, change the first >= value from *80* to *75* the second value to *50* the third value to *25* and the fourth value to *10* Compare your screen with Figure 3, and then click **OK** to close the New Formatting Rule dialog box.

> You can use the New Formatting Rule dialog box to create custom conditional formatting rules.

6. With the range still selected, click **Format Painter**, and apply the formatting to **O5:P9**. Decrease the zoom of the window to 100%, and then AutoFit **columns N:P**. Compare your screen with Figure 4.

> In this manner, you can create custom icon sets. Here, cells N5 and P5 reflect sales at 75 percent or higher; O5, N6, and P6 reflect sales at 25 percent but less than 50 percent; and the remaining cells reflect sales at 10 percent or less.

7. **Save** 🖫 the workbook.

■ **You have completed Skill 3 of 10**

► Formulas can be inserted into conditional formatting rules so that cells display formatting based on the results of those rules.

1. Select cell **K10**. In the **Styles group**, click **Conditional Formatting**, and then click **New Rule**.

2. In the **New Formatting Rule** dialog box, under **Select a Rule Type**, click **Use a formula to determine which cells to format**. Compare your screen with **Figure 1**.

3. Under **Edit the Rule Description**, in the **Format values where this formula is true** box, type =K10>2000

4. Click the **Format** button. In the **Format Cells** dialog box, on the **Font tab**, under **Font style**, click **Bold**.

5. Click the **Color arrow**, and then under **Standard Colors**, click the sixth color— **Green**. Click **OK**, and then compare your screen with **Figure 2**.

This rule applies the desired formatting only when the value in cell K10 is greater than 2,000—the desired number of advance tickets sold. If true, the cell will be green and bold.

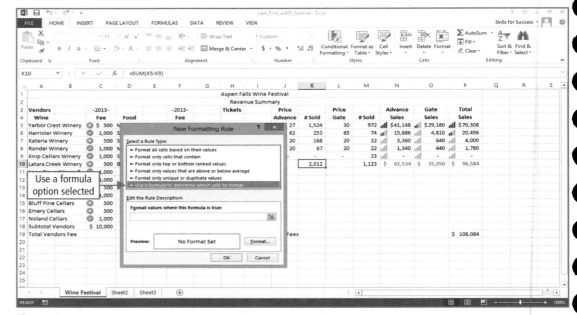

Figure 1

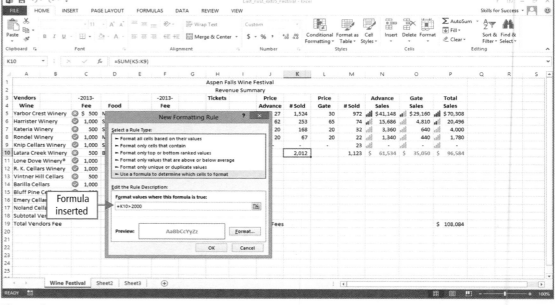

Figure 2

■ **Continue to the next page to complete the skill**

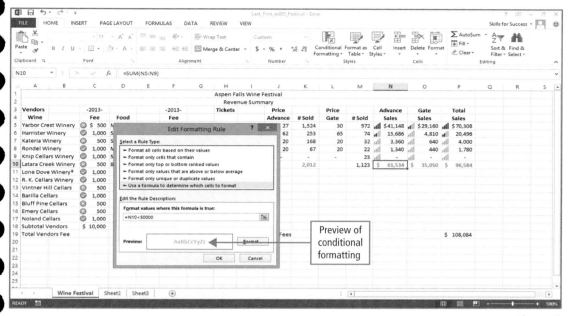

Figure 3

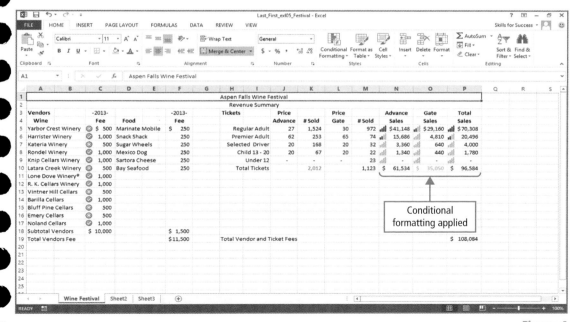

Figure 4

6. Click **OK** to close the New Formatting Rule dialog box and apply formatting.

   Because K10 is 2,012, which is greater than 2,000, the text format is bold and green.

7. Click cell **N10**. Click **Conditional Formatting**, and then click **Manage Rules**. In the **Conditional Formatting Rules Manager** dialog box, click the **Edit Rule** button.

8. In the **New Formatting Rule** dialog box, under **Select a Rule Type**, the rule **Use a formula to determine which cells to format** should be selected. Edit the formula to =N10<50000

9. Click the **Format** button. In the **Format Cells** dialog box, click the **Color arrow**, and then in first row, click the tenth color—**Orange, Accent 6**. Click **OK**, and then compare your screen with **Figure 3**.

   The preview box displays how the cell will be formatted when its value is less than $50,000.

10. Click **OK** two times. View the formatting change in the range **O10:P10**. Click cell **A1** and then compare your screen with **Figure 4**.

    The estimated ticket sales were $50,000; values less than $50,000 appear in orange.

11. Save 💾 the workbook.

■ **You have completed Skill 4 of 10**

▶ Cells can be deleted or inserted without affecting an entire column or row—but you need to specify in which direction the remaining cells will move.

▶ Column widths and cell ranges can be adjusted to fit text as needed.

1. AutoFit **column A**. Select **column B**. On the **Home tab**, in the **Cells group**, click the **Delete arrow**, and then click **Delete Sheet Columns**. Compare your screen with **Figure 1**.

   Alternately, right-click the column and then, from the shortcut menu, click **Delete**.

2. Select cell **A3**. In the **Cells group**, click the **Insert arrow**, and then click **Insert Sheet Rows**.

   A row is inserted above and the text in row 3 is moved to row 4. Rows and columns can be deleted or inserted by selecting a cell, row, or column.

3. Select the range **G14:O19**. In the **Cells group**, click the **Delete arrow**, and then click **Delete Cells**. In the **Delete** dialog box, verify the **Shift cells up** option is selected. Compare your screen with **Figure 2**, and then click **OK**.

   The range of cells is deleted and the cells that contain text are moved up.

■ **Continue to the next page to complete the skill** ➧

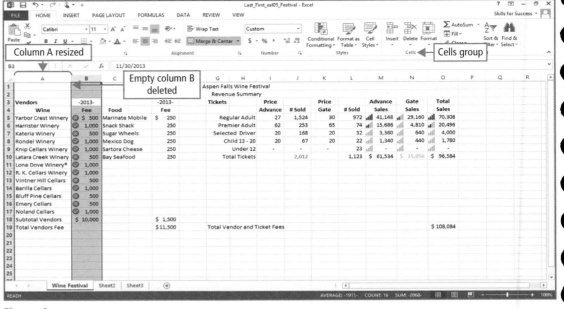

Figure 1

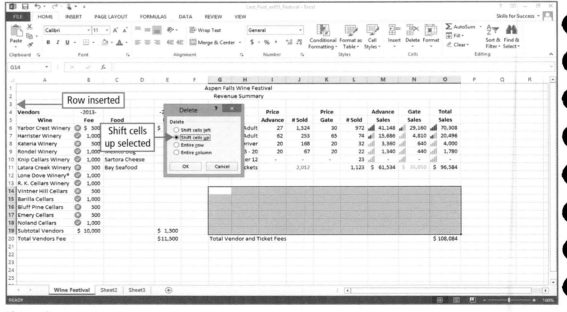

Figure 2

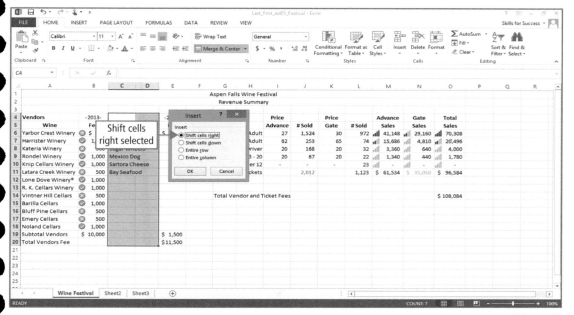

Figure 3

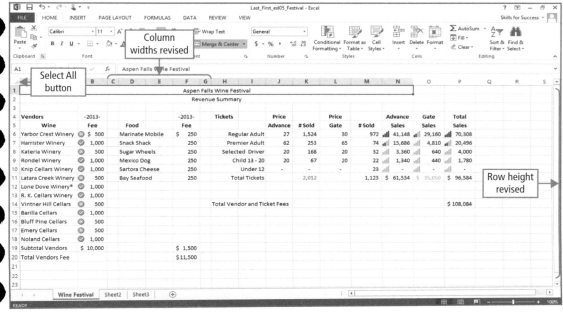

Figure 4

4. Select the range **C4:D20**. In the **Cells group**, click the **Insert arrow**, and then click **Insert Cells**. In the **Insert** dialog box, verify the **Shift cells right** option is selected. Compare your screen with Figure 3, and then click **OK**.

   Cells are inserted and the cells that contain text are moved to the right.

5. Select and delete **column C**. With **column C** selected, press and hold Ctrl, and then click **column G**. Release Ctrl.

6. In the **Cells group**, click the **Format** button, and under **Cell Size**, click **Column Width**. In the **Column Width** dialog box, type 3.00 and then click **OK**. AutoFit **columns F, O,** and **P**.

7. Click the **Select All** button. In the **Cells group**, click the **Format** button, and under **Cell Size**, click **Row Height**. In the **Row Height** dialog box, type 16.5 and then click **OK**. Select cell **A1**. Compare your screen with Figure 4.

8. **Save** the workbook.

■ **You have completed Skill 5 of 10**

▶ Recall that a **cell fill color**—also known as a **background color**—is the shading assigned to a cell.

▶ A **cell border**—decorative lines that can be applied to worksheet cells—is added to differentiate, emphasize, or group cells.

1. Select the range **A4:A5**, press and hold Ctrl, click the range **H4:I5**, and then release Ctrl.

2. On the **Home tab**, in the **Font group**, click the **Fill Color arrow** 🎨 ▾, and then in the fourth row, click the first color—**White, Background 1, Darker 25%**. Select cell **A1**, and then compare your screen with **Figure 1**.

3. Select the range **A19:F20**. In the **Font group**, click the **Fill Color button** 🎨 ▾. Select cell **A1**, and compare your screen with **Figure 2**.

> The color calls attention to the vendor fees totals. The cell fill color is now the default fill color and can be applied until changed.

4. Select the range **H11:P11**, and then click the **Fill Color button** 🎨 ▾. Repeat this step to apply the formatting to **H14:P14**.

> The color calls attention to the *Total Tickets* sold, and the *Total Vendor and Ticket Fees*.

■ **Continue to the next page to complete the skill** ▶

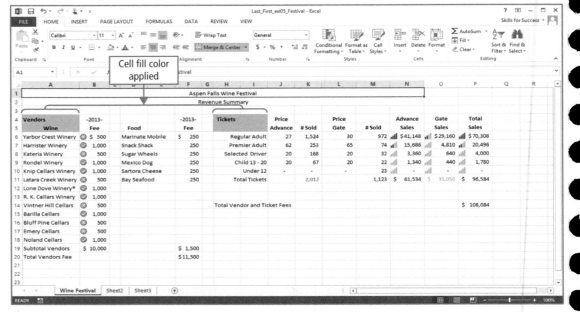

Figure 1

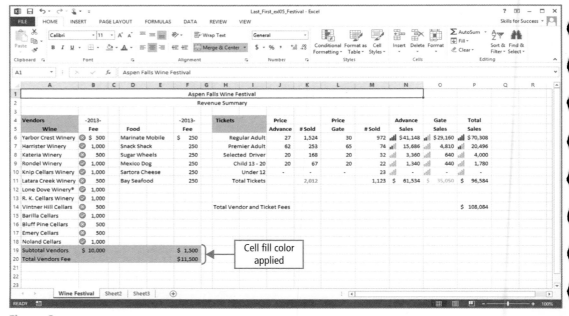

Figure 2

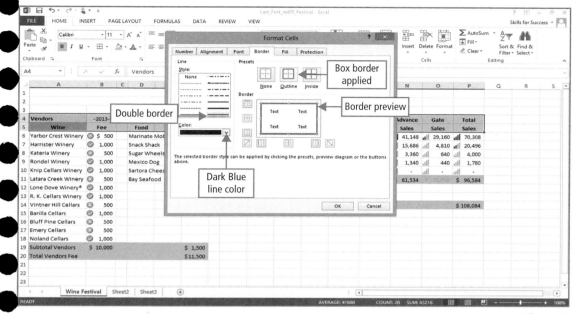

Figure 3

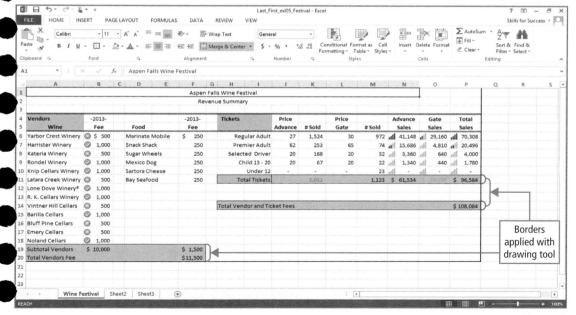

Figure 4

5. Select the range **A4:P5**. Click the **Bottom Border arrow** ⊞ ▾, and then click **More Borders** to open the **Format Cells** dialog box.

6. On the **Border tab**, under **Line Style**, click the last option in the second column—**double line**. Click the **Color arrow**, and under **Standard Colors** click the ninth option—**Dark Blue**.

7. Under **Presets**, click **Outline**. Compare your screen with **Figure 3**, and then click **OK**.

8. In the **Font group**, click the **More Borders arrow** ⊞ ▾. Under **Draw Borders**, click **Line Color**, and then under **Standard Colors** click the ninth option—**Dark Blue**.

   The mouse pointer now appears as a pencil, which is the Handwriting pointer.

9. With the Handwriting pointer ✏, drag to select the ranges **A19:F20**, **H11:P11**, and then **H14:P14**. Click Esc to turn the **Line Color** off.

10. Select the range **A1:P20**. In the **Font group**, click to open the **More Borders arrow** ⊞ ▾. Under **Borders**, select the eighth option—**Thick Box Border**. Click cell **A1**, and then compare your screen with **Figure 4**.

11. **Save** 🖫 the workbook.

■ **You have completed Skill 6 of 10**

▶ A *style* is a group of formatting choices that can be applied in a single step.

▶ Some cell styles already exist as part of the Cell Styles gallery.

▶ Styles can be created and saved as part of the workbook file.

1. Select the range **A1:P2**. On the **Home tab**, in the **Styles group**, click the **Cell Styles** button. Under **Titles and Headings**, click the **Title** style. AutoFit **rows 1:2**, and then select the range **A1:P1**. In the **Alignment group**, double-click **Merge & Center**. Select the range **A2:P2**. In the **Alignment group**, double-click **Merge & Center**, and then select cell **A3**.

2. In the **Styles group**, click the **Cell Styles** button, and below the **Cell Styles** gallery, click **New Cell Style**.

3. In the **Style** dialog box, in the **Style name** field, replace the existing value with Wine Style and then compare your screen with **Figure 1**.

4. Click the **Format** button. In the **Format Cells** dialog box, click the **Number tab**, and then under **Category**, click **Text**.

   The *Text format* treats the cell value as text even when the cell contains numbers.

5. On the **Alignment tab**, under **Text Alignment**, click the **Horizontal arrow**, and then click **Left (Indent)**. Under **Indent**, change to 1 and then compare your screen with **Figure 2**.

6. On the **Font tab**, under **Font**, scroll down and click **Arial**, and then change the **Size** to **11**. Click the **Color** arrow, and click **Automatic** color. Click **OK** two times.

■ Continue to the next page to complete the skill ▶

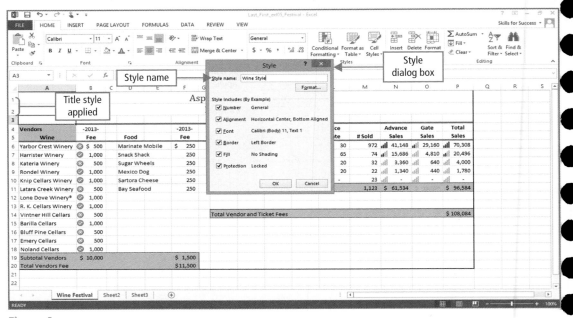

Figure 1

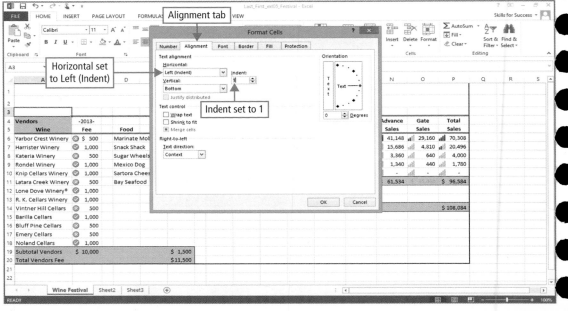

Figure 2

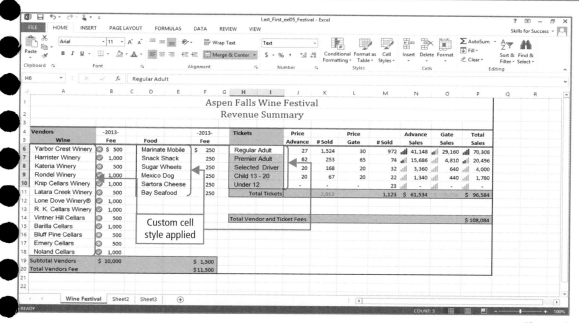

Figure 3

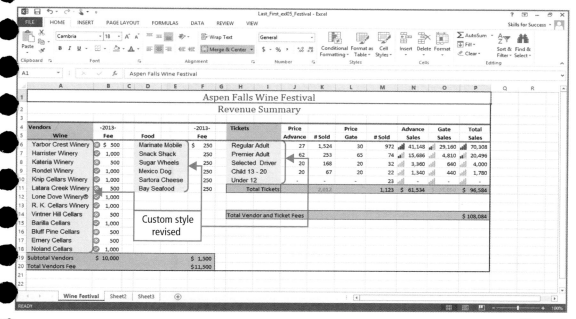

7. Select the range **A6:A18**. In the **Styles group**, click **Cell Styles**, and under **Custom**, click **Wine Style**. AutoFit column **A**.

> The custom cell style formatting is applied to the range.

8. Repeat this technique to apply the custom cell style to ranges **D6:E11** and **H6:I10**, and then compare your screen with **Figure 3**.

9. In the **Styles group**, click the **Cell Styles** button. Under **Custom**, right-click **Wine Style**, and then click **Modify**. Click the **Format** button, and then click the **Fill tab**. Under **Background Color**, in the gallery, in the second row, click the fifth color—**Blue**, **Accent 1**, **Lighter 80%**. Click the **Border** tab, and in the **Border** preview click the left border to deselect it. Click **OK** two times, and then select cell **A1**. Compare your screen with **Figure 4**.

> The custom cell style is saved with the workbook and can be applied as often as needed within the workbook.

10. Save 🖫 the workbook.

■ **You have completed Skill 7 of 10**

Figure 4

Format Cells and Worksheets | **Microsoft Excel Chapter 5** • **189**

▶ Recall that a theme is a set of colors, fonts, lines, and fill effects that can be applied to entire worksheets or to individual cells.

▶ Themes can be customized by changing the colors, fonts, and effects assigned to them. Care should be taken to choose color combinations that look professional.

1. Select cell **A3**. On the **Page Layout tab**, in the **Themes group**, click the **Fonts** button, and then compare your screen with **Figure 1**.

   A font theme consists of two fonts, one for titles and one for text. In Excel, most styles assign the same font to both.

2. Below the Fonts gallery, click **Customize Fonts**.

3. In the **Create New Theme Fonts** dialog box, in the **Heading font** box, verify that **Cambria** displays in the box.

   When the new theme is applied, all heading cell styles will display in the Cambria font.

4. Click the **Body font arrow**, scroll up the displayed list, and then click **Arial**.

   The default font face and size for Excel 2013 is Calibri, size 11. When you change the body font, you change the default font for the workbook. Here, the default font has been changed to Arial.

   Under Sample, a sample of the selected font choices displays for the heading and body font styles.

5. In the **Name** field, replace the existing text with Festival Theme Compare your screen with **Figure 2**.

■ Continue to the next page to complete the skill ▶

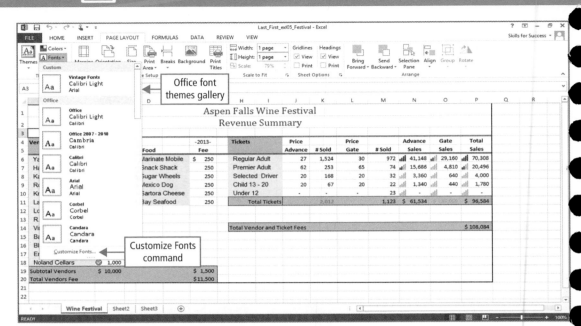

Figure 1

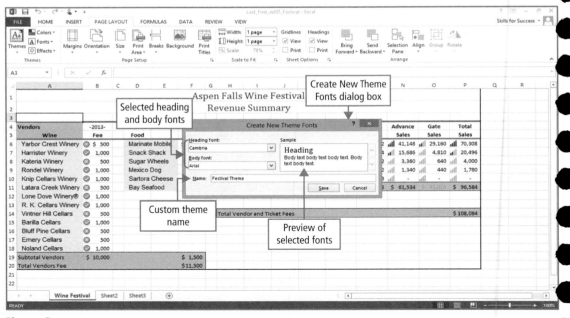

Figure 2

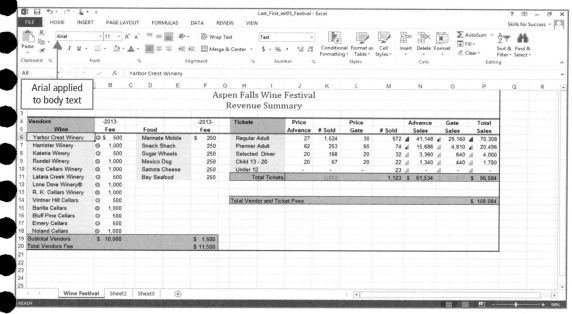

Figure 3

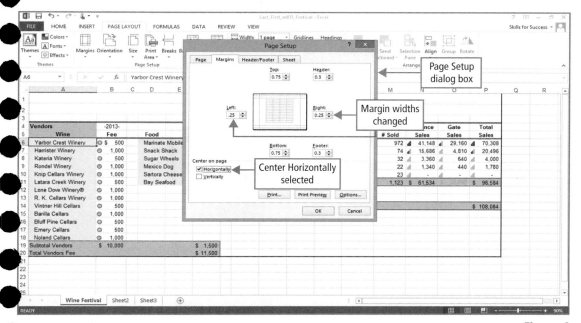

Figure 4

6. Click **Save** to save the custom font theme. If necessary, adjust column widths, select the **Home tab**, and then select cell **A6**. Decrease the **Zoom** to **90%**. Compare your screen with Figure 3.

> In the worksheet, the body fonts are formatted as Arial.

7. On the **Page Layout tab**, in the **Themes group**, click the **Fonts** button. Verify that the *Festival Theme* displays at the top of the displayed gallery, and then click the **Fonts** button again to close the gallery.

8. In the **Page Setup group**, click the **Margins** button, and then below the gallery, click **Custom Margins**.

9. In the **Page Setup** dialog box, on the **Margins tab**, replace the **Left** value with 0.25 and the **Right** value with 0.25

> Reducing margins is a way to include all of the data on the printed page without having to decrease the size of the worksheet.

10. Under **Center on page**, click the **Horizontally** check box, and then compare your screen with Figure 4.

> This setting will center the spreadsheet on the printed page horizontally.

11. Click **OK**, and then **Save** 🖫 the workbook.

■ **You have completed Skill 8 of 10**

▶ A **watermark** is a graphic inserted into a workbook background. Watermarks are typically inserted into headers.

▶ Background colors can be applied to ranges of cells to add interest to a worksheet.

1. On the **Insert tab**, in the **Text group**, click the **Header & Footer** button. Click in cell **A1**, and then decrease the **Zoom** to **80%**. Select *Click to add Header* in the center header, as shown in **Figure 1**.

2. On the **Design tab**, in the **Header & Footer Elements group**, click the **Picture** button.

3. In the **Insert Pictures** dialog box, navigate to the student data files for this chapter. Select **exl05_FestivalLogo**, and then click **Insert**.

> Recall that when objects are inserted into headers or footers, they are represented by fields. Here, *&[Picture]* represents the picture that was just inserted.

4. Click in the area above the **Header** to deactivate the **Header & Footer** area, and to display the watermark as shown in **Figure 2**.

> Any picture can be used as a watermark. By adding an image to the header, it is displayed behind the data on the spreadsheet instead of on top of the data.

5. Click the **View tab**, and then in the **Workbook Views group**, click **Normal**.

> Recall that header and footer elements do not display in Normal view.

■ **Continue to the next page to complete the skill**

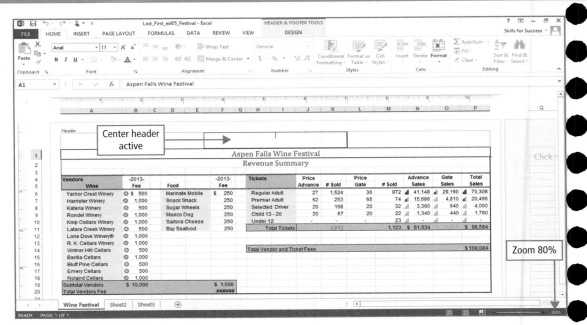

Figure 1

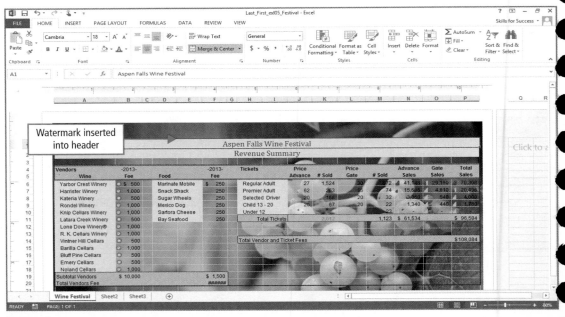

Figure 2

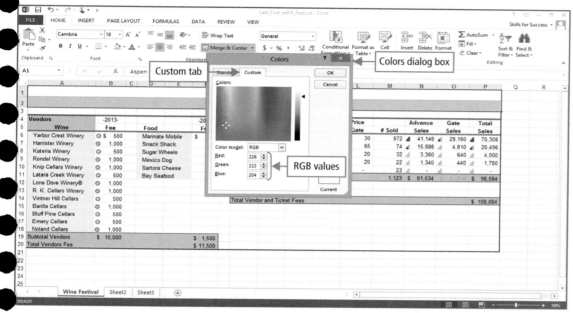

Figure 3

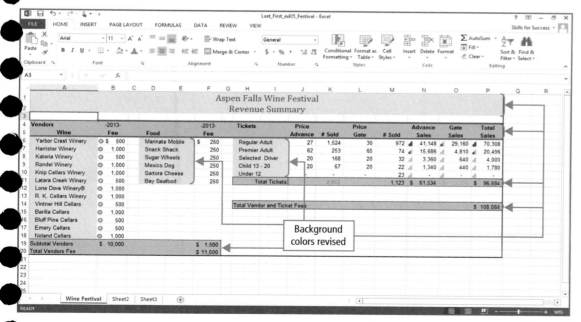

Figure 4

6. Select the range **A1:P2**. On the **Home tab**, in the **Font group**, click the **Fill Color arrow** 🖌️, and then below the colors, click **More Colors**. In the **Colors** dialog box, click the **Custom tab**. Replace the **Red** value with 226 the **Green** value with 222 and the **Blue** value with 204

   In this manner, colors can be created that are not available in the gallery. *RGB values* are constructed from combinations of red, green, and blue.

7. Compare your screen with Figure 3, and then click **OK**.

8. Select the range **A6:A18**. In the **Font group**, click the **Fill Color** button. Repeat the technique to revise the fill color for **D6:E11** and **H6:I10**.

9. Select the range **A19:F20**. Click the **Fill Color arrow**, and then in the gallery, under **Theme Colors**, in the third row, click the third color—**Tan, Background 2, Darker 25%**. Repeat the technique to revise the fill color for the ranges **H11:P11**, **H14:P14**, and **A4:P5**. Click an empty cell, and then compare your screen with Figure 4.

10. Save 🖫 the workbook.

- **You have completed Skill 9 of 10**

▶ **Gridlines** are lines that run horizontally and vertically across a worksheet and intersect to create cells.

▶ Gridlines are useful when working with a spreadsheet, but they can be hidden after the worksheet is completed.

1. On the **Page Layout tab**, in the **Sheet Options group**, clear the **Gridlines View** check box. Compare your screen with **Figure 1**.

2. Select the range **A6:F18**, press and hold ⌈Ctrl⌉, and then select the range **H6:P10**. Release ⌈Ctrl⌉.

3. On the **Home tab**, in the **Font group**, click the **Font Settings Dialog Box Launcher** ⌈⌉. In the **Format Cells** dialog box, click the **Border tab**.

4. In the **Format Cells** dialog box, under **Style**, be sure that the last line style in the left column is selected. Click the **Color arrow**, and then under **Theme Colors**, in the third row, click the first color—**White, Background 1, Darker 15%**.

5. Under **Presets**, click the **Inside** button, and then compare your screen with **Figure 2**. Click **OK**, to close the **Format Cells** dialog box.

By selecting an inside border, the color is applied only to the inside borders.

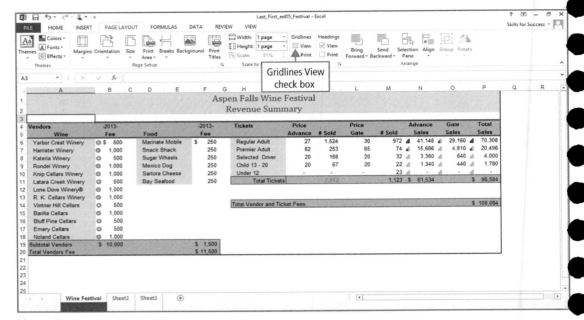

Figure 1

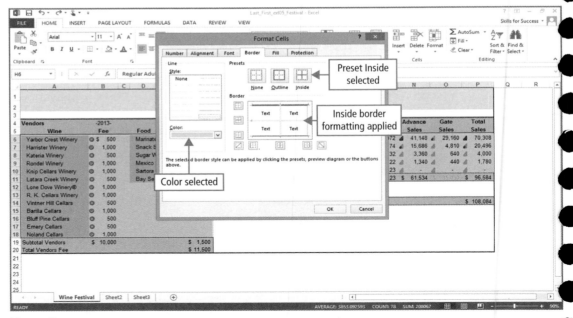

Figure 2

■ Continue to the next page to complete the skill ▶

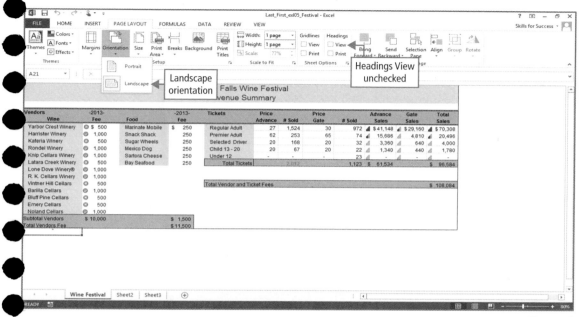

Figure 3

6. Select the range **A1:P20**. On the **Home tab**, in the **Font group**, click the **Thick Box Border** arrow, and then click the seventh option, **Outside Borders**.

7. Select cell **A21**. On the **Page Layout tab**, in the **Sheet Options group**, clear the **Headings View** check box.

8. In the **Page Setup group**, click the **Orientation** button, and verify that **Landscape** is selected. Compare your screen with **Figure 3**.

9. Display the **File tab**, and then click **Print**. Compare your screen with **Figure 4**.

10. **Save** 🖫 the workbook, and then **Close** ✕ Excel. Submit the workbook as directed by your instructor.

✔ **DONE!** You have completed Skill 10 of 10, and your workbook is complete!

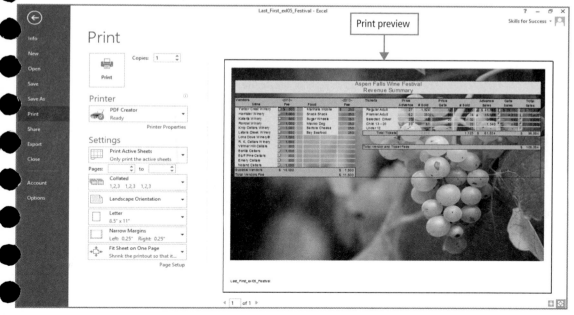

Figure 4

The following More Skills are located at **www.pearsonhighered.com/skills**

More Skills Copy Styles Between Workbooks

Because custom styles are saved only in the workbook in which they are created, they are not automatically available in other workbooks. However, you can copy cell styles from other workbooks into the workbook you are currently working with. In this way, you can use cell styles to consistently format worksheets within your organization.

In More Skills 11, you will copy cell styles from another workbook and then apply those styles.

To begin, open your web browser, navigate to www.pearsonhighered.com/skills, locate the name of your textbook, and then follow the instructions on the website.

More Skills Draw Borders

You can draw borders directly in cells. You can select the border formatting that you need, and then click or drag along the cell edges to apply the border where you need it. In this manner, you can quickly apply borders.

In More Skills 12, you will practice drawing borders in worksheet cells. You will select different colors and line styles, and then drag to apply the borders to various cell ranges.

To begin, open your web browser, navigate to www.pearsonhighered.com/skills, locate the name of your textbook, and then follow the instructions on the website.

More Skills Convert Comma-Separated Text into Columns

When importing data from other sources, a column may have two values separated by commas. For example, both first and last names may be presented in a single column separated by a comma. When this happens, you can convert the text into two or more columns.

In More Skills 13, you will convert a single column of data containing two names into two separate columns.

To begin, open your web browser, navigate to www.pearsonhighered.com/skills, locate the name of your textbook, and then follow the instructions on the website.

More Skills Create Screen Shots

Screen shots can be inserted directly into an Excel worksheet without using an external image-capturing program. The Take a Screenshot tool captures an image from your computer and inserts it directly into Excel, where it can be manipulated and saved.

In More Skills 14, you will open a workbook and a website, and then use the Take a Screenshot tool to capture a portion of the web page, insert it into the worksheet, and then change the color of the image.

To begin, open your web browser, navigate to www.pearsonhighered.com/skills, locate the name of your textbook, and then follow the instructions on the website.

Please note that there are no additional projects to accompany the More Skills Projects, and they are not covered in End-of-Chapter projects.

The following table summarizes the **SKILLS AND PROCEDURES** covered in this chapter.

Skills Number	Task	Step	Icon	Keyboard Shortcut
1	Insert symbols	Insert tab → Symbols group → Symbol		
1	Create custom number formats	Home tab → Number group → Number Format Dialog Box Launcher → Number tab	⬛	
2	Copy formatting with Format Painter	Select the text format to copy → click Format Painter to copy once and double-click to copy more than once → select the text to be formatted	🖌	
3	Write conditional formatting rules	Home tab → Styles group → Conditional Formatting → New Rule		
4	Manage conditional formatting rules	Home tab → Styles group → Conditional Formatting → Manage Rules		
5	Delete rows	Click row number → Home tab → Cells group → Delete arrow → Delete Sheet Rows		Ctrl + Minus (-)
5	Delete columns	Click column letter → Home tab → Cells group → Delete arrow → Delete Sheet Columns		Ctrl + Shift + Minus (-)
6	Create cell borders	Select the range → Home tab → Font group → Border button	⊞ ▾	
7	Create cell styles	Home tab → Styles group → Cell Styles → New Cell Style		
8	Create custom fonts	Page Layout tab → Themes group → Fonts → Customize Fonts		
8	Apply custom fonts	Page Layout tab → Themes group → Fonts → click customized font name		
9	Insert watermarks	Insert tab → Text group → Header & Footer → Design tab → Header & Footer Elements group → click Picture		
10	View/hide gridlines	Page Layout tab → Sheet Options group → Gridlines → View check box		
10	View/hide row and column headings	Page Layout tab → Sheet Options group → Headings → View check box		

Key Terms

Online Help Skills

1. Start **Excel 2013**, and then in the upper-right corner of the Excel window, click the **Help** button ⟨ ? ⟩.

2. In the **Excel Help** window **Search help** box, type conditional formatting and then press ⟨ Enter ⟩.

3. In the search results, click **Add**, **change**, **find**, **or clear conditional formats**. Read the article's introduction, and then below **What do you want to do?** click **Use a formula to determine which cells to format**. Compare your screen with Figure 1.

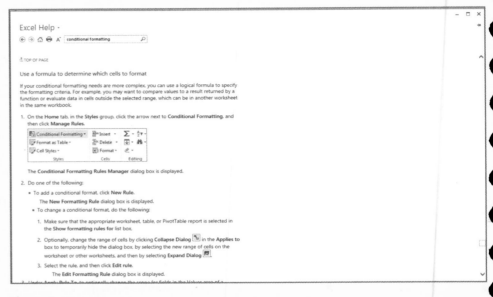

Figure 1

4. Read the section to answer the following questions: What type of formula can be used to specify conditional formatting criteria? What types of cell references are automatically inserted when using conditional formatting?

Matching

Match each term in the second column with its correct definition in the first column by writing the letter of the term on the blank line in front of the correct definition.

____ **1.** Decorative lines that can be applied to worksheet cells.

____ **2.** A set of design elements, including backgrounds, colors, and fonts, that are applied to a spreadsheet.

____ **3.** Treats a cell value as text even when the cell contains numbers.

____ **4.** Small graphics that visually represent a cell's value in relation to other cells.

____ **5.** A group of formatting choices that can be applied in a single step.

____ **6.** A tool that copies formatting from one cell to another.

____ **7.** Characters that must be inserted and are not available on the keyboard.

____ **8.** The shading assigned to a cell.

____ **9.** By default, lines that run horizontally and vertically across a worksheet and intersect to create cells.

____ **10.** Formatting that changes the appearance of a cell or range when one or more conditions are true.

A Gridlines

B Format Painter

C Cell borders

D Fill color

E Icon set

F Conditional formatting

G Text format

H Symbol

I Theme

J Style

Multiple Choice (MyITLab®)

Choose the correct answer.

1. Which of the following is a character such as the degree symbol or trademark symbol that is a frequently used symbol located on a shorter list and not found on the keyboard?
   A. Wingding
   B. Insert
   C. Special character

2. Which of the following specifies the year with four digits?
   A. [Color]
   B. yyyy
   C. mm

3. Which of the following specifies a placeholder for a digit?
   A. #
   B. 0
   C. mm

4. Once a symbol is inserted into a cell, it can be formatted like this workbook element.
   A. Text
   B. Image
   C. Style

5. You must specify in which direction to move the surrounding cells whenever you perform this operation on a worksheet.
   A. Format
   B. Insert
   C. Copy

6. Which of the following is a location where custom styles are saved?
   A. Application
   B. Workbook
   C. Desktop

7. Header and footer elements do not display in this view.
   A. Page Setup
   B. Print Preview
   C. Normal

8. A graphic that is inserted into a document background is called which of the following?
   A. Watermark
   B. Logo
   C. Cell Style

9. A watermark is typically inserted into this area of the page.
   A. Header
   B. Column
   C. Cell

10. Colors constructed from a combination of red, green, and blue are called which of the following?
    A. RGB values
    B. Colorscale
    C. HEX

Topics for Discussion

1. You have added conditional formatting that displays icon sets. Do you think these special formats add to or detract from the data's meaning? Why?

2. In this chapter, you placed borders and shading in cells and then hid the gridlines and column and row headings. Compare this format with one that displays only gridlines and headings but does not display borders and shading. Which format do you think is easiest for others to read? Why?

Skills Review

MyITLab®
Grader

To complete this project, you will need the following files:

- exl05_SRTourism
- exl05_SRLogo

You will save your file as:

- Last_First_exl05_SRTourism

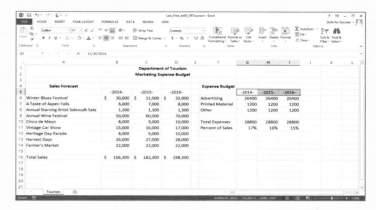

Figure 1

1. Start **Excel 2013**, and open the student data file **exl05_SRTourism**. Save the workbook in your chapter folder as Last_First_exl05_SRTourism

2. Select the range **B5:D5**. In the **Number group**, click the **Number Dialog Box Launcher**, and then under **Category**, click **Custom**. In the **Type** box, replace the existing value with -yyyy- In the **Clipboard group**, click the **Format Painter**, and then select the range **G5:I5**. Compare your screen with **Figure 1**.

3. Select the range **B6:D6**. In the **Clipboard group**, double-click the **Format Painter** button. Apply the format to the ranges **G6:I6** and **G10:I10**. Click the **Format Painter** button.

4. Select cell **B7**. Click the **Format Painter**, and apply the format to **G7:I8**.

5. Select the range **A6:D14**. Press and hold [Ctrl], and select the range **F6:I8**. In the **Font group**, click the **Fill Color button arrow**, and then under **Theme Colors**, in the second row, click the ninth color—**Blue, Accent 5, Lighter 80%**. In the **Font group**, click the **Bottom Border arrow**, and then click **Thick Box Border**. Click the **Thick Box Border arrow**, and then click **More Borders**. Click the **Color arrow**, and then under **Theme Colors**, in the sixth row, click the ninth color—**Blue, Accent 5, Darker 50%**. Click **OK**, and click an empty cell. Compare your screen with **Figure 2**.

6. Select the range **G11:I11**. Click **Conditional Formatting**, point to **Icon Sets**, and then click **More Rules**. In the **New Formatting Rule** dialog box, under **Edit the Rule Description**, click the **Icon Style arrow**, click **3 Symbols (Uncircled)**, click the **Reverse Icon Order** button, and then click **OK**.

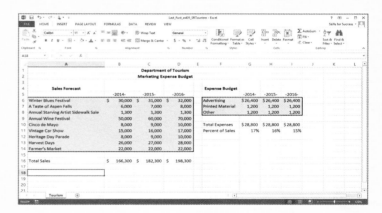

Figure 2

■ Continue to the next page to complete this Skills Review ▶

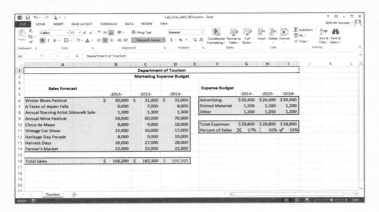

Figure 3

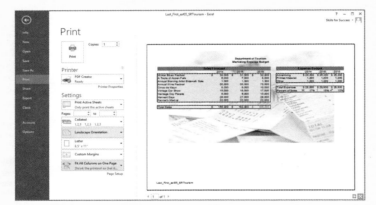

Elenathewise / Fotolia

Figure 4

7. Select the range **B16:D16**. In the **Styles group**, click **Conditional Formatting**, and then click **Manage Rules**. Click **Edit Rule**, and in the **Format values where this formula is true** box, replace the text with =B16>185000

8. Click the **Format** button. On the **Font tab**, under **Font style**, click **Bold**. Click the **Color arrow**. In the gallery, under **Standard Colors**, click the sixth color—**Green**, and then click **OK** three times.

9. Select the range **A16:D16**, press and hold ⌃Ctrl, and select the range **F10:I11**. On the **Font tab**, click the **Fill Color** button arrow. Under **Theme Colors**, click the second row, ninth color—**Blue, Accent 5, Lighter 80%**. Click the **More Borders arrow**, and click **Thick Box Border**. Select cell **A1**, and then compare your screen with Figure 3.

10. On the **Home tab**, in the **Styles group**, click **Cell Styles**, and then click **New Cell Style**. In the **Style name** box, type Tourism Style

11. Click **Format**. Click the **Number tab**, and then under **Category**, click **Text**. Click the **Alignment tab**. Under **Text Alignment**, click the **Horizontal arrow**, and then click **Center Across Selection**. Click the **Font tab**, and then under **Font** click **Arial**, and then under **Size** click **12**. Click the **Fill tab**, and then click the sixth color in the first column. Click **OK** two times.

12. Select the range **A4:D4**, and in the **Styles group**, click **Cell Styles**, and then under **Custom**, click **Tourism Style**. Select the range **F4:I4**, and then repeat the above instructions to apply the **Tourism Style**.

13. Select the range **A1:I2**. Click the **Cell Styles arrow**, and under **Titles and Headings**, click **Title**.

14. On the **Page Layout tab**, in the **Themes group**, click **Fonts**, and then click **Customize Fonts**.

15. Click the **Heading font arrow**, and then click **Cambria**. Click the **Body font arrow**, and then click **Arial**. In the **Name** box, type Tourism Fonts and then click **Save**.

16. On the **Insert tab**, in the **Text group**, click **Header & Footer**. On the **Design tab**, in the **Header & Footer Elements group**, click **Picture**. In the student data files for this chapter, locate and click **exl05_SRLogo**, and then click **Insert**. Click in the space above the header to view the watermark.

17. On the **Page Layout tab**, in the **Sheet Options group**, under **Gridlines**, clear the **View** check box. Under **Headings**, clear the **View** check box.

18. **Save** the workbook. Click the **File tab**, and then click **Print**. Compare your screen with Figure 4.

19. Submit your workbook as directed by your instructor.

 DONE! You have completed the Skills Review

Skills Assessment 1

MyITLab®
Grader

To complete this project, you will need the following files:

- exl05_SA1Travel
- exl05_SA1Logo

You will save your file as:

- Last_First_exl05_SA1Travel

---

1. Start **Excel 2013**, and then open the student data file **exl05_SA1Travel**. Save the file in the **Excel Chapter 5** folder as Last_First_exl05_SA1Travel

2. For the range **A1:D16**, apply an **Orange**, **Accent 2**, **Lighter 80%** fill color. Insert a new **column A**, and then resize the column width to **3.5**.

3. Use **Format Painter** to copy the format in cell **C4** to the range **C16:E16**. Select the range **C5:C15**, and then copy the format to **D5:E15**.

4. Select cell **E4**, and then create a new conditional format rule with the following condition: =E4<0 When the condition is true, display the cell text as **Bold** and **Red**. Use **Format Painter** to apply the formatting in cell **E4** to the range **E5:E16**.

5. In the range **E4:E15**, apply the **3 Arrows (Colored)** icon set.

6. Create a new **Cell Style** named Travel Style Set the **Horizontal** alignment to **Center Across Selection**. Set the **Font** to **Arial**, size **18**. Set the font color to **Dark Blue**. On the **Fill tab**, under **Background Color** click **No Color**. Apply the **Travel Style** to the range **B1:E1**.

7. Select the range **B3:E16**, apply a **Thick Box Border** with the **Green, Accent 6, Darker 50%** color. Apply a **thin line inside** border, **Green, Accent 6, Darker 50%**. AutoFit **columns C:E**.

8. Create a new **Theme font**. Name the new theme font Travel Font Apply **Cambria** for the **Heading font**, and then **Arial** for the **Body font**.

9. Apply the **Heading 4** cell style to the range **C3:E3**, and then to cell **B16**. Apply **Travel Style** to **B2:E2**, and then set the font to size **12**. AutoFit **column B**.

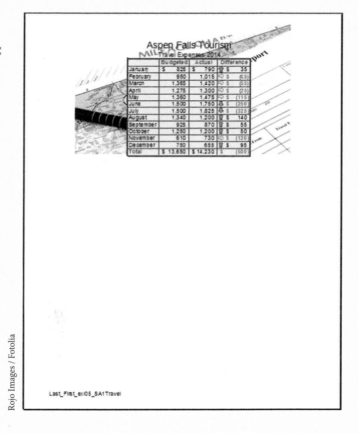

Figure 1

10. Display the header and footer, and in the middle header, insert a watermark using the file **exl05_SA1Logo**. Switch to **Normal view**, and then select cell **A1**.

11. **Print Preview** the worksheet, and compare the completed workbook with **Figure 1**. **Save** the workbook, and then submit it as directed by your instructor.

DONE! You have completed Skills Assessment 1

Skills Assessment 2

To complete this project, you will need the following file:

- exl05_SA2Attendance

You will save your file as:

- Last_First_exl05_SA2Attendance

---

1. Start **Excel 2013**, and then open the student data file **exl05_SA2Attendance**. Save the file in the **Excel Chapter 5** folder as Last_First_ exl05_SA2Attendance

2. Select cell **A4**. Create a new **Cell Style** named Event Style For the style, apply the custom number format mmmm-yyyy Select the range **A4:A15**, and then apply the **Event Style**. Set the width of **column A** to **15.00**.

3. Use the **Format Painter** to copy the format from cell **B4** to the range **B5:D16**.

4. Select the range **D4:D15**, and then apply the **3 Signs** icon set conditional formatting.

5. Select the range **A3:D16**, and apply a **Green, Accent 6, Lighter 60%** fill color to the range. Insert a new column **A**, and then resize columns **A** and **F** to **6**.

6. Create a new **Cell Style** named Event2 Style with the following formatting: **Center Across Selection**; **Cambria**, size **14**; and a font color **Blue-Gray, Text 2, Darker 25%**. Apply a thick **Dark Red** border along the **bottom** edge of the cell only. Select the range **B2:E2**, and then apply the **Event2 Style**.

7. Insert a new row **1**, and then resize the row to **20**.

8. Create a new **Cell Style** named Total Style Format the style with a double border, **Blue, Accent 5, Darker 50%** to the **top** of the cell only. Format the two sides with a thin line **Blue, Accent 5, Darker 50%** border. Set the fill color to **Light Blue**. Set the number format to **Number** with **0 decimal places**, **Use 1000 Separator (,)**, and then set the **Alignment** to **Horizontal General**. Select the range **B17:E17**, and apply the **Total Style.**

9. Select the range **A1:F18**, and then apply a **Thick Box Border**. Select the range **B2:E17**, apply a **Dark Red, Thick Outline** border. Apply a **Dark Red** thin inside border to **B4:E16**.

10. Apply the **Title style** to the range **B2:E2**. Create a new **Theme font** called Event Fonts and then set the **Heading** to **Cambria** and the **Body** to **Arial**.

11. **Print Preview** the worksheet, and then compare with Figure 1.

12. **Save** the workbook, and then submit it as directed by your instructor.

 DONE! You have completed Skills Assessment 2

Aspen Falls Tourism			
Event Attendance 2014			
	Estimated	Actual	Variance
January-2014	2,000	1,755	(245)
February-2014	6,500	6,875	375
March-2014	1,500	1,365	(135)
April-2014	2,600	2,900	300
May-2014	1,300	1,200	(100)
June-2014	1,550	1,350	(200)
July-2014	1,800	2,100	300
August-2014	425	645	220
September-2014	600	475	(125)
October-2014	2,200	2,675	475
November-2014	2,800	2,665	(135)
December-2014	4,400	4,150	(250)
Total	27,675	28,155	480

Last_First_exl05_SA2Attendance

Figure 1

Visual Skills Check

To complete this project, you will need the following file:

- exl05_VSCount

You will save your file as:

- Last_First_exl05_VSCount

Start **Excel 2013**, and open the student data file **exl05_VSCount**. Save the workbook in your chapter folder as Last_ First_exl05_VSCount Format the worksheet as shown in **Figure 1**. Format, merge, and center the worksheet titles—**Century Schoolbook**, size **16**, **Bold**, **Green**, **Accent 6**, **Darker 50%**. Copy the number formatting in the range **B5:B9** to **C5:E9**. For the range **A1:E9**, apply **White**, **Background 1**, **Darker 25%** fill color. Apply a **Green**, **Accent 6**, **Darker 50%** thick box border around the range **A1:E9**, and then a thick top and bottom **Green**, **Accent 6**, **Darker 50%** border to **A3:E3**. Apply a thin **Green**, **Accent 6**, **Darker 50%** bottom border to **A4:E4**. Apply a **Light Green** thin inside border to the range **A5:E9**. Apply the **Red – Yellow – Green Color Scale** conditional formatting to the ranges **C5:C8** and **E5:E8**. Create a new conditional formatting rule in **D5:D8** using the **3 Triangles Icon Style**. In **A9:E9**, apply a **Green**, **Accent 6**, **Darker 25%** fill color. **Print Preview** the worksheet, and then **Save** the workbook, and submit it as directed by your instructor.

 DONE! You have completed Visual Skills Check

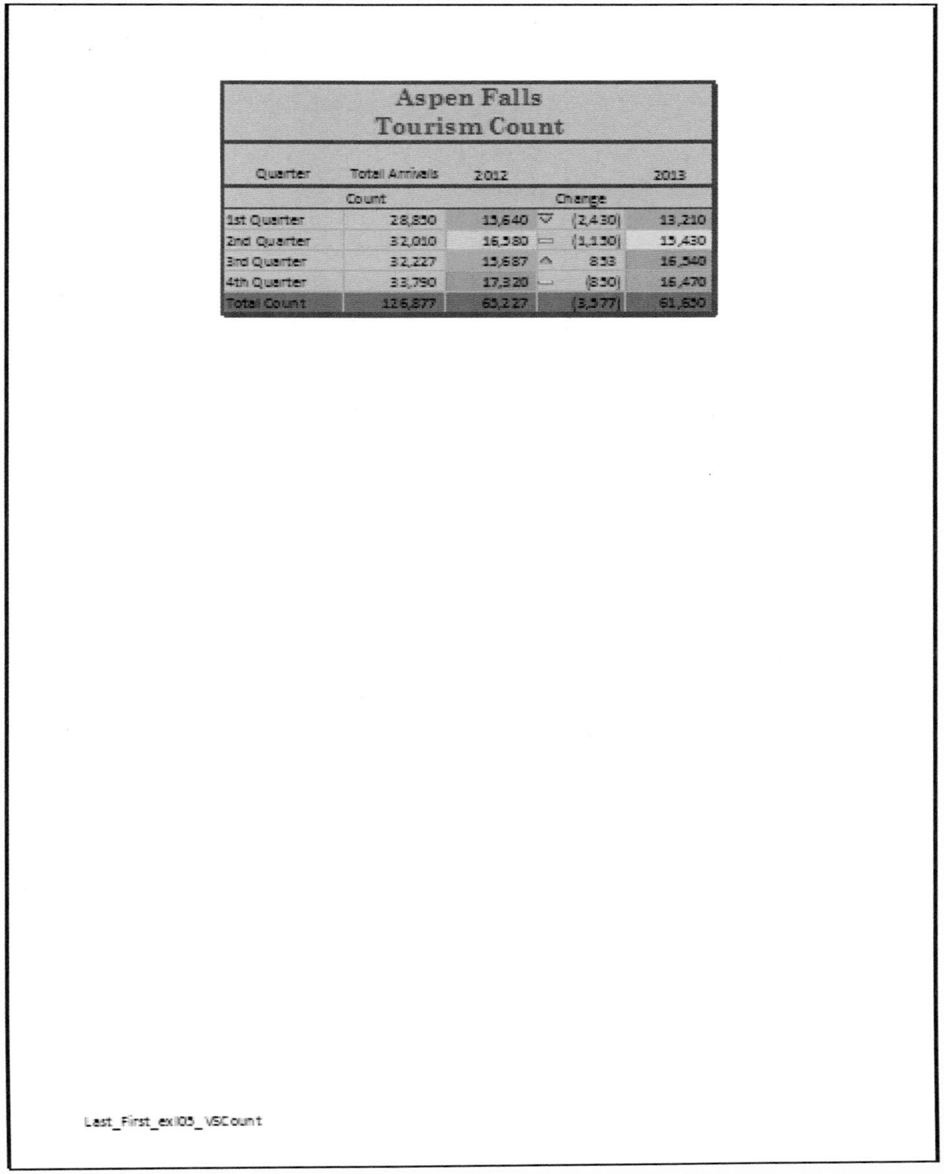

Aspen Falls Tourism Count				
Quarter	Total Arrivals	2012		2013
	Count	Change		
1st Quarter	28,850	15,640 ▽	(2,430)	13,210
2nd Quarter	32,010	16,580 ▭	(1,150)	15,430
3rd Quarter	32,227	15,687 △	853	16,540
4th Quarter	33,790	17,320 ▭	(850)	16,470
Total Count	126,877	65,227	(3,577)	61,650

Last_First_exl05_VSCount

Figure 1

My Skills

To complete this project, you will need the following file:

- **exl05_MYGrades**

You will save your file as:

- **Last_First_exl05_MYGrades**

1. Start **Excel 2103**, and open the student data file **exl05_MYGrades**. Save the workbook in your chapter folder as Last_First_exl05_MYGrades

2. In the first cell replace *Student Name* with your first and last names.

3. Create a new **Cell Style** named Grades Style with the following formatting: **Center Across Selection**, **Arial**, size **16**, and a font color of **Green**, **Accent 6**. Select the range **A1:E2**, and then apply the **Grades Style**.

4. Insert cells in **A3:A15**, as shown in Figure 1.

5. Apply a **Conditional Formatting 3 Symbols (Circled)** icon set that shows whether each grade exceeds, meets, or is below the grade intended for each course.

6. Use the **Format Painter** to copy the formatting from **Courses** to **Semester** and **Grades**.

7. Create a new **Custom Font** named Grades Font Select **Arial** for the heading and body fonts. AutoFit columns if needed.

8. Select the entire range of the data cells. Apply a **Thick Box Border**, and then apply the fill color **Blue-Gray**, **Text 2**, **Lighter 80%**.

9. Hide the worksheet **Gridlines** and **Headings**. **Print Preview** the worksheet.

10. Compare the completed workbook with Figure 1. **Save** the workbook, and then submit it as directed by your instructor.

 DONE! You have completed My Skills

Figure 1

Skills Challenge 1

To complete this project, you will need the following file:

- exl05_SC1Spending

You will save your file as:

- Last_First_exl05_SC1Spending

The Aspen Falls Bureau of Tourism is trying to analyze tourism spending. Start **Excel 2013**, and then open the file **exl05_SC1Spending**. Save the workbook in your chapter folder as Last_First_exl05_SC1Spending Edit the custom style Spending Style applied to the worksheet headings. Apply formatting using more professional fonts, font color, and fill color. Edit the custom font Tourism Fonts, selecting fonts that are more appropriate for a business document. Edit the Labels

cell style so that the borders, cell shading, and alignments are consistent with the formatting practiced in the chapter. For the Variance column, apply conditional formatting so that the busiest years can be identified easily. AutoFit columns, and delete columns and rows as needed. Save the workbook, and then submit it as directed by your instructor.

 DONE! You have completed Skills Challenge 1

Skills Challenge 2

To complete this project, you will need the following file:

- exl05_SC2Growth

You will save your file as:

- Last_First_exl05_SC2Growth

Tourism Director Todd Austin would like to compare Aspen Falls's growth with growth data for your city. Go to http://quickfacts.census.gov/qfd/index.html and search for the state, and then city in which you live. To find data for 10 years you will also need to click the Browse Data Sets for (city), at the upper-right corner of the table, and then select Historical population counts. If no data exists for your city, choose another nearby location. Start **Excel 2013**, open the file **exl05_SC2Growth**, and then save the workbook in your

chapter folder as Last_First_exl05_SC2Growth Enter the data provided from the website. Utilizing techniques practiced in this chapter, apply conditional formatting that visually represents the population changes in your area. Apply cell styles, background colors, and borders to the spreadsheet in a manner consistent with the techniques used in this chapter. Save the workbook, and then submit it as directed by your instructor.

 DONE! You have completed Skills Challenge 2

CHAPTER 6

Insert Advanced Functions and Create Scenarios

- ▶ Functions are used to perform complex operations easily—for example, you can manipulate text to calculate the future value of assets.

- ▶ Analysis tools are used to perform what-if analyses and to determine which variables need to be changed in order to meet certain criteria.

- ▶ Future value can be calculated by using the FV function, when the interest rate is constant.

- ▶ Cell ranges can be calculated using only the cells that meet specified criteria.

- ▶ Text functions are used to capitalize the beginning of proper nouns, and to join text into one cell.

- ▶ Values can be retrieved by using lookup tables to determine a value.

- ▶ Logical functions are used to determine if values meet certain criteria.

- ▶ Array formulas can be used to calculate multiple ranges into one cell or a range of cells.

Picture-Factory / Fotolia

Aspen Falls City Hall

In this chapter, you will support Janet Neal, the Aspen Falls finance director, by editing an existing workbook and using Excel functions and formulas to calculate and analyze payroll-related expenses. Janet's responsibilities include planning, organizing, and controlling financial resources, and this workbook will assist her with predicting the present and future value of liabilities.

Excel workbooks can contain multiple sheets from which data can be copied and pasted between worksheets. Businesses and organizations often use Excel workbooks to create analyses for strategic planning and to predict future financial decisions. Functions can be used to insert values from tables, and a lookup function can used to return the correct rate from a table.

In this project you will incorporate functions and formulas to calculate wages based on one or multiple criteria. You will also use text functions to join text, convert text, and paste values. You will practice using logical functions to determine certain criteria and use lookup functions to determine rates needed to calculate taxes and retirement deductions. You will also calculate the future value of assets and perform what-if analyses based on scenarios to help Janet and other stakeholders make financial planning decisions. Finally, you will use array formulas to perform calculations using multiple cell ranges.

Time to complete all 10 skills – 60 to 90 minutes

Student data file needed for this chapter:

exl06_Payroll

You will save your workbook as:

Last_First_exl06_Payroll

Outcome

Using the skills in this chapter, you will be able to create worksheets like this:

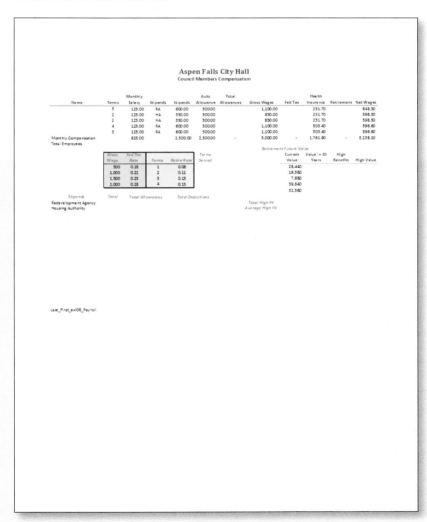

SKILLS

Skills 1-10 Training

At the end of this chapter, you will be able to:

Skill 1 Modify Text Using Text Functions

Skill 2 Use Paste Options to Change Underlying Values

Skill 3 Look Up Data Using Lookup Functions

Skill 4 Edit Conditions in Logical Functions

Skill 5 Use COUNTA and COUNTIF Functions

Skill 6 Perform What-If Analyses Using Scenario Manager

Skill 7 Estimate Future Value

Skill 8 Insert Array Formulas

Skill 9 Calculate Conditional Sums

Skill 10 Calculate Conditional Averages

MORE SKILLS

Skill 11 Use Web Functions

Skill 12 Use Solver

Skill 13 Delete Duplicate Records

Skill 14 Use External Data Links to Update Data

▶ The **CONCATENATE** function is a text function used to join the text in two cells into one cell.

▶ The **PROPER** function converts text to title case—the first letter of each word is capitalized.

1. Start **Excel 2013**. Open the file **exl06_ Payroll**. On the **File tab**, click **Save As**, and then click **Browse**. In the **Save As** dialog box, navigate to the location where you are saving your files. Click **New folder**, type Excel Chapter 6 and then press Enter two times. Name the workbook Last_ First_exl06_Payroll and then press Enter.

2. Click the **Employees** worksheet tab, and then select cell **M2**.

3. On the **Formulas tab**, in the **Function Library group**, click the **Text** button, and then click **CONCATENATE**. Compare your screen with Figure 1.

4. In the **Function Arguments** dialog box, click in the **Text1** box, and then click cell **B2**. If necessary, move the dialog box. Press Tab to move the insertion point to the **Text2** box.

5. In the **Text2** box, press the SpaceBar, and then press Tab to move to the **Text3** box. Notice the quotation marks inserted around the blank space in the **Text2** box.

   In function arguments, text must be enclosed in quotation marks. If they are not inserted, they will be added automatically. A **string** is any sequence of letters and numbers and is designated by quotation marks.

6. With the insertion point in the **Text3** box, click cell **C2**. Compare your screen with Figure 2.

■ **Continue to the next page to complete the skill**

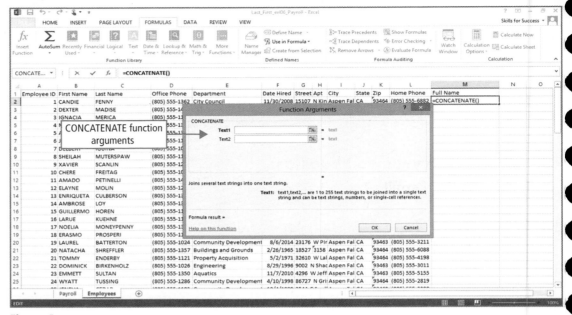

Figure 1

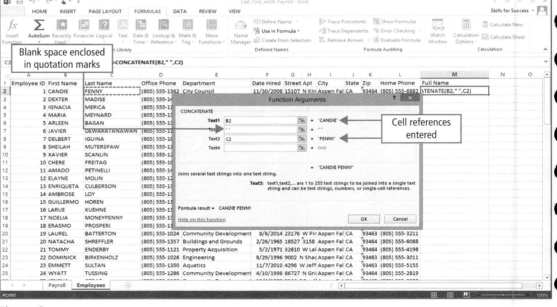

Figure 2

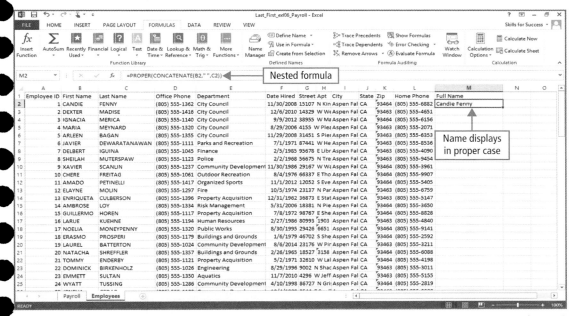

Figure 3

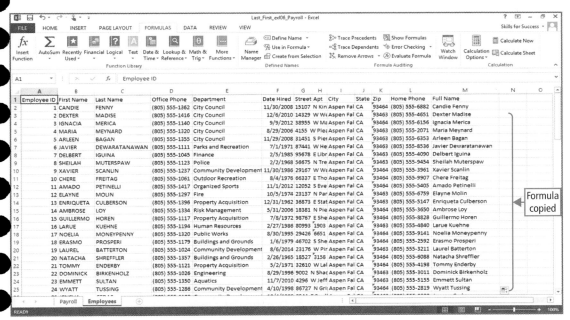

Figure 4

7. Click **OK** to close the dialog box. Notice the displayed value in cell **M2**.

The CONCATENATE function combined the First Name and Last Name values into a single string. For readability, a blank space was inserted between the two fields.

8. With cell **M2** selected, click in the formula bar, and then position the insertion point between the equal sign (=) and the word CONCATENATE.

9. Type PROPER(Make sure to include the left open parenthesis after *PROPER,* and then press [End] to move the insertion point to the end of the expression in the formula bar. Add a closing parenthesis character) and then press [Enter]. Select cell **M2**, and then compare your screen with **Figure 3**.

A *nested function* is a function placed inside another function. Here, the CONCATENATE function is nested within the PROPER function. The text is first concatenated, and then the PROPER function converts the result to title case.

10. With cell **M2** still selected, point to the fill handle, and then with the ➕ pointer, drag down to cell **M103**. Press [Ctrl] + [Home], and then compare your screen with **Figure 4**.

11. **Save** 🖫 the workbook.

■ **You have completed Skill 1 of 10**

EXL 6-2
VIDEO

▶ When a cell or a group of cells is copied and then pasted into a new location, the formatting and underlying values of the original cell are pasted.

▶ You can use Paste Special to modify the formatting or underlying values of the contents being pasted.

1. In the **Employees** worksheet, select the range **M2:M6**. On the **Home tab**, in the **Clipboard group**, click **Copy** 📋.

2. Click the **Payroll** worksheet tab, and then select cell **A5**.

3. In the **Clipboard group**, click the **Paste** button. Point to the error message button ⬥ ▾ but do not click, and then read the message that displays as shown in **Figure 1**.

The error indicator, error value (*#REF!*), and error message all indicate a problem with the function in the pasted cells. Here, the underlying values of the copied and pasted cells contain functions that concatenate text and convert it to title case. In the new location, these functions now refer to the wrong cells. Common error values are summarized in **Figure 2**.

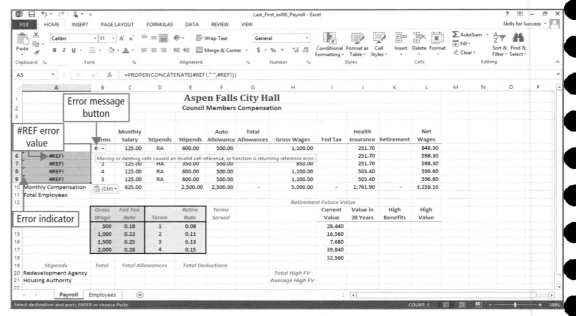

Figure 1

Common Excel Error Values

Error Message	Error
#DIV/0!	Indicates that a number is being divided by zero
#N/A	When using a Lookup function, this displays if there is no match
#NAME?	Refers to formula text that Excel does not recognize in a formula
#REF?	Indicates that the referenced cells do not contain any data
#VALUE	Indicates that a formula contains the wrong type of data—for example, text instead of numbers

Figure 2

■ Continue to the next page to complete the skill ▶

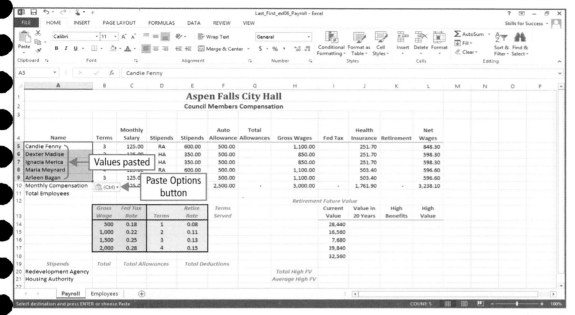

Figure 3

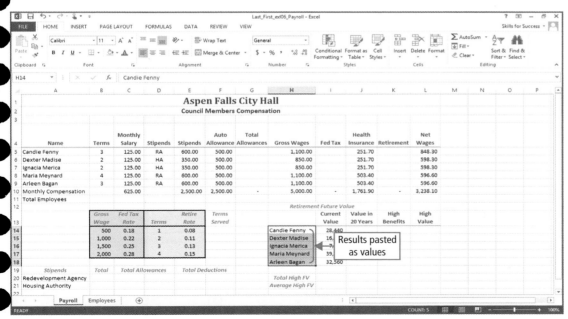

Figure 4

4. Below and to the right of the range just pasted, click the **Paste Options** button. In the **Paste Options gallery**, under **Paste Values**, click the first button—**Values (V)**—and then compare your screen with Figure 3.

  The Values paste option pastes the displayed values of the copied cells instead of their underlying formulas. In this manner, the Paste Options button can change the underlying values when pasting cells.

5. Select cell **H14**, and in the **Clipboard group**, click the **Paste arrow**. At the bottom of the **Paste gallery**, click **Paste Special**.

6. In the displayed **Paste Special** dialog box, under **Paste**, select **Values**, and then click **OK**. Press Esc, and then compare your screen with Figure 4.

  In this manner, you can choose a Paste Special option before pasting the contents.

7. Click cell **A1**, and then **Save** the workbook.

■ **You have completed Skill 2 of 10**

EXL 6-3
VIDEO

▶ *Lookup functions* are used to find values that are stored in *lookup tables*—data organized into rows and columns in such a way that values can be easily retrieved.

▶ The *VLOOKUP* function finds values in a lookup table. The function searches down the table's first column.

1. Select cell **I5**. On the **Formulas tab**, in the **Function Library group**, click the **Lookup & Reference** button, and then click **VLOOKUP**.

2. In the **Function Arguments** dialog box, with the insertion point in the **Lookup_value** box, type H5 Press [Tab] to move the insertion point to the **Table_array** box, and then compare your screen with **Figure 1**.

   The VLOOKUP function will search the lookup table for the Gross Wage value in cell H5.

3. In the **Table_array** box, click the **Collapse Dialog box** button ▦, drag through the range **B14:C17**, and then press [F4]. Click the **Expand Dialog box** button ▦, and then compare your screen with **Figure 2**.

   Recall that when you press [F4], you create an absolute cell reference. Here, the lookup table is the range B14:C17. Referring to the lookup table using absolute cell references enables you to copy the cell reference to other cells without altering the cell references to the lookup table.

4. Press [Tab] to move the insertion point to the **Col_index_num** box, and then type 2

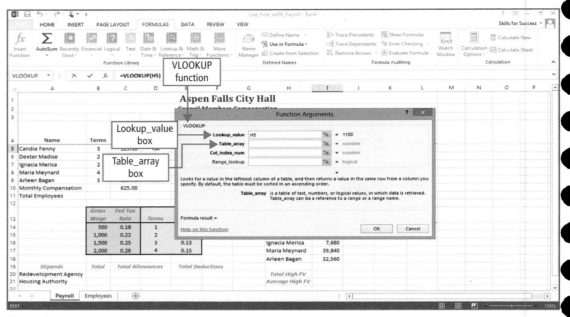

Figure 1

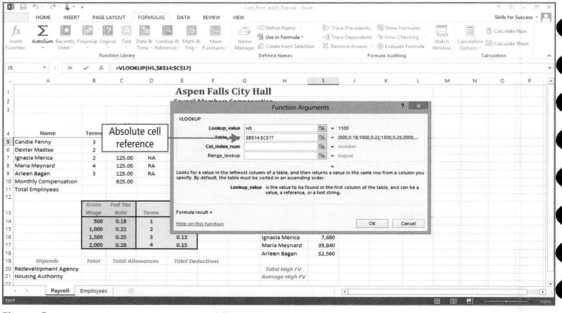

Figure 2

■ **Continue to the next page to complete the skill**

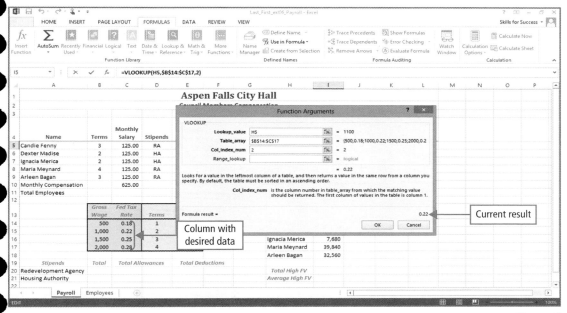

Figure 3

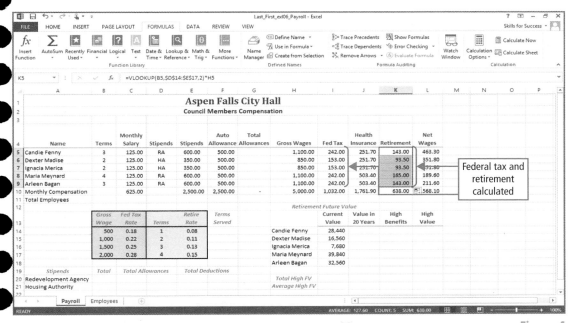

Figure 4

5. Compare your screen with **Figure** 3.

The VLOOKUP function searches the data table (B14:C17) for the value in cell H5. When it finds the value, it returns the value in the data table's second column (Col_index_num). The values in the first column of the table must be sorted in ascending order.

6. Click **OK**. In the **formula bar**, place the insertion point at the end of the formula, type *H5 and then click **Enter** ✔. Verify the value displayed is *242.00*—the result of gross wages times the tax rate for gross wages between 1,000 and 1,500. Copy the formula to the range **I6:I9**.

7. Select cell **K5**. In the **Function Library group**, click the **Lookup & Reference** button, and then click **VLOOKUP**. With the insertion point in the **Lookup_value** box, type B5 and then press ⎯Tab⎯.

8. Click the **Table_array Collapse Dialog** button 🔢, and then drag to select the range **D14:E17**. Press F4, and then click the **Expand Dialog box** button 📇. Press ⎯Tab⎯. In the **Col_index_num** box, type 2 and then click **OK**.

9. Ensure that cell **K5** is selected. In the formula bar, type *H5 at the end of the formula, and then click **Enter** ✔. Copy the formula to the range **K6:K9**, and then compare your screen with **Figure** 4.

10. **Save** 🖫 the workbook.

■ **You have completed Skill 3 of 10**

▶ **Logical functions** are used to create formulas that test whether a condition is true or false.

1. Select cell **K14**, and then on the **Formulas tab**, in the **Function Library group**, click the **Logical** button. In the displayed list, click **AND**, and then compare your screen with **Figure 1**.

    The **AND** function evaluates two conditions. When both conditions are true, the displayed value is TRUE.

2. In the **Function Arguments** dialog box, in the **Logical1** box, type J5>=255 Notice that this condition is FALSE.

3. Press Tab , and then in the **Logical2** box, type K5>125 Notice that this condition is TRUE. Compare your screen with **Figure 2**.

    Candie Fenny's health benefits deductions are less than $255 and her retirement benefits deductions are greater than $125. The benefits are being evaluated to see whether they meet both of the criteria. In this instance only one condition meets the criteria.

4. Click **OK**. In cell **K14**, notice that the displayed value is FALSE, indicating that Candie Fenny does not pay high benefits.

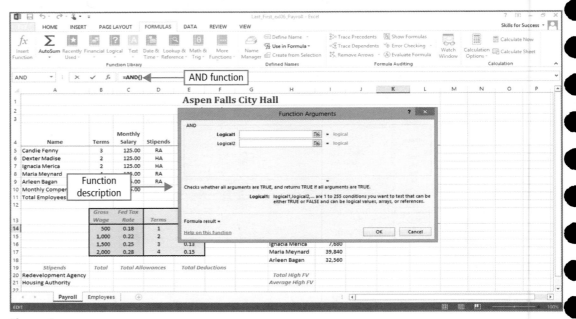

Figure 1

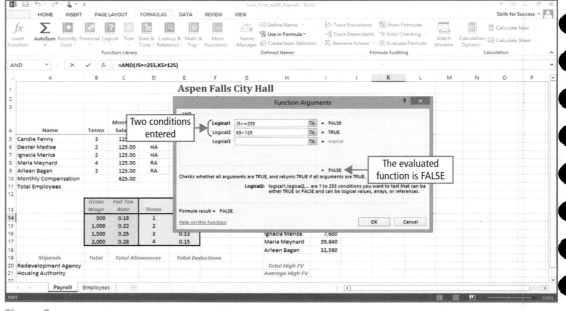

Figure 2

■ **Continue to the next page to complete the skill** ▶

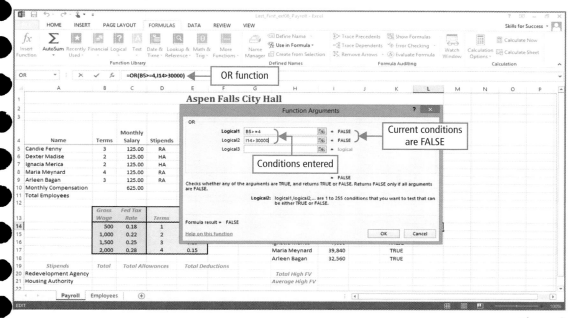

Figure 3

Common Excel Logical Functions	
Function	**Description**
AND	Displays TRUE when all of the conditions are true
IF	Performs a test to determine when one of the specified conditions is true
IFERROR	Displays a a message of your choice when there is an error in the formula. When there is not an error, it displays the result of the formula
NOT	Evaluates the opposite of a condition. For example, NOT<5 returns TRUE when the condition is not less than five
OR	Displays TRUE if any one of the conditions is TRUE

Figure 4

5. **AutoFill** the function in **K14** down through **K18**.

   The values in K15:K16 are also FALSE because Dexter Madise and Ignacia Merca have low retirement and health insurance deductions. Maria Meynard and Arleen Bagan both have retirement deductions greater than $125 and health insurance deductions greater than $255, so the values returned are TRUE.

6. Select cell **L14**, and then in the **Function Library group**, click the **Logical** button. In the displayed list, click **OR**.

   The **OR** function evaluates two conditions. If one condition is true, the displayed value is TRUE.

7. In the **Function Arguments** dialog box, in the **Logical1** box, type B5>=4 Notice that this condition returns FALSE.

8. Press Tab, and then in the **Logical2** box, type I14>30000 Notice that this condition also returns FALSE. Compare your screen with **Figure 3**.

9. Click **OK**. **AutoFill** the function in **L14** down through **L18**.

   The values in L14:L16 are FALSE because they don't meet either of the criteria; however, the values in L17:L18 are TRUE, even though the terms for Arleen Bagan do not meet those specified. Logical functions can be combined with each other or with many other functions to create a formula that is carefully designed to display the required information. Logical functions are summarized in **Figure 4**.

10. **Save** 🖫 the workbook.

■ **You have completed Skill 4 of 10**

▶ The **COUNTA** function is used to count the number of cells containing specified values. When no values are specified, the number of cells in a range that are not blank are counted.

▶ The **COUNTIF** function is used to count the number of cells in a range that meet a specified condition. The condition might be a number, an expression, or text. When using COUNTIF, you need to specify the criterion that determines which cells in a range should be counted.

1. Select cell **B11**. On the **Formulas tab**, in the **Function Library group**, click **More Functions**. In the list, point to **Statistical**, and then click **COUNTA**. Compare your screen with Figure 1.

> COUNTA is an example of a *statistical function*—it is used to describe a collection of data such as totals, counts, and averages.

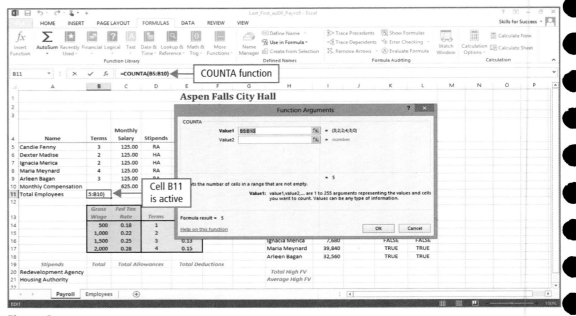

Figure 1

2. In the **Function Arguments** dialog box, place the insertion point in the **Value1** box, and replace the existing text with A5:A9 Compare your screen with Figure 2, and then click **OK**.

3. Select cell **F14**. In the **Function Library group**, click the **More Functions** button, point to **Statistical**, and then click **COUNTIF**.

■ Continue to the next page to complete the skill ➡

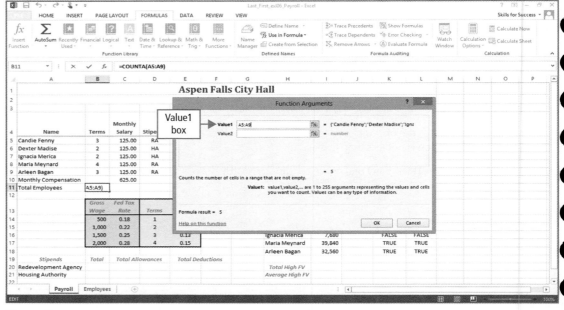

Figure 2

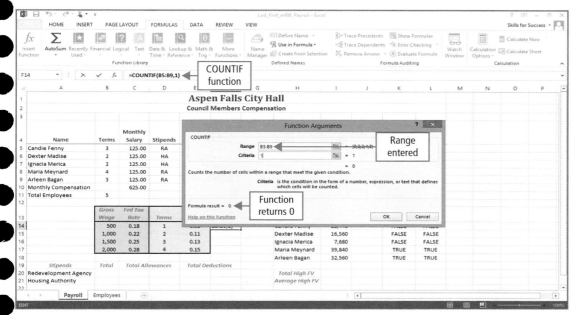

Figure 3

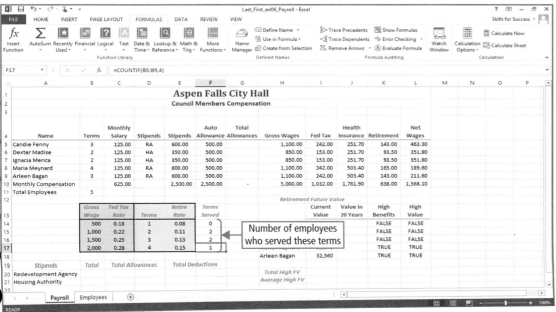

Figure 4

4. In the **Function Arguments** dialog box, place the insertion point in the **Range** box, if necessary, drag to select the range **B5:B9**, and then press ⟨Tab⟩.

5. In the **Criteria** box, type 1 Compare your screen with Figure 3, and then click **OK**.

Here, the COUNTIF function is used to count the number of cells with the value *1* in the range B5:B9. It returns the result of zero (0), which is displayed in the Function Arguments dialog box as a preview.

6. Select cell **F15**. In the **Function Library group**, click the **Recently Used** button, and then click **COUNTIF**. With the insertion point in the **Range** box, drag to select the range **B5:B9**, and then press ⟨Tab⟩. In the **Criteria** box, type 2 and then click **OK**.

7. In **F16**, repeat the technique just practiced to insert a function that counts the number of times the value **3** is in the range **B5:B9**.

8. Select cell **F17**, repeat the technique just practiced to insert a function that counts the number of times the value **4** is in the range **B5:B9**. Compare your screen with Figure 4.

9. Save 💾 the workbook.

■ **You have completed Skill 5 of 10**

▶ The **what-if analysis** is a set of tools that change the values in cells to show how those changes affect the outcome of other formulas on the worksheet.

▶ In a what-if analysis, each set of assumptions is called a **scenario**, which is a set of values that Excel can save and automatically substitute in cells.

▶ You can use Scenario Manager to save different groups of assumptions, and then switch to those scenarios to view the results.

---

1. Select the range **E14:E17**. On the **Data tab**, in the **Data Tools group**, click the **What-If Analysis** button, and then click **Scenario Manager**. If necessary, move the **Add Scenario** dialog box to the right to see the data in **E14:E17**.

    Before creating a scenario, you should select the cells that will change. Here, the Retire Rate values will be amended to show how the changes will affect the payroll.

2. In the **Scenario Manager** dialog box, click **Add**. Compare your screen with **Figure 1**.

3. In the **Add Scenario** dialog box, in the **Scenario name** box, type Reduced Contributions and then press Tab .

4. In the **Changing cells** box, verify that **E14:E17** is displayed, and then press Tab . Compare your screen with **Figure 2**.

    Because the range E14:E17 was selected when Scenario Manager was opened, the Changing cells box displays that range.

■ **Continue to the next page to complete the skill** ▶

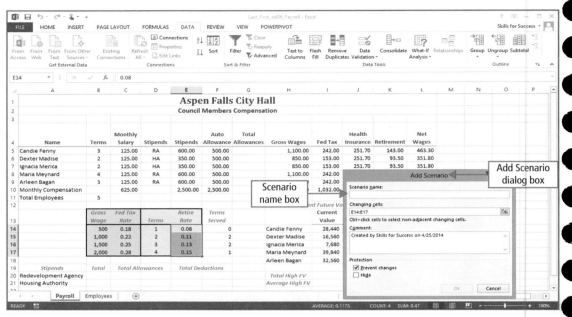

Figure 1

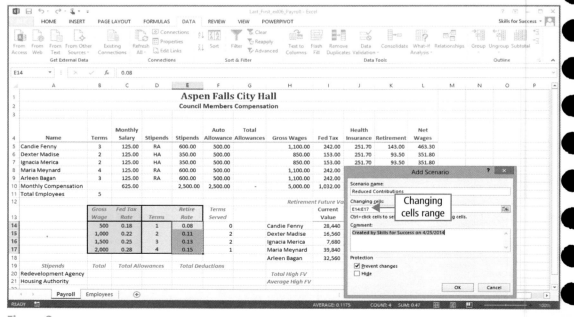

Figure 2

Figure 3

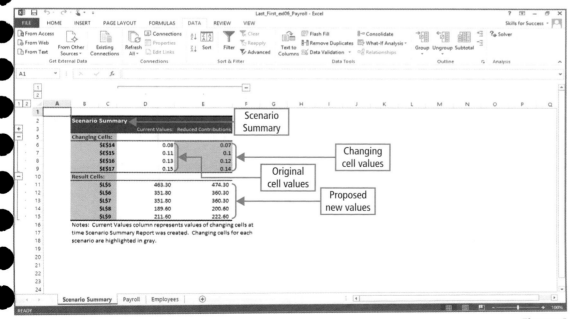

Figure 4

5. In the **Comment** box, replace the existing text with Analyzes retirement rate reductions for council members

   A comment helps to recall the scenario assumptions and purpose.

6. Click **OK** to open the **Scenario Values** dialog box, and then compare your screen with Figure 3.

   The Scenario Values dialog box displays the current values in the range E14:E17. These values will be replaced with scenario values.

7. In the **Scenario Values** dialog box, in the box for **$E$14**, change the value to .07 Press Tab, and change the value for **$E$15** to .10 Press Tab, and then change the value for **$E$16** to .12 In the **$E$17** box, change the value to .14 Click **OK**.

   Assuming these new values, final wages for each week can be calculated and presented as a proposal.

8. In the **Scenario Manager** dialog box, click **Summary**. In the **Scenario Summary** dialog box, in the **Result cells** box, type L5:L9 Click **OK**.

9. If necessary, display the **Scenario Summary** worksheet, and then compare your screen with Figure 4.

   The Scenario Summary worksheet displays the original and the Reduced Contributions scenario values. In this scenario, some net wages increased while others decreased.

10. Display the **Payroll** worksheet. Notice that none of the values in the range **E14:E17** changed on the original worksheet.

11. **Save** 🖫 the workbook.

■ **You have completed Skill 6 of 10**

▶ The ***future value*** of an asset, such as an investment or a home, is its value at the end of a period of time.

▶ The future value of an asset can be calculated when constant payments are made over time and the interest rate remains fixed.

1. On the **Payroll** worksheet, select cell **J14**.

2. On the **Formulas tab**, in the **Function Library group**, click the **Financial** button. If necessary, scroll down the displayed list, and click **FV**. Compare your screen with **Figure 1**.

The FV function requires three arguments: the interest rate for each payment, the total number of payments, and the payment amount. When calculating the future value of an investment, the present value of the investment can also be entered here. The Type argument also is optional. It is either 0 or 1; if omitted, it is assumed to be 0. This indicates payments are made at the end of the period.

3. In the displayed **Function Arguments** dialog box, in the **Rate** box, type 4.8%/12 and then press Tab. Compare your screen with **Figure 2**.

Here, the annual interest rate of 4.8% is divided by 12 to calculate the interest rate for each monthly payment.

4. In the **Nper** box, type 12*20 and then press Tab to move to the Pmt box.

The monthly payments to the Council Members' Retirement account will be made for 20 years. The total number of payments—Nper—equals 12 multiplied by 20.

■ **Continue to the next page to complete the skill**

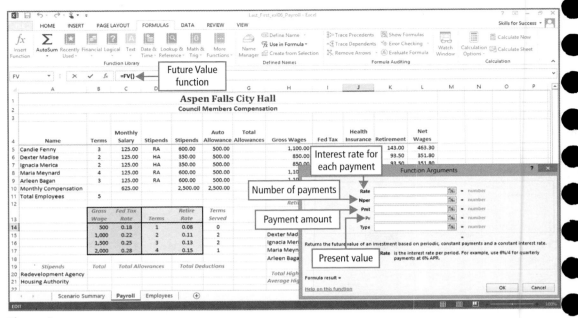

Figure 1

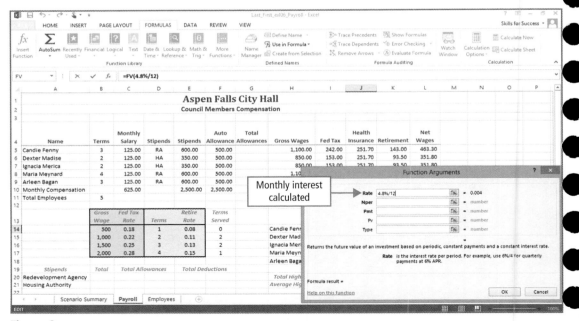

Figure 2

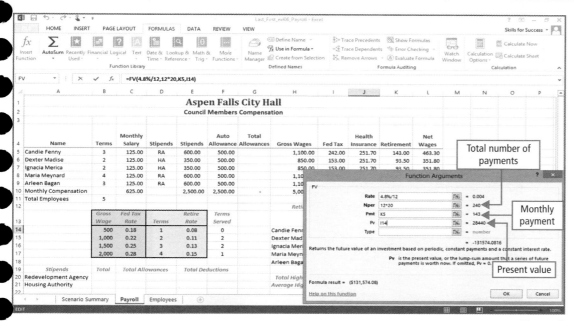

Figure 3

Common Financial Functions	
Function	**Description**
FV	The value of an investment or asset at some point in the future
NPER	The total number of payments made over the term of a loan or the total number of contributions made to an investment
PV	The value of an investment or a loan at the beginning of its term
PMT	The amount of money being paid to reduce a loan value or increase the value of an asset
RATE	The interest earned by an investment or the interest paid for a loan

Figure 4

5. In the **Pmt** box, type K5 and then press Tab to move to the PV box.

6. In the **PV** box, type I14 and then compare your screen with **Figure 3**.

   The present value of this investment is the current value that is in cell I14—Candie Fenny's retirement account.

7. Click **OK** to close the dialog box. AutoFit **column J**.

8. With cell **J14** selected, place the insertion point in the **formula bar** between the equal sign (=) and **FV**. Type - (minus sign), move the insertion point to the end of the formula, and then press Enter.

   In financial formulas, payments are typically represented as negative numbers. Placing a negative sign before the formula converts the payments and future values into positive numbers.

9. **AutoFill** the function in **J14** down through **J18**.

   Common financial functions are summarized in **Figure 4**.

10. **Save** 🖫 the workbook.

■ **You have completed Skill 7 of 10**

▶ An **array** is a collection of data typically arranged in multiple columns and rows. Most workbooks arrange data in arrays.

▶ An **array formula** can perform calculations across multiple items in an array. For example, you can use an array formula to calculate the sum of the values in one column multiplied by the sum of the values in another column.

1. If necessary, select the **Payroll** worksheet, and then select the range **G5:G9**.

   Because array formulas are applied to a range of cells, you should first select the range in which the array formula will be inserted.

2. Type = to begin the function. Type E5:E9 then type + and then type F5:F9 Press and hold Ctrl and Shift, and then press Enter. Compare your screen with Figure 1.

   When you enter a formula using the Ctrl + Shift + Enter keyboard shortcut, the formula is enclosed with braces ({ and }) to signify that it is an array formula. Here, the results of the array formula are the same as adding the values in E5:E9 and F5:F9. However, with an array formula, the formula is the same in every row. In this manner, array formulas provide greater consistency than using AutoFill to write separate formulas.

3. Select cell **D20**. Type an = to begin the sum function, and then type the word sum followed by a left parenthesis: (Compare your screen with Figure 2.

■ Continue to the next page to complete the skill

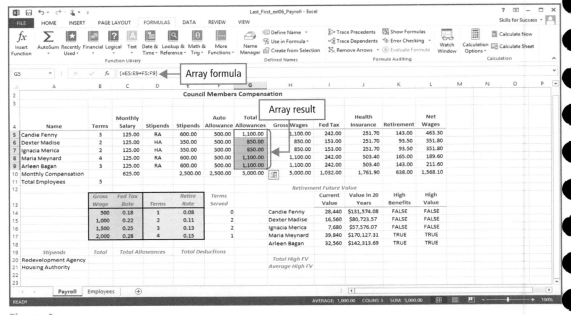

Figure 1

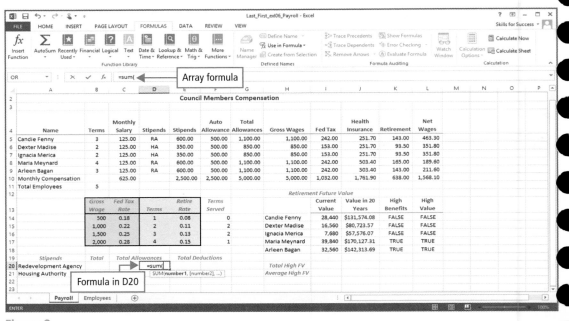

Figure 2

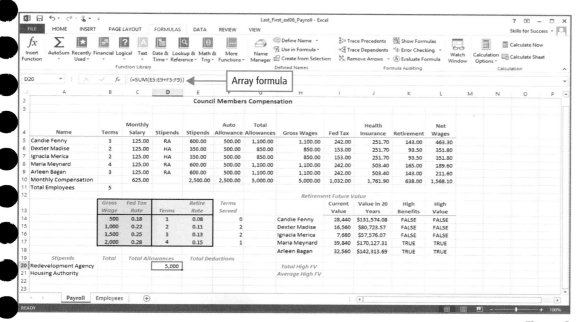

Array formula

Figure 3

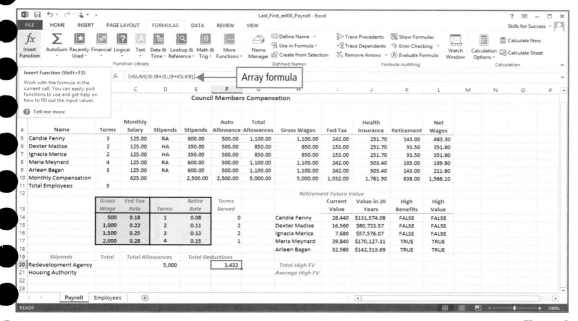

Array formula

Figure 4

4. Select the range **E5:E9**, and then type +
Select the range **F5:F9**, and then type the
right parenthesis:)

5. Press and hold the Ctrl and Shift keys,
and then press Enter. Compare your
screen with **Figure 3**.

In D20, the formula {=SUM(E5:E9+F5:F9)}
appears in the formula bar, and represents
the total number of allowances for the
month.

6. Select the cell **F20**. Type = to begin the
sum function, and then type the word
sum followed by a left parenthesis: (

7. Select the range **I5:I9**, and then type +
Select the range **J5:J9**, and then type +

8. Select the range **K5:K9**, and then type the
right parenthesis:)

9. Press and hold the Ctrl and Shift keys,
and then press Enter. Compare your
screen with **Figure 4**.

In F20, the formula {=SUM(I5:I9+J5:J9
+K5:K9)} appears in the formula bar, and
represents the total number of deductions
for the month.

10. **Save** 🖫 the workbook.

■ **You have completed Skill 8 of 10**

▶ The **SUMIF** function adds the cells in a range that meet a specified condition.

▶ The **SUMIFS** function adds the cells in a range that meet multiple conditions.

1. On the **Payroll** worksheet, select cell **B20**.

2. On the **Formulas tab**, in the **Function Library group**, click the **Math & Trig** button. Scroll down the displayed list, and then click **SUMIF**. Compare your screen with **Figure 1**.

3. In the **Function Arguments** dialog box, with the insertion point in the **Range** box, type D5:D9 and then press ⎀Tab⎀.

   In the SUMIF function, the Range argument defines the range to be tested by the criteria. Here, the Range lists the stipends to be evaluated.

4. In the **Criteria** box, type RA and then press ⎀Tab⎀.

   Here, only the cells where the job category equals RA will be added.

5. In the **Sum_range** box, type E5:E9 and then compare your screen with **Figure 2**. Click **OK**.

6. Select cell **B21**. Repeat the steps you just learned to create a **SUMIF** function applying the same **Range** and **Sum_range**, but replacing the **Criteria** with HA

7. Select cell **I20**. On the **Formulas tab**, in the **Function Library group**, click the **Math & Trig** button. Scroll down the displayed list, and then click **SUMIFS**.

■ Continue to the next page to complete the skill ▶

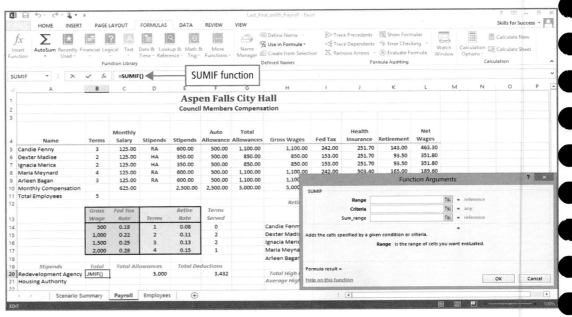

Figure 1

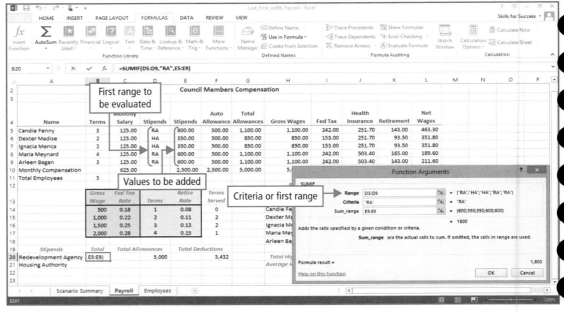

Figure 2

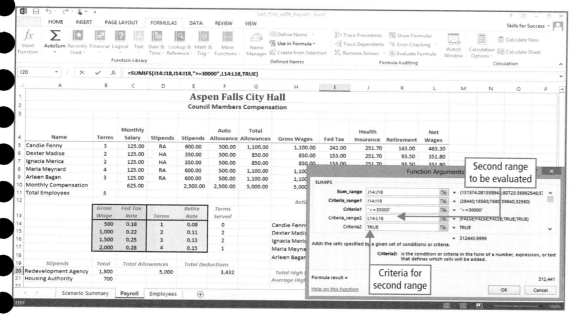

Figure 3

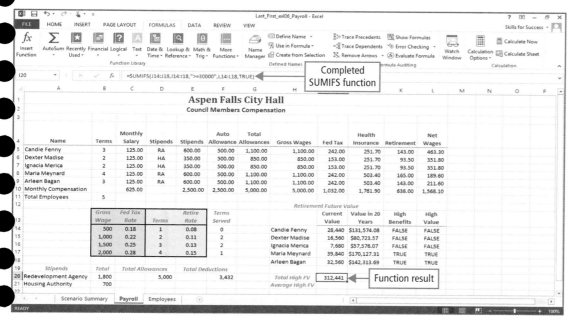

Figure 4

8. In the **Function Arguments** dialog box, with the insertion point in the **Sum_range** box, type J14:J18 and then press Tab .

   In the SUMIFS function, the Sum_range argument contains the values to be added. In this exercise, the Sum_range argument lists Future Retirement Value.

9. In the **Criteria_range1** box, type I14:I18 and then press Tab .

   Criteria_range1 is the range that will be evaluated for the specified condition.

10. In the **Criteria1** box, type >=30000 and then press Tab .

    Criteria1 is a condition or criteria in the form of a number, an expression, or text that defines which cells will be added.

11. In the **Criteria_range2** box, type L14:L18 and then press Tab .

    Criteria_range2 is the range that will be evaluated for the second criteria.

12. In the **Criteria2** box, type TRUE Compare your screen with **Figure 3**.

    Criteria2 is a condition or criteria in the form of a number, an expression, or text that defines which cells will be added for the second criteria.

13. Click **OK**, and then notice the value of cell **I20** is *312,441*, which is the sum of **J17:J18**. Compare your screen with **Figure 4**.

14. **Save** 🖫 the workbook.

■ **You have completed Skill 9 of 10**

▶ The ***AVERAGEIFS*** function is used to calculate the average of cells specified by a given set of conditions or criteria.

1. On the **Payroll** worksheet, select cell **I21**.

2. On the **Formulas tab**, in the **Function Library group**, click **More Functions**. In the list, point to **Statistical**, and then click **AVERAGEIFS**. Compare your screen with Figure 1.

3. In the **Function Arguments** dialog box, with the insertion point in the **Average_ range** box, type J14:J18 and then press Tab.

   In the AVERAGEIFS function, the Average_ range argument contains the values to be averaged.

4. In the **Criteria_range1** box, type I14:I18 and then press Tab.

   Criteria_range1 is the range that will be evaluated for the specified condition.

5. In the **Criteria1** box, type >=20000 and then press Tab. Compare your screen with Figure 2.

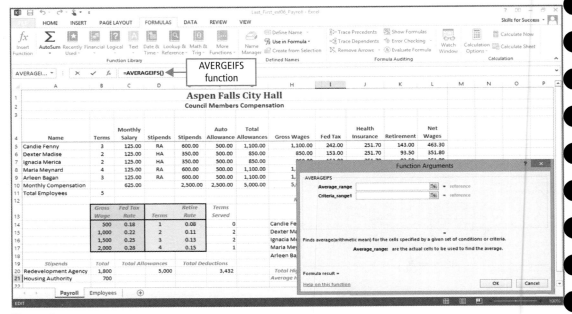

Figure 1

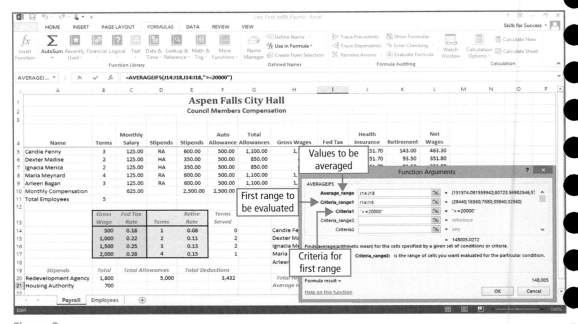

Figure 2

■ Continue to the next page to complete the skill ▶

6. In the **Criteria_range2** box, type L14:L18 and then press Tab.

   Criteria_range2 is the range that will be evaluated for the second criteria.

7. In the **Criteria2** box, type TRUE Compare your screen with **Figure 3**.

8. Click **OK**, and then notice that the value of cell **I21** is *156,220*, which is the average of **J17:J18**. Compare your screen with **Figure 4**.

9. Select cell **A1**, **Save** 🖫 the workbook, and then **Close** ✕ Excel.

10. Submit the workbook as directed by your instructor.

 DONE! You have completed Skill 10 of 10, and your workbook is complete!

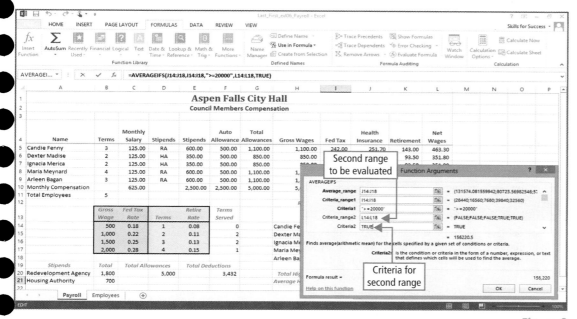

Figure 3

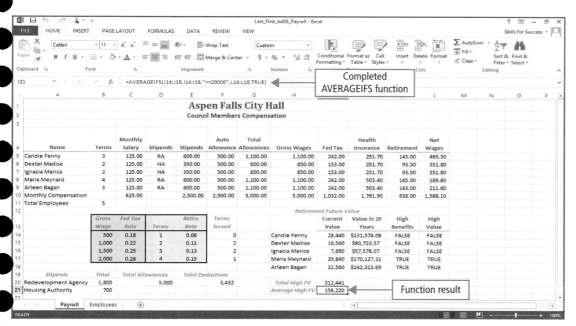

Figure 4

The following More Skills are located at **www.pearsonhighered.com/skills**

More Skills Use Web Functions

With Web Services you can exchange data between different programs and different platforms. Your program can publish its function or message to the rest of the world.

In More Skills 11, you will use the ENCODEURL function to link postal codes as parameters to a web query, and then use FILTERXML functions to provide city, state, and weather data.

To begin, open your web browser, navigate to www.pearsonhighered.com/skills, locate the name of your textbook, and then follow the instructions on the website.

More Skills Use Solver

The Solver tool allows you to change multiple values to achieve a desired goal. Solver can also find a solution within limitations that you set—such as a maximum value a cell can be changed to. Before using Solver, you must install it as an Excel add-in.

In More Skills 12, you will install the Solver add-in, and then use Solver to determine the rate to change to reach a desired retirement savings amount.

To begin, open your web browser, navigate to www.pearsonhighered.com/skills, locate the name of your textbook, and then follow the instructions on the website.

More Skills Delete Duplicate Records

Excel workbooks that contain large amounts of tabular data might have rows with duplicate values. Duplicated rows can cause errors that lead to inaccurate information. You can search for and remove duplicates using the Remove Duplicates tool.

In More Skills 13, you will open a workbook with a number of duplicate records. You will use the Remove Duplicates tool to remove the duplicate records.

To begin, open your web browser, navigate to www.pearsonhighered.com/skills, locate the name of your textbook, and then follow the instructions on the website.

More Skills Use External Data Links to Update Data

You can automatically connect to external databases on the Internet to update workbook data. You can then use the data as if it had been entered directly into the workbook.

In More Skills 14, you will open a workbook and create a link to a web-based database of stock prices. You will then use the

values obtained from the database to calculate the current value of an investment.

To begin, open your web browser, navigate to www.pearsonhighered.com/skills, locate the name of your textbook, and then follow the instructions on the website.

Please note that there are no additional projects to accompany the More Skills Projects, and they are not covered in End-of-Chapter projects.

The following table summarizes the **SKILLS AND PROCEDURES** covered in this chapter.

Skills Number	Task	Step
1	Join text	Formulas tab → Function Library group → Text → CONCATENATE
1	Convert text to title case	Formulas tab → Function Library group → Text → PROPER
3	Calculate totals based on criteria	Formulas tab → Function Library group → Math & Trig → SUMIFS
4	Use lookup functions	Formulas tab → Function Library group → Lookup & Reference → VLOOKUP
4	Use logical function AND	Formulas tab → Function Library group → Logical → AND
4	Use logical function OR	Formulas tab → Function Library group → Logical → OR
5	Insert COUNTIF functions	Formulas tab → Function Library group → More Functions → Statistical → COUNTIF
6	Create and save scenarios	Data tab → Data Tools group → What-If Analysis → Scenario Manager → Add → Enter Name
7	Calculate future value	Formulas tab → Function Library group → Financial → FV → Enter Rate, Nper, Pmt, and Present Value
8	Create array formulas	Press [Ctrl] + [Shift] + [Enter] after writing the desired formula
9	Calculate totals based on criteria	Formulas tab → Function Library group → Math & Trig → SUMIF Formulas tab → Function Library group → Math & Trig → SUMIFS
10	Calculate averages based on criteria	Formulas tab → Function Library group → More Functions → Statistical → AVERAGEIFS

Key Terms

Online Help Skills

1. Start **Excel 2013**, and then in the upper-right corner of the Excel window, click the **Help** button [?].

2. In the **Excel Help** window **Search help** box, type what-if analysis and then press [Enter].

3. Scroll down, and click **Use Goal Seek to find a result by adjusting an input value**. Compare your screen with Figure 1.

Figure 1

4. Read the section to answer the following question: When should you use the Goal Seek tool, and when should you use the Solver?

Matching

Match each term in the second column with its correct definition in the first column by writing the letter of the term on the blank line in front of the correct definition.

___ **1.** A function that returns TRUE if *any* argument is true and returns FALSE if *both* arguments are false.

___ **2.** A function that counts the number of specified cells in a range.

___ **3.** A function placed inside another function.

___ **4.** A function that is used to find values which are stored in a table in a spreadsheet.

___ **5.** A function that displays TRUE only when both of the conditions are true.

___ **6.** A function that averages values based on multiple conditions.

___ **7.** A function that describes a collection of data; for example, COUNTA and COUNTIF.

___ **8.** A function that returns and displays either TRUE or FALSE.

___ **9.** A set of saved assumptions that can be used to view the results if those assumed values were accepted.

___ **10.** The function used to calculate the value of an investment or asset at some point in the future.

A AND

B AVERAGEIFS

C COUNTA

D FV

E Logical function

F Lookup function

G Nested function

H OR

I Scenario

J Statistical function

Multiple Choice

Choose the correct answer.

1. This option is used to change the formatting or underlying values of cells as they are pasted.
   A. Paste
   B. Paste Special
   C. Copy

2. This function is used to convert text to title case.
   A. CONCATENATE
   B. PROPER
   C. SUBSTITUTE

3. This function is used to count the number of cells in a range that meet a certain criteria.
   A. COUNTA
   B. SUM
   C. COUNTIF

4. This tool is used to change cells to see how those changes affect a desired outcome.
   A. Goal Seek analysis
   B. What-if analysis
   C. Data table

5. This is the correct format to calculate a monthly interest rate.
   A. rate/12
   B. rate/6
   C. rate/18

6. In Future Value functions, enter 0 or 1 in this box to indicate if payments are due at the beginning or end of the period.
   A. Type
   B. PV
   C. Rate

7. This function is used to join text from separate cells and columns.
   A. LINK
   B. CONCATENATE
   C. JOIN

8. The amount of money being paid to reduce a loan value or increase the value of an asset.
   A. PV
   B. PMT
   C. NPER

9. This error indicates that the referenced cell does not contain any data.
   A. #VALUE
   B. #N/A
   C. #REF

10. This type of formula performs calculations across multiple ranges.
    A. COUNTIF
    B. Array
    C. Scenario

Topics for Discussion

1. When inputting assumed values in a what-if analysis, you can copy and paste the results into separate worksheets or save them as scenarios using Scenario Manager. Which method do you think would be most effective, and why?

2. In Skill 8, you used an array formula. The same results could have been obtained by entering a regular formula and filling it down the column. Compare the two methods, and then discuss the advantages and disadvantages of each method.

Skills Review

To complete this project, you will need the following file:

- exl06_SRTaxes

You will save your file as:

- Last_First_exl06_SRTaxes

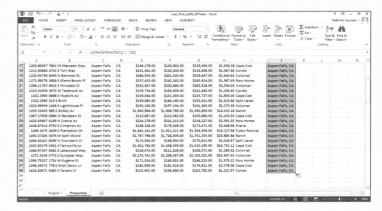

Figure 1

1. Start **Excel 2013**, and open the file **exl06_SRTaxes**. Save the workbook in your chapter folder as Last_First_exl06_SRTaxes

2. Display the **Properties** worksheet. Select cell **C2**. On the **Formulas tab**, in the **Function Library group**, click the **Text** button, and then click **PROPER**. In the **Text** box, type ASPEN FALLS and then click **OK**. **Copy** the formula in **C2** down through **C38**.

3. Select cell **J2**. On the **Formulas tab**, in the **Function Library group**, click the **Text** button, and then click **CONCATENATE**. In the **Text1** box, type C2 In the **Text2** box, add a comma, then a space. In the **Text3** box, type D2 and then click **OK**. AutoFit **column J**, and then **copy** the formula down through cell **J38**. Compare your screen with **Figure 1**.

4. Copy the range **J2:J15**. Display the **Region 1** worksheet, and then select cell **D3**. Display the **Home tab**. In the **Clipboard group**, click the **Paste arrow**, and then under **Paste Values**, click the first option, **Values (V)**.

5. Select cell **F3**. On the **Formulas tab**, in the **Function Library group**, click **Lookup & Reference**, and then click **VLOOKUP**. In the **Lookup_value** box, type E3 In the **Table_array** box, type $C$19:$D$24 In the **Col_index_num** box, type 2 and then click **OK**. Click in the **formula bar**, and then at the end of the formula type *E3 Press [Enter], and then copy the formula down through **F16**. Compare your screen with **Figure 2**.

Figure 2

■ **Continue to the next page to complete this Skills Review** ▶

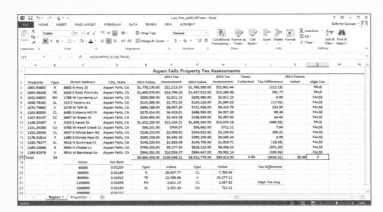

Figure 3

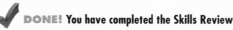

Figure 4

6. Select cell **H3**. Insert a **VLOOKUP** function. In the **Lookup_value** box, type G3 In the **Table_array** box, type $C$19:$D$24 In the **Col_index_num** box, type 2 and then click **OK**. In the **formula bar**, at the end of the formula type *G3 Press ⎡Enter⎤, and then copy the formula down through **H16**.

7. Click cell **L3**. In the **Function Library group**, click **Logical**, and then click **AND**. In the **Logical1** box, type F3>10000 In the **Logical2** box, type H3>10000 Click **OK**.

8. Fill down the formula in cell **L3** through cell **L16**.

9. Select cell **B17**. In the **Function Library group**, click **More Functions**, point to **Statistical**, and then click **COUNTA**. Ensure **column B** is visible. With the insertion point in the **Value1** box, drag to select the range **B3:B16**, and then click **OK**.

10. Select cell **L17**. In the **Function Library group**, click **More Functions**, point to **Statistical**, and then scroll down the list and click **COUNTIF**. With the insertion point in the **Range** box, drag to select the range **L3:L16**, and then press ⎡Tab⎤. In the **Criteria** box, type TRUE and then click **OK**. Compare your screen with Figure 3.

11. Select cell **K3**. In the **Function Library group**, click **Financial**, and then click **FV**. In the **Rate** box, type .015 In the **Nper** box, type 12*.5 In the **Pmt** box, type 0 In the **Pv** box, type H3 and then click **OK**. With cell **K3** selected, in the **formula bar** place the insertion point between the equals sign (=) and **FV**, and then type - (minus sign) and press ⎡Enter⎤. Copy the formula down through **K16**.

12. Select cell **I3**. Type = Select the range **F3:F16**, and then type + Select the range **H3:H16**, press and hold the ⎡Ctrl⎤ and ⎡Shift⎤ keys, and then press ⎡Enter⎤. Select cell **I3** and copy the formula down through cell **I16**.

13. Select cell **J20**. Type =sum followed by a left parenthesis: (Select the range **J3:J16**, followed by a right parenthesis:) Press and hold the ⎡Ctrl⎤ and ⎡Shift⎤ keys, and then press ⎡Enter⎤.

14. Select cell **J23**. On the **Formulas tab**, in the **Function Library group**, click **More Functions**. In the list, point to **Statistical**, and then click **AVERAGEIFS**.

15. In the **Average_range** box, type I3:I16 In the **Criteria_range1** box, type I3:I16 In the **Criteria1** box, type >=30000 In the **Criteria_range2** box, type L3:L16 In the **Criteria2** box, type TRUE and then click **OK**. Compare your screen with Figure 4.

16. **Save** the workbook, and then submit it as directed by your instructor.

✓ **DONE! You have completed the Skills Review**

Skills Assessment 1

To complete this project, you will need the following file:

- exl06_SA1Bonds

You will save your file as:

- Last_First_exl06_SA1Bonds

Aspen Falls Finance Department
Bond Investments Report

		Bonds Sold							
Year	Invested Amount	Interest Rate	Term	FV	Purpose	Investor ID	Investor Name	Lucrative
2012	2,150,000	3.25%	12	$ 3,155,871	Sewer	3	Millon Financial	TRUE
2013	3,200,000	4.00%	10	$ 4,736,782	Roads	8	Cita Bank	TRUE
2014	1,450,000	4.35%	15	$ 2,746,343	Airport	16	Walls Savings	FALSE
2015	5,300,000	2.80%	12	$ 7,382,326	Roads	8	Cita Bank	TRUE
2016	4,500,000	3.65%	18	$ 8,579,461	Sewer	11	Feni Investments	FALSE
Total	16,600,000			$ 26,600,783		5		

	Number	Value			Investors		
Total Road Bonds	2	$ 12,119,108		3	millon	financial	Millon Financial
Total Sewer Bonds	2	$ 11,735,332		8	cita	bank	Cita Bank
Total Airport Bonds	1	$ 2,746,343		11	feni	investments	Feni Investments
Value After Investment		$ 10,000,783		16	walls	savings	Walls Savings

Average FV of Bonds	$ 5,320,157

1. Start **Excel 2013**, and then open the file **exl06_SA1Bonds**. Save the workbook in your chapter folder as Last_ First_exl06_SA1Bonds

2. In cell **E6**, enter a **Future Value (FV)** function with the following arguments: For the **Rate** enter C6 and for **Nper** enter D6 The **Pmt** should be left blank, and for the **PV** enter -B6 Copy the function down through cell **E10**.

3. In cell **I14**, insert the **CONCATENATE** function to combine the following: **G14**, a space character, and then **H14**. In the function, nest the **PROPER** function so that title case is applied to the text. Copy the function down through cell **I17**, and then AutoFit **column I**.

4. In cell **H6**, insert the **VLOOKUP** function using G6 for the **Lookup_value**, $F$14:$I$17 for the **Table_array**, and 4 for the **Col_ index_num**. Copy the function down through cell **H10**. AutoFit **column H**.

5. In **B14**, insert a function that counts the number of times the word *Roads* displays in **F6:F10**. Use the same function in **B15:B16**, substituting the appropriate **Criteria**.

6. In cell **C14**, insert the **SUMIF** function using $F$6:$F$10 as the **Range**, Roads as the **Criteria**, and $E$6:$E$10 as the **Sum_range**. Use the same function in the range **C15:C16**, substituting the appropriate **Criteria**.

7. In cell **C17**, insert an **Array** formula using the **FV** and the Invested Amount to calculate the Value After Investment.

8. In cell **F11**, insert the **COUNTA** function to count the number of bond investments.

9. From the **Data tab**, start the **What-If Analysis Scenario Manager**. Add a scenario named Investments Set the range **C6:C10** as the **Changing cells**, and then click **OK**. In the **Scenario Values** dialog boxes, replace the current value in box 1 with .04 in box 2 with .045 in box 3 with .047 in box 4 with .03 and in box 5 with .038 Click **OK**. Click **Summary**; the **Result cells** should be **E11**, and then click **OK**.

Scenario Summary

	Current Values:	Investments
Changing Cells:		
$C$6	3.25%	4.00%
$C$7	4.00%	4.50%
$C$8	4.35%	4.70%
$C$9	2.80%	3.00%
$C$10	3.65%	3.80%
Result Cells:		
$E$11	$26,600,783	$27,661,782

Notes: Current Values column represents values of changing cells at time Scenario Summary Report was created. Changing cells for each scenario are highlighted in gray.

Figure 1

10. On the **Bonds** worksheet, in cell **I6**, insert the **Logical** function **AND** using C6<=0.04 as **Logical1** and D6<=15 as **Logical2**. Click **OK**. Copy the function down through cell **I10**.

11. In cell **C19**, insert the **AVERAGEIFS** function using $E$6:$E$10 as the **Average_range**, $E$6:$E$10 as the **Criteria_range1**, and then >=2000000 as the **Criteria1**. Use $D$6:$D$10 as the **Criteria_range2**, and then >=10 as the **Criteria2**. Click **OK**. Compare your screen with **Figure 1**.

12. **Save** the workbook, and then submit it as directed by your instructor.

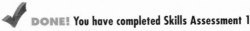 **DONE! You have completed Skills Assessment 1**

Skills Assessment 2

To complete this project, you will need the following file:

- exl06_SA2WaterDisputes

You will save your file as:

- Last_First_exl06_SA2WaterDisputes

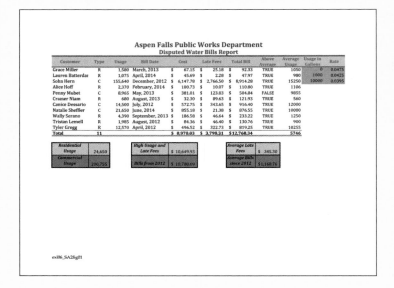

Aspen Falls Public Works Department
Disputed Water Bills Report

exl06_SA2fig01

1. Start **Excel 2013**, and then open the file **exl06_SA2WaterDisputes**. Save the workbook in your chapter folder as Last_First_exl06_SA2WaterDisputes

2. Display the **Customers** worksheet. Select cell **F2**. Using the **Formulas tab**, insert the **Text** function **CONCATENATE**. For **Text1** use D2 for **Text2** add a comma and then a space, and then for **Text3** use E2 Click **OK**. Add the **PROPER** function to the result. Copy the function in cell **F2** down through cell **F12**.

3. Copy the range **F2:F12**. Click the **Report** worksheet tab, and then select cell **D4**. Use the **Values (V)** option under **Paste Values** to paste the values.

4. Select cell **E4**. Insert a **VLOOKUP** function. For the arguments, use C4 for the **Lookup_value**, $J$4:$K$6 for the **Table_array**, and 2 for the **Col_index_num**. Click **OK**. At the end of the formula, type *C4 and then press Enter. Copy the function down through cell **E14**.

5. Select cell **E17**. Insert the **SUMIFS** function. Use G4:G14 as the **Sum_range**, C4:C14 as the **Criteria_range1**, >10000 as the **Criteria1**, F4:F14 as the **Criteria_range2**, and >300 as the **Criteria2**. Click **OK**.

6. Select cell **H17**. Insert the **AVERAGEIFS** function. Use F4:F14 as the **Average_range**, F4:F14 as the **Criteria_range1**, >0 as the **Criteria1**, G4:G14 as **Criteria_range2**, and then >0 as **Criteria2**. Click **OK**.

7. Select cell **H18**. Insert the **AVERAGEIFS** function. Use G4:G14 as the **Average_range**, G4:G14 as the **Criteria_range1**, >0 as the **Criteria1**, Customers!E2:E12 as the **Criteria_range2**, and then >=2012 as the **Criteria2**. Click **OK**.

8. Select cell **B15**. Insert the **COUNTA** function to calculate the number of disputed water bills. Compare your screen with Figure 1.

9. **Save** the workbook, and then submit it as directed by your instructor.

Customer ID	Type	Customer	Month	Year	Bill Date
C-1436	R	Grace Miller	MARCH	2013	March, 2013
C-1598	R	Lauren Batterdar	APRIL	2014	April, 2014
D-6983	C	Sohn Hern	DECEMBER	2012	December, 2012
F-7690	R	Alice Hoff	FEBRUARY	2014	February, 2014
V-3491	C	Penny Mubet	MAY	2013	May, 2013
H-3491	R	Cramer Niam	AUGUST	2013	August, 2013
G-4509	C	Canice Dessario	JULY	2012	July, 2012
V-1106	C	Natalie Sheffler	JUNE	2014	June, 2014
G-5609	R	Wally Serano	SEPTEMBER	2013	September, 2013
W-9087	R	Tristan Lemell	AUGUST	2012	August, 2012
Z-9723	R	Tyler Gregg	APRIL	2012	April, 2012

Figure 1

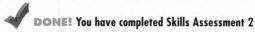

DONE! You have completed Skills Assessment 2

Visual Skills Check

To complete this project, you will need the following file:

- exl06_VSPermits

You will save your file as:

- Last_First_exl06_VSPermits

Start **Excel 2013**, and open the file **exl06_VSPermits**. Save the workbook in your chapter folder as Last_First_exl06_VSPermits In the range **B4:B12**, use the appropriate statistical function to determine the number of permits sold using the **Permit Data** worksheet, based on each project. In the range **C4:C12**, use the **SUMIFS** function to determine the fees per type of project greater than 0. In the range **D4:D12**, use the **AND** function to calculate if the 3rd Quarter met or exceeded the projected **Total Number of Permits** of **10** and projected **Fees per Permit** of **$2,000**. In **G5:I21**, use **SUMIFS** and the **Permit Data** worksheet to calculate the total fees collected each day of the month based on the criteria of **Month** and **Day**. In **J22** use an **Array** formula to calculate the total fees collected for the 3rd Quarter using the day data by month. Compare your screen with **Figure 1**. Save the workbook, and then submit it as directed by the instructor.

DONE! You have completed Visual Skills Check

Aspen Falls City Hall
Permits 3rd Quarter 2014

Permit Type	Total Number of Permits	Fees per Permit	Projected	Projects by Month/Day	July	August	September
Addition	14	$ 3,276.46	TRUE	Total	$ 5,376.42	$ 2,899.12	$ 4,664.66
Carport	3	$ 948.32	FALSE	1	1,144.76	296.01	-
Fence	15	$ 742.50	FALSE	2	-	-	1,045.48
Deck	3	$ 866.64	FALSE	6	1,049.67	346.50	648.61
Garage	3	$ 907.90	FALSE	8	-	-	526.21
Remodel	22	$ 2,732.20	TRUE	10	491.54	-	1,012.83
Roof	7	$ 1,539.85	FALSE	12	900.45	-	-
Sprinkler System	2	$ 372.00	FALSE	13	-	99.00	1,148.99
Windows	6	$ 1,554.33	FALSE	15	-	99.00	-
Total	75	$ 12,940.20		17	369.99	99.00	282.54
				19	408.67	302.00	-
				21	518.25	-	-
				23	-	550.52	-
				24	362.79	-	-
				26	-	116.00	-
				28	-	58.00	-
				29	130.30	-	-
				30	-	933.09	-
				Total			$ 12,940.20

Figure 1

Figure 1

Figure 2

My Skills

To complete this project, you will need the following file:

- exl06_MYSavings

You will save your file as:

- Last_First_exl06_MYSavings.

1. Start **Excel 2013**, and then open the file **exl06_MYSavings**. Save the workbook in your chapter folder as Last_First_exl06_ MYSavings

2. In the first cell replace *Student Name* with your first and last names.

3. In cell **C5**, create the future value of the savings account using a rate of 4%/12 the number of payments as 12 and a monthly payment of 100 The present value of the account is included in the worksheet. Edit the formula and enter a - (minus sign) between = and FV.

4. Copy the formula for each year and then determine the amount of interest earned each year, taking into account that you are depositing $100 each month, and then create the total ending balance of the account for each year.

5. Create a scenario using the **What-If Analysis** tool that will analyze the future value if the present value is $1000 and whose result is based on the total at the end of five years (using the **SUM** function).

6. On the **Savings FV** worksheet, in cell **C11**, create the future value of the savings account using a **Rate** of 3.5%/12 number of payments of 12 and a monthly payment of 200. Edit the formula and enter a - (minus sign) between = and FV. The present value of the account is included in the worksheet.

7. Copy the formula for each year and then determine the amount of interest earned each year taking into account that you are depositing $200 each month, and then create the total ending balance of the account for each year (using the **SUM** function).

8. Create a scenario using the **What-If Analysis** tool that will analyze the future value if the present value is $1000 and whose result is based on the total at the end of five years. Compare your completed worksheet with Figure 1.

9. Select the **Savings FV** worksheet tab, and then compare your completed worksheet with Figure 2.

10. **Save** the workbook, and then submit it as directed by your instructor.

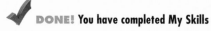

DONE! You have completed My Skills

Skills Challenge 1

To complete this project, you will need the following file:

- exl06_SC1Retirement

You will save your file as:

- Last_First_exl06_SC1Retirement

Start **Excel 2013**, and then open the file **exl06_SC1Retirement**. Save the workbook in your chapter folder as Last_First_exl06_SC1Retirement On the Symbols worksheet, use a function in the range D2:D11 that combines the text in the Symbol1 and Symbol2 columns to display a four-character symbol. Copy the range D2:D11, and paste only the values into the range F5:F14 of the Projections worksheet. On the Projections

worksheet, in the range E5:E14, calculate the future value of the investments in 20 years, assuming monthly payments are made every month and the return is fixed as specified in the worksheet. Save the workbook, and then submit it as directed by your instructor.

 DONE! You have completed Skills Challenge 1

Skills Challenge 2

To complete this project, you will need the following file:

- exl06_SC2Services

You will save your file as:

- Last_First_exl06_SC2Services

Start **Excel 2013**, and then open the file **exl06_SC2Services**. Save the workbook in your chapter folder as Last_First_exl06_SC2Services Using skills learned from this chapter, insert a formula in the range D4:D15 that calculates the increase/decrease in spending from 2013 to 2014. Use a formula practiced in the chapter to enter the Total Spending for 2013

and 2014 in C17. In D17, insert a formula that calculates the total increase/decrease using 2013 and 2014 actual data. Insert a statistical function in A16 to count the number of services. Save the workbook, and then submit it as directed by your instructor.

 DONE! You have completed Skills Challenge 2

CHAPTER 7

Work with Data and Audit Formulas

▶ You can import data into Excel from a variety of file formats and then analyze and manipulate that data.

▶ When errors occur in a formula, Excel provides tools to locate and fix the source of the error.

▶ You can sort and filter data to make it easier to manipulate and analyze.

▶ You can easily add subtotals to Excel worksheets.

▶ You can use sorting and conditional formatting to customize data as a table.

Apops/Fotolia

Aspen Falls City Hall

In this chapter, you will support Leah Kim, the Aspen Falls Parks and Recreation Director. You will assist her with editing an existing workbook and using Excel functions and data analysis tools to calculate and analyze financial loss for personal enrichment classes offered through the Recreation Division. This workbook will assist Leah in evaluating class participation, as well as break-even points for classes and future profits.

Businesses and organizations often use Excel workbooks for data analysis. Two different types of tables used to analyze data are Excel tables and data tables. Excel tables are created to more easily manage and analyze a range of data using formatting, sorting, filtering, totals, and formulas. Data tables analyze a range of cells and show how changing one or two variables in formulas can affect the formula results. Using subtotal as part of a table provides a sum of filtered and summarized data. Custom filtering is used to filter data in a column based on more than one condition. Tools are also available to identify, analyze, and repair formula errors.

In this project you will import data from a text file and use that data to incorporate functions and data analysis tools to analyze class profit and losses. You will sort data based on conditions, and summarize data using subtotals. You will use Excel tools to evaluate formulas and determine if there are formula errors. Using analysis tools you will revise values in existing formulas. You will evaluate data using cell ranges to determine possible scenarios based on changes in values and convert the ranges to allow filtering based on multiple conditions. Finally, you will create custom table formatting to enhance the readability of the data.

Time to complete all 10 skills – 60 to 90 minutes

Student data files needed for this chapter:

exl07_Classes
exl07_ClassesData

You will save your workbooks as:

Last_First_exl07_Classes
Last_First_exl07_ClassesSnip1
Last_First_exl07_ClassesSnip2

Outcome

Using the skills listed in this chapter, you will be able to create worksheets like these:

SKILLS

MyITLab®
Skills 1-10 Training

At the end of this chapter, you will be able to:

Skill 1 Import Data from Text Files
Skill 2 Apply Advanced AutoFilters
Skill 3 Sort Data Using Conditional Formatting
Skill 4 Sort Data and Use the Subtotal Tool to Summarize Data
Skill 5 Trace and Evaluate Formulas
Skill 6 Audit Formulas Using Cell Watch
Skill 7 Create One-Variable Data Tables
Skill 8 Create Two-Variable Data Tables
Skill 9 Generate Custom Table Styles
Skill 10 Convert Tables to Ranges

MORE SKILLS

Skill 11 Create Amortization Tables
Skill 12 Use the ROUND Function
Skill 13 Use Information Functions
Skill 14 Sort Tables Based on Multiple Criteria

EXL 7-1
VIDEO

► Data can be imported into a workbook from a **_delimited text file_**—a file in which the data in each column is separated by an identifying character such as a comma, a space, or a tab stop.

1. Start **Excel 2013**. Open the student data file **exl07_Classes**. On the **File tab**, click **Save As**, and then click **Browse**. In the **Save As** dialog box, navigate to the location where you are saving your files. Click **New folder**, type Excel Chapter 7 and then press Enter two times. Name the file Last_First_exl07_Classes and then press Enter .

2. Take a few moments to familiarize yourself with the text file shown in **Figure 1**.

   The data in the text file, which can be opened in Microsoft Word, is organized into rows and columns by using tab stops. A tab stop, indicated by an arrow, has been inserted to indicate each new column. The paragraph character at the end of each row indicates where a new row begins. In this manner, tabular data can be represented in a **_text file_**—a file that stores only the text characters but not the formatting or tables.

3. In the **Classes** worksheet, click cell **A6**. On the **Data tab**, in the **Get External Data group**, click the **From Text** button. In the **Import Text File** dialog box, navigate to the student data files for this chapter. Compare your screen with **Figure 2**.

4. Select **exl07_ClassesData**, and then click the **Open** button.

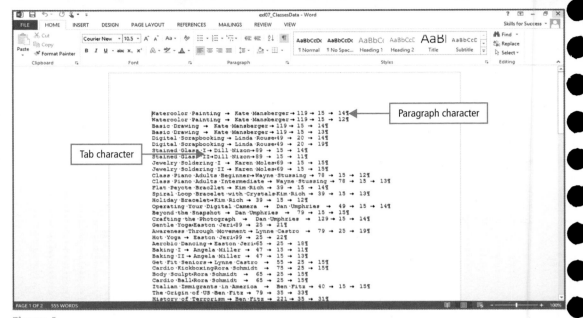

Figure 1

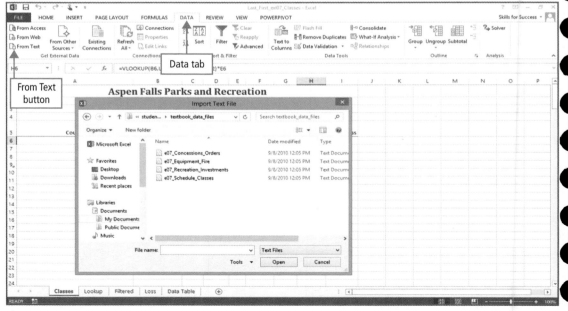

Figure 2

■ **Continue to the next page to complete the skill**

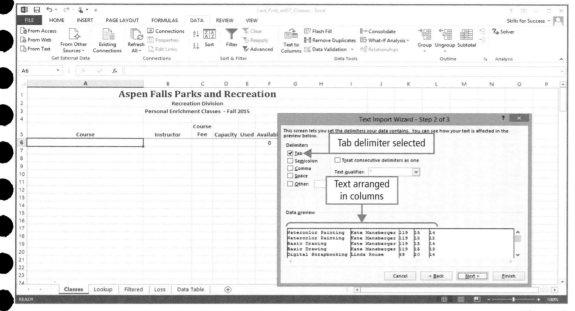

Figure 3

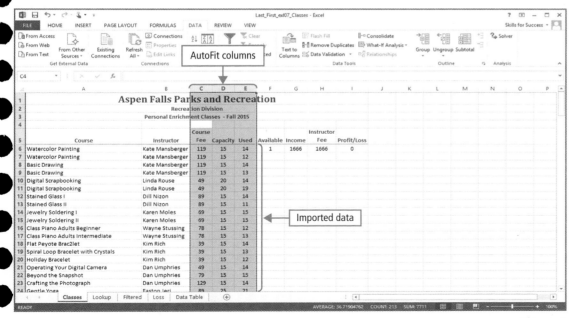

Figure 4

5. In the **Text Import Wizard - Step 1 of 3**, under **Original data type**, verify that the **Delimited** option button is selected, and then click **Next**.

6. In the **Text Import Wizard - Step 2 of 3**, under **Delimiters**, verify that the **Tab** check box is selected. Compare your screen with **Figure 3**.

   Under Data preview, the data is arranged into columns. The wizard uses the tab delimiter to determine in which column to place each value in the text file.

7. Click **Next**. In the **Text Import Wizard - Step 3 of 3**, under **Column data format**, verify that **General** is selected.

   This step allows you to select each column and then set the data format. General format converts numeric values to numbers, date values to dates, and all remaining values to text.

8. Click **Finish**. In the **Import Data** dialog box, verify that the **Existing worksheet** option button is selected and that the box displays the text =$A$6, and then click **OK** to insert the text file into the worksheet starting in cell A6. AutoFit columns as needed, and then compare your screen with **Figure 4**.

   The data was inserted into the worksheet. Each tab resulted in a new column, and each paragraph mark resulted in a new row.

9. **Save** 🖫 the workbook.

■ **You have completed Skill 1 of 10**

▶ EXL 7-2
VIDEO

▶ You can sort data by text, numbers, or dates, or by a custom list that includes colors or icon sets.

▶ Custom filters can be written using your own criteria, and then combined with other filters to apply multiple criteria.

1. If necessary, select cell **A6**. On the **Data tab**, in the **Sort & Filter group**, click **Filter**.

2. In cell **B5**, click the **Filter arrow** ▣. Point to **Text Filters**, and then click **Custom Filter**.

3. In the **Custom AutoFilter** dialog box, click the **arrow** in the box to the right of **equals**, type j and then click **Jules Casarillo**.

4. Click the **Or** option button. In the box below *equals*, click the **arrow**, and then click **equals**. Click the **arrow** in the box next to *equals*, type li and then click **Lisa Render**. Compare your screen with Figure 1, and then click **OK**.

   Or is a logical operator and evaluates two conditions. The custom filter will display only the rows where either *Jules Casarillo* or *Lisa Render* is the instructor.

5. In cell **C5**, click the **Filter arrow** ▣. Point to **Number Filters**, and then click **Greater Than or Equal To**. In the box next to *is greater than or equal to,* type 50 Click **OK**, and then compare your screen with Figure 2.

   When you apply filters to multiple columns, only the records that meet the criteria for both filters display. Here, only the Course Fees greater than or equal to 50 for Jules Casarillo and Lisa Render display.

■ **Continue to the next page to complete the skill** ➤

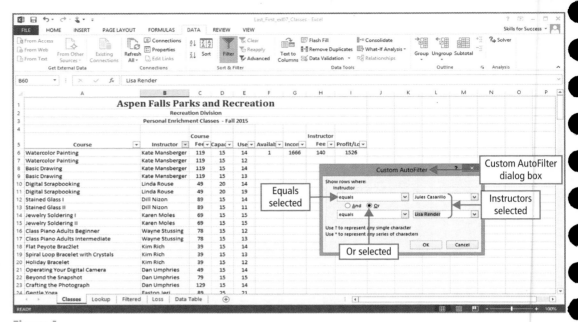

Figure 1

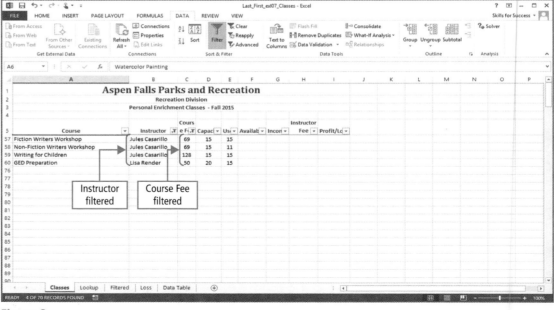

Figure 2

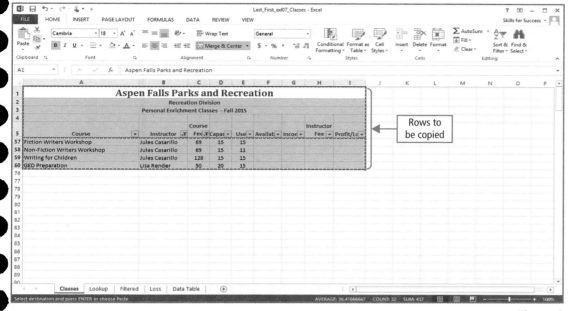

Figure 3

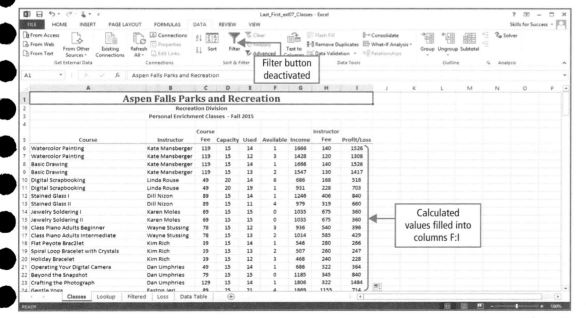

Figure 4

6. Select the range **A1:I60**. On the **Home tab**, in the **Clipboard group**, click **Copy** 📋. Compare your screen with **Figure 3**.

When copying filtered records, only the displayed rows are copied. Here, only the four filtered rows were copied to the clipboard.

7. Click the **Filtered** worksheet tab. With cell **A1** selected, on the **Home tab**, in the **Clipboard group**, click **Paste**.

The pasted rows are renumbered and are no longer filtered.

8. Click the **Classes** worksheet tab, and press Esc. On the **Data tab**, in the **Sort & Filter group**, click the **Filter** button to remove the custom filter.

9. Select cell **A6**, and then click the **Filter** button again. In cell **A5**, click the **Filter arrow**. Point to **Text Filters**, and then click **Begins With**.

10. In the dialog box, in the box to the right of *begins with*, type Basic and then click **OK**.

11. In cell **E5**, click the **Filter arrow** 🔽. Point to **Number Filters**, and then click **Less Than or Equal To**. In the box to the right of *is less than or equal to*, type 15 and then click **OK**.

12. Select and copy the range **A5:I71**.

13. Click the **Filtered** worksheet tab, select cell **A11**, and paste the data.

14. Click the **Classes** worksheet tab, and press Esc. On the **Data tab**, in the **Sort & Filter group**, click the **Filter** button.

15. Select the range **F6:I6**. AutoFill the functions in **F6:I6** down through **I75**. Select cell **A1**, and then compare your screen with **Figure 4**.

16. **Save** 💾 the workbook.

■ **You have completed Skill 2 of 10**

▶ EXL 7-3
VIDEO

▶ Data can be sorted based on the conditional formatting applied to each cell in a column. For example, when icon sets are applied to a column, you can sort the column by the icon set applied to each cell instead of the underlying numeric values in those cells.

1. On the **Classes** worksheet tab, select the range **I6:I75**.

2. On the **Home tab**, in the **Styles group**, click **Conditional Formatting**. Point to **Icon Sets**, and then click **More Rules**.

3. In the **New Formatting Rule** dialog box, under **Edit the Rule Description**, click the first **arrow** below **Type**, and then click **Number**. In the first box below **Value**, replace the existing value with 750

4. Click the second arrow below **Type**, and then click **Number**. In the second box below **Value**, verify that *0* displays. Compare your screen with **Figure 1**, and then click **OK**.

   There is no option to change the third icon because all of the possible options are taken into consideration by changing the first two values.

5. Verify the range **I6:I75** is still selected, and then click the **Data tab**. In the **Sort & Filter group**, click the **Sort** button. Read the **Sort Warning** message box. Verify that the **Expand the selection** option button is selected, and then click **Sort**. Compare your screen with **Figure 2**.

   Expanding the selection will ensure that the row data does not become separated. If the selection is not expanded, only the selected column is sorted.

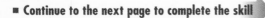

■ **Continue to the next page to complete the skill** ▶

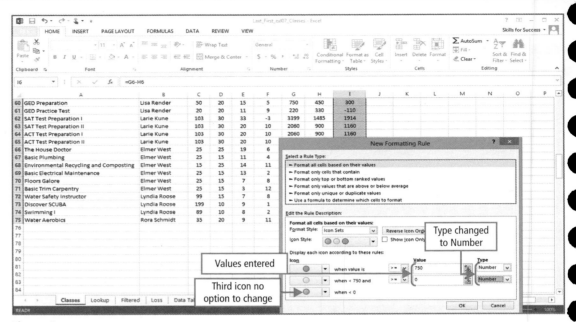

Figure 1

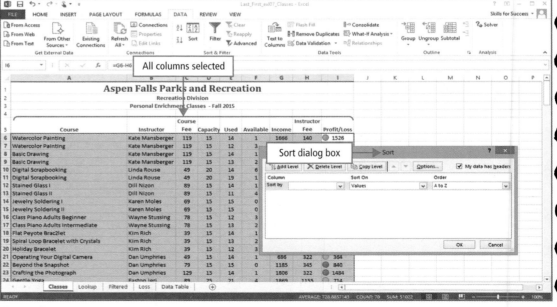

Figure 2

Figure 3

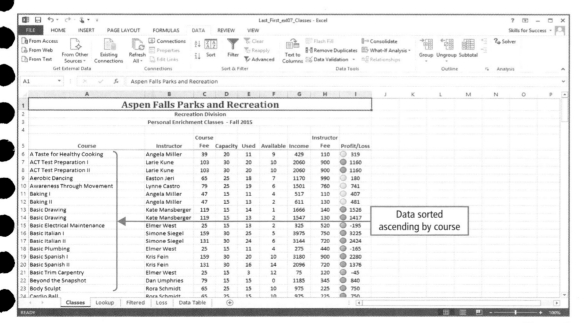

Figure 4

6. In the **Sort** dialog box, under **Column**, click the **Sort by arrow**, and then click **Profit/Loss** to sort the rows by that column.

7. Click the **Sort On arrow**, and then click **Cell Icon**. Click the **Order arrow**, and then click the red icon. In the last box, verify that **On Top** is displayed. Compare your screen with Figure 3, and then click **OK**.

   The cells with the red icons are now at the top of the list. These cells indicate classes that have lost money.

8. Select the range **A1:I19**. On the **Home tab**, in the **Clipboard group**, click the **Copy** button 🗐.

   The worksheet titles and the first fourteen rows of data are copied to the clipboard.

9. Display the **Loss** worksheet tab. Verify that cell **A1** is selected, and then in the **Clipboard group**, click the **Paste** button.

10. Display the **Classes** worksheet tab, and then select the range **A6:I75**. On the **Data tab**, in the **Sort & Filter group**, click the **Sort** button. In the **Sort** dialog box, click the **Sort by arrow**, and then click **Course**.

11. Click the **Sort On arrow**, and then click **Values**. In the **Order** box, verify that *A to Z* is displayed, and then click **OK** to sort the *Course* column in ascending order. Click cell **A1**, and then compare your screen with Figure 4.

   When a sort order is not specified, the rows are sorted in ascending order. Here, the rows were sorted alphabetically (A to Z) by course.

12. **Save** 🖫 the workbook.

■ **You have completed Skill 3 of 10**

▶ When data is grouped, you can use the Excel Subtotal tool to display summary statistics—sums and counts, for example—for each group.

▶ Before adding subtotals to tabular data, the rows need to be sorted by the column being subtotaled.

1. On the **Classes** worksheet tab, select cell **B6**. On the **Data tab**, in the **Sort & Filter group**, click the **Sort A to Z** button. Compare your screen with **Figure 1**.

   The rows are now grouped by Instructor. When sorted in this manner, the Subtotal tool can provide subtotals for each instructor.

2. Select cell **A6**. In the **Outline group**, click **Subtotal**.

3. In the **Subtotal** dialog box, click the **At each change in arrow**, and then click **Instructor**. Verify that the **Use function** box displays *Sum*. Under **Add subtotal to**, click as necessary to select the **Income**, **Instructor Fee**, and **Profit/Loss** check boxes. Compare your screen with **Figure 2**.

   Subtotals will be displayed for each instructor and will include the Course Income, the Instructor Fees, and the Profit/Loss columns.

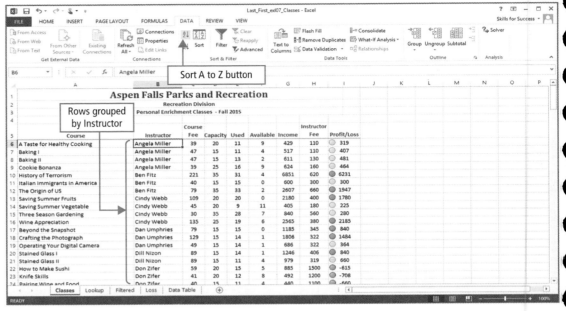

Figure 1

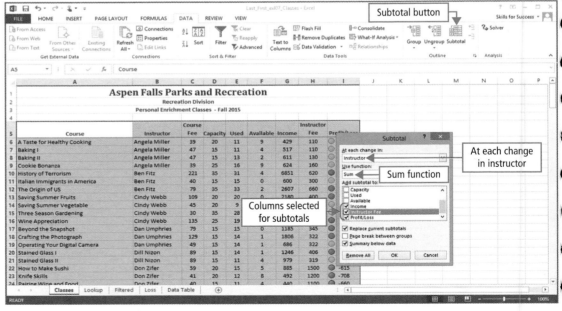

Figure 2

■ **Continue to the next page to complete the skill** ▶

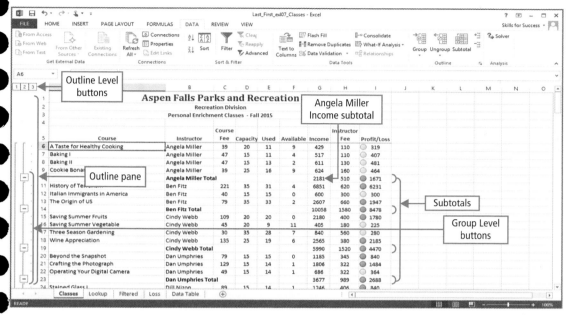

Figure 3

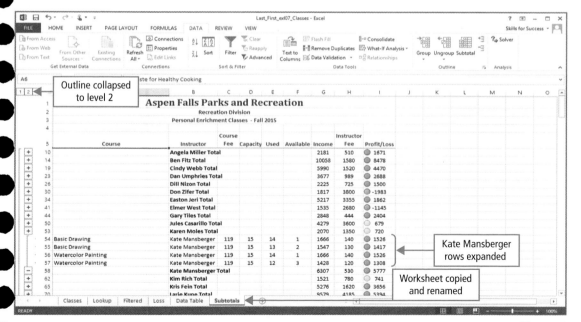

Figure 4

4. Click **OK**, and then compare your screen with **Figure 3**.

> The result may take several seconds to complete. The table is organized as an outline with three levels, and the Outline pane is displayed. For each instructor, the specified columns display subtotals. For example, the *Course Income* for Angela Miller's four classes, as shown in cell G10, is *2181*.

5. In the **Outline** pane, click the **Outline Level 2** button ☐2☐ to display just the totals for each instructor.

6. In the **Outline** pane, to the left of row **58**, click the **Expand** button ☐+☐ to display all of the rows for Kate Mansberger.

> In this manner, details for individual subtotals can be expanded or collapsed.

7. Right-click the **Classes** worksheet tab, and then in the shortcut menu that displays, click **Move or Copy**. In the **Move or Copy** dialog box, under **Before sheet**, click **(move to end)**. Select the **Create a copy** check box, and then click **OK**.

8. Right-click the **Classes (2)** worksheet tab, and click **Rename**. Type Subtotals press ☐Enter☐, and then compare your screen with **Figure 4**.

9. Click the **Classes** worksheet tab, and then on the **Data tab**, in the **Outline group**, click the **Ungroup arrow**. In the list, select **Clear Outline**.

10. Click cell **A6**, and then on the **Data tab**, in the **Sort & Filter group**, click the **Sort A to Z** button ☐A↓Z☐.

11. **Save** ☐💾☐ the workbook.

■ **You have completed Skill 4 of 10**

▶ Tracing the precedents or dependents of a cell helps you evaluate worksheet formulas and is useful when trying to determine the cause of an error.

▶ A **precedent** is any cell value that is referred to in a formula and a function. A **dependent** is any cell value that depends on the value in a given cell.

1. On the **Classes** worksheet, select cell **G6**. On the **formula bar**, change the formula to =A6*E6 Press Enter.

   The #VALUE! error value indicates that the formula contains the wrong type of data. The error displays in cells G6 and I6 because cell A6 contains a text value. Excel cannot perform mathematical calculations when one of the values being multiplied is formatted as text.

2. Select cell **G6**. On the **Formulas tab**, in the **Formula Auditing group**, click **Trace Precedents** and then click **Trace Dependents**. Compare your screen with **Figure 1**.

   The precedents are indicated by blue lines with blue dots indicating the cells used in the formula. The dependents are indicated by a red line.

3. In the **Formula Auditing group**, click the **Evaluate Formula** button. In the **Evaluate Formula** dialog box, click **Step In**. Compare your screen with **Figure 2**.

   The Evaluate Formula dialog box is used to evaluate each part of a formula in a step-by-step process. The underlying formula in cell G6 displays and cell A6 is highlighted to indicate that it is the cell being evaluated in this step.

■ Continue to the next page to complete the skill ▶

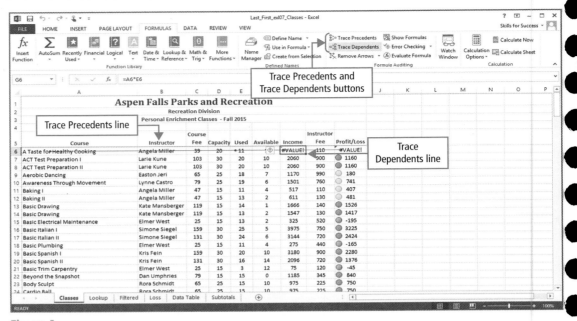

Figure 1

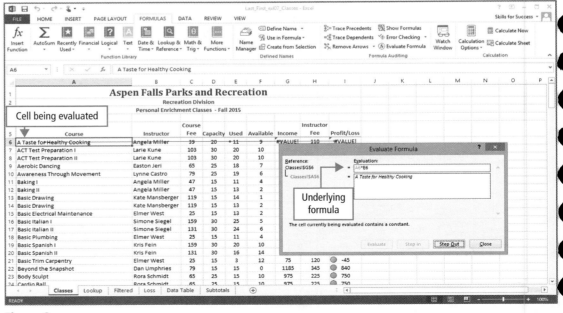

Figure 2

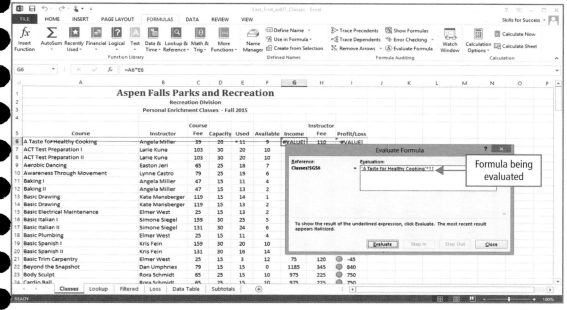

Figure 3

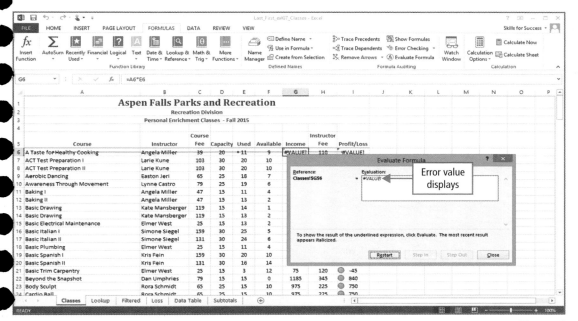

Figure 4

4. Notice that cell **A6** contains a text value, *A Taste for Healthy Cooking,* and then click the **Step Out** button. Click **Step In**, notice that cell **E6** contains a numeric value, *11,* and then click **Step Out**. Compare your screen with Figure 3.

   The Evaluation box indicates the steps evaluated to this point by displaying actual values and underlining each part of the formula that has been evaluated. Here *"A Taste for Healthy Cooking"*11* has been evaluated. In this manner, each step in a formula can be analyzed.

5. Click the **Evaluate** button, and then compare your screen with Figure 4.

   The Evaluation box displays an error value in place of the information that was previously displayed. The error value helps you locate the exact cell causing the error value.

6. If necessary, drag the **Evaluate Formula** dialog box down so that both trace lines display.

7. Using the skills you previously practiced, create a full-screen snip. **Save** 🖫 the snip in your **Excel Chapter 7** folder as Last_First_exl07_ClassesSnip1 and then **Close** ⊠ the **Snipping Tool** window.

8. In the **Evaluate Formula** dialog box, click **Close**. In the **Formula Auditing group**, click the **Remove Arrows** button to remove the trace lines.

9. In cell **G6**, change the formula back to =C6*E6 and then press Enter . Select cell **A1**.

10. **Save** 🖫 the workbook.

■ **You have completed Skill 5 of 10**

> ▶ EXL 7-6
> VIDEO

- ▶ The **Watch Window** displays cells and the formulas in those cells when they are not visible on the screen.

- ▶ The Watch Window does not change when you scroll in the worksheet, and you can move or dock it as needed.

1. On the **Classes** worksheet, select cell **H12**. On the **Formulas tab**, in the **Formula Auditing group**, click the **Watch Window** button.

2. In the **Watch Window**, click **Add Watch**. If needed, move the **Add Watch** dialog box to view both windows. Compare your screen with **Figure 1**.

3. In the **Add Watch** dialog box, verify that the value *=Classes$H$12* displays, and then click **Add**.

4. Select cell **I7**. In the **Watch Window**, click **Add Watch**, and then in the **Add Watch** dialog box click **Add**. If necessary, resize the **Watch Window** to display all of the **VLOOKUP** formula, as shown in **Figure 2**.

   The underlying formulas for the two cells are added to the Watch Window display. In this manner, multiple cells can be added to the Watch Window.

■ **Continue to the next page to complete the skill**

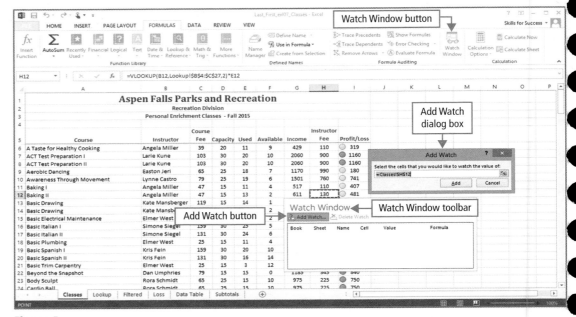

Figure 1

Figure 2

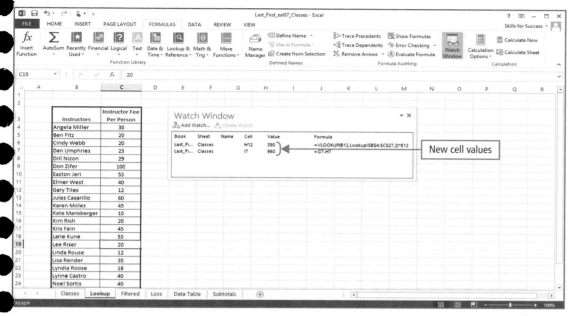

Figure 3

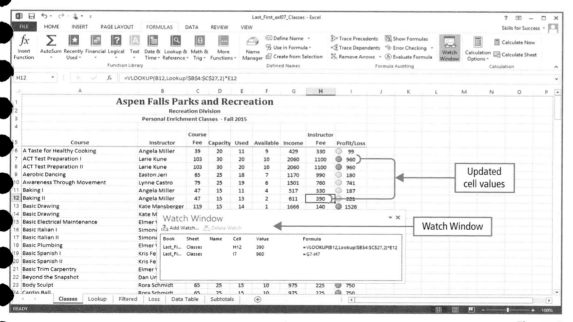

Figure 4

5. Select the **Lookup** worksheet. Move the **Watch Window** so that the upper left corner is in cell **E3**. In the **Watch Window**, notice that the **Value** column for cell **H12** displays *130*.

6. In cell **C4**, type 30 In the **Watch Window**, watch the **Value** for cell **H12**, and then press [Enter]. Notice the value changes from *130* to *390*.

   The Watch Window is used to view changes in cells that are not currently displayed in the worksheet.

7. In cell **C18**, replace the existing value with 55 and then press [Enter]. Notice that the **Value** of cell **I7** on the **Watch Window** changes from *1160* to *960*, as shown in **Figure 3**.

8. Display the **Classes** worksheet. Verify that the value in cell **H12** is *390* and that the value in cell **I7** is *960*, as shown in **Figure 4**. If necessary, move the **Watch Window** as shown in the figure.

9. Using the skills you previously practiced, create a full-screen snip. **Save** 🔲 the snip in your **Excel Chapter 7** folder as Last_First_e07_ClassesSnip2 and then **Close** ☒ the **Snipping Tool** window.

10. **Close** ☒ the **Watch Window**, and then select cell **A1**.

11. **Save** 🔲 the workbook.

■ **You have completed Skill 6 of 10**

▶ In Excel, a ***data table*** is a range of cells set up to show how changing one or two values in a formula will affect the formula's results.

▶ Data tables are used to perform what-if analyses and can contain one or two variables. A ***one-variable data table*** changes one value in a formula using input from either a row or a column.

1. Select the **Data Table** worksheet tab, and then select cell **B9**. Type =G6 and then press Enter.

2. In cell **B10**, type 3 and then press Enter. In cell **B11**, type 4.5% Press Enter. In cell **B12**, type 1200 Press Enter, and then compare your screen with **Figure 1**.

   These values reflect an investment earning 4.5 percent interest per year. The initial investment is the class profit of *$44,770*, and monthly payments of $1,200 will be added for three years.

3. With cell **B13** selected, on the **Formulas tab**, in the **Function Library group**, click **Financial**. If necessary, scroll down, and then click **FV**.

4. In the dialog box, in the **Rate** box, type B11/12 In the **Nper** box, type B10*12 In the **Pmt** box, type -B12 In the **Pv** box, type -B9 and then compare your screen with **Figure 2**.

   The result of the future value function indicates that the initial investment will grow to *$97,387.28* if the investment earns 4.5 percent and monthly payments of $1,200 are made. Recall that the initial amount invested and the payment amount should be negative values because the money is an outflow—money being paid out to the investment.

■ Continue to the next page to complete the skill ▶

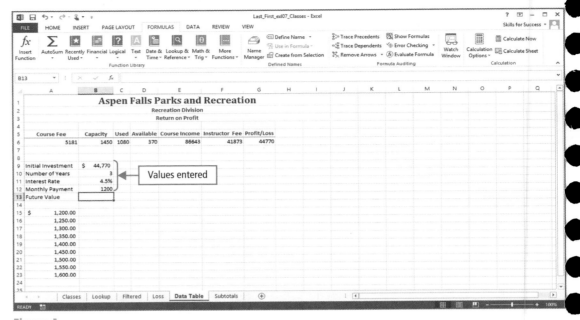

Figure 1

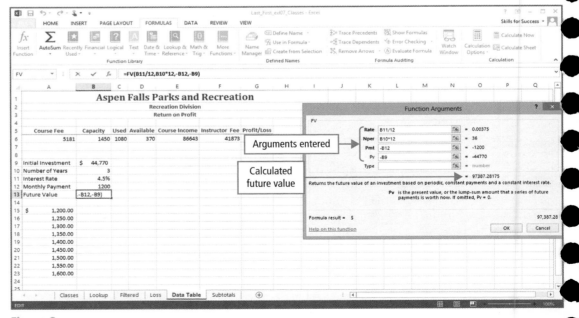

Figure 2

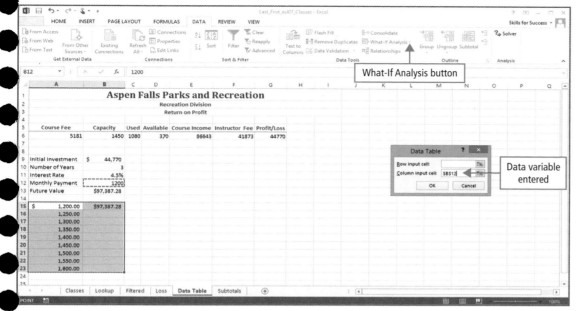

Figure 3

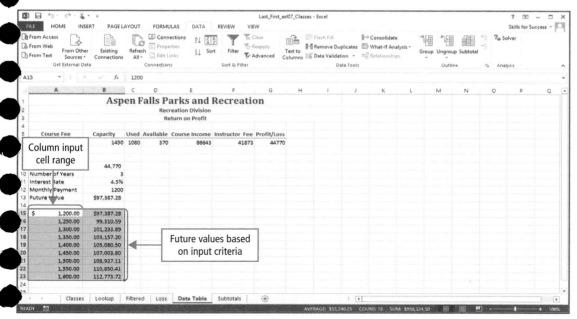

Figure 4

5. Click **OK**. Select cell **B15**, type =B13 and then press Enter. Resize the width of column **B** to **13**.

> A data table must be built from an underlying formula. Here, the results of the future value formula in cell B13 will be the data table's underlying function.

6. Select the range **A15:B23**. On the **Data tab**, in the **Data Tools group**, click the **What-If Analysis** button, and then click **Data Table**.

7. In the **Data Table** dialog box, click the **Column input cell** box, and then click cell **B12**. Press F4 if necessary to change to an absolute cell reference, as shown in **Figure 3**.

> The Monthly Payment value in cell B12 represents the variable that will be changed using the values in the first column of the data table.

8. Click **OK**, and then compare your screen with **Figure 4**.

> For each row in this data table, the payment value used in the FV function (B12) was changed to the corresponding value in column A. For example, in cell B17, the future value of the investment with a payment of *$1,300* would be *$101,233.89*.

9. Select cell **A1**. **Save** 🖫 the workbook.

■ **You have completed Skill 7 of 10**

▶ EXL 7-8
VIDEO

▶ A **two-variable data table** uses two inputs—one from a column and one from a row.

▶ Two-variable data tables display the results across a range of cells.

1. On the **Data Table** worksheet tab, select cell **E15**, type =B13 and then press Enter.

    Cell E15 will contain the underlying formula for a two-variable data table.

2. In cell **E16**, type 1.0% and then press Enter. In cell **E17**, type 1.5% and then press Enter.

3. Select the range **E16:E17**, and then on the **Home tab**, in the **Number group**, click the **Decrease Decimal** button one time. With the range **E16:E17** still selected, drag the fill handle down through cell **E23** to fill the series. Compare your screen with Figure 1.

    In the range E16:E23, the values will be the different interest rates used as the column input in a data table.

4. Click cell **F15**, type 1 and then press Tab. In cell **G15**, type 2 Select the range **F15:G15**, and then drag the fill handle to the right through cell **J15**. Compare your screen with Figure 2.

    The range F15:J15 will display the number of years used as the row input in the data table.

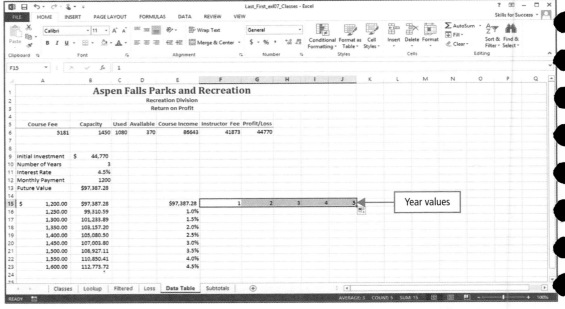

Figure 1

Figure 2

■ Continue to the next page to complete the skill ▶

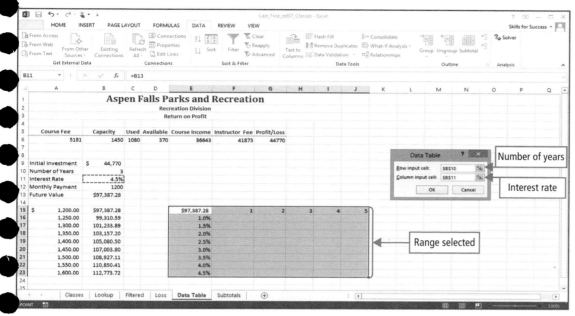

Figure 3

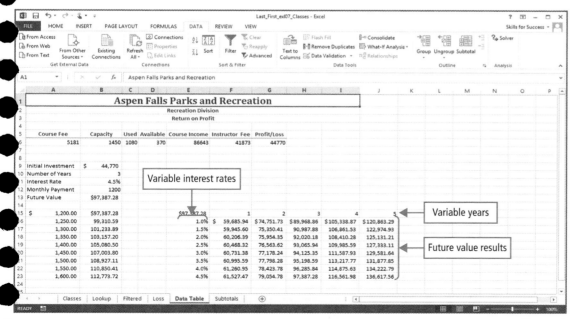

Figure 4

5. Select the range **E15:J23**. On the **Data tab**, in the **Data Tools group**, click **What-If Analysis**, and then click **Data Table**.

6. In the **Data Table** dialog box, with the insertion point in the **Row input cell** box, click cell **B10**—the number of years the investment payments will be made. Press Tab.

7. With the insertion point in the **Column input cell** box, click cell **B11**—the interest rate earned by the investment. Compare your screen with **Figure 3**.

    In this data table, the Row input cell is equal to the number of years, and the Column input cell is equal to the interest rate.

8. Click **OK**. AutoFit columns as necessary. Select cell **A1**, and compare your screen with **Figure 4**.

    A data table displays the results of its underlying function using two different variables. Here, the future value of the investment is calculated using the different interest rates in column E and the different years in row 15. For example, the future value of the investment after five years at 4.0 percent interest is $134,222.79.

9. **Save** the workbook.

■ **You have completed Skill 8 of 10**

▶ A *table style* is a collection of table formatting options that can be applied to a range with a single click.

▶ Quick styles are displayed in a gallery with a small sample image of the style called a *thumbnail*.

1. Click the **Loss** worksheet tab. Drag to select the range **A5:I19**. On the **Home tab**, in the **Styles group**, click **Format as Table**, and then in the gallery, click **New Table Style**.

2. In the **New Table Style** dialog box, in the **Name** box, type Classes Compare your screen with **Figure 1**.

   You use the New Table Styles dialog box to create custom table styles that you name and format yourself.

3. In the **New Table Style** dialog box, under **Table Element**, verify that **Whole Table** is selected, and then click the **Format** button.

4. In the **Format Cells** dialog box, click the **Border tab**. Under **Line**, in the **Style** box, click the next to last style in the right column—the solid thick line. Click the **Color arrow**, and then under **Theme colors**, click the fourth color in the first row—**Dark Blue**, **Text 2**. Under **Presets**, click **Outline**. Compare your screen with **Figure 2**.

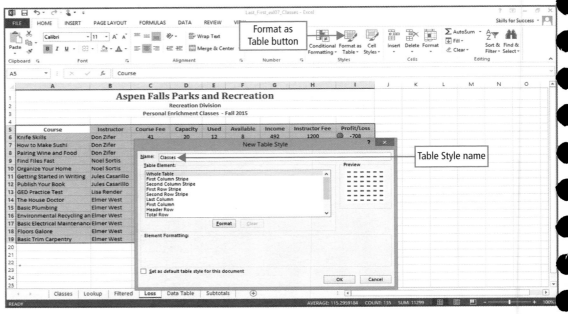

Figure 1

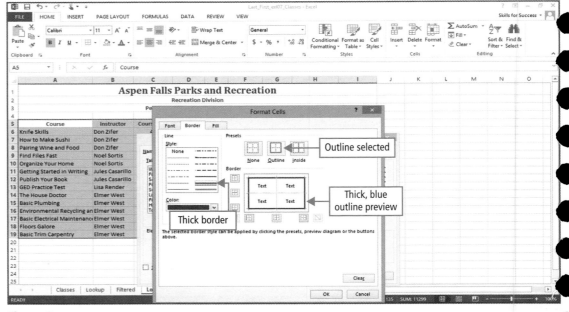

Figure 2

■ Continue to the next page to complete the skill ▶

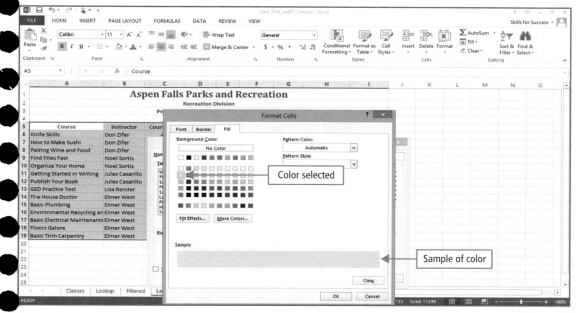

Figure 3

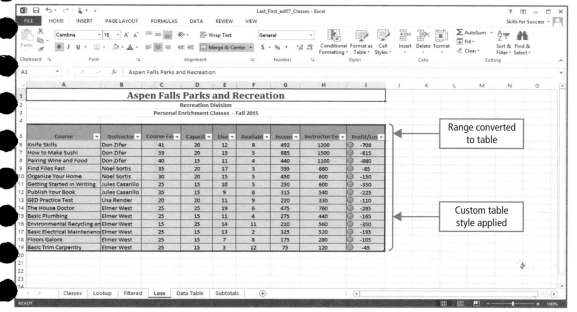

Figure 4

5. In the **Style** box, click the last style in the left column—the thin solid line, and then under **Presets**, click **Inside**.

6. Click the **Fill tab**. Under **Background Color**, click the first color in the third row. Compare your screen with Figure 3, and then click **OK**.

7. In the **New Table Style** dialog box, under **Table Element**, click **Header Row**, and then click the **Format** button.

8. In the **Format Cells** dialog box, on the **Fill tab**, under **Background Color**, click the first color in the fifth row, and then click **OK**.

9. In the **New Table Style** dialog box, **Preview** the formatting, and then click **OK**.

10. With the range **A5:I19** still selected, in the **Styles group**, click **Format as Table**. In the **Table Styles** gallery, under **Custom**, point to the thumbnail to display the name in the ScreenTip—*Classes*. Click the *Classes* thumbnail to apply the style.

11. In the **Format As Table** dialog box, verify that the **Where is the data for your table** box displays =$A$5:$I$19. Verify the **My table has headers** check box is selected, and then click **OK**. Select cell **A1**, and then compare your screen with Figure 4.

    The custom table style is applied to the specified range, and the range is converted into an Excel table. Darker shading has been applied to the header row.

12. **Save** 🖫 the workbook.

■ **You have completed Skill 9 of 10**

▶ When a table is converted to a range, the table functions are removed and the formatting remains.

▶ Tables can be expanded or decreased using the Resize Table tool.

1. Select the **Classes** worksheet tab, and click cell **B6**. On the **Data tab**, in the **Sort & Filter group**, click **Sort A to Z** ↓. If necessary, in the **Outline group**, click the **Subtotal** button, and then in the **Subtotal** dialog box, click **Remove All**.

2. Select the range **A1:I17**. On the **Home tab**, in the **Clipboard group**, click **Copy** 🖹.

3. Click the **New Sheet** button ⊕. If necessary, select cell **A1**. On the **Home tab**, in the **Clipboard group**, click **Paste**, and then compare your screen with **Figure 1**.

4. Right-click the **Sheet1** tab, click **Rename**, and then type Range Press ⏎. AutoFit columns as needed.

5. On the **Home tab**, in the **Styles group**, click **Format as Table**. In the **Table Styles gallery**, under **Custom**, point to the thumbnail to display the name in the ScreenTip—*Classes*. Click the *Classes* thumbnail to apply the style.

6. In the **Format As Table** dialog box, in the **Where is the data for your table** box, select the range A5:I17, and then click the **My table has headers** check box.

7. Click **OK**, and then compare your screen with **Figure 2**.

The range is formatted as an Excel table with filter and sort buttons in the header row.

■ **Continue to the next page to complete the skill**

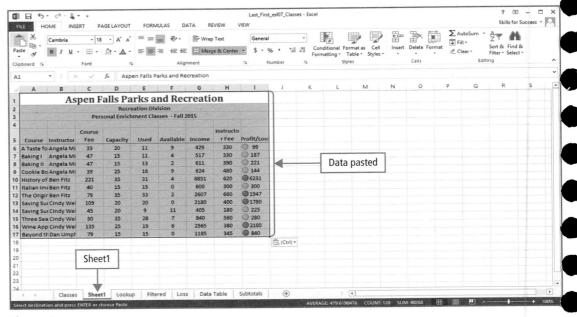

Figure 1

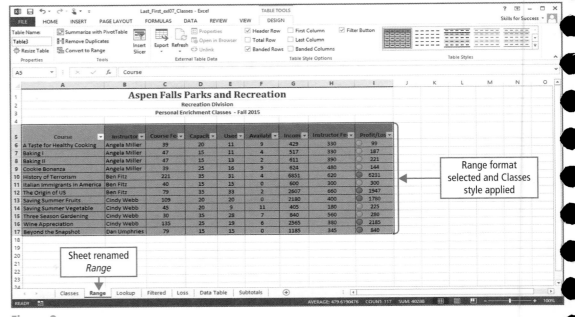

Figure 2

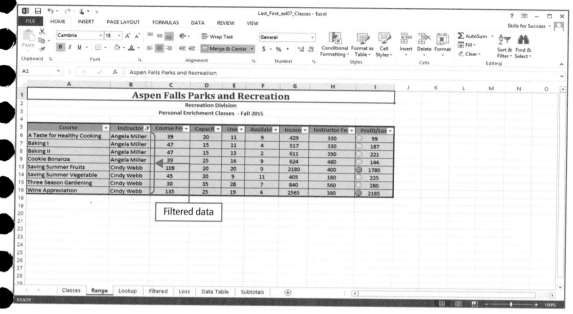

Figure 3

8. In cell **B5**, click the **Filter arrow**. In the **Filter gallery**, clear the **(Select All)** check box, and then select the *Angela Miller* and *Cindy Webb* check boxes. Click **OK**. Select cell **A1**, and then compare your screen with Figure 3.

9. Select cell **A5**. On the **Design tab**, in the **Tools group**, click **Convert to Range**. Read the message that displays, and then click **Yes**. Select cell **A1**, and then compare your screen with Figure 4.

   The table is converted to a range. The filter that had been applied is removed; however, the formatting of the table remains.

10. Select the **Classes** worksheet, and then click cell **A1**. Right-click the **Classes** worksheet tab, and then click **Select All Sheets**. Insert the file name in the left footer. Right-click the **Classes** worksheet tab, and then click **Ungroup Sheets**. Return to **Normal** view.

11. **Save** 🖫 the workbook. Submit the workbook and the snips as directed by your instructor.

   ✔ **DONE! You have completed Skill 10 of 10, and the workbook is complete!**

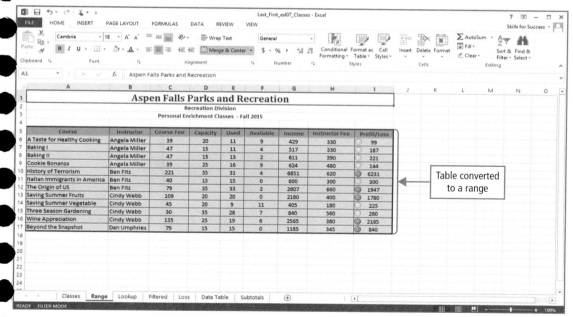
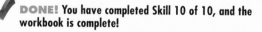

Table converted to a range

Figure 4

More Skills

The following More Skills are located at **www.pearsonhighered.com/skills**

More Skills Create Amortization Tables

An amortization table is a useful tool that allows you to keep track of the payments made on an investment. A well-designed amortization table will display the amount of principal and interest that are paid each month along with the remaining balance on the principal.

In More Skills 11, you will create an amortization table showing the payments on a 72-month loan with an initial principal amount of $57,000 and an interest rate of 1.99 percent.

To begin, open your web browser, navigate to www.pearsonhighered.com/skills, locate the name of your textbook, and then follow the instructions on the website.

More Skills Use the ROUND Function

You use the ROUND function to round a number to a specified number of decimal places. This function is often used to display numbers as whole numbers instead of showing the decimal places.

In More Skills 12, you will open a workbook and then use the ROUND, ROUNDUP, and ROUNDDOWN functions to change the way numbers are displayed so that numbers with large numbers of digits to the right of the decimal point are easier to read.

To begin, open your web browser, navigate to www.pearsonhighered.com/skills, locate the name of your textbook, and then follow the instructions on the website.

More Skills Use Information Functions

Excel has a collection of functions that are used to provide you with information about the data that is contained within a workbook. The ISODD and ISERROR functions evaluate data and provide true or false results.

In More Skills 13, you will use both the ISODD and ISERROR functions to calculate values that are used to calculate another value.

To begin, open your web browser, navigate to www.pearsonhighered.com/skills, locate the name of your textbook, and then follow the instructions on the website.

More Skills Sort Tables Based on Multiple Criteria

In Excel, you can sort a table based on as many criteria as needed. The criteria can be values, cell colors, or icons.

In More Skills 14, you will sort a table based on multiple criteria.

To begin, open your web browser, navigate to www.pearsonhighered.com/skills, locate the name of your textbook, and then follow the instructions on the website.

Please note that there are no additional projects to accompany the More Skills Projects, and they are not covered in End-of-Chapter projects.

The following table summarizes the **SKILLS AND PROCEDURES** covered in this chapter.

Skills Number	Task	Step	Icon
1	Import text file	Data tab → Get External Data group → From Text → Select file	
2	Apply Advanced AutoFilter	Data tab → Sort & Filter group → Filter	
3	Sort data using conditional formatting	Home tab → Styles group → Conditional Formatting	
4	Sort data	Data tab → Sort & Filter group → Sort	
4	Sort data A to Z	Data tab → Sort & Filter group → Sort A to Z	
4	Subtotal data	Data tab → Outline group → Subtotal → Select field to sort by	
5	Trace precedents	Formulas tab → Formula Auditing group → Trace Precedents	
5	Trace dependents	Formulas tab → Formula Auditing group → Trace Dependents	
6	Evaluate formulas	Formulas tab → Formula Auditing group → Watch Window → Add Watch	
7	Create one-variable data table	Data tab → Data Tools group → What-If Analysis → Data Table → Enter input row or column address	
8	Create two-variable data table	Data tab → Data Tools group → What-If Analysis → Data Table → Enter input row and column address	
9	Create table styles	Home tab → Styles group → Format as Table → New Table Style	
9	Apply table styles	Home tab → Styles group → Format as Table → Custom → Click thumbnail	
9	Format data as a table	Home tab → Styles group → Format as Table	
10	Convert tables to ranges	Home tab → Design tab → Tools group → Convert to Range	

Key Terms

Online Help Skills

1. Start **Excel 2013**, and then in the upper right corner of the Excel window, click the **Help** button ⟦?⟧. In the **Help** window, click the **Maximize** ⟦□⟧ button.

2. Click in the search box, type data tables and then press ⟦Enter⟧. In the search results, click **Calculate multiple results by using a data table**.

3. Read the article's introduction, and then below **In this article**, click **Data table basics**. Compare your screen with Figure 1.

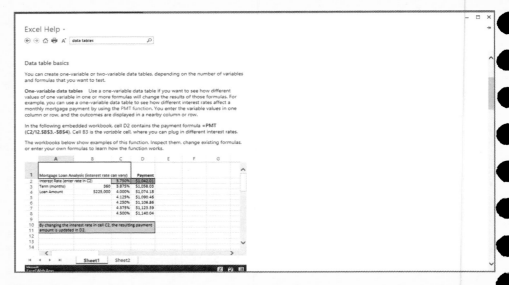

Figure 1

4. Read the section to answer the following questions: How many different what-if analysis tools are available in Excel? Which what-if analysis tool should you use if you want to analyze more than two variables?

Matching

Match each term in the second column with its correct definition in the first column by writing the letter of the term on the blank line in front of the correct definition.

___ **1.** A file that stores the text characters, but not the formatting or tables.

___ **2.** A logical operator that returns true if either of the criteria is true.

___ **3.** A tool that displays summary statistics for grouped data in an outline format.

___ **4.** An error value indicating that the wrong type of data is being used in a formula.

___ **5.** A process that analyzes a function by stepping into and out of each part of the function.

___ **6.** A toolbar that provides information about selected cells when those cells are not currently displayed on the screen.

___ **7.** A range of calculations based on a single underlying formula that uses rows and/or columns as inputs.

___ **8.** The Data Table command can be found by clicking this button.

___ **9.** A type of data table that takes input from a row and input from a column.

___ **10.** Table styles that you create and name display in the gallery under this category.

A #VALUE

B Custom

C Data table

D Evaluate Formula

E Or

F Subtotal

G Text file

H Two-variable

I Watch Window

J What-If Analysis

Multiple Choice

Choose the correct answer.

1. The type of file in which the data in each field is separated by a comma, a space, or a tab stop.
   A. Delimited
   B. Plain
   C. Comma-separated

2. This command displays only rows that meet a specified condition.
   A. Arranger
   B. Sorter
   C. Filter

3. When you use Subtotals, details can be expanded or collapsed using this.
   A. Outline Level
   B. Filter
   C. Group

4. This is the name for a cell value that is referred to by a function in another cell.
   A. Dependent
   B. Precedent
   C. Variable

5. This type of cell's value is contingent on the value in a given cell.
   A. Dependent
   B. Precedent
   C. Variable

6. This type of data table is created using input from either a row or a column.
   A. One-variable
   B. Two-variable
   C. Complex-variable

7. This is a collection of formatting options that can be applied with a single click.
   A. Style template
   B. Quick style
   C. Table style

8. This is a small sample image of a style.
   A. Thumbnail
   B. Live preview
   C. Preview

9. Select this option to remove filters from a table while keeping the table.
   A. Sort
   B. Convert to Range
   C. Format as Table

10. Tables can be expanded or decreased using this tool.
    A. Reduce Table
    B. Resize Table
    C. Expand Table

Topics for Discussion

1. What kind of information do you think a small business or organization would have in a text file or a database that would need to be imported into a spreadsheet?

2. For what purposes would you use the filter and sort tools when you work with spreadsheets?

Skills Review

MyITLab®
Grader

To complete this project, you will need the following files:

- exl07_SRConcessions
- exl07_SRConcessionsData

You will save your files as:

- Last_First_exl07_SRConcessions
- Last_First_exl07_SRConcessionsSnip1
- Last_First_exl07_SRConcessionsSnip2
- Last_First_exl07_SRConcessionsSnip3

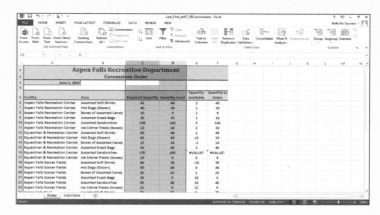

Figure 1

1. Start **Excel 2013**, and open the file **exl07_SRConcessions**. Save the workbook in your chapter folder as Last_First_exl07_SRConcessions

2. On the **Order** worksheet, select cell **A6**. On the **Data tab**, in the **Get External Data group**, click **From Text**. In the **Import Text File** dialog box, locate **exl07_SRConcessionsData**, and then click **Import**. In the **Text Import Wizard - Step 1 of 3**, click **Finish**, and then in the **Import Data** dialog box, click **OK**. AutoFit columns as needed, and then compare your screen with Figure 1.

3. Select cell **B6**, and then on the **Data tab**, in the **Sort & Filter group**, click **Sort A to Z**.

4. Select cell **E7**. On the **Formulas tab**, in the **Formula Auditing group**, click **Trace Precedents**, and then click **Trace Dependents**. Click **Evaluate Formula**. In the **Evaluate Formula** dialog box, click **Evaluate**, and then click **Step In**. Click **Step Out**, and then click **Evaluate**.

5. Create a full-screen snip. **Save** it in your chapter folder as Last_First_exl07_SRConcessionsSnip1 and then close the Snipping Tool. Compare your screen with Figure 2.

Figure 2

6. In the **Evaluate Formula** dialog box, click **Close**. On the **Formulas tab**, in the **Formula Auditing group**, click **Remove Arrows**. Verify cell **E7** is selected, and then type =C7-D7 and press Enter.

7. Select cell **E22**, and then in the **Formula Auditing group**, click **Watch Window**. In the **Watch Window**, click **Add Watch**, and then in the **Add Watch** dialog box, click **Add**. Add cell **E9** to the **Watch Window**. Select cell **D9**, type 22 and then press Enter. Create a full-screen snip. **Save** it in your **Excel Chapter 7** folder as Last_First_exl07_SRConcessionsSnip2 and then close the Snipping Tool. Close the **Watch Window**.

■ Continue to the next page to complete this Skills Review ▶

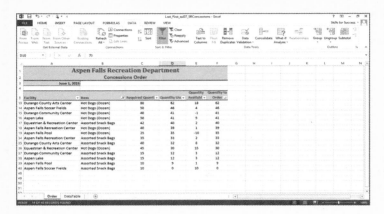

Figure 3

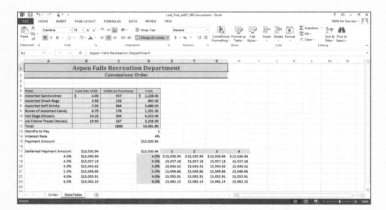

Figure 4

8. On the **Data** tab, in the **Sort & Filter** group, click **Filter**. Click the cell **B5 Filter arrow**, point to **Text Filters**, and then click **contains**. In the dialog box, in the first row click the second box **arrow**, and then click **Assorted Snack Bags**. Click the **Or** option button. Under **Or**, click the first box **arrow**, and then click **contains**. Click the second box **arrow**, and then click **Hot Dogs (Dozen)**. Click **OK**.

9. In the **Sort & Filter group**, click **Sort**. In the dialog box, under **Column**, click the **Sort by arrow**, and then click **Quantity to Order**. Under **Order**, click **Largest to Smallest**, and then click **OK**. Compare your screen with Figure 3.

10. Create a full-screen snip. **Save** it in your **Excel Chapter 7** folder as Last_First_exl07_SRConcessionsSnip3 and then close the Snipping Tool.

11. In the **Sort & Filter group**, click **Filter**. Select cell **B6**. In the **Sort & Filter group**, click **Sort A to Z**. In the **Outline** group, click **Subtotal**. In the dialog box, under **At each change in**, click the **arrow**, and then select **Item**. Click **OK**. Click the **Outline Level 2**.

12. On the **DataTable** worksheet, select the range **A17:B23**. In the **Data Tools group**, click **What-If Analysis**, and then click **Data Table**. In the dialog box, click in the **Column input cell** box, and then click cell **D14**. Click **OK**. Select the range **D17:H23**. Click **What-If Analysis**, and then click **Data Table**. In the dialog box, click in the **Row input cell** box, and then click cell **D13**. Click in the **Column input cell** box, and then click cell **D14**. Click **OK**. AutoFit columns **E:H**.

13. Select the range **A5:D12**. On the **Home tab**, in the **Styles group**, click **Format as Table**, and then click **New Table Style**. In the dialog box, in the **Name** box, type Concessions Click **Format**, and then in the dialog box, click the **Border tab**. Under **Style**, ensure the last style in the left column is selected. Click the **Color arrow**, and then under **Theme colors**, click the sixth color in the first row—**Red**, **Accent 2**. In the **Presets** area, click **Outline**, and then under **Style**, click the last style in the first column. In the **Presets** area, click **Inside**. Click the **Fill tab**. Click the sixth color in the second row, and then click **OK**. Under **Table Element**, click **Header Row**, and then click **Format**. In the dialog box, on the **Fill tab**, click the first color in the third row. Click **OK** two times.

14. In the **Styles group**, click **Format as Table**, and then under **Custom**, click **Concessions**. In the dialog box, click **OK**.

15. On the **Design** tab, in the **Tools** group, click **Convert to Range**. In the message box, click **Yes**. Click cell **A1**, and then compare your screen with Figure 4.

16. **Save** the workbook, and then submit the workbook and the snips as directed by your instructor.

 DONE! You have completed the Skills Review

Skills Assessment 1

To complete this project, you will need the following files:

- exl07_SA1Investments
- exl07_SA1InvestmentsData

You will save your files as:

- Last_First_exl07_SA1Investments
- Last_First_exl07_SA1InvestmentsSnip1
- Last_First_exl07_SA1InvestmentsSnip2
- Last_First_exl07_SA1InvestmentsSnip3

1. Start **Excel 2013**, and open the file **exl07_SA1Investments**. Save the workbook in your chapter folder as Last_First_exl07_SA1Investments

2. Select cell **A6**, and then using all the wizard defaults, import the data in the delimited text file **exl07_SA1InvestmentsData**. AutoFit columns **A:E**.

3. In the range **A5:E18**, sort the **Interest Rate** by **Cell Icon**, and set the **Order** so that the green circle is on top.

4. Filter the range **A5:E18** so that only the rows where the **Account Type** for **Money Market** displays. For the range, add a **Number Filter** so that the interest rate is less than 2.75%

5. Create a full-screen snip. **Save** it in your chapter folder as Last_First_exl07_SA1InvestmentsSnip1 and then close the Snipping Tool window.

6. Remove all filters, and then sort the range **A6:E18** in ascending order by **Facility**. Add subtotals to provide a sum for the **Balance** column at each change in **Facility**. AutoFit columns if needed.

7. For cell **E6**, display the **Trace Precedents** line. Use the **Evaluate Formula** dialog box to step through the process. Click **Step In** and **Step Out** one time each, and then click **Evaluate**. Move the **Evaluate Formula** dialog box so that the **Precedent** line displays, and then create a full-screen snip. **Save** it in your chapter folder as Last_First_exl07_SA1InvestmentsSnip2 and then close the Snipping Tool window. Close the **Evaluate Formula** dialog box. Click **Remove Arrows**.

8. Add cell **E13** to the **Watch Window**. Select cell **D13**, type 4.75 and then press Tab. Create a full-screen snip, **Save** it in your chapter

folder as Last_First_exl07_SA1InvestmentsSnip3 and then close the Snipping Tool window. **Close** the **Watch Window**.

9. Select the range **A5:E25**, and then create a new table style. **Name** the style Investments For the **Whole Table**, apply the following **Outline** and **Inside** borders: select the last line style in the left column. For the color, apply the fourth color in the top row. On the **Fill tab**, click the first color in the third row. Close all open dialog boxes, and then apply the new table style to the range. Click **Yes** in the message box. Convert the table to a normal range. AutoFit the columns. Click cell **A1**, and then compare your screen with **Figure 1**.

10. **Save** the workbook, and then submit the workbook and the snips as directed by your instructor.

 DONE! You have completed Skills Assessment 1

Aspen Falls Parks and Recreation
Capital Improvement Investments
June 30, 2015

Account Type	Facility	Balance	Interest Rate	Future Value
Stock Fund	Arts Center	$15,000.00	4.28%	22,797.82
Money Market	Arts Center	$8,700.00	1.05%	9,657.89
	Arts Center Total	$23,700.00		
Stock Fund	Golf	$11,525.00	2.79%	15,168.35
Money Market	Golf	$54,832.00	2.15%	67,829.37
	Golf Total	$66,357.00		
Stock Fund	Parks	$18,550.00	4.28%	28,193.30
Stock Fund	Parks	$45,529.00	4.75%	72,414.98
Money Market	Parks	$878,346.00	3.20%	1,203,236.67
	Parks Total	$942,625.00		
Money Market	Pool	$7,500.00	2.75%	$ 9,837.38
Savings	Pool	$68,000.00	2.79%	89,496.55
	Pool Total	$75,500.00		
Savings	Recreation Center	$6,391.00	3.95%	9,414.86
Savings	Recreation Center	$14,500.00	1.55%	16,910.92
Money Market	Recreation Center	$19,000.00	2.33%	23,909.54
	Recreation Center To	$39,891.00		
Savings	Tennis	$105,250.00	2.18%	130,517.45
	Tennis Total	$105,250.00		
	Grand Total	$1,253,323.00		

Last_First_exl07_SA1Investments

Figure 1

Skills Assessment 2

To complete this project, you will need the following file:

- exl07_SA2Endowment

You will save your files as:

- Last_First_exl07_SA2Endowment
- Last_First_exl07_SA2EndowmentSnip

1. Start **Excel 2013**, and open the file **exl07_SA2Endowment**. Save the workbook in your chapter folder as Last_First_exl07_SA2Endowment

2. In cell **A9** of the **Endowment** worksheet, insert the **FV** function. Type B6/12 for the **Rate**, B7*12 for the **Nper**, and -B5 for the **Pv**.

3. For the range **A9:G20**, create a two-variable data table that uses the term for the row input and the interest rate for the column input. AutoFit columns as needed.

4. Click the **Rental** worksheet. Create a new table style with the name Rental For the **Inside** border for the **Whole Table**, apply the last line style in the left column, and apply the color **Olive Green**, **Accent 3**. Use the same color and the next-to-last line in the right column for the **Outline** border. On the **Fill tab**, click the third color in the first row, and then click **OK**. For the **Rental** table style, for the table's **Header Row**, on the **Fill tab**, assign the third color in the second row.

5. Select the range **A5:F12**, and apply the **Rental** custom table style.

6. For the range **A5:F12**, apply a custom **Number Filter** so that only the rows where the **Income** value **is greater than or equal to $250,000** and **is less than or equal to $500,000** display.

7. Create a full-screen snip. **Save** it in your chapter folder as Last_First_exl07_SA2EndowmentSnip1 and then close the Snipping Tool window.

8. Remove all filters. Convert the table **A5:F12** to a range.

9. Click the **Table** worksheet tab. Select cell **C6**, and then click **Sort A to Z**. Use the **Subtotal** command to sum the **Net** column for each change in **Rate**. AutoFit **column F**. Collapse the subtotals to level 2. Compare your worksheets with **Figure 1**.

10. **Save** the workbook, and then submit the workbook and the snips as directed by your instructor.

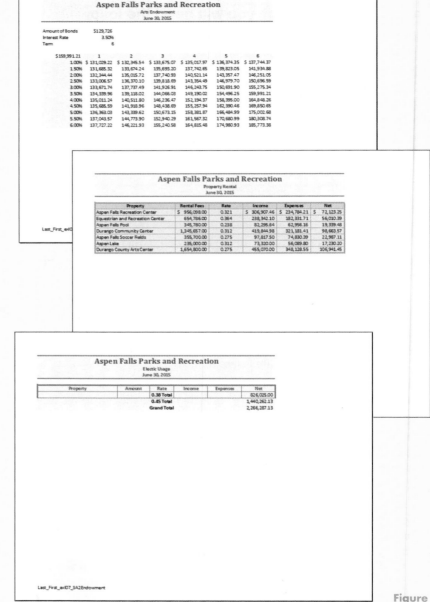

Figure 1

 DONE! You have completed Skills Assessment 2

Visual Skills Check

To complete this project, you will need the following files:

- exl07_VSInventory
- exl07_VSInventoryData

You will save your file as:

- Last_First_exl07_VSInventory

Start **Excel 2013**, and open the file **exl07_VSInventory**. Save the workbook in your chapter folder as Last_First_exl07_VSInventory Select cell **A4** and import the data from **exl07_VSInventoryData**. Create a custom table style named Inventory with borders and shading similar to the table shown in Figure 1. Apply the table style to the table, and then convert the table to a range. Use the **Subtotal** tool to organize and summarize the data as shown in Figure 1. **Save** the workbook and then submit it as directed by your instructor.

DONE! You have completed Visual Skills Check

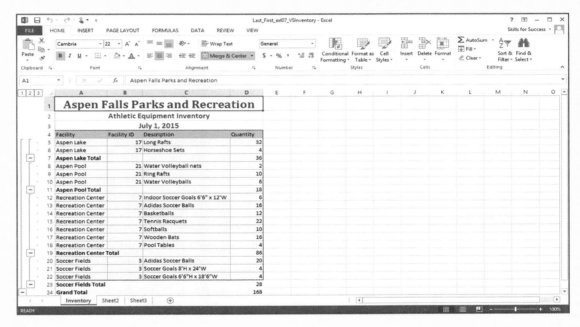

Figure 1

Figure 1

Figure 2

My Skills

To complete this project, you will need the following file:

- exl07_MYBudget

You will save your file as:

- Last_First_exl07_MYBudget

1. Start **Excel 2013**, and open the file **exl07_MYBudget**. Save the workbook in your chapter folder as Last_First_exl07_MYBudget

2. In the first cell of the **Budget** worksheet, replace *Student Name* with your first and last names.

3. Enter your Net Income (income after taxes) for July, August, and September.

4. Enter your expense data for July, August, and September for all expenses. If you do not have these expenses, use the Internet to search for the data and enter estimated data for the area in which you live.

5. Using skills practiced in this chapter, create a table style using the name Budget with the following formatting: thick line **Blue-Gray**, **Text 2**, **Outline** border, thin line **Blue**, **Accent 1 Inside** border, fill color first row, third color. Add a **Header Row** using fill color second row, third color.

6. Apply the **Budget** table style to the range **A4:E19** and then click cell **A1**. Compare the worksheet with Figure 1.

7. Select the **Savings tab**. Replace *Student Name* with your first and last names.

8. In cell **B5**, type the current interest rate for your savings account.

9. In cell **B7**, use the **FV** function to create the result using B5/12 for the **Rate**, B4*12 for **Nper**, –B6 for **Pmt**, and –B3 for **Pv**.

10. Create a **What-if Analysis** one-variable data table for the range **A8:B20** using **B6** as the **Column input**.

11. Select cell **A1**, and then compare the worksheet with Figure 2. **Save** the workbook, and then submit it as directed by your instructor.

DONE! You have completed My Skills

Skills Challenge 1

To complete this project, you will need the following file:

- exl07_SC1Claims

You will save your file as:

- Last_First_exl07_SC1Claims

Aspen Falls tracks employee health care claims on a yearly basis in an effort to reduce costs and promote employee well-being. Start **Excel 2013**, and then open the student data file **exl07_SC1Claims**. Save the workbook in your chapter folder as Last_First_exl07_SC1Claims Format the range A4:F106 as a table, using skills practiced in the chapter to create a new table style with the name Claims Apply the following: a thick Dark Blue outline border and thin inside border using the same color. Apply the following fill color: first row, third color. For the Header Row, apply the fill color in the second row, third

color. Remove all external data ranges. Using the trace and evaluation tools, locate and fix the four errors in the table. Sort the table in ascending order by Code, and Convert the table to a range to retain the formatting. Subtotal both the Fee and Co-Pay 15% columns by Code. Collapse the subtotals to level 2, and then AutoFit column E. Save the workbook with the filter applied, and then submit it as directed by your instructor.

 DONE! You have completed Skills Challenge 1

Skills Challenge 2

To complete this project, you will need the following file:

- exl07_SC2Triathalon

You will save your file as:

- Last_First_exl07_SC2Triathalon

Aspen Falls tracks racers in its annual Women's Triathlon in an effort to provide the results to racing magazines. Start **Excel 2013**, and then open the file **exl07_SC2Triathalon**. Save the workbook in your chapter folder as Last_First_exl07_SC2Triathalon Sort the Total Time from smallest to largest. Copy the range A1:H21 and paste it into a new worksheet named Top 20 Resize the columns A:H to the width 11. Apply the following to the Top 20 worksheet: a Subtotal at each

change in Bracket by Total Time, and the Level 2 Outline, which will show the Total Time by Bracket. Then Sort the Bracket column in ascending order. Select cell A1 of the 2014 Females worksheet. Save the workbook with the filter applied, and then submit it as directed by your instructor.

 DONE! You have completed Skills Challenge 2

CHAPTER 8

Manage and Present Data Visually

- ► Excel functions can be used to edit data imported from other files.
- ► You can use legends to help users understand charted data.
- ► You can use a graphic representation to signify trends in data.
- ► You can insert text into shapes to provide additional information about data in a chart.

- ► You can combine data from multiple worksheets into one worksheet.
- ► Excel provides preformatted charts that can be edited to fit your needs.
- ► Excel workbooks can be shared through email or by storing on a secure, web-based application.

Minerva Studio / Fotolia

Aspen Falls City Hall

In this chapter, you will support Janet Neal, the Finance Director of Aspen Falls. You will assist her with editing an existing workbook using text functions, chart tools, and Excel templates to manipulate employee expense data, and then save workbooks in different formats to share via email and web-based services. This workbook will assist Janet with evaluating employee expenses for upper management through charts to predict possible future expenses and trends and to compare employees' expenses.

Businesses and organizations often use Excel workbooks to manipulate data downloaded from other file types. When data is imported into an Excel workbook it can be edited to repair the data or to create new data. The data can then be represented visually using different chart views and elements.

In this project you will open files saved in other file types, and use text functions to edit data to create employee passwords and delete extra spaces entered incorrectly. You will edit and create charts incorporating legends, trendlines, data ranges, data labels, and alternate data views. Additionally, you will create dual axis charts to compare data and create chart templates. You will edit an Excel template to create an employee expense report template and combine data from other worksheets into a worksheet within the workbook. Finally, you will save the workbook as different file types in order to share with others through email, the Internet, and SkyDrive.

Time to complete all 10
skills – 60 to 90 minutes

Student data files needed for this chapter:

exl08_Expenses   exl08_CityHallExpenses

exl08_EmployeeExpenses

You will save your workbooks as:

Last_First_exl08_Expenses
Last_First_exl08_ExpensesPdf
Last_First_exl08_ExpenseSnip1
Last_First_exl08_ExpensesTxt
Last_First_exl08_ExpensesXml
Last_First_exl08_ExpensesXls

Outcome

Using the skills listed in this chapter, you will be able to create worksheets like these:

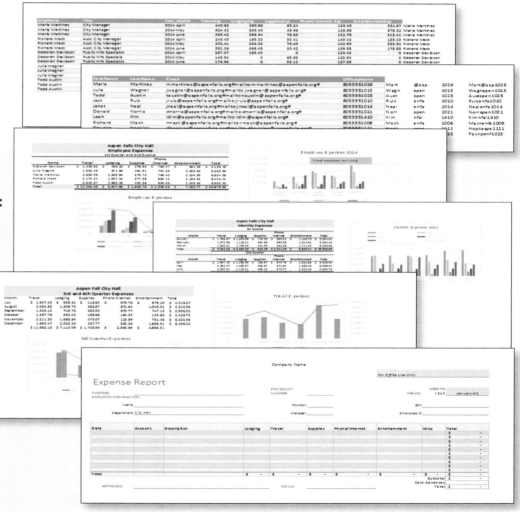

SKILLS

Skills 1-10 Training

At the end of this chapter, you will be able to:

Skill 1 Import and TRIM Data from Non-native Files
Skill 2 Use LEFT, RIGHT, and MID Functions
Skill 3 Add Legends and Data Series to Charts
Skill 4 Enhance Charts with Trendlines and Text Boxes
Skill 5 Modify Excel Worksheet Templates
Skill 6 Consolidate Worksheet Data
Skill 7 Construct Dual Axis Charts
Skill 8 Create and Edit Custom Chart Templates
Skill 9 Edit and Save Excel File Type Versions
Skill 10 Send Workbook Files via Email and SkyDrive

MORE SKILLS

Skill 11 Modify Charts and Graph Parameters
Skill 12 Insert and Edit SmartArt Charts
Skill 13 Embed Worksheet Data in a Web Page
Skill 14 Present a Workbook Online

EXL 8-1 VIDEO

- In Excel, you can open ***non-native files***—formats that are not current Excel 2013 files—including previous versions, text files, and data tables.

- When text data is imported or copied into Excel, extra spaces can sometimes be included with the data.

- The ***TRIM*** function is a text function used to remove all spaces from a text string except for single spaces between words.

1. Start **Excel 2013**. Open the student data file **exl08_Expenses**. On the **File tab**, click **Save As**, and then click **Browse**. In the **Save As** dialog box, navigate to the location where you are saving your files. Click **New folder**, type Excel Chapter 8 and then press Enter two times. Name the file Last_First_exl08_Expenses and then press Enter.

2. If necessary, select the **Data** worksheet and click cell **A1**. On the **File tab**, click **Open**. Navigate to the student data files for this chapter. At the bottom right of the **Open** dialog box click the **file extension arrow** and choose **All Files**. Compare your screen with Figure 1, and then open the file **exl08_CityHallExpenses**.

3. In the **Microsoft Excel Security Notice** dialog box, read the information, and then click **Enable**.

   When you link a file to an external file, Excel recognizes potential security issues.

4. In the **Select Table** dialog box, click to select the **2nd Qtr Employee Expenses** table. Compare your screen with Figure 2, and then click **OK**.

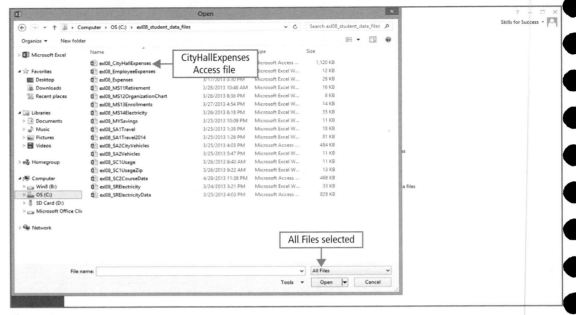

Figure 1

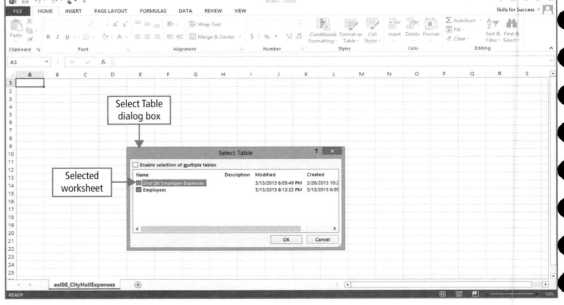

Figure 2

■ **Continue to the next page to complete the skill**

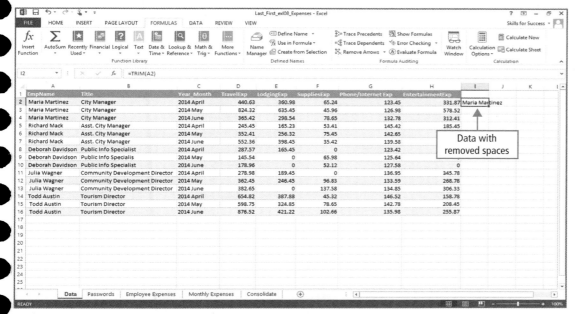

Figure 3

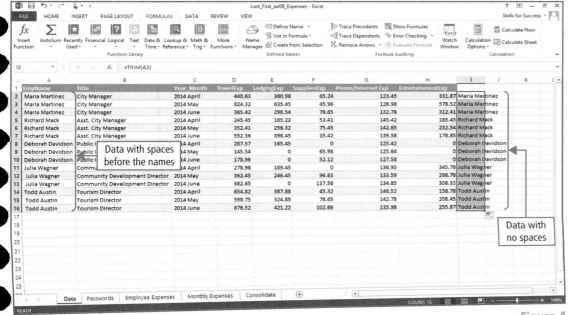

Figure 4

5. In the **Import Data** dialog box, verify **Existing worksheet** is selected and the box displays =$A$1, and then click **OK**.

6. Select **B1:I16**. On the **Home tab**, in the **Clipboard group**, click **Copy** 📋. Click the Excel icon on the taskbar, and navigate to the **Last_First_exl08_Expenses** window. In the **Data** worksheet, ensure cell **A1** is selected. In the **Clipboard group**, click the **Paste Options arrow**. In the **Paste Options gallery**, under **Paste**, click the sixth button 🔲—**Keep Source Column Widths (W)**.

7. Close the **Book1** Excel file without saving. In the **Microsoft Excel** dialog box, read the information, and then click **No**.

8. Click cell **I2**, and then click the **Formulas tab**. In the **Function Library group**, click the **Text** button, and then click **TRIM**.

9. In the **Function Arguments** dialog box, in the **Text** box, type A2 and then click **OK**. Compare your screen with **Figure 3**.

    Maria Martinez is the data that was evaluated. The spaces before the name were removed.

10. With **I2** selected, drag the fill handle down through cell **I16**. Compare your screen with **Figure 4**.

    The data in column A has extra spaces before it; the data in column I does not.

11. On the **Home tab**, in the **Clipboard group**, click the **Copy** button, and select cell **A2**. Click the **Paste Options arrow**. In the **Paste Options gallery**, under **Paste Values**, click the first button 📋—**Values (V)**.

    You are replacing data that has extra spaces. When pasting cells that contain functions, using Paste Values pastes values, not functions.

12. Select cell **A1**, and then **Save** 💾 the workbook.

▪ **You have completed Skill 1 of 10**

EXL 8-2 VIDEO

▶ When text data is imported or copied into an Excel worksheet, characters from these cells can be extracted to create new data.

▶ The **LEFT** function returns a specified number of characters starting from the left side of the data.

▶ The **RIGHT** function returns a specified number of characters starting from the right side of the data.

▶ The **MID** function returns a specified number of characters starting from a specified position in the data.

1. Select the **Passwords** worksheet. Click cell **A1**. On the **File tab**, click **Open**. Navigate to the student data files for this chapter. At the bottom of the **Open** dialog box, verify **All Files** is selected, and then open the file **exl08_CityHallExpenses**.

2. In the **Microsoft Excel Security Notice** dialog box, click **Enable**.

3. In the **Select Table** dialog box, click the **Employees** table. Compare your screen with **Figure 1**, and then click **OK**.

4. In the **Import Data** dialog box, verify that the **Existing worksheet** option button is selected, and that the box displays the text =$A$1, and then click **OK**.

5. Select the range **B1:E11**. Click the **Home tab**, and in the **Clipboard group**, click **Copy**. Click the **Excel** icon on the taskbar, and navigate to the **Last_First_exl08_Expenses** window. In the **Passwords** worksheet, using the method you learned in Skill 1, paste the data using —**Keep Source Column Widths (W)**. Compare your screen with **Figure 2**.

■ **Continue to the next page to complete the skill**

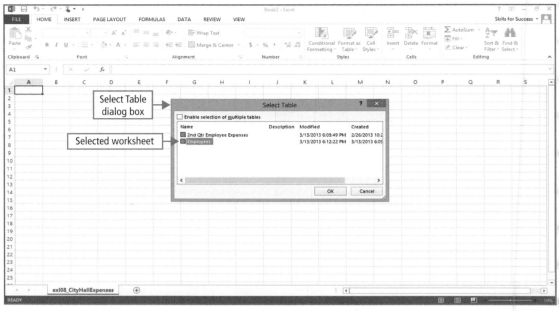

Figure 1

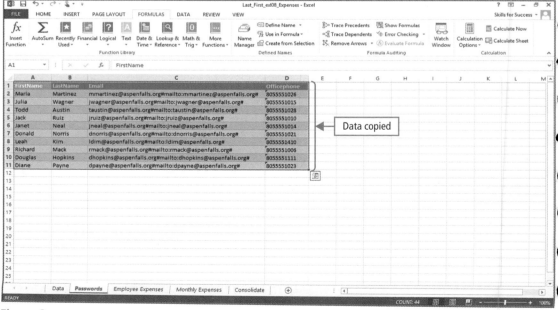

Figure 2

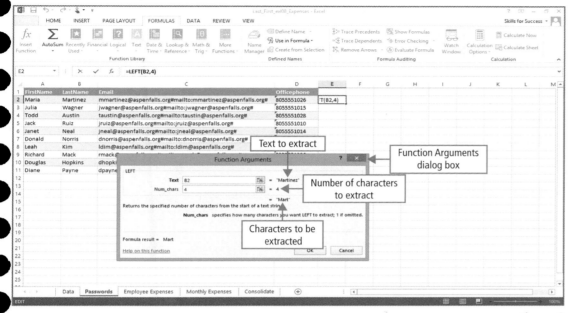

Figure 3

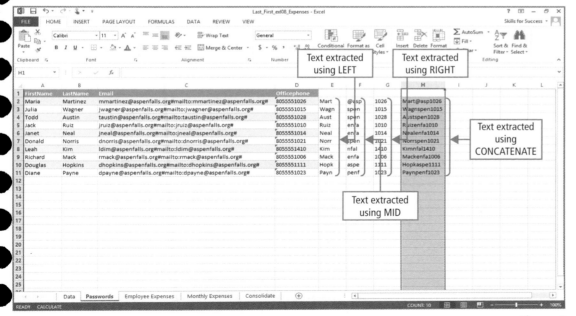

Figure 4

6. Select cell **E2**, and then click the **Formulas tab**. In the **Function Library group**, click the **Text** button, and then click **LEFT**.

7. In the **Function Arguments** dialog box, in the **Text** box, type B2 and then press Tab. In the **Num_chars** box, type 4 Compare your screen with **Figure 3**, and then click **OK**.

8. Select cell **F2**. In the **Function Library group**, click the **Text** button, and then click **MID**.

9. In the **Function Arguments** dialog box, in the **Text** box, type C2 and then press Tab. In the **Start_num** box, type 10 and then press Tab. In the **Num_chars** box, type 4 Click **OK**.

10. Select cell **G2**. In the **Function Library group**, click the **Text** button, and then click **RIGHT**.

11. In the **Function Arguments** dialog box, in the **Text** box, type D2 and then press Tab. In the **Num_chars** box, type 4 and then click **OK**.

12. Select cell **H2**. In the **Function Library group**, click the **Text** button, and then click **CONCATENATE**.

13. In the **Function Arguments** dialog box, in the **Text1** box, type E2 and then press Tab. In the **Text2** box, type F2 press Tab, and then in the **Text3** box, type G2 Click **OK**.

14. Select the range **E2:H2**, and then drag the fill handle down through cell **H11**. AutoFit **column H**, and then compare your screen with **Figure 4**.

    New passwords have been created for all the employees.

15. Close the **Book2** Excel file without saving the file.

16. Select cell **A1**, and then **Save** 💾 the workbook.

■ **You have completed Skill 2 of 10**

▶ A chart *legend* helps users to interpret or understand charted data.

▶ In a chart, the *data series*—related data points that are plotted in a chart—originate from worksheet rows and columns.

▶ Each data series has a unique outline color. One or more data series can be plotted in charts; however, pie charts have only one data series.

1. Click the **Employee Expenses** worksheet, and then click the **Employee Expenses 2014** chart. On the **Design tab**, in the **Chart Layouts group**, click the **Add Chart Element** button. In the list, click **Legend**, and then point to **Bottom**. Compare your screen with **Figure 1**, and then click **Bottom**.

   The legend is inserted at the bottom of the chart.

2. With the chart still selected, in the **Data group**, click the **Select Data** button. In the **Select Data Source** dialog box, click the **Collapse Dialog** button 📊.

3. Select the range **B4:F9**, click the **Expand Dialog** button 📊, and then click **OK**.

   The chart has two new data series: Phone Internet and Entertainment.

4. With the chart still selected, in the **Data group**, click the **Select Data** button. In the **Select Data Source** dialog box, note the **Horizontal (Category) Axis Labels**, and compare your screen with **Figure 2**.

   The horizontal axis labels are currently represented by 1, 2, 3, 4, and 5.

5. Under **Horizontal (Category) Axis Labels**, click the **Edit** button. Select the range **A5:A9**, and then click **OK** two times.

■ Continue to the next page to complete the skill ▶

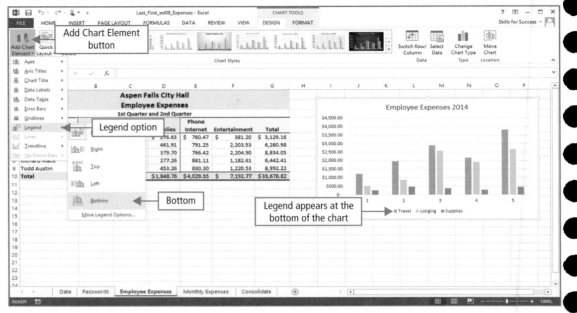

Figure 1

Figure 2

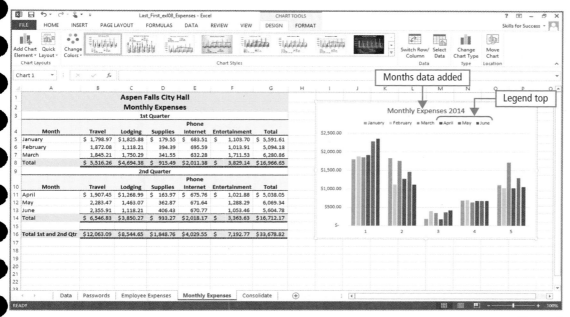

Figure 3

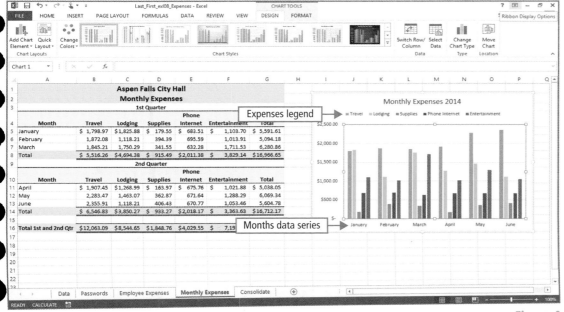

Figure 4

6. Select the **Monthly Expenses** worksheet, and then click the **Monthly Expenses 2014** chart. On the **Design tab**, in the **Chart Layouts group**, click the **Add Chart Element** button. In the list, click **Legend**, and then click **Top**.

7. With the chart still selected, in the **Data group**, click the **Select Data** button. In the **Select Data Source** dialog box, click the **Collapse Dialog** button ▦, and then press and hold the Ctrl key. Select the range **A11:F13**, and then click the **Expand Dialog** button ▦. Click **OK**. Compare your screen with **Figure 3**.

> The series data for April, May, and June is included in the chart.

8. In the **Data group**, click the **Select Data** button. In the **Select Data Source** dialog box, under **Horizontal (Category) Axis Labels**, click the **Edit** button.

9. Select the range **B4:F4**, and then in the **Axis Labels** dialog box, click **OK** two times.

10. In the **Data group**, click the **Switch/Row Column** button. Compare your screen with **Figure 4**.

> The data labels are switched, the horizontal axis is now the months and the legend is the expense labels. The chart now shows the expenditures categorized by month instead of expense.

11. Select cell **A1**, and then **Save** ▦ the workbook.

■ **You have completed Skill 3 of 10**

▶ When data is graphed, the data can forecast expenses and other outcomes for the next quarter, or next year, and project expected results for a data series.

▶ A *trendline* is a graphic representation of trends in a data series. It is used for problem prediction.

▶ To provide additional information in a chart, insert a *text box*—a rectangular object on a worksheet or chart in which you can type text.

1. Select the **Employee Expenses** worksheet, and then click the **Employee Expenses 2014** chart. On the **Design tab**, in the **Chart Layouts group**, click the **Add Chart Element** button. In the list, click **Trendline**, and then compare your screen with **Figure 1**.

   The Trendline gallery displays the types of trendlines. Select trendlines based on how the data appears to be graphed. Some types of trendlines are *Linear* (data points follow nearly a straight line), *Exponential* (data points create a symmetric arc), *Linear Forecast* (data points follow a straight line with a two-period forecast), and *Moving Average* (data points follow a smooth curve to show data fluctuations).

2. Click **Linear Forecast**. In the **Add Trendline** dialog box, ensure **Travel** is selected, and then click **OK**. Compare your screen with **Figure 2**.

   The trendline is added to the chart and shows a straight line going up based on the increase in travel expenses. The trendline also is added to the legend.

■ Continue to the next page to complete the skill

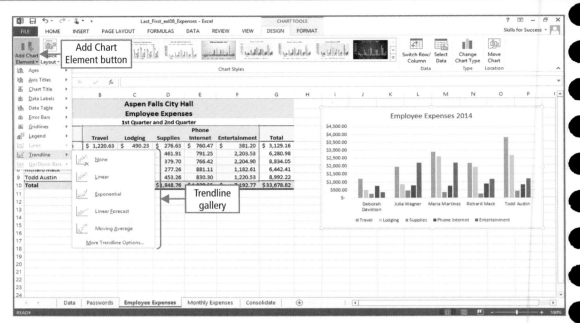

Figure 1

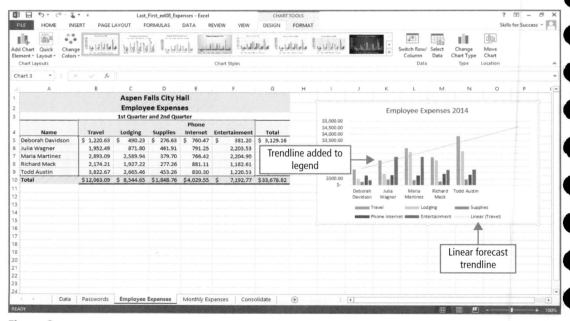

Figure 2

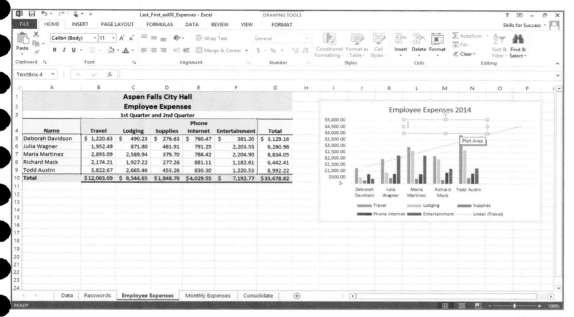

Figure 3

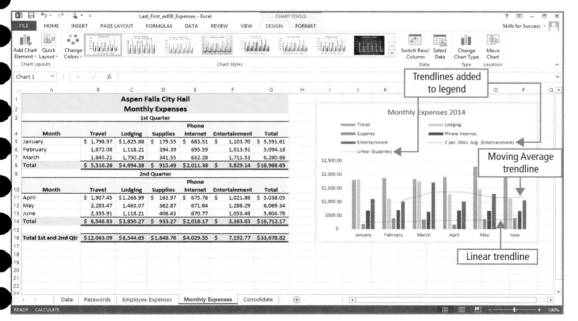

Figure 4

3. With the chart still selected, click the **Format tab**, and in the **Insert Shapes group**, click **Text Box** ⌨.

4. Place the cursor in the chart on the *$5,000* line, where it intersects with the left side of column **L**. Drag the cursor to the right of column **N**, and then down to *$4,000*. Compare your screen with **Figure 3**.

5. With the text box selected, type Travel expenses are rising Click the **Format tab**. In the **Shape Styles group**, click the **Shape Fill arrow**, and then click the eighth color in the top row—**Gold, Accent 4**. Select the text in the text box, and then in the **WordArt Styles group**, click the first style—**Fill – Black, Text 1, Shadow**.

6. Select the **Monthly Expenses** worksheet, and then click the **Monthly Expenses 2014** chart. Click the **Design tab**. In the **Chart Layouts group**, click the **Add Chart Element** button. In the list, click **Trendline**, and then click **Moving Average**. In the **Add Trendline** dialog box, click **Entertainment**, and then click **OK**.

   The trendline is added to the chart and shows a fluctuation in Entertainment expenses from month to month.

7. In the **Chart Layouts group**, click the **Add Chart Element** button. In the list, click **Trendline**, and then click **Linear**. In the **Add Trendline** dialog box, click **Supplies**, and then click **OK**. Compare your screen with **Figure 4**.

   The trendline is added to the chart and shows nearly a straight line. Supplies costs are similar from month to month.

8. Select cell **A1**, and then **Save** 🖫 the workbook.

■ **You have completed Skill 4 of 10**

EXL 8-5
VIDEO

- To save time or to standardize, Excel provides preformatted worksheets and charts.
- A **worksheet template** is a workbook with content and formatting that you use as a model to create other similar workbooks or worksheets.
- Worksheet templates can be edited to meet an organization's specifications.

1. On the **File tab**, click **New**.

   The categories for available Excel templates are shown.

2. In the **New** window, click the **Expense** link, and then click the second **Expense report**. Compare your screen with Figure 1, and then click **Create**.

3. Right-click the **Expense Report** worksheet tab and select **Move or Copy**. In the **Move or Copy** dialog box, under *To book:* click the arrow next to the *Expense report1* text box, and then click **Last_First_exl08_Expenses**. Under *Before sheet:*, click **(move to end)**, and then click **OK**.

4. In the **Last_First_exl08_Expenses** window, ensure the **Expense Report** worksheet is selected. On the **View tab**, in the **Workbook Views group**, click **Normal**.

5. Click cell **J4**. Click in the **formula bar**, delete the text *PAY* and the space after it, and then press Tab. In cell **K4**, replace the existing text with MONTH YEAR and then press Tab.

6. Click cell **L4**. On the **Home tab**, in the **Number group**, click the **Number Format Dialog Box Launcher** ⊡. In the **Format Cells** dialog box, under **Category**, ensure **Date** is selected. Under **Type**, scroll down and click **March-12**. Click **OK**, and then compare your screen with Figure 2.

■ **Continue to the next page to complete the skill**

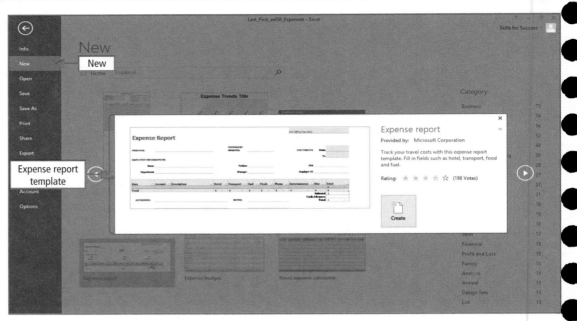

Figure 1

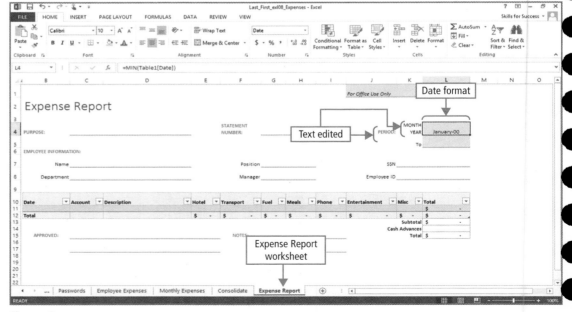

Figure 2

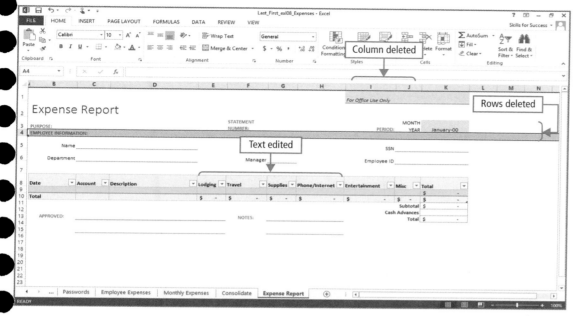

Figure 3

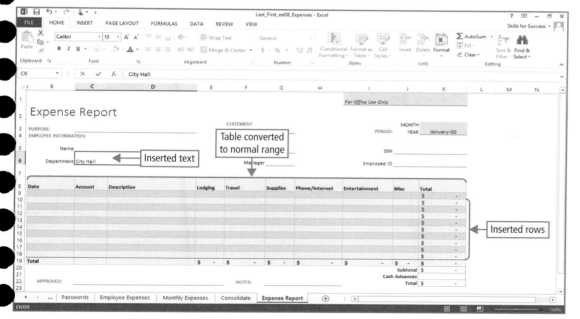

Figure 4

7. Click cell **E10**. Replace the existing text with Lodging and then press Tab. In cell **F10**, replace the existing text with Travel and then press Tab. In cell **G10**, replace the existing text with Supplies and then press Tab. AutoFit **column G**. Click cell **I10**. Replace the existing text with Phone/Internet and then press Tab. AutoFit **column I**.

8. Select **column H**. In the **Cells group**, click the **Delete** button to delete the column. Select **row 3**. In the **Cells group**, click the **Delete** button to delete the row, and then AutoFit **row 2**. Select **row 4**. In the **Cells group**, click the **Delete** button to delete the row. Compare your screen with **Figure 3**.

9. Select **row 10** through **row 18**. In the **Cells group**, click the **Insert** button to insert eight additional rows, and then click in one of the newly created cells.

10. Click the **Design tab**. In the **Tools group**, click **Convert to Range**, and then click **Yes** to convert to a normal range.

11. Select the range **B9:B18**. In the **Number group**, click the **Number Format Dialog Box Launcher** 🔲. Under **Category**, select **Date**, and then under **Type**, click **3/14/12**. Click **OK**.

12. Select **row 24**. In the **Cells group**, click the **Delete** button to delete the signature lines in the row.

13. Select cell **C6**, and then type City Hall Compare your screen with **Figure 4**.

14. Select cell **B1**, and then **Save** 🔲 the workbook.

■ **You have completed Skill 5 of 10**

▶ EXL 8-6
VIDEO

▶ Data can be combined into one worksheet from worksheets in the same workbook or other workbooks.

▶ The **Consolidate** command is used to summarize and report results from separate worksheets.

▶ You can consolidate worksheet data by position or by category.

1. On the **File tab**, in the list, select **Open**. Navigate to the student data files for this chapter, and then open **exl08_EmployeeExpenses**.

2. In the taskbar, click the **Excel** icon, and then click the **Last_First_exl08_Expenses** window. Select the **Consolidate** worksheet, and then click cell **A3**.

3. Click the **Data tab**, and then in the **Data Tools group**, click the **Consolidate** button. Compare your screen with Figure 1.

4. In the **Consolidate** dialog box, verify that **Sum** is selected as the **Function**. For the **Reference**, click the **Browse** button, navigate to the student data files, and then double-click **exl08_EmployeeExpenses**.

5. Click the **Collapse Dialog** button. On the taskbar, select the **exl08_EmployeeExpenses** file, and then in the **3rd Qtr** worksheet select **A3:F6**. In the **Consolidate - Reference** dialog box, click the **Expand Dialog** button.

6. In the **Consolidate** dialog box, click **Add**. Compare your screen with Figure 2.

Figure 1

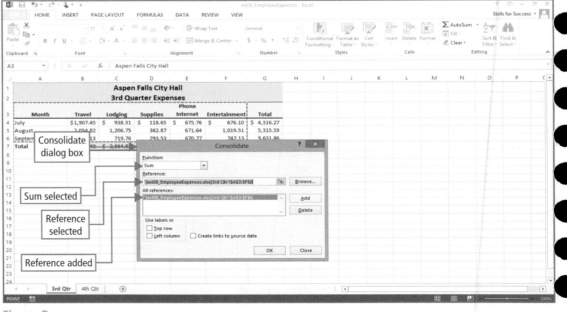

Figure 2

■ **Continue to the next page to complete the skill**

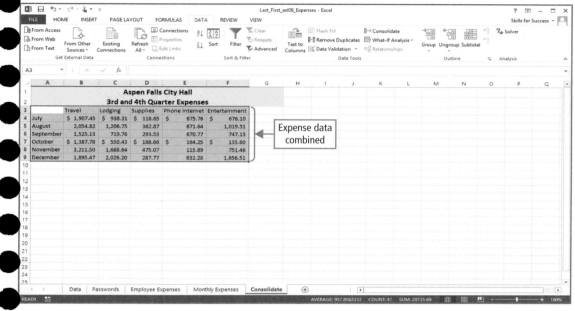

Figure 3

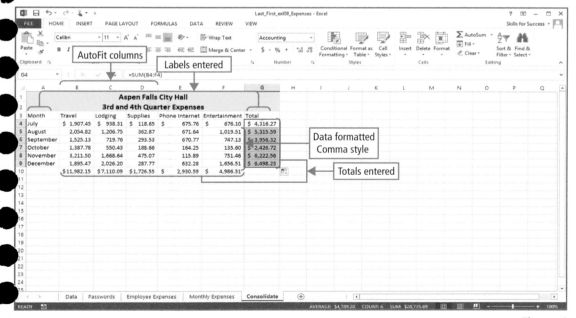

Figure 4

7. Click the **Browse** button. Navigate to the student data files, and then double-click **exl08_EmployeeExpenses**. Click the **Collapse Dialog** button. In the taskbar, select the **exl08_ EmployeeExpenses** file, and then in the **4th Qtr** worksheet select **A3:F6**. In the **Consolidate - Reference** dialog box, click the **Expand Dialog** button.

8. In the **Consolidate** dialog box, click **Add**, and then under **Use Labels in**, ensure that the **Top row** and **Left column** check boxes are checked. Click **OK** to close the **Consolidate** dialog box.

   Checking the top row and left column check boxes ensures that the labels will be included in the consolidation.

9. Close the **exl08_EmployeeExpenses** workbook. Compare your screen with Figure 3.

   The Consolidate worksheet appears with the combined data from the 3rd and 4th Qtr worksheets.

10. Click cell **A3**, and type Month

11. Select the range **B5:F9**. Click the **Home tab**, and then in the **Number group**, click **Comma Style**.

12. Click cell **B10**. In the **Editing group**, click **AutoSum** , and then press Enter. Using the fill handle in cell **B10**, drag over to **F10**. AutoFit **columns B:D**.

13. Select cell **G3**, and then type Total Click cell **G4**. In the **Editing group**, click **AutoSum** , and then press Enter. Using the fill handle in cell **G4**, drag down to **G9**. Compare your screen with Figure 4.

14. Select cell **A1**, and then **Save** the workbook.

■ **You have completed Skill 6 of 10**

▶ EXL 8-7
VIDEO

▶ Values in a 2-D chart can vary widely from data series to data series, or have mixed types of data.

▶ In a *dual axis chart*, one or more data series is plotted on a secondary vertical axis.

▶ The secondary vertical axis reflects the value series.

1. In the **Consolidate** worksheet, select the range **A3:B9**, press and hold the Ctrl key, and then select **G3:G9**. Click the **Insert tab**. In the **Charts group**, click **Insert Column Chart**, and then under **2-D Column**, select the first option in the first row—**Clustered Column**.

2. Drag the chart so that the top left corner is positioned in cell **I2**. Compare your screen with **Figure 1**.

3. In the chart, click the *Chart Title*. Replace the text with Travel Expenses

4. In the chart, click the **Total** data series.

   In the chart, the data series columns for Total should be selected.

5. On the **Design tab**, in the **Type group**, click the **Change Chart Type** button. In the **Change Chart Type** dialog box, click the second option at the top—**Clustered Column - Line on Secondary Axis**.

6. Under **Choose the chart type and axis for your data series**, verify that the check box under **Secondary Axis** for **Total** is checked. Compare your screen with **Figure 2**, and then click **OK**.

   The secondary axis is added showing the travel data and how it compares to the Total Expenses.

▪ **Continue to the next page to complete the skill**

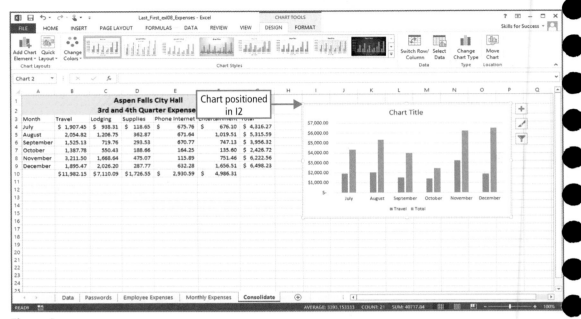

Figure 1

Figure 2

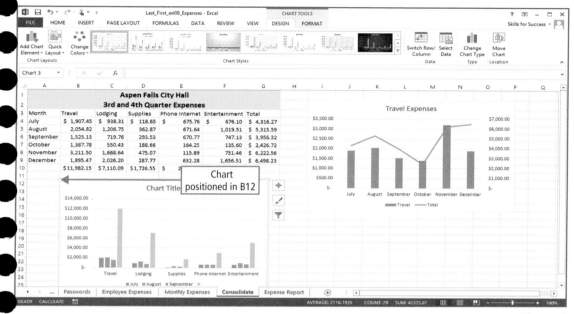

Figure 3

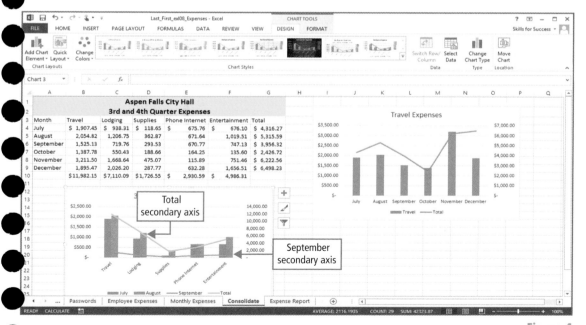

Figure 4

7. Select the range **A3:F6**, press and hold the ⎡Ctrl⎤ key, and then select **A10:F10**. On the **Insert tab**, in the **Charts group**, click **Insert Column Chart** ▮▼, and then under **2-D Column**, select the first option in the first row—**Clustered Column**.

8. Drag the chart's top left corner to cell **B12**. Compare your screen with **Figure 3**.

   The chart compares the 3rd Qtr expenses and total expenses for 3rd and 4th Qtr.

9. In the chart, click *Chart Title*. Replace the text with 3rd Quarter Expenses

10. On the **Design tab**, in the **Data group**, click **Select Data**. In the **Select Data Source** dialog box, under **Legend Entries (Series)**, click **<blank series>**, and then click **Edit**. In the **Edit Series** dialog box, in the **Series name** text box, replace the text with Total and then click **OK** two times.

11. In the chart, select the **Total** data series. The data series columns for Total should be selected.

12. In the **Type group**, click the **Change Chart Type** button. In the **Change Chart Type** dialog box, click the second option at the top—**Clustered Column - Line on Secondary Axis**.

13. Under **Choose the chart type and axis for your data series**, ensure that all have the **Clustered Column** selected as the **Chart Type** except for **September** and **Total**. Under **Secondary Axis**, ensure that only **September** and **Total** are selected, and then click **OK**. Compare your screen with **Figure 4**.

   An additional secondary axis shows the comparison of September data related to the Total Expenses.

14. Select cell **A1**, and then **Save** 🖫 the workbook.

■ **You have completed Skill 7 of 10**

▶ To save time formatting charts, you can reuse a chart that you created, and save that chart as a template.

▶ A *chart template* is a custom chart type that you can apply like any other chart type.

1. In the **Consolidate** worksheet, right click on the **3rd Quarter Expenses** chart. In the shortcut menu, click **Save as Template**.

2. In the **Save Chart Template** dialog box, replace the **File name** with Dual Axis Chart Ensure the **Save as type** is **Chart Template Files**. Compare your screen with Figure 1, and then click **Save**.

   The chart template will be saved as a .crtx file.

3. Click the **Employee Expenses** worksheet. Right-click on the **Employee Expenses 2014** chart. In the shortcut menu, click **Save as Template**.

4. In the **Save Chart Template** dialog box, replace the **File name** with Trendline Chart Ensure that the **Save as type** is **Chart Template Files**. Compare your screen with Figure 2, and then click **Save**.

   In the Save Chart Template dialog box, the Dual Axis Chart appears as a saved template.

5. In the **Employee Expenses** worksheet, select the range **A4:F9**.

6. Click the **Insert tab**. In the **Charts group**, click the **See All Charts Dialog box launcher** ⌐, and then click the **All Charts tab**.

■ Continue to the next page to complete the skill ▶

Figure 1

Figure 2

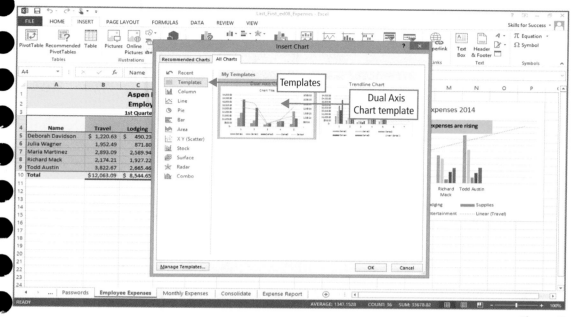

Figure 3

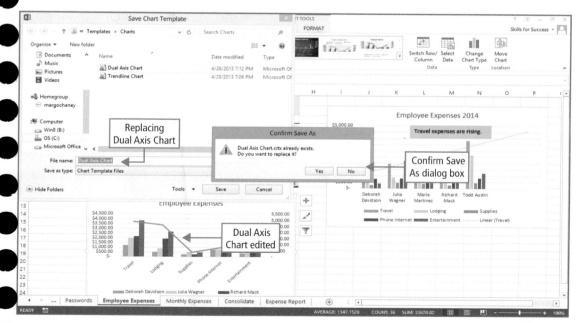

Figure 4

7. In the list, click **Templates**, and then compare your screen with **Figure 3**.

> The two chart templates you previously saved should appear in this dialog box.

8. In the **Insert Chart** dialog box, click the first option—**Dual Axis Chart**, and then click **OK**.

9. Drag the chart so that the top left corner is positioned in cell **B12**.

10. Click the *Chart Title*. Replace the text with Employee Expenses

11. On the **Design tab**, in the **Type group**, click the **Change Chart Type** button. In the **Change Chart Type** dialog box, under **Choose the chart type and axis for your data series**, ensure that each data series has the **Clustered Column** selected as the **Chart Type** except for **Maria Martinez**. Under **Secondary Axis**, ensure that only the **Maria Martinez** check box is selected, and then click **OK**.

12. Ensure the chart is selected, and in the **Chart Styles group**, click the **Change Colors** button. In the gallery, under **Colorful**, select the third option—**Color 3**.

13. Right-click on the **Employee Expenses** chart, in the shortcut menu, and click **Save as Template**.

14. In the **Save Chart Template** dialog box, click **Dual Axis Chart**. Ensure the **Save as type** is **Chart Template Files**, and then click **Save**. Compare your screen with **Figure 4**.

15. In the **Confirm Save As** dialog box, read the message, and then click **Yes**.

> Because you are replacing the previous template with a new version, confirmation is requested.

16. Select cell **A1**, and then **Save** 🔲 the workbook.

■ **You have completed Skill 8 of 10**

▶ Software is updated to improve the software and meet the needs of the user market.

▶ A **software version** is the software release or format.

▶ A **file type**—the standard way information is encoded for storage in a computer file—is designated for each software version.

1. Click the **Data** worksheet. On the **File tab**, click **Save As**. In the **Save As** dialog box, navigate to the location where you are saving your files. Click the **Excel Chapter 8** folder. Name the file Last_First_exl08_ExpensesXls and then in the **Save As type** box, click the arrow.

2. In the menu, select the fourth option—**Excel 97-2003 Workbook**. Compare your screen with **Figure 1**, and then click **Save**.

   The list contains several file types. This file type can be opened by any user with a previous version of Excel; however, with newer versions of Excel, additional formatting and tools may make it difficult to transfer exact data and formatting into previous versions. There are several other file type versions compatible with Excel to save the integrity of your data. Common Excel file types are summarized in the table in **Figure 2**.

3. In the **Microsoft Excel - Compatibility Checker** dialog box, read the message, and then uncheck the **Check compatibility when saving this workbook** check box and click **Continue**.

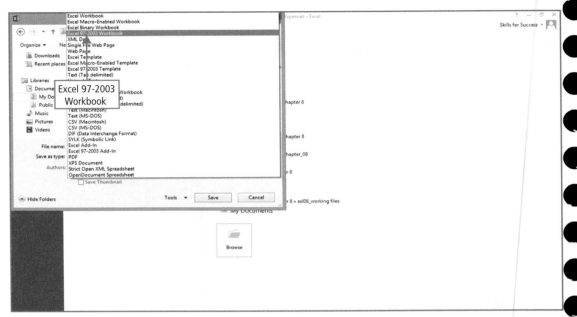

Figure 1

Common Excel File Type Versions		
Format	**Extension**	**Description**
Excel Workbook	.xlsx	Default XML file format for Excel 2013, 2010, and 2007.
Template	.xltx	Default file format for an Excel template for 2013, 2010, and 2007.
Excel 97-2003 Workbook	.xls	Binary file format for Excel 97—Excel 2003.
CSV	.csv	Saves workbook as a comma-delimited text file for use on another Windows operating system, and makes sure that tab characters, line breaks, and other characters are interpreted correctly. Saves only the active sheet.
DIF	.dif	Saves only the active sheet.
DBF.3/DBF.4	.dbf	Users can open dBase formats in Excel, but users can't save an Excel file to dBase format.
OpenDocument	.ods	Files can be opened in spreadsheet applications that use the OpenDocument Spreadsheet format, such as Google Docs and OpenOffice.org Calc.
PDF	.pdf	A format that preserves document formatting and enables file sharing. When the PDF format file is viewed online or printed, it keeps the format that users intended.
Text	.txt	Saves a workbook as a tab-delimited text file for use on another Windows operating system. Tab characters, line breaks, and other characters are interpreted correctly.
XML	.xml	A file format that transports and stores data. The most common tool for data transmissions between all sorts of applications.

Figure 2

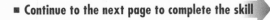
■ **Continue to the next page to complete the skill** ▶

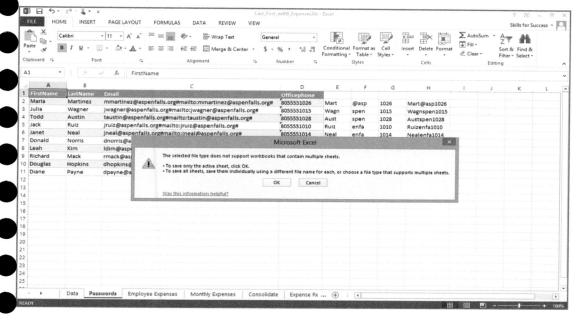

Figure 3

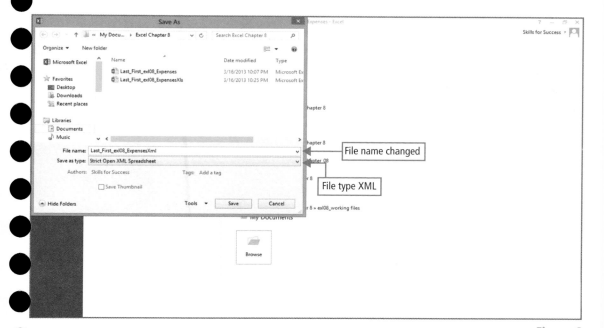

Figure 4

4. Click the **Passwords** worksheet. On the **File tab**, click **Save As**. In the **Save As** dialog box, navigate to the **Excel Chapter 8** folder. Name the file Last_First_exl08_ExpensesTxt and then in the **Save As type** box, click the arrow. In the list, select the eleventh option—**Text (Tab delimited)**—and then click **Save**.

5. In the **Microsoft Excel** dialog box, read the message, and then compare your screen with Figure 3. Click **OK**, click **Yes**, and then close the workbook without saving the changes.

   Text (Tab delimited) will save only the current worksheet in a file format that separates the data columns with tab characters.

6. Open the **Last_First_exl08_Expenses** file. Click the **Consolidate** worksheet. On the **File tab**, click **Save As**. In the **Save As** dialog box, navigate to the **Excel Chapter 8** folder. Name the file Last_First_exl08_ExpensesPdf and then in the **Save As type** box, click the arrow. In the list, select the fourth option from the bottom—**PDF**. Accept the default settings, and then click **Save**. If the file opens in PDF view, close the PDF to go back to the **Last_First_exl08_Expenses** file.

7. On the **File tab**, click **Save As**. In the **Save As** dialog box, navigate to the **Excel Chapter 8** folder. Name the file Last_First_exl08_ExpensesXml and then in the **Save As type** box, click the arrow. In the list, select the second option from the bottom—**Strict Open XML Spreadsheet**—and then compare your screen with Figure 4. Click **Save**.

8. Click the **Data** worksheet. Click cell **A1**, and then **Save** 🖫 the workbook. Close the file.

■ **You have completed Skill 9 of 10**

▶ If your organization uses Outlook, you can share workbooks through the E-mail command in Excel.

▶ When workbooks are shared through email, multiple users can simultaneously edit the workbook; however, any changes will need to be merged.

▶ **SkyDrive** is a secure online application used to store and share files.

▶ Workbooks can be uploaded directly to SkyDrive through the Share command in Excel.

1. Open the **Last_First_exl08_Expenses** workbook. On the **File tab**, click **Share**, and then ensure that the **Invite People** option is selected. Compare your screen with Figure 1.

    This option allows you to save your file to SkyDrive and then share it with others.

2. Click **Save To Cloud**. In the **Save As** window click the first option—**SkyDrive**—and then click **Browse**. If you do not see the Browse button, you may need to log into your Live account.

    When you installed your Office 2013 software you were instructed to register for SkyDrive or enter your account information.

3. In the **Save As** dialog box, click **New folder**. Name the folder Excel Chapter 8 click **Open** two times, and then click **Save**. Compare your screen with Figure 2.

    When you invite people to see a file, you need to share it to SkyDrive first in order for them to access it from the Web.

4. Under **Invite People**, in the **Type names or e-mail addresses** box, type janet.neal@ aspenfalls.org

■ **Continue to the next page to complete the skill**

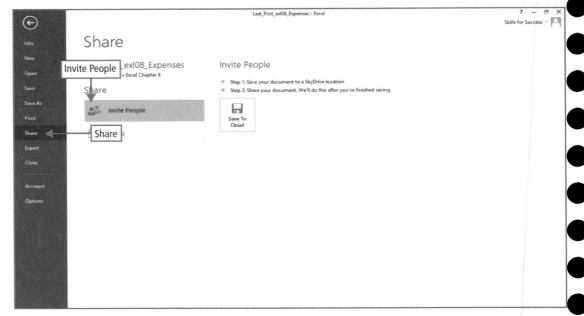

Figure 1

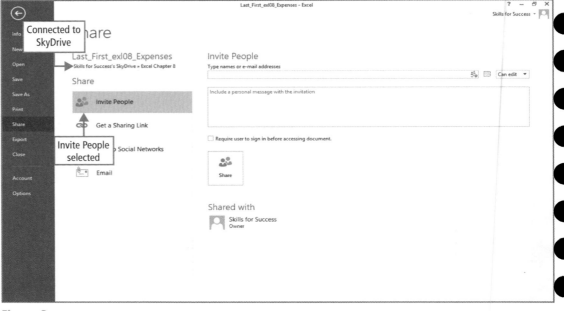

Figure 2

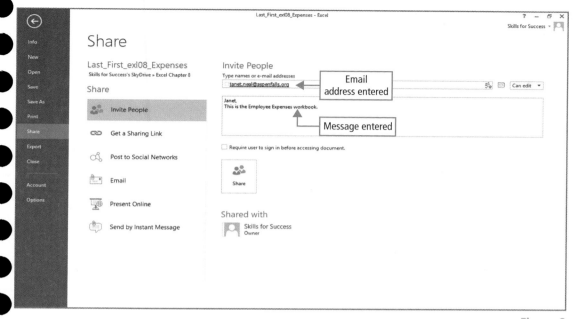

Figure 3

Share File Using Email

Sent as Format	Description
Attachment	Excel file is attached to an Outlook email and anyone can edit.
Link	File can be edited by multiple users at the same time and everyone can view the changes.
PDF	File is created as a PDF file, and attached to Outlook email. Layout, formatting, and images can't be easily edited.
XPS	File is created as an XPS file, and attached to Outlook email. Layout, formatting, and images can't be easily edited.
Internet Fax	Fax service provider is required, but fax machine is not required.

Figure 4

5. In the **Include a personal message with the invitation** box, type Janet, press Enter, and then type This is the Employee Expenses workbook. Compare your screen with **Figure 3**.

6. Create a full-screen snip. **Save** the snip in your **Excel Chapter 8** folder as Last_First_exl08_ExpensesSnip1 and then **Close** the **Snipping Tool** window.

7. Under **Invite People**, click **Share**. In the **Sharing Information** dialog box, read the message, and then click the link **Click here for the additional authentication step**. You may not need to authenticate if you have previously completed this step; if so, skip to step 9.

   The authentication process is a security precaution to verify the identity of the person sharing the file.

8. In the **Live** login screen, enter your username and password for SkyDrive. In the **Help us fight junk email** window, read the message, and enter the characters. In the **Thanks for Solving the Puzzle** window, click **Close**, and then click **Proceed**.

   In the Share window, under Shared with, you will see an icon with the user's name and picture (if they have uploaded a picture).

9. In the **Share** window, click **Email**, and note the options available. The options are explained in the table in **Figure 4**.

   An Outlook account is needed to send files by email.

10. Return to the workbook view, and then select cell **A1**. **Save** the workbook, and then **Close** Excel. Submit the workbook, files, and snip as directed by your instructor.

DONE! You have completed Skill 10 of 10, and your workbook is complete!

The following More Skills are located at **www.pearsonhighered.com/skills**

More Skills Modify Charts and Graph Parameters

When you create a workbook that includes charts, you might need to add elements to the charts that can affect the relationship of the charted data to assist with the evaluation of the data.

In More Skills 11, you will modify a chart and include additional data variables.

To begin, open your web browser, navigate to www.pearsonhighered.com/skills, locate the name of your textbook, and then follow the instructions on the website.

More Skills Insert and Edit SmartArt Charts

Several SmartArt organizational layouts are designed to visually represent the relationships in an organizational hierarchy. The available layouts can be resized, recolored, and reformatted to fit the information.

In More Skills 12, you will insert a hierarchical organization chart and add text and shapes to the chart.

To begin, open your web browser, navigate to www.pearsonhighered.com/skills, locate the name of your textbook, and then follow the instructions on the website.

More Skills Embed Worksheet Data in a Web Page

Excel spreadsheets can be published as web pages to share calendars, schedules, and other data with others. Your users have the ability to interact with tables and data, and to sort and filter the data to find information.

In More Skills 13, you will publish a table that allows users to sort and filter the data.

To begin, open your web browser, navigate to www.pearsonhighered.com/skills, locate the name of your textbook, and then follow the instructions on the website.

More Skills Present a Workbook Online

Workbooks can be presented and shared online with others in real time for meetings or discussions. Using a Lync account, you can allow others to view your presentation and take control of your workbook.

In More Skills 14, you will download Lync and then begin the meeting by inviting attendees.

To begin, open your web browser, navigate to www.pearsonhighered.com/skills, locate the name of your textbook, and then follow the instructions on the website.

Please note that there are no additional projects to accompany the More Skills Projects, and they are not covered in End-of-Chapter projects.

The following table summarizes the **SKILLS AND PROCEDURES** covered in this chapter.

Skills Number	Task	Step	Icon
1	Import non-native files	File tab → Open → All files → Select file → Enable	
1	TRIM data	Formulas tab → Function Library group → Text → TRIM → Text	🅰
2	Extract data from LEFT	Formulas tab → Function Library group → Text → LEFT → Characters	🅰
2	Extract data from RIGHT	Formulas tab → Function Library group → Text → RIGHT → Text → Characters	🅰
2	Extract data from MID	Formulas tab → Function Library group → Text → MID → Text → Characters	🅰
3	Add legend to chart	Chart Tools → Design tab → Chart Layouts group → Add Chart Element → Legend → Position	
3	Add data series to charts	Chart Tools → Design tab → Data group → Select Data → Chart data range	▦
3	Add data series labels to charts	Chart Tools → Design tab → Data group → Select Data → Edit	
3	Switch axis data	Chart Tools → Design tab → Switch Row/Column	▦
4	Add trendline to charts	Chart Tools → Design tab → Chart Layouts group → Add Chart Element → Trendline → Type	📊
4	Insert text box	Chart Tools → Format tab → Insert Shapes group → Text box	abl
5	Modify Excel templates	File tab → New → Select template style → Create	
6	Consolidate worksheet data	Data tab → Data Tools group → Consolidate → Function → Reference → Add	▤
7	Construct dual axis charts	Chart Tools → Design tab → Type group → Change Chart Type → Choose the chart type and axis for your data series	📊
8	Create chart templates	Select chart → Right click → Save as Template → File name → Save as type: Chart Template Files	📊
8	Edit chart templates	Insert tab → See All Charts dialog box launcher → All Charts tab → Templates → Type	
9	Save Excel file versions	File tab → Save As → Navigate to Place → Save as type	
10	Save Excel file to SkyDrive	File tab → Share → Invite People → Save to Cloud → SkyDrive → Browse → Save	☁
10	Share Excel file via SkyDrive	File tab → Share → Enter Email → Share	👥
10	Share Excel file via email	File tab → Share → Email → Choose Email Option	

Key Terms

Online Help Skills

1. Start **Excel 2013**, and then in the upper right corner of the Excel window, click the **Help** button ?. In the **Help** window, click the **Maximize** button.

2. Click in the search box, type Excel charts and then press Enter. In the search results, click **Available chart types**.

3. Read the article's introduction, and then below **Click a chart type to learn more about it**, click **Combo charts**. Compare your screen with Figure 1.

Figure 1

4. Read the section to answer the following questions: What are the advantages of using a combo chart? What types of combo charts are available?

Matching

Match each term in the second column with its correct definition in the first column by writing the letter of the term on the blank line in front of the correct definition.

___ **1.** Formats that are not current Excel versions, but can be opened in the current version.

___ **2.** A text function used to remove spaces from a text string, except for a single space between words.

___ **3.** A text function used to return a specified number of characters starting from a specified point in the data.

___ **4.** Helps users to interpret or understand charted data.

___ **5.** Related data points that are plotted in a chart.

___ **6.** A graphic representation of trends in a data series.

___ **7.** A rectangular object that can be inserted into a worksheet or chart to accommodate text.

___ **8.** Data points that create a symmetric arc.

___ **9.** A software release or format.

___ **10.** A secure online application used to store and share files.

A Data series

B Exponential trendline

C Legend

D MID function

E Non-native files

F SkyDrive

G Software version

H Text box

I Trendline

J TRIM function

Multiple Choice

Choose the correct answer.

1. Returns a specified number of characters from the left side of data.
   - **A.** LEFT function
   - **B.** TRIM function
   - **C.** RIGHT function

2. Used to return a specified number of characters starting from the right side of the data.
   - **A.** MID function
   - **B.** RIGHT function
   - **C.** TRIM function

3. Data points that follow a nearly straight line.
   - **A.** Linear trendline
   - **B.** Moving Average trendline
   - **C.** Exponential trendline

4. Data line that follows a straight line with a two-period forecast.
   - **A.** Linear trendline
   - **B.** Moving Average trendline
   - **C.** Linear Forecast trendline

5. Data points that follow a smooth curve to show data fluctuations.
   - **A.** Exponential trendline
   - **B.** Moving Average trendline
   - **C.** Linear trendline

6. A workbook with content and formatting that can be used as a model and edited as needed.
   - **A.** Worksheet template
   - **B.** Text box
   - **C.** Trendline

7. Used to summarize and report results from separate worksheets.
   - **A.** RIGHT function
   - **B.** Linear trendline
   - **C.** Consolidate

8. One or more data series plotted on a secondary vertical axis.
   - **A.** Linear trendline
   - **B.** Dual axis chart
   - **C.** Trendline

9. A custom chart type that can be applied like other chart types.
   - **A.** Chart template
   - **B.** File type
   - **C.** Text box

10. A standard way that information is encoded for storage in a computer file.
    - **A.** File type
    - **B.** Worksheet template
    - **C.** Chart template

Topics for Discussion

1. In this chapter, you have seen a workbook into which data from a non-native file was inserted. Discuss other situations in which this might be useful to organizations.

2. In this chapter you used trendlines to predict or show data trends. For what other types of information would trendlines be useful to predict data trends?

Skills Review

MyITLab®
Grader

To complete this project, you will need the following files:

- exl08_SRElectricity
- exl08_SRElectricityData

You will save your workbook as:

- Last_First_exl08_SRElectricity

1. Start **Excel 2013**, and open the file **exl08_SRElectricity**. If necessary, select **Continue**. Save the workbook in your chapter folder as Last_First_exl08_SRElectricity

2. In the **Data** worksheet, ensure cell **A1** is selected. On the **File tab**, click **Open**. Navigate to your student data files. At the bottom of the **Open** dialog box, change the option to **All Files**, and then open the file **exl08_SRElectricityData**. Click to **Enable** the security notice. In the **Select Table** dialog box, select the **Residents** table, and then click **OK** two times.

3. Select **B1:G25**. On the **Home tab**, click **Copy**. In the **taskbar**, select the **Last_First_exl08_SRElectricity** window. Click cell **A1**, select the **Paste** arrow, and then click **Paste Options—Keep Source Column Widths (W)**. Close the **Book1** Excel file without saving. Click **No** to delete the information on the Clipboard. Compare your screen with **Figure 1**.

4. Click cell **G2**, and then click the **Formulas tab**. In the **Function Library group**, click the **Text** button, and then click **TRIM**. In the **Function Arguments** dialog box, in the **Text** box, type A2 and then click **OK**. Drag the fill handle down through cell **G25**. Copy the range **G2:G25**. Click on cell **A2**. On the **Home tab**, in the **Clipboard group**, click **Paste Options**. Under **Paste Values**, click the first button—**Values (V)**.

5. Click cell **I2**. Click the **Formulas tab**. In the **Function Library group**, click the **Text** button, and then click **LEFT**. In the **Function Arguments** dialog box, in the **Text** box, type A2 and then press Tab. In the **Num_chars** box, type 4 and then click **OK**. Drag the fill handle down through cell **I25**.

6. Click cell **J2**, and then repeat the Step 5 using **RIGHT**, **Text** F2 and **Num_chars** 4 Drag the fill handle down through cell **J25**. Compare your screen with Figure 2.

7. Select cell **K2**. In the **Function Library group**, click the **Text** button, and then click **CONCATENATE**.

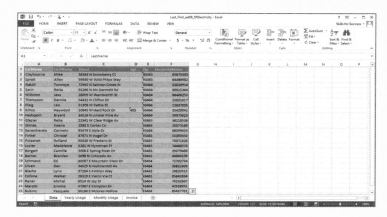

Figure 1

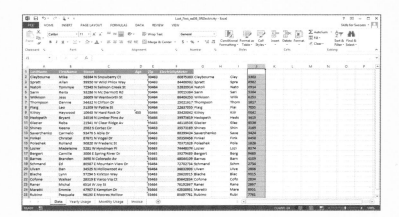

Figure 2

■ Continue to the next page to complete this Skills Review ▶

Figure 3

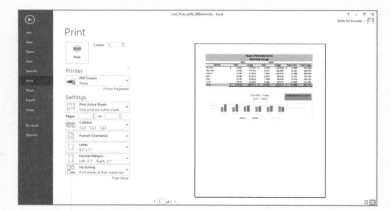

Figure 4

8. In the **Function Arguments** dialog box, in the **Text1** box, type I2 press ⎡Tab⎤, and then in the **Text2** box, type J2 Click **OK**. Drag the fill handle down through cell **K25**, and then AutoFit **column K**. Select cell **A1**.

9. Click on the **Yearly Usage** worksheet, and select the **Yearly Usage 2012–2015** chart. Click the **Design tab**. In the **Chart Layouts group**, click **Add Chart Element**. In the list, click **Legend**, and then click **Bottom**. In the **Data group**, click the **Select Data** button. In the **Select Data Source** dialog box, under **Horizontal (Category) Axis Labels**, click the **Edit** button, and then select the range **A5:A8**. Click **OK** twice.

10. Select the **Yearly Fees 2012–2015** chart. In the **Type group**, click **Change Chart Type**. On the **All Charts tab**, click **Combo**, and then click **Clustered Column - Line on Secondary Axis**. Under **Choose the chart type and axis for your data series**, ensure the **Chart Type** for **Total Fees** is **Line** and the **Secondary Axis** box is checked, and then click **OK**. Compare your screen with Figure 3.

11. Display the **Monthly Usage** worksheet and select the **Monthly Usage 2013–2014** chart. On the **Design tab**, in the **Chart Layouts group**, click **Add Chart Element**, point to **Trendline**, and then click **Linear Forecast**. In the **Add Trendline** dialog box, click **2014**, and then click **OK**. Click the **Format tab**, and in the **Insert Shapes group**, click **Text Box**. Place the cursor in the chart in the top right corner at the border of **columns E** and **F**, and then drag over to the right edge of the chart and down to the 2013–2014 line. In the text box, type Usage decreased in 2014 In the **Shape Styles group**, click the **Shape Fill** arrow. Under **Theme Colors**, click the tenth color in the first row—**Green, Accent 6**. On the **Home tab**, in the **Alignment group**, click **Center**. Select cell **A1**.

12. On the **File tab**, click **New**, and then next to **Suggested searches** click **Invoice**. In the **New window**, scroll down and select **Invoice tracker**. Click **Create**. Select the range **B3:I18**, and then on the **Home tab**, in the **Clipboard group**, click **Copy**. Navigate to the **Last_First_exl08_SRElectricity** window, display the **Invoice** worksheet, and then in cell **A1** paste the range using **Keep Source Column Widths (W)**. Close the **Invoice Tracker1** workbook without saving the file. Click **No** to delete the information on the Clipboard.

13. Display the **Monthly Usage** worksheet. **Save** the workbook. Click the **File tab**, and then click the **Print tab**. Compare your screen with Figure 4. Submit the workbook as directed by your instructor.

 DONE! You have completed the Skills Review

Skills Assessment 1
MyITLab®
Grader

To complete this project, you will need the following files:

- exl08_SA1Travel
- exl08_SA1Travel2014

You will save your files as:

- Last_First_exl08_SA1Travel
- Last_First_exl08_SA1TravelPdf
- Last_First_exl08_SA1TravelSnip1

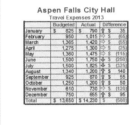

1. Start **Excel 2013**, and open the file **exl08_SA1Travel**. Save the file in your chapter folder as Last_First_exl08_SA1Travel

2. In the **Travel 2013** worksheet, add a legend to the chart, and position it at the top of the chart. Edit the legend to include **Budgeted**, **Actual**, and **Difference** as the **Legend Entries (Series)**. Edit the **Horizontal (Category) Axis Labels** to include the range **A4:A15**.

3. Change the chart type to **Clustered Column - Line on Secondary Axis**. Ensure the **Difference** is the secondary axis **Line**. Select cell **A1**.

4. Display the **Travel 2014** worksheet. In cell **A3**, consolidate the data from the range **A1:D13** from the **Mileage** worksheet and **A1:D13** from the **Lodging** worksheet in the **exl08_SA1Travel2014** file. Ensure the labels are selected as the **Top row** and **Left column**.

5. Select the range **A3:D15**, and then create a **Column chart** using the **Trendline Chart** template located in **My Templates** (this template was created in Skill 8). Position the top left edge of the chart in cell **F3**. Change the chart title to Travel Expenses 2014

6. Edit the trendline, replacing it with a **Moving Average** trendline, and then change the chart colors to **Color 4**, and the style to **Style 8**. Replace the text in the text box with Travel expenses peak in July and August Resize the textbox so all the text fits on one line.

7. **Save** the chart as a new template with the name Moving Average Chart Select cell **A1**.

8. **Save** the worksheet as a PDF file with the name Last_First_exl08_SA1TravelPdf

9. **Save** the workbook to the **Excel Chapter 8** folder in **SkyDrive**, and then share it with janet.neal@aspenfalls.org In the message box, type Janet, press Enter, then type I am sharing the completed Travel

Expenses workbook for 2013 through 2014. Press Enter, and then type your first and last names. Require the user to sign in to access the document. Take a screenshot using the Windows Snipping Tool, and then save the file as Last_First_exl08_SA1TravelSnip1 **Share** the file, and then return to Normal view. Compare your workbook with **Figure 1**.

10. **Save** the workbook. Submit the workbook, snip, and PDF file as directed by your instructor.

Figure 1

 DONE! You have completed Skills Assessment 1

Skills Assessment 2

To complete this project, you will need the following files:

- exl08_SA2Vehicles
- exl08_SA2CityVehicles

You will save your workbook as:

- Last_First_exl08_SA2Vehicles

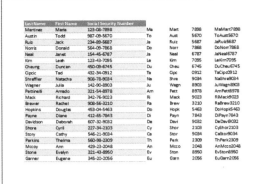

1. Start **Excel 2013**, and open the file **exl08_SA2Vehicles**. Save the file in your chapter folder as Last_First_exl08_SA2Vehicles

2. Open the **exl08_SA2CityVehicles** table, and then import the data from the **Employees** worksheet. Select the range **B1:D23**, and then copy and paste the range using **Keep Source Column Widths (W)** into cell **A1** of the **Codes** worksheet in the **Last_First_exl08_SA2Vehicles** file. Close the **Book1** table without saving.

3. In cell **D2**, use the **LEFT** function to extract the first two characters from the employee's **First Name**. In cell **E2**, use the **LEFT** function to extract the first four characters from the employee's **Last Name**. In cell **F2**, use the **RIGHT** function to extract the last four characters from the employee's **Social Security Number**.

4. In cell **G2**, use the **CONCATENATE** function to create a code combining **D2**, **E2**, and **F2**. AutoFill **D2:G2** down through **G23**. AutoFit **column G**. Click cell **A1**.

5. Click on the **Vehicles** worksheet. Select the range **A3:C10**. Create a **Column chart** using the **Clustered Column - Line on Secondary Axis** on the **All Charts**, **Combo** tab. **Vehicle Quantity** should be graphed as the secondary axis line chart. Position the top left edge of the chart in cell **E2**. Change the chart title to Vehicle Inventory 2014

6. Move the legend to the **Top**, and then **save** the chart as a new template with the name Dual Axis Line Chart

7. Create a new Excel worksheet based on the **Travel expense calculator** template. Move it to the end of the **Last_First_exl08_SA2Vehicles** file. Replace the title in **B1** with Aspen Falls Expense Log Select cell **A1**.

8. **Save** the workbook to the **Excel Chapter 8** folder in **SkyDrive**. Return to Normal view, and then compare your workbook with Figure 1.

Figure 1

9. **Save** the workbook, and then submit the workbook as directed by your instructor.

✓ **DONE! You have completed Skills Assessment 2**

Visual Skills Check

To complete this project, you will need the following:

- exl08_VSFair (Access)
- New blank workbook

You will save your workbook as:

- Last_First_exl08_VSCityFair

Start **Excel 2013,** and then open a blank workbook. Save the workbook in your chapter folder as Last_First_exl08_VSCityFair To create the worksheet shown in **Figure 1**, copy the data from the Revenue table located in the student file for this project—**exl08_VSFair**. Do not copy the table's RevID data. In Excel, paste the data into the range A1:G6.

Add labels, formatting, and AutoSums as shown in **Figure 1**. Center headings. Use Accounting and Comma formats with 2 decimal places. Ensure that all data is visible. Insert a Dual Axis chart, Clustered Column - Line on Secondary Axis, with bottom legend, as shown in **Figure 1**. Use Colorful chart Color 4. Save the workbook, and submit it as directed by your instructor.

✔ **DONE! You have completed Visual Skills Check**

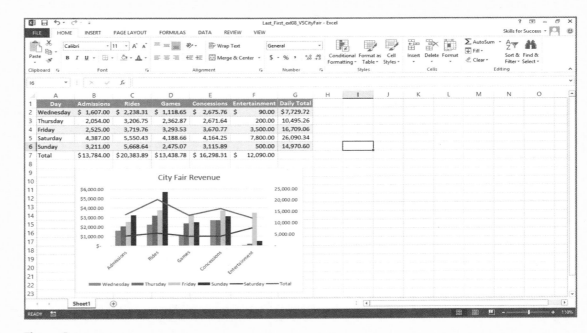

Figure 1

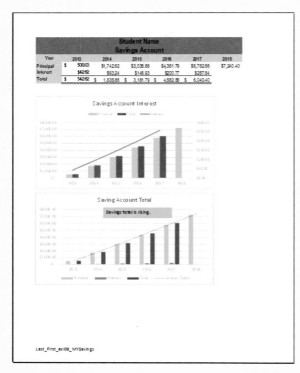

Last_First_exl08_MYSavings

Figure 1

My Skills

To complete this project, you will need the following file:

- exl08_MYSavings

You will save your file as:

- **Last_First_exl08_MYSavings**

1. Start **Excel 2013**, and open the file **exl08_MYSavings**. Save the file in your chapter folder as Last_First_exl08_MYSavings

2. In the first cell of the **Savings** worksheet, replace *Student Name* with your first and last names.

3. Select the range **A3:G6**, and then insert a **Dual Axis Column** chart using the **Dual Axis Chart** template that was created in Skill 8.

4. Move the chart to position the top left corner in cell **A9**.

5. Replace the title with the name Savings Account Interest Move the legend to the **Top**.

6. Remove the **Year** from the **Legend Entries**. Edit the **Horizontal Axis** to include the range **B3:G3**.

7. Select the range **A3:G6**, and then insert a **Column** chart using the **Trendline Chart** template that was created in Skill 8.

8. Move the chart to position the top left corner in cell **A24**.

9. Replace the title with the name Savings Account Total

10. Remove the **Year** from the **Legend Entries**. Edit the **Horizontal Axis** to include the range **B3:G3**.

11. Add a **Linear** trendline based on the **Total**, and then replace the text in the text box with Savings total is rising.

12. Select cell **A1**, and then **Save** the workbook. Compare the worksheet with Figure 1. Submit the workbook as directed by your instructor.

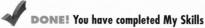 **DONE! You have completed My Skills**

Skills Challenge 1

To complete this project, you will need the following files:

- exl08_SC1Usage
- exl08_SC1UsageZip

You will save your workbook as:

- Last_First_exl08_SC1Usage

Aspen Falls Public Works tracks electricity usage and fees on a yearly basis in an effort to predict monthly trends. Start **Excel 2013**, and then open the student data file **exl08_SC1Usage**. Save the file in your chapter folder as Last_First_exl08_SC1Usage Open the student data file **exl08_SC1UsageZip**. In cell A11 of the **Last_First_exl08_SC1Usage** file, import the data from the **exl08_SC1UsageZip** workbook, using the skills practiced in the chapter. Consolidate the data from the 93464

and 93465 worksheets into the usage 2013-2014 worksheet. The data from the worksheets should be added and include the month labels in the left column. Close the **exl08_SC1UsageZip** file without saving. Save the **Last_First_exl08_SC1Usage** workbook, and then submit it as directed by your instructor.

 DONE! You have completed Skills Challenge 1

Skills Challenge 2

To complete this project, you will need the following file:

- exl08_SC2CourseData

You will save your file as:

- Last_First_exl08_SC2CourseID

Aspen Falls city employees have the benefit of being able to complete business courses at the local community college. If they earn a C or better in a business class, they can submit the tuition for reimbursement. Use the data file provided to search the business classes available. Start **Excel 2013**. Using the All Files option, open the file **exl08_SC2CourseData**, and move the data to a new worksheet before Sheet1 in the open Excel file. Save the file in your chapter folder as Last_First_exl08_SC2CourseID Convert the data to a normal range. Trim the extra spaces from the Major ID data, and then replace the data with the trimmed data. In the next column, create the

beginning of the course identification using the first four letters of the Major data. In the next column, create the middle of the course identification using the last three letters of the Major ID. In the next column, create the end of the course identification using the three numbers in the middle of Course Number. To create the Course ID, concatenate columns F through H. Ensure all of the column widths fit the data. Save the workbook, and then submit it as directed by your instructor.

 DONE! You have completed Skills Challenge 2

CHAPTER 9

Link and Analyze Data in PivotTables and PivotCharts

▶ You can import and relate large amounts of data from multiple file sources, rapidly perform information analysis, and easily share insights.

▶ PivotTable reports are used to dynamically summarize and analyze large amounts of data.

▶ You can use PivotTable and PivotChart reports to place category data in both rows and columns to produce a variety of results in the value fields.

▶ Using PivotTable reports, you can perform various calculations on data to provide different types of results in the value fields.

▶ PivotChart reports graphically display the results that are calculated in PivotTable reports.

▶ You can filter PivotTable reports and PivotChart reports to show only the data that meets criteria you specify.

▶ You can use Power View to represent data using various chart explorations and visualizations.

Mangostock / Fotolia

Aspen Falls City Hall

In this chapter, you will support Cyril Shore, Planning Council Director. The Planning Council examines and uses demographic data to plan for new services, communities, and schools. The council analyzes data on housing tenure, transportation, and salaries to determine if there is a need for such things as additional rental and ownership communities, public transportation and sidewalk access, and educators in the public school system.

You can use Excel to connect to data sources from relational databases, multidimensional sources, and text files. Once the connection is established, the data in Excel updates automatically without reconnecting to the data source. In Excel, imported data can be analyzed using database tools, statistical queries, and visualization tools that summarize the data across multiple categories.

In this project, you will create a new workbook by connecting data sources from Access and Excel files. You will apply filters to demographic data from Aspen Falls to analyze average income, household size, housing tenure, and commuting methods. Similarly, you will calculate and filter government salaries to summarize education salary information. You will also create charts and use other data visualization tools to assist with presenting the data.

Time to complete all 10
skills – 60 to 90 minutes

Student data files needed for this chapter:

exl09_CensusData (Access)
exl09_EmploymentData (Excel)
exl09_DemographicsPicture (JPG)

You will save your workbook as:

Last_First_exl09_Census

Outcome

Using the skills listed in this chapter, you will be able
to create worksheets like these:

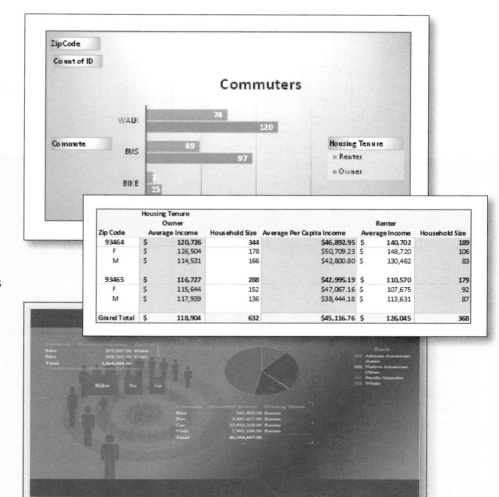

SKILLS

MyITLab®
Skills 1-10 Training

At the end of this chapter, you will be able to:

Skill 1   Use PowerPivot to Link Data to Access Databases
Skill 2   Create PivotTable Reports
Skill 3   Change PivotTable Report Views
Skill 4   Change Calculation Types and Format PivotTable Reports
Skill 5   Create PivotTable Report Calculated Fields
Skill 6   Group and Filter PivotTable Reports
Skill 7   Use Slicers to Filter PivotTable Reports
Skill 8   Create PivotChart Reports from External Data Sources
Skill 9   Create PivotChart Reports Using Power View
Skill 10 Use Power View to Format PivotChart Reports

MORE SKILLS

Skill 11 Import and Export XML Data
Skill 12 Add Cube Functions Using the PowerPivot Add-In
Skill 13 Update Calculations Manually
Skill 14 Use the Inquire Add-In

► To analyze large volumes of data from various sources, you can use **PowerPivot**—an Office Professional Plus Excel add-in—to perform powerful data analysis and to create sophisticated data models.

► An Excel **add-in** is a file that adds functionality to Excel, usually in the form of new functions.

► A **data model** is a collection of tables with relationships.

1. Start **Excel 2013**, and then open a blank workbook. Click the **File tab**, click **Options**, and then click **Add-Ins**. At the bottom of the **Excel Options** dialog box, click the **Manage arrow**, and then compare your screen with **Figure 1**. (Your list of add-ins may vary.) From the list, click **COM Add-ins**, and then click the **Go** button.

2. In the **COM Add-ins** dialog box, select the **Microsoft Office PowerPivot for Excel 2013** check box, and then click **OK** to add the PowerPivot tab to the Ribbon.

   If you do not have permission to install the PowerPivot add-in, you will not be able to complete this project.

3. Click the **PowerPivot tab**, and then in the **Data Model group**, click **Manage**. Compare your screen with **Figure 2**.

   In the PowerPivot for Excel dialog box, you can import and filter data as you add it to your file. You can also create relationships between tables, and enrich the data with calculations and expressions.

■ **Continue to the next page to complete the skill**

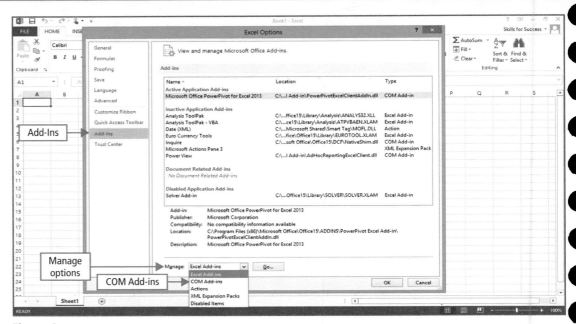

Figure 1

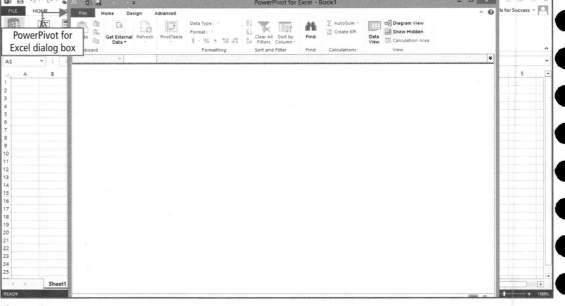

Figure 2

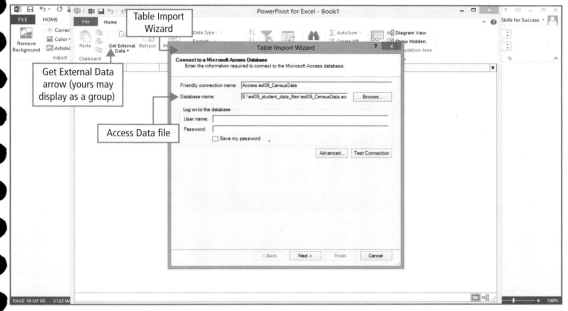

Figure 3

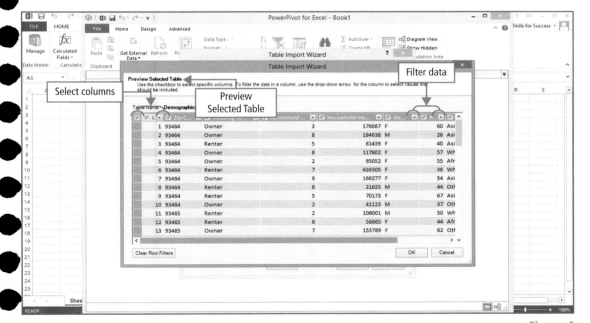

Figure 4

4. In the **PowerPivot for Excel** window, on the **Home tab**, in the **Get External Data group**, click **From Database**, and then click **From Access**. In the **Table Import Wizard**, click **Browse**. Navigate to the student data files for this chapter, click the Access file **exl09_CensusData**, and then click **Open**. Compare your screen with Figure 3, and then click **Next**.

5. In the **Table Import Wizard**, under **Choose How to Import the Data**, verify the **Select from a list of tables and views to choose the data to import** option button is selected, and then click **Next**.

6. In the wizard, under **Select Tables and Views**, select the **Demographics** check box, and then click **Preview & Filter**. Compare your screen with Figure 4, and then click **OK**.

   In Preview Selected Table you can select columns to import. The data can also be filtered using the drop-down arrows.

7. Click **Finish**, wait for the import, and then **Close** the Table Import Wizard.

8. If necessary, resize the PowerPivot for Excel window. Click the **File** button, and then from the list, click **Save As**. In the **Save As** dialog box, navigate to the location where you are saving your files. Click **New folder**, type Excel Chapter 9 and then press Enter two times. Name the file Last_First_exl09_Census and then click **Save**.

   The data imported to PowerPivot is saved in the workbook; however, it is not visible until you select Manage.

■ **You have completed Skill 1 of 10**

▶ A ***PivotTable report*** is an interactive way to summarize, explore, and analyze data.

▶ PivotTable reports group, filter, and sort large amounts of data so that you can quickly create different views of the same data.

1. Click the **Manage** button to view the PowerPivot data.

    The table stores demographic data ***records***—collections of related information that displays in a single row in a database table—from a survey of 1,000 Aspen Falls citizens.

2. In the **PowerPivot for Excel** window, on the **Home tab**, in the **Get External Data group**, click **From Other Sources**. In the **Table Import Wizard**, scroll down, and then under **Text Files**, click **Excel File**. Compare your screen with **Figure 1**, and then click **Next**.

3. Click **Browse**, navigate to the student data files for this chapter, and then open the file **exl09_EmploymentData**. Select the **Use first row as column headers** check box, and then click **Next**.

4. In the wizard, under **Select Tables and Views**, verify that the **Employment** is selected, click **Finish**, wait for the import, and then click **Close**.

    The Employment worksheet is added to the PowerPivot window.

5. Click the **Demographics** worksheet. On the **Home tab**, click the **PivotTable arrow**, and then click **PivotTable**.

    A PivotTable report can be placed in a new worksheet or an existing worksheet. By default, New Worksheet is selected.

6. In the **Insert Pivot** dialog box, click **Existing Worksheet**, and then click **OK**. Compare your screen with **Figure 2**.

■ **Continue to the next page to complete the skill**

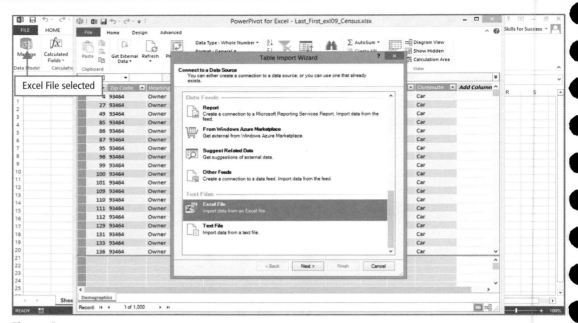

Figure 1

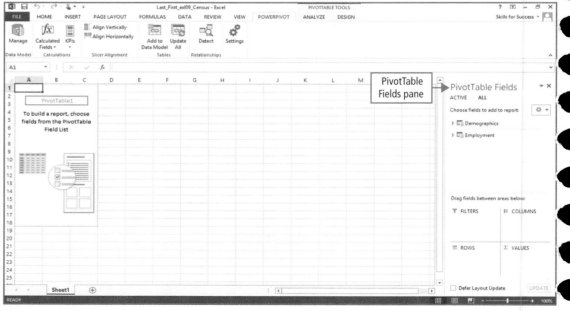

Figure 2

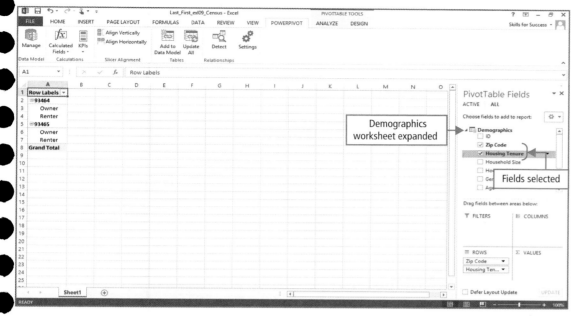

Figure 3

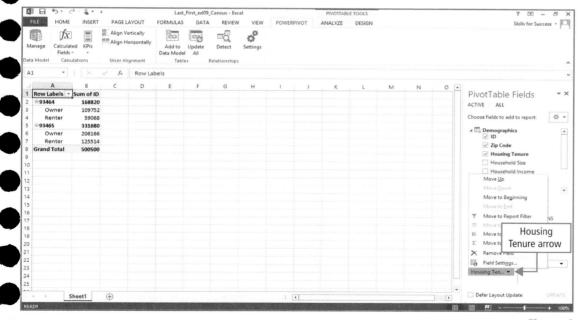

Figure 4

7. In the **PivotTable Fields** pane, under **Choose fields to add to report**, expand ▷ **Demographics**, and then select the **Zip Code** and **Housing Tenure** check boxes. Compare your screen with **Figure 3**.

In a database, *fields*—categories of data—are organized into columns. In a PivotTable report, fields can be organized in either rows or columns. *Row labels* are the fields used to categorize the data by rows. In this PivotTable report, the *Zip Code* field displays in rows and will group the data in the PivotTable report.

8. In the **PivotTable Fields** pane, under **Choose fields to add to report**, in the **Demographics** area, select the **ID** check box.

The *Sum of ID* values are *PivotTable values*—the fields for which summary statistics are calculated.

9. Under **Drag fields between areas below**, in the **Rows** box, click the **Housing Tenure arrow**, and then compare your screen with **Figure 4**.

The list of field options is displayed.

10. Click cell **C1**, and then rename the **Sheet1** worksheet tab as Housing Tenure

If you select a cell that is not a cell in the PivotTable, the PivotTable Fields pane is hidden.

11. **Save** 🖫 the workbook.

■ **You have completed Skill 2 of 10**

▶ EXL 9-3
VIDEO

▶ You can quickly change how data is presented in PivotTable reports.

▶ The PivotTable Fields pane is used to change fields from rows to columns, to add or remove fields, and to change the fields used to calculate values.

1. Click cell **A3** to select the PivotTable report and display the PivotTable Fields pane.

   You can also display PivotTable Fields by clicking the Field List button on the Analyze tab, in the Show group.

2. At the bottom of the **PivotTable Fields** pane, click the **Housing Tenure arrow**, and then click **Move to Column Labels** to move the *Housing Tenure* values to the columns in the worksheet. Compare your screen with **Figure 1**.

3. In the **Values** box, click the **Sum of ID arrow**, and then click **Value Field Settings**. In the **Value Field Settings** dialog box, under **Summarize value field by**, click **Count**, and then click **OK**.

   The values in the worksheet are changed to the number of owners and renters for each postal code and the grand total for each.

4. Click cell **A2**, replace the text with Zip Code and then press Enter . Click cell **B1**, replace the text with Housing Tenure and then press Enter .

5. In the **PivotTable Fields** pane, under **Choose fields to add to report**, select **Gender**. Compare your screen with **Figure 2**.

   The Gender field is added to the Rows section of the PivotTable Fields pane. The data displayed is the number of households within each postal code, grouped by gender.

▪ **Continue to the next page to complete the skill** ➤

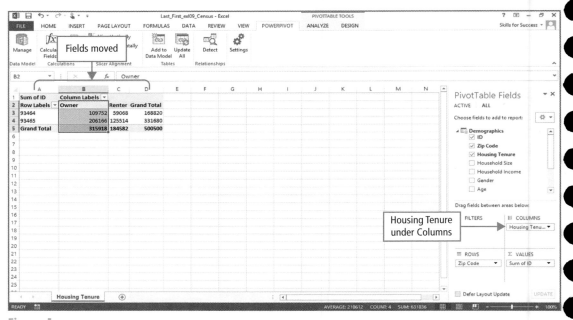

Figure 1

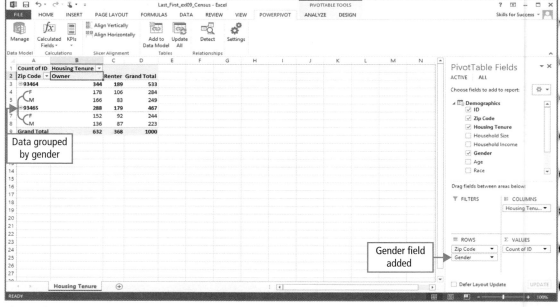

Figure 2

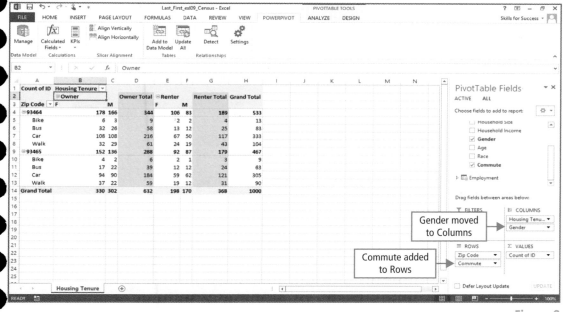

Figure 3

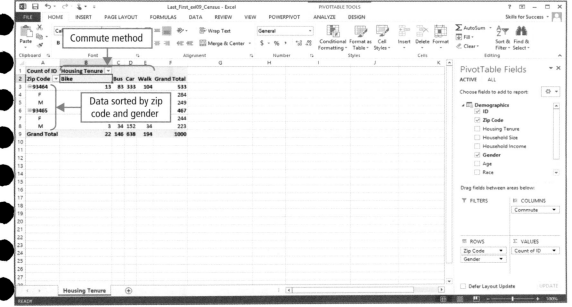

Figure 4

6. In the **PivotTable Fields** pane, under **Drag fields between areas below**, drag **Gender** from the **Rows** box to the **Columns** box.

   The PivotTable report now shows the number of households headed by each gender for each housing tenure.

7. In the **PivotTable Fields** pane, under **Choose fields to add to report**, drag the **Commute** field into the **Rows** box, and then compare your screen with **Figure 3**.

   Within each Zip Code and Housing Tenure, the PivotTable displays how many individuals own or rent their homes, how many households are headed by males or females, and how each household commutes to work. In this manner, PivotTable reports can change how data is summarized.

8. In the **PivotTable Fields** pane, drag the **Gender** field from the **Columns** box into the **Rows** box.

9. Drag the **Commute** field from the **Rows** box into the **Columns** box.

10. In the **Columns** box, click the **Housing Tenure arrow**, and then select **Remove Field**. Compare your screen with **Figure 4**.

    This chart shows the method by which each household within a particular postal code commutes to work. It also shows the total males and females who are designated as the head of households within each zip code.

11. In the **PivotTable Fields** pane, under **Choose fields to add to report**, select the **Housing Tenure** and **Household Income** check boxes, and then clear the **Commute** check box.

12. Save 🖫 the workbook.

■ **You have completed Skill 3 of 10**

► By default, PivotTable reports summarize fields by calculating a total for each group. Other summary statistics, including count, average, minimum, or maximum, can also be calculated.

► PivotTable reports are formatted by applying PivotTable styles.

1. In the **PivotTable Fields** pane, drag **Housing Tenure** from the **Rows** box to the **Columns** box, and then position the field above the **Values** field.

2. Click cell **C3**, and then click the **Analyze tab**. In the **Active Field group**, click **Field Settings**, and then compare your screen with Figure 1.

3. In the **Value Field Settings** dialog box, under **Summarize value field by**, click **Average**, and then click the **Number Format** button.

4. In the **Format Cells** dialog box, under **Category**, click **Accounting**. In the **Decimal places** box, change the value to **0**, and then click **OK**.

5. In the **Value Field Settings** dialog box, in the **Custom Name** box, replace the existing value with Average Income Compare your screen with Figure 2, and then click **OK**.

In this manner, you can customize value fields to calculate different summary statistics and display different number formats.

6. In the **PivotTable Fields** pane, in the **Values** box, click the **Count of ID arrow**, and then click **Remove Field**.

7. Click cell **A3**, and then click the **Design tab**. In the **Layout group**, click the **Blank Rows** button, and then click **Insert Blank Line after Each Item**.

■ **Continue to the next page to complete the skill** ➤

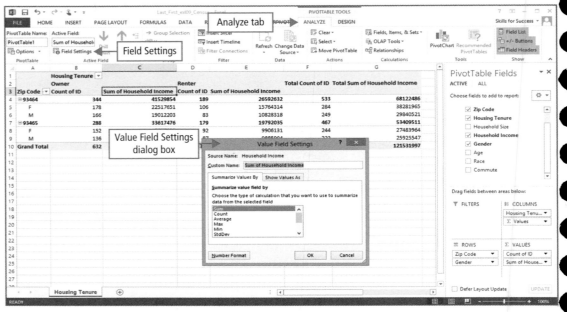

Figure 1

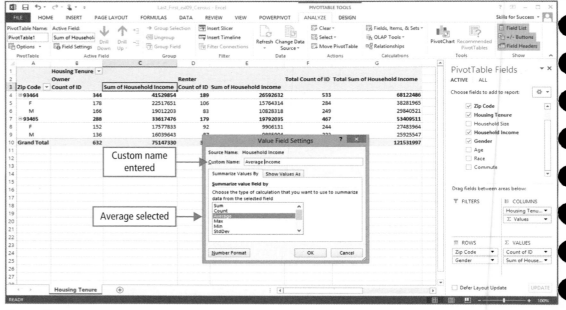

Figure 2

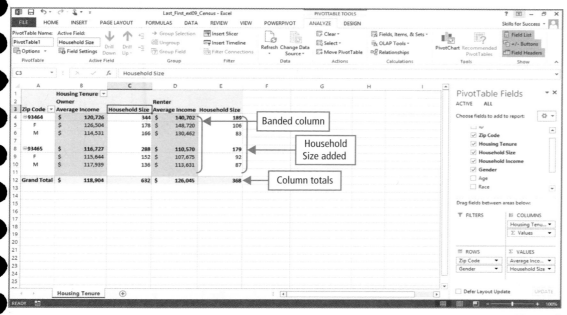

Figure 3

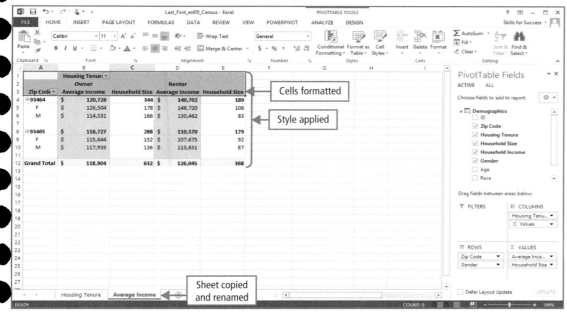

Figure 4

8. In the **PivotTable Style Options group**, select the **Banded Columns** check box.

Banded columns visually separate the data, making the information easier to read.

9. In the **Layout group**, click the **Grand Totals** button, and then click **On for Columns Only**.

10. In the **PivotTable Fields** pane, under **Choose fields to add to report**, select the **Household Size** check box.

11. Click cell **C3**, and then click the **Analyze tab**. In the **Active Field group**, click **Field Settings**, click **Count**, and then change the custom name to Household Size Click **OK**, and then compare your screen with **Figure 3**.

This pivot shows the average household income for each zip code area, arranged by household size. It further compares the average income based on the gender of the head of the household.

12. Click the **Design tab**. In the **PivotTable Styles group**, click the **More** button ⏷. In the gallery, under **Light**, click the style in the third row, sixth column—**Pivot Style Light 19**.

13. Select the range **A1:E3**. On the **Home tab**, in the **Alignment group**, click **Center** ☰.

14. Right-click the **Housing Tenure** worksheet tab, and then click **Move or Copy**. In the **Move or Copy** dialog box, under **Before sheet**, select **(move to end)**, select the **Create a copy** check box, and then click **OK**.

15. Rename the **Housing Tenure (2)** worksheet tab as Average Income and then compare your screen with **Figure 4**.

16. Save ☐ the workbook.

■ **You have completed Skill 4 of 10**

▶ A *calculated field* is a data field whose values are derived from formulas that you create. PivotTable fields can be included in these formulas.

▶ A calculated column needs to be created in the PowerPivot window before it can be added to a PivotTable in a worksheet. Calculated columns work much like the formulas and functions in normal Excel cells.

1. Click the **PowerPivot tab**, and then in the **Data Model group**, click the **Manage** button. Click the **Design tab**, and then in the **Columns group**, click the **Add** button.

2. With the insertion point in the **formula bar**, type an equal sign (=). Click the **Household Income** field name, and then in the **formula bar**, type a slash (/). Click the **Household Size** field name. Compare your screen with Figure 1, and then press Enter.

3. Double-click the **CalculatedColumn1** field name, type Per Capita Income and press Enter. Click the **Home tab**, and then in the **Formatting group**, click **Apply Currency Format $ ▾**. Click **$ English (United States)**. Compare your screen with Figure 2.

   The formula divides Household Income by Household Size to determine the per capita income of each household.

4. On the Quick Access Toolbar, click the **Switch to Workbook** button. Display the **Housing Tenure** worksheet. In the **PivotTable Fields** pane, expand **Demographics**, and scroll down, if necessary, and select the **Per Capita Income** check box.

■ **Continue to the next page to complete the skill**

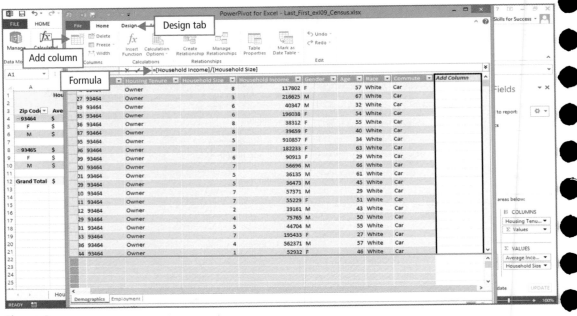

Figure 1

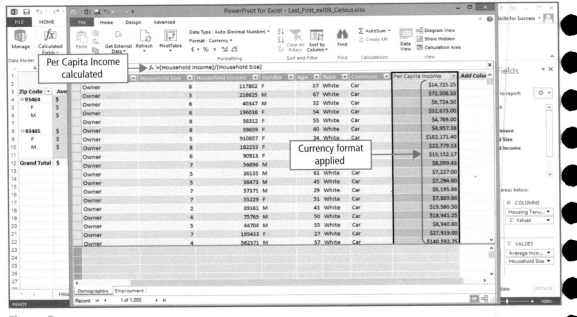

Figure 2

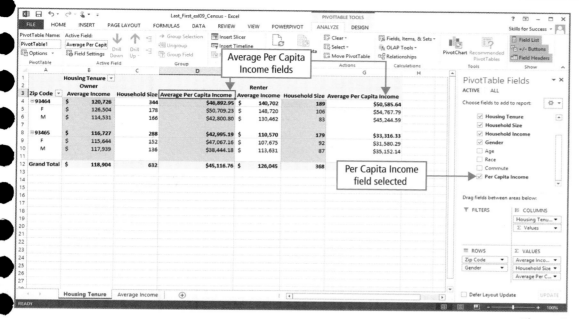

Figure 3

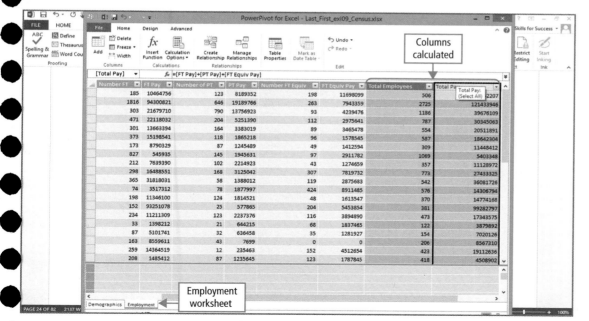

Figure 4

5. Click cell **D3**. On the **Analyze tab**, in the **Active Field group**, click the **Field Settings** button.

6. In the **Value Field Settings** dialog box, click **Average**. In the **Custom Name** box, type Average Per Capita Income and then click **OK** to change the calculated field in the PivotTable report. Compare your screen with Figure 3.

7. Right-click the **Housing Tenure** worksheet tab, and then click **Move or Copy**. In the **Move or Copy** dialog box, under **Before sheet**, select **(move to end)**, select the **Create a copy** check box, and then click **OK**.

8. Rename the **Housing Tenure (2)** worksheet as Per Capita Income

9. Click the **PowerPivot tab**, and then in the **Data Model group**, click the **Manage** button. Display the **Employment** worksheet. Click the **Design tab**, and then in the **Columns group**, click the **Add** button.

10. With the insertion point in the **formula bar**, type an equal sign (=). Click the **Number FT** field name, and then in the **formula bar**, type a plus sign (+). Click the **Number of PT** field name, type a plus sign (+), and then click the **Number FT Equiv** field name. Press Enter.

11. Double-click the **CalculatedColumn1** field, type Total Employees and press Enter.

12. On the **Design tab**, in the **Columns group**, click the **Add** button. Repeat the previous instructions to create a calculated field named Total Pay that adds **FT Pay**, **PT Pay**, and **FT Equiv Pay** field names. Compare your screen with Figure 4.

13. **Save** 🔡 the workbook.

■ **You have completed Skill 5 of 10**

▶ PivotTable report groups can be collapsed or expanded to show or hide the details for each group.

▶ Recall that *filtering* displays only the data that satisfies conditions you specify. In a PivotTable report, AutoFilter can filter data by rows or by columns.

1. Display the **Housing Tenure** worksheet. Select cell **A4**, and then on the **Analyze tab**, in the **Show group**, verify that the **Field List** button is selected. In the **PivotTable Fields** pane, under **Choose fields to add to report**, expand **Demographics**, clear the **Gender** and **Household Size** check boxes, and then select the **Race** check box.

2. In cell **A4**, click the **Collapse** ☐ button to collapse the row, and then in **A6** click the **Collapse** ☐ button.

   A minus symbol ☐ indicates that a group can be collapsed. A plus symbol ☐ indicates that a group can be expanded.

3. Right-click cell **A4**. From the shortcut menu, point to **Expand/Collapse**, and then click **Expand**.

   The rows are expanded to show the full details for the category.

4. With cell **A4** still selected, click the **Collapse** ☐ button to collapse the row again. Compare your screen with Figure 1.

5. With cell **A4** still selected, click the **Expand** ☐ button to expand the details for the 93464 Zip Code category. Compare your screen with Figure 2.

■ Continue to the next page to complete the skill

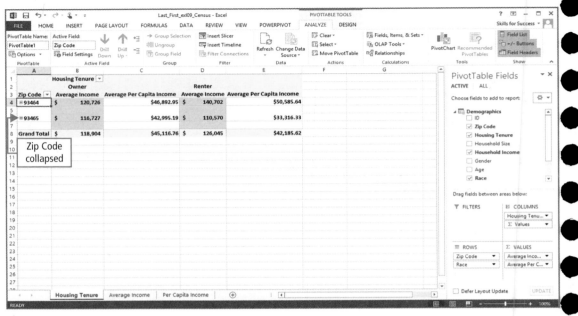

Figure 1

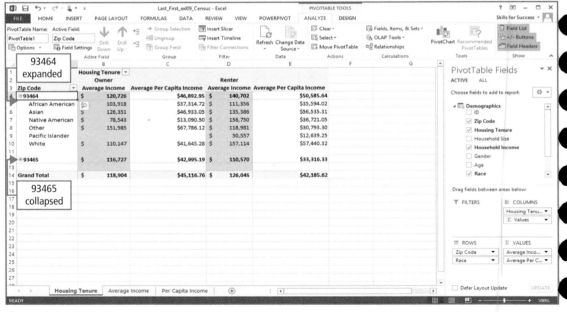

Figure 2

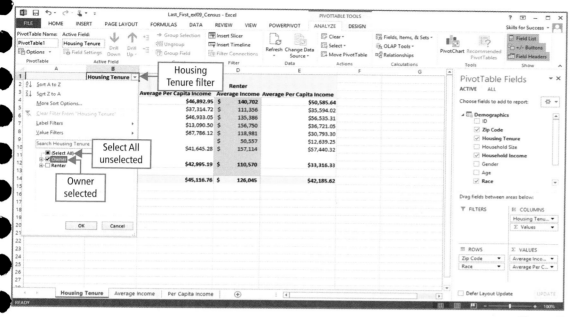

Figure 3

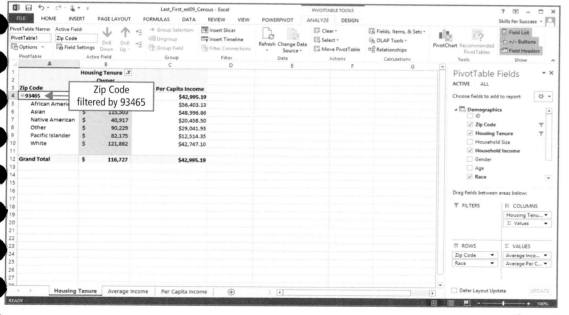

Figure 4

6. Select cell **B1**, and then click the **Housing Tenure filter arrow** ▾. In the AutoFilter list, clear the **Select All** check box, and then select the **Owner** check box. Compare your screen with Figure 3, and then click **OK**.

The filter displays only the column where the race is by owner.

7. Select cell **A3**, and then click the **Zip Code filter arrow** ▾. In the AutoFilter list, clear the **Select All** check box, select the **93465** check box, and then click **OK**. In **A4**, click the **Expand** ⊞ button, and then compare your screen with Figure 4.

The filter is applied to the PivotTable rows so that only the summary data for the selected Zip Code displays.

8. Right-click the **Housing Tenure** worksheet tab, and then click **Move or Copy**. In the **Move or Copy** dialog box, under **Before sheet**, click **(move to end)**. Select the **Create a copy** check box, and then click **OK**.

9. Rename the new worksheet Filtered Race

10. Display the **Housing Tenure** worksheet. Click the **Zip Code filter arrow** ▾, select the **Select All** check box, and then click **OK**. Select the **Housing Tenure filter arrow** ▾, select the **Select All** check box, and then click **OK**.

11. On the **Analyze tab**, in the **Show group**, click **Field List** to close the **PivotTable Fields** pane.

12. Select cell **A1**, and then **Save** 🖫 the workbook.

■ **You have completed Skill 6 of 10**

▶ A **slicer** is a tool that is used to filter data in PivotTable views.

▶ Slicers filter data based on distinct values in columns.

1. Display the **Housing Tenure** worksheet. Select cell **A4**. On the **Analyze tab**, in the **Filter group**, click **Insert Slicer**.

2. In the **Insert Slicers** dialog box, select the **Commute** check box, select the **Gender** check box, and then click **OK**.

   Two slicers are created. One filters the data based on gender; the other filters the data based on the commute method.

3. Select the **Gender** slicer. Drag the slicer so that the upper left corner is positioned in cell **G1**. Move the **Commute** slicer so that the upper left corner is positioned in cell **G15**. Compare your screen with **Figure 1**.

4. In the **Gender** slicer, click the **M** slice.

   The data in the PivotTable report is now filtered to show only the results when the commuter is a male.

5. In the **Commute** slicer, click **Bus**, and then compare your screen with **Figure 2**.

   The data in the PivotTable report is filtered so that only the information related to male commuters who take the bus to work is displayed. For this Slicer Style, each selected slice has a single blue bar and the slices that are not selected have a white background. This is true for each Light Style; depending on the color selected the bars will change color. For the Dark Styles, the slices not selected will be gray.

■ **Continue to the next page to complete the skill** ▶

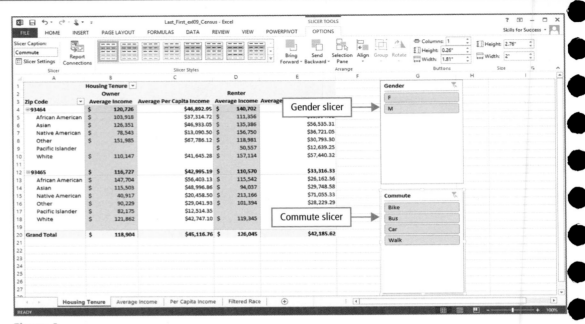

Figure 1

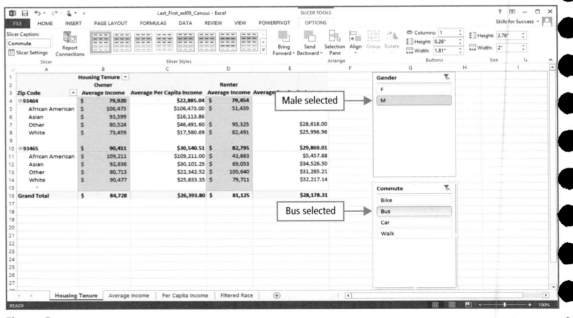

Figure 2

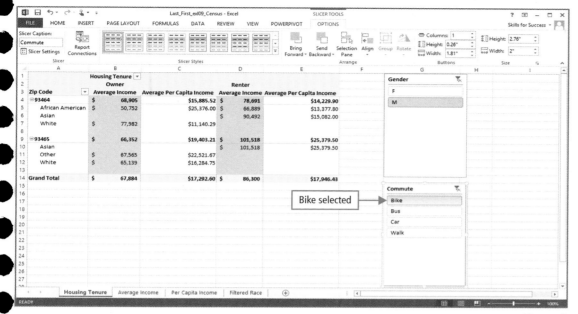

Figure 3

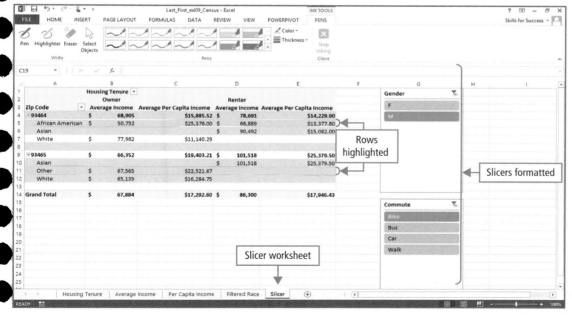

Figure 4

6. In the **Commute** slicer, click **Bike**. The PivotTable report now displays only male commuters who ride a bike to work. Compare your screen with **Figure 3**.

7. Press Ctrl, and then click the **Gender** slicer. On the **Options tab**, in the **Slicer Styles group**, click **More** ▾, and then under **Dark**, click **Slicer Style Dark 6**.

8. Right-click the **Housing Tenure** worksheet tab, and then click **Move or Copy**. In the **Move or Copy** dialog box, under **Before sheet**, click **(move to end)**. Select **Create a copy**, and then click **OK**.

9. Rename the new worksheet Slicer

10. On the **Slicer** worksheet, click the **Review tab**. In the **Ink group**, click **Start Inking**. If you do not have an Ink group, right-click a blank area of the ribbon, and select **Customize the Ribbon**. Click **New Group**, and then **Rename**. In the dialog box, type Inking and click **OK**. Under **Choose commands from**, click **All Commands**. Scroll down and click **Start Inking**, and then click **Add**. Click **OK**. In the **Write group**, click **Highlighter**.

11. Move the pointer into the worksheet. It will turn into a yellow rectangle. Drag to highlight **A5:E5** and **A11:E11**. Click **Stop Inking**. Compare your screen with **Figure 4**.

    If your line does not appear straight, in the Write group, click the Eraser button, and then repeat the previous instructions.

12. In the **Gender** slicer, click **Clear Filter** 🔻. The values in the cells change. In the **Commute** slicer, click **Clear Filter** 🔻.

13. Right-click the **Gender** slicer title bar, and then click **Remove Gender**. Right-click the **Commute** slicer title bar, and then click **Remove Commute**.

14. **Save** 🖫 the workbook.

■ **You have completed Skill 7 of 10**

▶ A **PivotChart report** is a dynamic visual representation of data. For example, you can assign any field to the value axis or category axis and then apply filters.

▶ The data source for a PivotChart can be an external file, such as a table in a database file.

1. On the **Housing Tenure** worksheet tab, click cell **F1**. On the **Insert tab**, in the **Charts group**, click the **PivotChart arrow**, and then click **PivotChart**.

2. In the **Create PivotChart** dialog box, select the **Use an external data source** option button. Click the **Choose Connection** button, and then in the **Existing Connections** dialog box, under **Connections in this Workbook**, select **Access exl09_CensusData**. Click **Open**.

3. In the **Create PivotChart** dialog box, select the **New Worksheet** option. Compare your screen with **Figure 1**, and then click **OK**.

   A PivotChart is created.

4. On the **Analyze tab**, in the **Show/Hide** group, click the **Field List** button. In the **PivotChart Fields** pane, under **Choose fields to add to report**, select the **ID**, **Zip Code**, and **Commute** check boxes.

5. In the **PivotChart Fields** pane, under **Drag fields between areas below**, select the **Sum of ID arrow**, and then click **Value Field Settings**. In the **Value Field Settings** dialog box, click **Count**, and then click **OK**. Compare your screen with **Figure 2**.

 ■ Continue to the next page to complete the skill

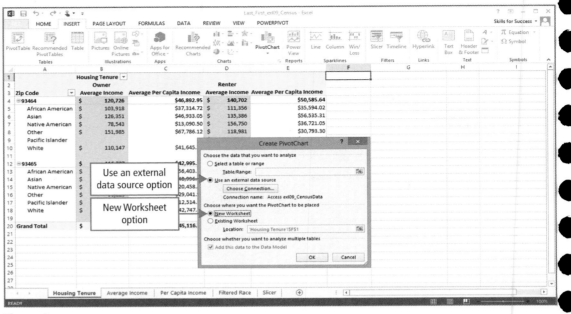

Figure 1

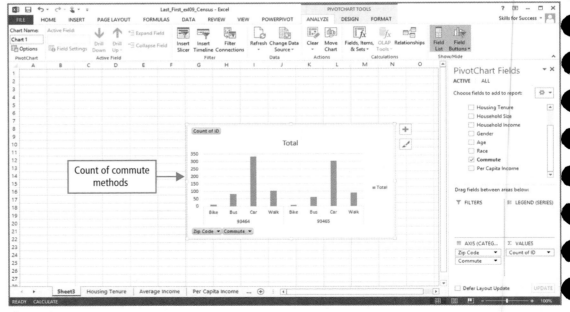

Figure 2

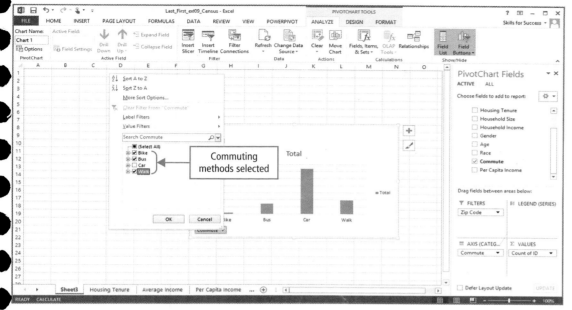

Figure 3

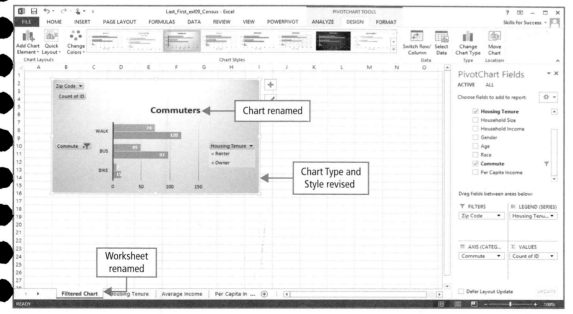

Figure 4

6. With the **PivotChart** selected, in the **PivotChart Fields** pane, under **Drag fields between areas below**, click **Zip Code**, and then drag it from the **Axis (Categories)** box into the **Filters** box.

7. In the **PivotChart**, click the **Commute filter arrow** |▾|, and then in the **AutoFilter** list, clear the **Select All** check box. Select the **Bike**, **Bus**, and **Walk** check boxes. Compare your screen with Figure 3, and then click **OK**.

   The chart displays the number of people who commute by bus, bike, and walk, filtered by their zip code.

8. With the **PivotChart** active, in the **PivotChart Fields** pane, drag **Housing Tenure** into the **Legend (Series)** box.

   When you know what type of field you need, you can drag it directly into the desired box, and it will be automatically selected in the PivotChart Fields.

9. On the **Design tab**, in the **Chart Layouts group**, click the **Add Chart Element** button, point to **Chart Title** and then click **Above Chart**. Replace the title with Commuters

10. In the **Type group**, click the **Change Chart Type** button. In the **Change Chart Type** dialog box, click **Bar**, and then click **OK**. In the **Chart Styles group**, click **Style 3**.

11. Move the **PivotChart** so that the upper left corner is located in **B2**, and then rename the worksheet tab as Filtered Chart Compare your screen with Figure 4.

12. Select cell **A1**, and then **Save** |💾| the workbook.

■ **You have completed Skill 8 of 10**

▶ EXL 9-9 VIDEO

▶ You can interact with data in Excel using ***Power View***—an interactive data exploration, visualization, and presentation add-in that encourages ad hoc reporting.

▶ Workbooks can contain only one data model. Multiple sheets can be created based on it.

▶ You can modify the internal data model without leaving the Power View sheet.

1. If Power View is already installed on your computer, move to step 3. On the **File tab**, click **Options**, and then click **Add-Ins**. At the bottom, click the **Manage arrow**, click **COM Add-ins**, and then click **Go**.

2. In the **COM Add-ins** dialog box, click the **Power View** check box, and then click **OK**.

   If you do not have permission to install the Power View add-in, you will not be able to complete this project.

3. On the **Insert tab**, in the **Reports group**, click **Power View**, and then compare your screen with Figure 1.

4. If Silverlight is already installed, your screen will look like Figure 2, and you can move to step 5; otherwise, click **Install *Silverlight***—a development tool for creating engaging, interactive user experiences for web and mobile applications. In the **View Download** dialog box, click **Run**. If asked about making changes, click **Yes**, and then click **Install Now**. Click **Close** two times, and then in the displayed message, click **Reload**. Compare your screen with Figure 2.

5. In the **Power View Fields** pane, expand **Employment**. Select **Government Function**, **FT Equiv Pay**, **FT Pay**, and **PT Pay**.

6. On the **Design tab**, in the **Switch Visualization group**, click **Bar Chart**, click **Clustered Bar**, and then click **Stacked Bar**.

■ **Continue to the next page to complete the skill** ▶

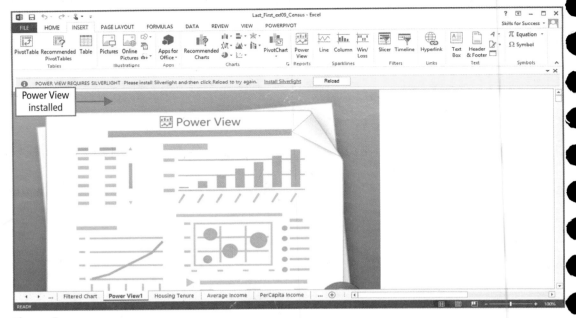

Figure 1

Figure 2

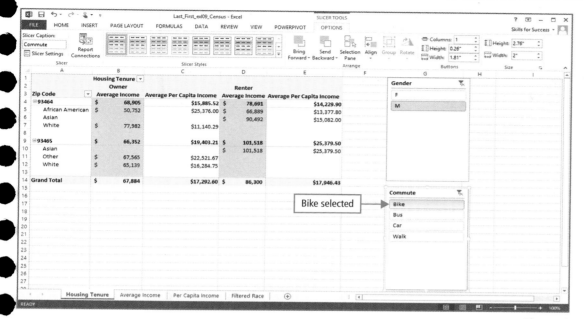

Figure 3

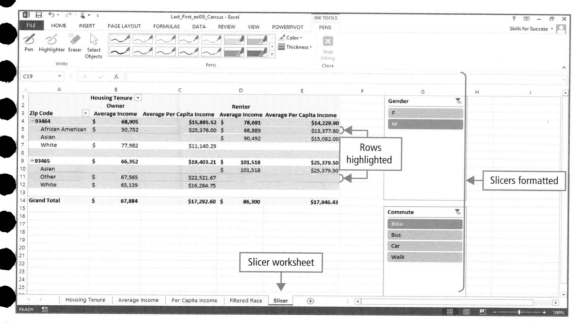

Figure 4

6. In the **Commute** slicer, click **Bike**. The PivotTable report now displays only male commuters who ride a bike to work. Compare your screen with Figure 3.

7. Press Ctrl, and then click the **Gender** slicer. On the **Options tab**, in the **Slicer Styles group**, click **More** ▼, and then under **Dark**, click **Slicer Style Dark 6**.

8. Right-click the **Housing Tenure** worksheet tab, and then click **Move or Copy**. In the **Move or Copy** dialog box, under **Before sheet**, click **(move to end)**. Select **Create a copy**, and then click **OK**.

9. Rename the new worksheet Slicer

10. On the **Slicer** worksheet, click the **Review tab**. In the **Ink group**, click **Start Inking**. If you do not have an Ink group, right-click a blank area of the ribbon, and select **Customize the Ribbon**. Click **New Group**, and then **Rename**. In the dialog box, type Inking and click **OK**. Under **Choose commands from**, click **All Commands**. Scroll down and click **Start Inking**, and then click **Add**. Click **OK**. In the **Write group**, click **Highlighter**.

11. Move the pointer into the worksheet. It will turn into a yellow rectangle. Drag to highlight **A5:E5** and **A11:E11**. Click **Stop Inking**. Compare your screen with Figure 4.

    If your line does not appear straight, in the Write group, click the Eraser button, and then repeat the previous instructions.

12. In the **Gender** slicer, click **Clear Filter** 🔖. The values in the cells change. In the **Commute** slicer, click **Clear Filter** 🔖.

13. Right-click the **Gender** slicer title bar, and then click **Remove Gender**. Right-click the **Commute** slicer title bar, and then click **Remove Commute**.

14. **Save** 🖫 the workbook.

■ **You have completed Skill 7 of 10**

► A ***PivotChart report*** is a dynamic visual representation of data. For example, you can assign any field to the value axis or category axis and then apply filters.

► The data source for a PivotChart can be an external file, such as a table in a database file.

1. On the **Housing Tenure** worksheet tab, click cell **F1**. On the **Insert tab**, in the **Charts group**, click the **PivotChart arrow**, and then click **PivotChart**.

2. In the **Create PivotChart** dialog box, select the **Use an external data source** option button. Click the **Choose Connection** button, and then in the **Existing Connections** dialog box, under **Connections in this Workbook**, select **Access exl09_CensusData**. Click **Open**.

3. In the **Create PivotChart** dialog box, select the **New Worksheet** option. Compare your screen with **Figure 1**, and then click **OK**.

   A PivotChart is created.

4. On the **Analyze tab**, in the **Show/Hide group**, click the **Field List** button. In the **PivotChart Fields** pane, under **Choose fields to add to report**, select the **ID**, **Zip Code**, and **Commute** check boxes.

5. In the **PivotChart Fields** pane, under **Drag fields between areas below**, select the **Sum of ID arrow**, and then click **Value Field Settings**. In the **Value Field Settings** dialog box, click **Count**, and then click **OK**. Compare your screen with **Figure 2**.

■ **Continue to the next page to complete the skill**

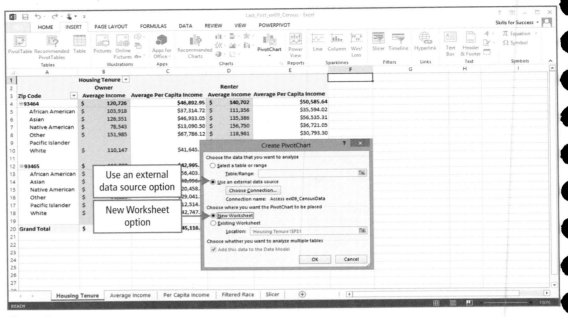

Figure 1

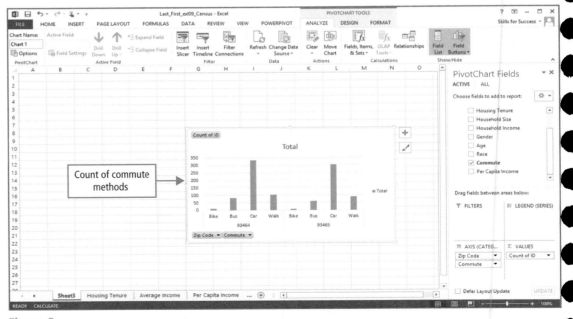

Figure 2

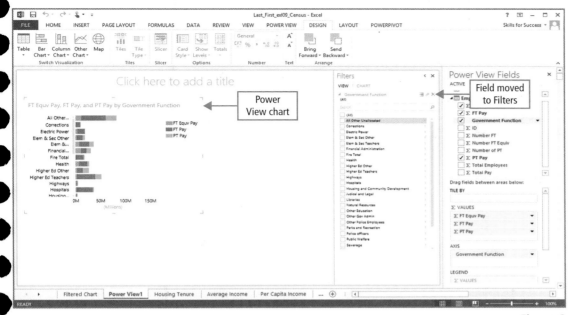

Figure 3

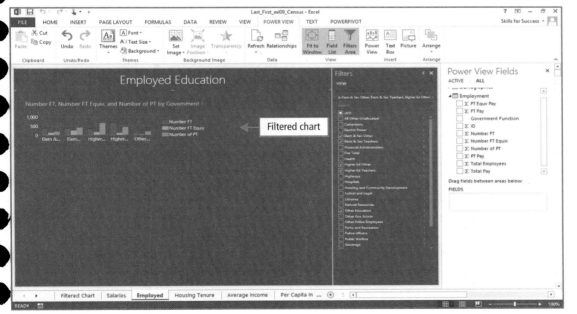

Figure 4

7. In the **Power View Fields** pane, drag **Government Function** to the **Filters** pane, and then compare your screen with Figure 3.

   Here, you have the ability to filter the chart based on employment functions.

8. In the **Filters** pane, select the following check boxes: **Elem & Sec Other**, **Elem & Sec Teachers**, **Higher Ed Other**, **Higher Ed Teachers**, and **Other Education**.

9. Replace the title text with Education Salaries

10. On the **Power View tab**, in the **Themes group**, click **Themes**, and then click the first option in the second column—**Theme2**. Click **Background**, and then click the first option in the third column—**Dark2 Solid**.

11. Rename the worksheet tab Salaries

12. On the **Power View tab**, in the **Insert group**, click **Power View**. In the **Power View Fields** pane, under **Employment**, select the following check boxes: **Government Function**, **Number FT**, **Number FT Equiv**, and **Number of PT**.

13. In the **Power View Fields** pane, drag **Government Function** to the **Filters** pane. Select the following check boxes: **Elem & Sec Other**, **Elem & Sec Teachers**, **Higher Ed Other**, **Higher Ed Teachers**, and **Other Education**.

14. On the **Design tab**, in the **Switch Visualization group**, click **Column Chart**, and then click **Clustered Column**.

15. Replace the title text with Employed Education Rename the worksheet tab Employed Compare your screen with Figure 4.

16. **Save** 🖫 the workbook.

■ **You have completed Skill 9 of 10**

► Many PivotChart elements can be formatted like other charts; however, with Power View you can incorporate additional visualizations like pictures and various chart arrangements.

1. On the **Power View tab**, in the **Insert group**, click the **Power View** button. In the **Power View Fields** pane, select the **Employment** collapse button to close it, and then select the **Demographics** expand button.

2. Select the **Commute**, **Household Income**, and **Zip Code** check boxes.

3. On the **Design tab**, in the **Tiles group**, click the **Tiles** button. In the chart, click the **Bike** chart tile. In the **Tiles group**, click the **Tile Type** button, and then click **Tile Flow**. Point to the lower right corner of the chart, and when the ⬚ arrow appears, drag down and to the right about .5 inches to resize the chart until the **Total** and **Zip Code** fields are viewable. Compare your screen with **Figure 1**.

4. Click the area to the right of the chart, and then in the **Power View Fields** pane, select the **Per Capita Income** and **Race** check boxes.

5. On the **Design tab**, in the **Switch Visualization group**, click **Other Chart**, and then click **Pie**. Point to the lower right corner of the chart, and when the ⬚ arrow appears, drag down and to the right until the legend is viewable. Compare your screen with **Figure 2**.

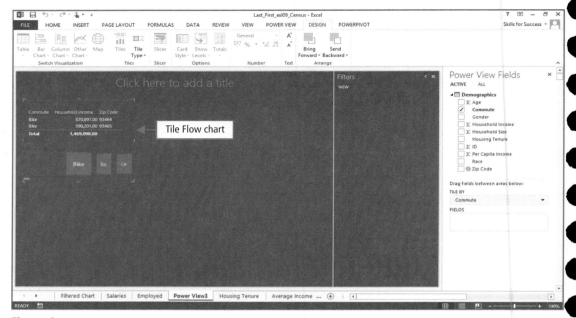

Figure 1

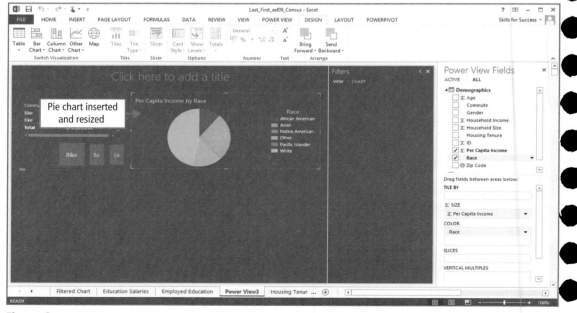

Figure 2

■ **Continue to the next page to complete the skill**

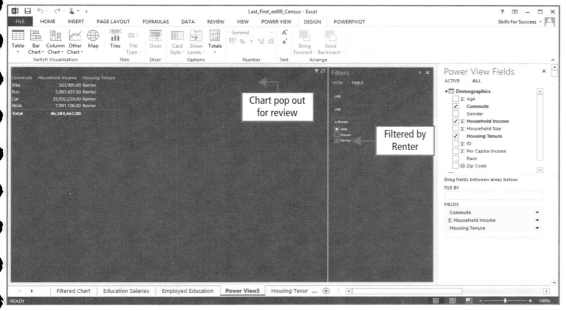

Figure 3

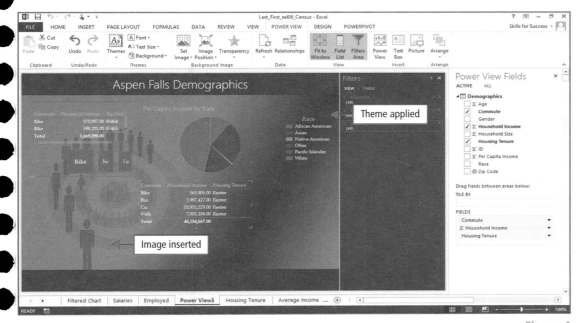

Figure 4

6. Click the area under the pie chart, and then in the **Power View Fields** pane, select the **Commute**, **Household Income**, and **Housing Tenure** check boxes. Point to the upper right corner of the chart, and then click **Show Filters** ▼. In the **Filters** pane, click **Housing Tenure**, and then select the **Renter** check box.

7. Point to the upper right corner of the chart, click **Pop out** ⌐⌐, and then compare your screen with Figure 3.

   In this view you only see this chart.

8. In the upper right corner of the chart window, click **Pop in** ⌐ to view the chart in the Normal view.

9. Replace the text in the chart title with Aspen Falls Demographics

10. On the **Power View tab**, in the **Background Image group**, click the **Set Image** button, and then click **Set Image**. Navigate to the student data files for this chapter, select **exl09_ DemographicsPicture**, and then select **Open**.

11. In the **Themes group**, click the **Themes arrow**, and then click the option in the sixth row, fourth column—**Executive** theme.

12. In the **Background Image group**, click the **Transparency** button, and then click **60%**. Compare your screen with Figure 4.

13. Rename the **PowerView3** worksheet Demographics **Save** 🖫 the workbook, and then submit it as directed by your instructor.

✔ **DONE! You have completed Skill 10 of 10, and your workbook is complete!**

The following More Skills are located at **www.pearsonhighered.com/skills**

More Skills Import and Export XML Data

XML is primarily known for transporting data between applications. Both Microsoft Excel and Microsoft Access support importing and exporting XML data.

In More Skills 11, you will copy a table created with Notepad into Excel 2013 and then format the table in Excel.

To begin, open your web browser, navigate to www.pearsonhighered.com/skills, locate the name of your textbook, and then follow the instructions on the website.

More Skills Add Cube Functions Using the PowerPivot Add-In

Once you have created PivotTable reports, you may need to perform other functions with the data that are not available with PivotTables. When you use Cube functions, each cell can contain its own formula and has the same flexibility as a standard Excel function.

In More Skills 12, you will import a table from a database and then format the table in Excel.

To begin, open your web browser, navigate to www.pearsonhighered.com/skills, locate the name of your textbook, and then follow the instructions on the website.

More Skills Update Calculations Manually

When you are working with complex formulas and large data sets, it may take a long time to recalculate the data. If you would like to validate the data before recalculation or calculate the data all at once, you can postpone the recalculation by setting the calculation to manual.

In More Skills 13, you will change the calculation to manually edit formulas and then recalculate the data using manual calculations.

To begin, open your web browser, navigate to www.pearsonhighered.com/skills, locate the name of your textbook, and then follow the instructions on the website.

More Skills 14 Use the Inquire Add-In

It is often necessary to compare versions of workbooks, analyze workbooks for problems or inconsistencies, or view links between workbooks and worksheets. Inquire is an add-in tool that has commands to perform all of these tasks.

In More Skills 14, you will analyze a workbook to view the number of sheets and formulas, create workbook diagrams to show relationships between worksheets and other workbooks, clean formatting from blank cells, and compare two similar workbooks to see the differences.

To begin, open your web browser, navigate to www.pearsonhighered.com/skills, locate the name of your textbook, and then follow the instructions on the website.

Please note that there are no additional projects to accompany the More Skills Projects, and they are not covered in End-of-Chapter projects.

The following table summarizes the **SKILLS AND PROCEDURES** covered in this chapter.

Skills Number	Task	Step	Icon
1	Link data to Access	PowerPivot tab → Data Model group → Manage → Get External Data → From Database → Browse → Select file	
2	Create PivotTable	Home tab → PivotTable arrow → PivotTable button	
3	Add fields to PivotTable	PivotTable Fields Pane → Expand worksheet → Select Fields	
3	Change PivotTable View	Drag fields between areas below → Select field arrow → Select where to move or click and drag the field to the view	
4	Change calculation types	Analyze tab → Active Fields group → Field settings → Function	
4	Edit PivotTable layout	Design tab → Layout group	
4	Edit PivotTable style	Design tab → PivotTable Styles group → More	
5	Create calculated field	PowerPivot tab → Data Model group → Manage → Design tab → Columns group → Add	
6	Show Field List	Analyze tab → Show group → Field List	
6	Group PivotTable reports	Click Expand/Collapse button	
6	Filter PivotTable reports	Click Filter arrow → AutoFilter List → Select option	
7	Insert slicer	Analyze tab → Filter group → Insert Slicer → Select Field(s) → In Slicer click option	
8	Create PivotChart from external data source	Insert tab → Charts group → PivotChart arrow → PivotChart → Use an external data source → Choose Communication → Select file	
9	Create PivotChart from PivotTable reports	Select PivotTable → Analyze tab → Tools group → PivotChart → Select chart type	
10	Format PivotChart reports	Select PivotChart Report → Format tab	

Key Terms

Online Help Skills

1. Start **Excel 2013**, and then in the upper right corner of the Excel window, click the **Help** button ⟨ ? ⟩. In the **Help** window, click the **Maximize** ⟨ □ ⟩ button.

2. Click in the search box, type Power View and then press ⟨ Enter ⟩. In the search results, click **Power View: Explore, visualize, and present your data**.

3. Read the article's introduction, and then below **In this article**, click **Creating charts and other visualizations**. Compare your screen with **Figure 1**.

Figure 1

4. Read the section to answer the following: What should you start with if you want to create a chart or visualization in Power View? When you convert a table to a visualization, how do you know what charts and visualizations are available to use for that table?

Matching

Match each term in the second column with its correct definition in the first column by writing the letter of the term on the blank line in front of the correct definition.

___ **1.** A file that increases Excel's functionality, usually in the form of new functions.

___ **2.** An interactive way to summarize, explore, and analyze data.

___ **3.** Categories of data organized into columns.

___ **4.** Located in the first column of a PivotTable report, these fields are used to categorize the rows.

___ **5.** Located along the top row of a PivotTable report, these fields are used to categorize the columns.

___ **6.** A new column or row whose values are derived from formulas that you create.

___ **7.** The technique used to display only the data that satisfies conditions you specify.

___ **8.** Indicates that a group can be collapsed.

___ **9.** A dynamic, visual representation of data.

___ **10.** An external data set used to create a PivotTable or PivotChart report, such as a table.

A Add-in

B Calculated field

C Column labels

D Data source

E Fields

F Filtering

G Minus symbol

H PivotChart report

I PivotTable report

J Row labels

Multiple Choice

Choose the correct answer.

1. An add-in used to perform powerful data analysis and to create sophisticated data models.
   A. Access database
   B. PivotTable report
   C. PowerPivot

2. A collection of tables within relationships.
   A. Data models
   B. Records
   C. Columns

3. Data can be imported into Excel from this source.
   A. Access database
   B. Word document
   C. PowerPoint presentation

4. Calculated fields work much like these items.
   A. Formulas
   B. Solutions
   C. Values

5. You click this to expand a collapsed group.
   A. Minus symbol
   B. Plus symbol
   C. Collapse All button

6. A tool used to filter data in PivotTable views.
   A. Minus symbol
   B. Expand All button
   C. Slicer

7. An interactive data exploration, visualization, and presentation experience.
   A. Access
   B. Power View
   C. Slicer

8. A powerful development tool for creating engaging, interactive user experiences for web and mobile applications.
   A. PowerPivot
   B. Silverlight
   C. PowerPoint

9. In the Create PivotTable dialog box, you specify this for the data.
   A. Source
   B. Records
   C. Values

10. If you use this tool in Power View you can view a visualization individually.
    A. Pop-out
    B. Filter
    C. Pop-in

Topics for Discussion

1. What are the advantages and disadvantages of using PivotTable or PivotChart reports to find meaning from large sets of data?

2. PivotTable and PivotChart reports are designed to be fluid—constantly changing as you work with the data. What problems might this cause, and what techniques could be used to avoid them?

Skills Review

To complete this project, you will need the following file:

- exl09_SRElectricity

You will save your workbook as:

- Last_First_exl09_SRPower

1. Start **Excel 2013**, open a blank workbook, and save it in your chapter folder as Last_First_exl09_SRPower

2. On the **PowerPivot tab**, in the **Data Model group**, click **Manage**. In the **Get External Data group**, click **From Database**, and then click **Microsoft Access**. In the **Table Import Wizard** dialog box, click **Browse**. Navigate to the student data files for this chapter, click **exl09_SRElectricity**, and then click **Open**. Click **Next** two times.

3. Under **Tables and Views**, select both tables, click **Finish**, and then click **Close**. Compare your screen with **Figure 1**.

4. Click the **PivotTable** button, select the **Existing Worksheet**, and then click **OK**. In the **PivotTables Fields** pane, expand the **Billing Cycles** worksheet, and then select **ElectricityUsage**. Expand the **Residents** worksheet, and then select the **Street** and **Zip** check boxes.

5. In the **Rows** box, drag **Zip** above the **Street** field. Click cell **B1**.

6. On the **Analyze tab**, in the **Active Field group**, click **Field Settings**. In the **Value Field Settings** dialog box, under **Summarize value field by**, click **Average**. In the **Custom Name** box, replace the text with Average Usage

7. Click **Number Format**. In the **Format Cells** dialog box, under **Category**, click **Number**, and then click **OK** two times.

8. In cell **A2**, click the **Collapse** button. In cell **A3**, click the **Collapse** button. Compare your screen with **Figure 2**.

9. Click the **PowerPivot tab**, and then in the **Data Model group**, click the **Manage** button. If necessary, select the **Billing Cycles** worksheet. On the **Design tab**, in the **Columns group**, click the **Add** button.

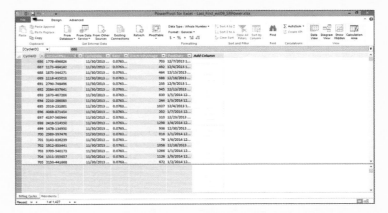

Figure 1

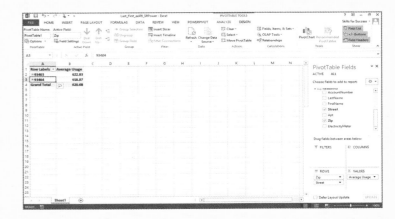

Figure 2

■ Continue to the next page to complete this Skills Review

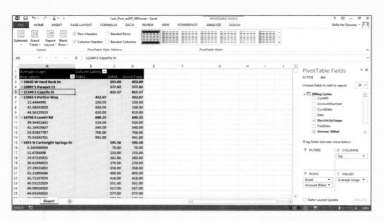

Figure 3

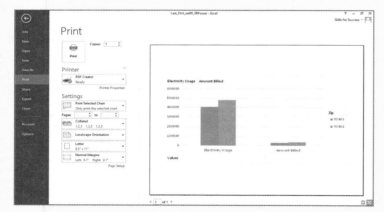

Figure 4

10. With the insertion point in the **formula bar**, type an equal sign (=). Click the **Rate** field, and then in the **formula bar** type an asterisk (*). Click the **Electricity Usage** field, and then press Enter.

11. Double-click the **CalculatedColumn1** field, type Amount Billed and then press Enter. Click the **Home tab**, and then in the **Formatting group**, click **Apply Currency Format**, and then click **$ English (United States)**. On the Quick Access Toolbar, click the **Switch to Workbook** button.

12. In the **PivotTables Fields** pane, expand the **Billing Cycles** worksheet, and select **Amount Billed**. Click cell **C1**. On the **Analyze tab**, in the **Active Field group**, select **Field Settings**. In the **Value Field Settings** dialog box, replace the **Custom Name** text with Amount Billed and then click **OK**.

13. On the **Design tab**, in the **PivotTable Styles group**, click the **More** button. Under **Medium**, click the seventh style in the third row—**Pivot Style Medium 21**.

14. In the **PivotTable Fields** pane, drag the **Zip** field from the **Rows** box into the **Columns** box, and then drag the **Amount Billed** field from the **Values** box into the **Rows** box.

15. In cell **A3**, click the **Collapse** button, and then collapse cells **A4** and **A5**. Compare your screen with Figure 3.

16. On the **Analyze tab**, in the **Filter group**, click **Insert Slicer**. Under **Residents**, select **Zip**, and then click **OK**. Drag the slicer so the upper left corner is positioned in **F2**. Select the **93463** slice. Rename the worksheet Slicer

17. Select cell **A1**. On the **PowerPivot tab**, in the **Data Model group**, click **Manage**. On the **Home tab**, click the **PivotTable arrow**, and then click **PivotChart**. In the **Insert Pivot** dialog box, click **OK**. Rename the sheet as Usage Chart

18. In the **PivotChart Fields List**, expand **Billing Cycles**, and then select **Electricity Usage** and **Amount Billed**. Expand **Residents**, and then select **Zip**. Move **Zip** from the **Axis (Category)** box into the **Legend** box, and then move **Values** into the **Axis (Category)** box.

19. Select the **PivotChart report**. On the **Design tab**, in the **Chart Styles group**, click the **More** button, and then in the second row, third column, click **Style 11**.

20. In the **PivotChart Fields** pane, modify the **Value field** settings to replace the *Sum of ElectricityUsage* with Electricity Usage and *Sum of Amount Billed* with Amount Billed

21. **Save** the workbook. Click the **File tab**, and then click the **Print tab**. Compare your screen with Figure 4. Submit the workbook as directed by your instructor.

DONE! You have completed the Skills Review

Skills Assessment 1

MyITLab®
Grader

To complete this project, you will need the following file:

- exl09_SA1Suppliers

You will save your workbook as:

- Last_First_exl09_SA1Suppliers

1. Start **Excel 2013**, open a blank workbook, and then save it in your chapter folder as Last_First_exl09_SA1Suppliers Using **PowerPivot**, import the Access table from **exl09_SA1Suppliers**.

2. In **PowerPivot**, using the **Suppliers** table as the data source, insert a PivotTable report into the worksheet. Rename the sheet as PivotTable

3. For the PivotTable, add **Supplier** as a column label, and **Date** and **Invoice** as row labels. In the **Rows** box, position **Date** above **Invoice**. Add **Amount** as a value field that calculates sums formatted as **Accounting** with **2** decimal places displayed.

4. Edit the layout of the data by inserting a blank line after each item. Change the PivotTable style to the sixth style in the first row under **Medium—Pivot Style Medium 6**. In cell **A1**, type Invoice Amount and then in **A2** type Suppliers

5. Select each of the date fields and collapse all of the fields to show only the totals for each month.

6. Copy the PivotTable worksheet and move it to the end of the workbook. Rename the worksheet Slicer Move **Supplier** to the **Rows** box above **Date** and then remove the blank line after each item.

7. Use a **Slicer** to display the **Supplier** showing the data for **Falls Catering**. Align the **Slicer** with the top left corner in cell **D2**. Apply the second style under **Dark—Slicer Style Dark 2**.

8. Using **PowerPivot**, insert a **PivotChart** into a new worksheet. Rename the worksheet PivotChart Move **Supplier** to **Legend (Series)**, **Date** to **Axis (Category)**, and **Amount** to **Values**.

9. Filter the **Date** to show only invoices for July through November.

10. Change the chart style to **Style 8**. Add a title above the chart and type Supplier Costs

11. Select cell **A1**. Compare your worksheets with **Figure 1**. **Save** the workbook, and then submit it as directed by your instructor.

Figure 1

✔ **DONE! You have completed the Skills Assessment 1**

Skills Assessment 2

To complete this project, you will need the following file:

- exl09_SA2Purchases

You will save your workbook as:

- Last_First_exl09_SA2Purchases

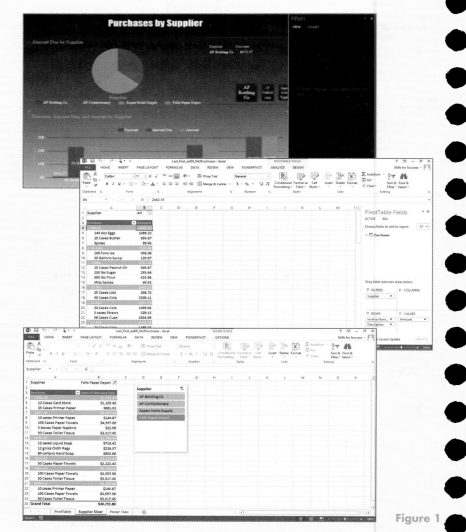

1. Start **Excel 2013**, open a blank workbook, and then save it in your chapter folder as Last_First_exl09_SA2Purchases

2. Using **PowerPivot**, import the **Purchases** worksheet from **exl09_ SA2Purchases**. Use the first row as column headers.

3. Insert a PivotTable report into the worksheet using **Purchases** as the source. Rename the worksheet PivotTable Filter by **Supplier**. In the **Rows** box, add **Invoice Number**, and then add **Description**. Add **Amount** to **Values**. In cell **A3**, type Invoices In cell **B3** type Amount Apply **Pivot Style Medium 7**.

4. In PowerPivot, add a calculated field named Discount that multiplies the **Amount** field by .02 Add another calculated field named Amount Due that subtracts **Discount** from **Amount**. Format both fields as **Currency** with **2** decimal places.

5. Copy the PivotTable worksheet and move it to the end of the workbook. Rename the worksheet Supplier Slicer Replace the **Amount** field with **Amount Due**. Use a **slicer** to display **Supplier** and filter **Falls Paper Depot**. Move the upper left corner of the **slicer** to cell **D2**. Apply **Slicer Style Dark 6**.

6. Display a new worksheet in **Power View**. Rename the worksheet Power View and the title Purchases by Supplier

7. Select **Amount Due** and **Supplier**, and format as a **Pie Chart**. Move the legend to the bottom of the chart, and drag the lower right sizing handle down and to the right until the **Supplier** legend is visible.

8. Close the **Filters** pane. Select the area to the right of the pie chart, and select **Supplier** and **Discount**. Apply **Tiles**, **Tile Flow** format. Resize the object using the lower right sizing handle until it is even with the bottom of the first chart and the right side is even with the Fields pane.

9. In the area below the pie chart add **Discount**, **Amount Due**, **Amount**, and **Supplier**. Apply the **Clustered Column Chart**. Drag the lower right sizing handle of the chart to the right until it touches the edge of the Fields pane, and then down to the bottom of the window.

Figure 1

Move the **legend** to the top, and add **data labels** to the center of the columns.

10. Change the **Theme** to **NewsPrint** and the **Background** to **Dark1 Vertical Gradient**.

11. Compare your worksheets with Figure 1. **Save** the workbook, and then submit it as directed by your instructor.

 DONE! You have completed Skills Assessment 2

Visual Skills Check

To complete this project, you will need the following file:

- exl09_VSGarden

You will save your workbook as:

- Last_First_exl09_VSGarden

Start **Excel 2013**, and then open a blank Excel workbook. Save the file in your chapter folder as Last_First_exl09_VSGarden Using PowerPivot, import the Inventory worksheet from exl09_VSGarden and use the first row as column headers. Use the imported data to create the report using the Chart and Table Horizontal option shown in **Figure 1**. Use the following directions as a guide. In PowerPivot, create a calculated column using the name Inventory Value The Inventory Value is calculated by multiplying the Cost Each by the Quantity in Stock. Apply the Pivot Style Medium 7 table style. Apply 3-D 100% Stacked Bar, and chart Style 3. Add the title Garden Inventory and then rename the worksheet Inventory Save the workbook and then submit it as directed by your instructor.

✔ **DONE! You have completed Visual Skills Check**

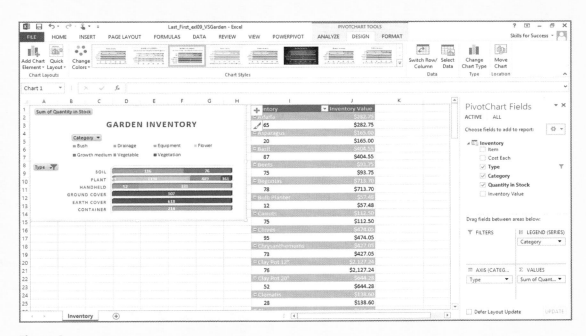

Figure 1

My Skills

To complete this project, you will need the following file:

- exl09_MYSalvage

You will save your workbook as:

- Last_First_exl09_MYSalvage

1. Start **Excel 2013** and open a blank workbook. Save the file in your chapter folder as Last_First_exl09_MYSalvage Using **PowerPivot**, import the **Salvage** worksheet from **exl09_MYSalvage** using the first row of the worksheet as column headers.

2. Add a calculated column that calculates the Net Weight subtracting the **Tare** from **Gross**.

3. Add a calculated column that calculates the Total Amount multiplying the **Price per Unit** by the **Net Weight**. Format as **Currency** with **2** decimal places.

4. Use **Power View** to create a **PivotChart** in the **Existing Worksheet**. Rename the sheet Salvage Chart

5. In the chart, add the **Date** to the **Legend**, **Description** to the **Axis**, and **Total Amount** to the **Values** fields. Format as a **Clustered Column Chart**.

6. Replace the chart title with Salvage Totals

7. Resize the chart to fill the window. Move the legend to the bottom of the chart.

8. Apply the **Aspect theme** and **Light2 Vertical Gradient background**.

9. **Save** the workbook. Compare the worksheets with **Figure 1**. Submit the workbook as directed by your instructor.

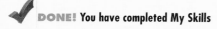 **DONE! You have completed My Skills**

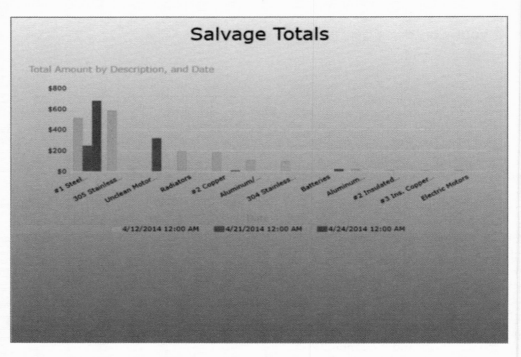

Salvage Totals

Total Amount by Description, and Date

4/12/2014 12:00 AM   4/21/2014 12:00 AM   4/24/2014 12:00 AM

Transaction #	Date	Description	Price per Unit	Gross	Tare	Net Weight	Total Amount	Add Column
1353716	4/12/2...	#1 Steel Unpr...	0.105	18700	13860	4840	$508.20	
1353716	4/12/2...	#2 Copper	2.65	69	0	69	$182.85	
1353716	4/12/2...	#2 Insulated ...	0.95	11	0	11	$10.45	
1353716	4/12/2...	#3 Ins. Coppe...	0.5	8	0	8	$4.00	
1353716	4/12/2...	304 Stainless ...	0.53	188	0	188	$99.64	
1353716	4/12/2...	305 Stainless ...	0.53	13860	12760	1100	$583.00	
1353716	4/12/2...	Aluminum Ra...	0.43	48	0	48	$20.64	
1353716	4/12/2...	Aluminum/C...	1.45	76	0	76	$110.20	
1353716	4/12/2...	Electric Motors	0.26	15	0	15	$3.90	
1353716	4/12/2...	Radiators	1.91	102	0	102	$194.82	
1353929	4/21/2...	#1 Steel Unpr...	0.105	15860	13480	2380	$249.90	
1353929	4/21/2...	Unclean Mot...	0.1	13480	10320	3160	$316.00	
1355641	4/24/2...	#1 Steel Unpr...	0.11	18920	12740	6180	$679.80	
1355641	4/24/2...	#2 Copper	2.58	2	0	2	$5.16	
1355641	4/24/2...	Batteries	0.27	88	0	88	$23.76	

Figure 1

Skills Challenge 1

To complete this project, you will need the following file:

- exl09_SC1Water

You will save your workbook as:

- Last_First_exl09_SC1Water

Aspen Falls Public Works provides water to the city. In an effort to meet the needs of the city, the department monitors water usage by postal code and month to ensure sufficient water is available. Each household's water usage for the months April, May, and June 2014 is recorded in **exl09_SC1Water**. Start **Excel 2013**, and then open a new workbook. Save the file in your chapter folder as Last_First_exl09_SC1Water Use PowerPivot to connect to the Excel data source exl09_SC1Water. Create and format PivotTable and PivotChart reports in the same worksheet using the skills practiced in the

chapter. Ensure the first row of data is used in the columns and import the table Water Data. Add fields to the chart and table that will provide information based on the average water usage by postal code for the months of April, May, and June. Apply an appropriate chart style to the chart and table style to the table. Enter an appropriate title for the chart and move the legend to the bottom of the chart. Rename the worksheet Water Usage Submit the workbook as directed by your instructor.

 DONE! You have completed Skills Challenge 1

Skills Challenge 2

To complete this project, you will need the following file:

- exl09_SC2Concessions

You will save your workbook as:

- Last_First_exl09_SC2Concessions

Aspen Falls Parks and Recreation Department purchases products for the concessions located in their parks. To determine the associated costs, it analyzes the amount of yearly purchases. The concessions purchases are recorded in **exl09_SC2Concessions**. Start **Excel 2013**, and then open a new workbook. Save the file in your chapter folder as Last_First_exl09_SC2Concessions Use PowerPivot to connect to the Access data source exl09_SC2Concessions. Add a calculated column that will provide the Total Cost for each order date and format the cost field. Create and format PivotTable and PivotChart reports in the same worksheet using the skills

practiced in the chapter. Add fields to the PivotTable report that will provide information based on the Total Cost by Date. Add fields to the PivotChart report that will provide the Total Cost of each Item represented as a percentage. Apply an appropriate chart style to the chart and a table style to the table. Enter an appropriate title for the chart. Rename the Sum of Total Cost field to Total Cost and rename Row Labels to Order Date Rename the worksheet Concessions Submit the workbook as directed by your instructor.

 DONE! You have completed Skills Challenge 2

CHAPTER 10

Secure and Share Workbooks

▶ You can personalize your version of Excel to identify a workbook's author.

▶ When you collaborate with others to build a workbook, each team member can add comments and you can track each change made. You can also protect the workbook so that only certain types of changes are allowed.

▶ You can create macros to automate common tasks with a single click.

▶ When sharing a workbook, you can track each member's changes so that you can accept or reject those changes at a later time.

▶ You can write validation rules so that only certain types of data can be entered, and you can protect the workbook so that only the cells you specify can be changed.

▶ Before sharing a workbook as a web page, you can search for and remove personal information from the workbook.

Mario Beauregard / Fotolia

Aspen Falls City Hall

In this chapter, you will review and revise a workbook for Evelyn Stone, the Aspen Falls Human Resources Director. Payroll is a function of the Human Resources Department, and the workbook contains the Fire Department employees' payroll data. It is essential that it is verified for accuracy to ensure that the payroll is calculated correctly and that promotions are timely.

When several employees collaborate on files, the ability to enter comments, approve modifications, and protect certain cells from being modified assists organizations with communication and helps prevent inaccuracies in the data.

In this project you will edit an existing workbook and create a final version to be posted as a web page. To begin, you will change the author of the workbook, review comments in the workbook, and then create new comments. You will create procedures to provide guidance to other editors of the workbook and you will accept and reject changes. To restrict certain cells from being edited you will protect cells from being modified and then create a series of steps that can be performed at the click of a button in order to save time when editing worksheets.

**Time to complete all 10
skills – 60 to 90 minutes**

Student data file needed for this chapter:

exl10_FireDept

You will save your files as:

Last_First_exl10_FireDept
Last_First_exl10_FireChanges
Last_First_exl10_FireSnip
Last_First_exl10_FireWeb
Last_First_exl10_FireMacro

Outcome

Using the skills listed in this chapter, you will be able
to create worksheets like these:

SKILLS
MyITLab®
Skills 1-10 Training

At the end of this chapter, you will be able to:

Skill 1 Modify Excel Options and Work with Comments
Skill 2 Add Data Validation Rules
Skill 3 Track Changes
Skill 4 Accept and Reject Tracked Changes
Skill 5 Merge Changes
Skill 6 Use the Document Inspector to Remove Personal Information
Skill 7 Save Workbooks as Web Pages
Skill 8 Unlock Cells and Protect Worksheets
Skill 9 Record Macros
Skill 10 Write Macros Using VBA

MORE SKILLS

Skill 11 Insert Form Controls
Skill 12 Add Macro Buttons to the Quick Access Toolbar
Skill 13 Modify the Ribbon
Skill 14 Assign Macros to Command Buttons

► Reviewer **comments** are descriptive text that you can add to cells without modifying the data in the worksheet.

► When collaborating on a project, reviewers can use comments to make suggestions.

► You can personalize your copy of Excel by changing the settings in the Excel Options dialog box.

1. **Start Excel 2013**, and then open the student data file **exl10_FireDept**. If the file opens in **Protected view**, click **Enable Editing**. On the **File tab**, click **Save As**, and then click **Browse**. In the **Save As** dialog box, navigate to the location where you are saving your files. Click **New folder**, type Excel Chapter 10 and then press [Enter] two times. Name the file Last_First_exl10_FireDept and then press [Enter].

2. Click the **File tab**, and then click **Options**. Compare your screen with **Figure 1**.

   The left side of the Excel Options dialog box displays option categories. By default, the General category is selected. The option categories are summarized in the table shown in **Figure 2**.

3. In the **Excel Options** dialog box, under **Personalize your copy of Microsoft Office**, note the current value in the **User name** box so that you can restore it later, if needed. If necessary, change the **User name** to your own first and last name, and then click **OK**.

   As comments are added to the worksheet, the user name identifies the comments' author.

■ **Continue to the next page to complete the skill**

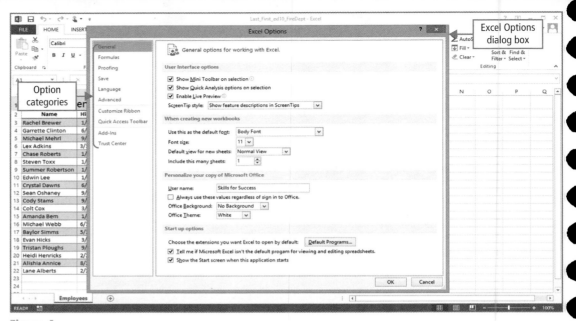

Figure 1

Excel Options Dialog Box	
Section	**Purpose**
General	Provides options to access the most commonly used settings.
Formulas	Provides options for how formulas are calculated and how errors are checked.
Proofing	Provides options for how spelling and grammar are checked.
Save	Provides options for how workbooks are saved.
Language	Provides options to set Office Language Preferences.
Advanced	Provides options to access 13 subcategories of options.
Customize Ribbon	Provides options to customize the Ribbon.
Quick Access Toolbar	Provides options to customize the Quick Access toolbar.
Add-Ins	Provides options to manage Excel Add-Ins.
Trust Center	Provides options to manage privacy and security.

Figure 2

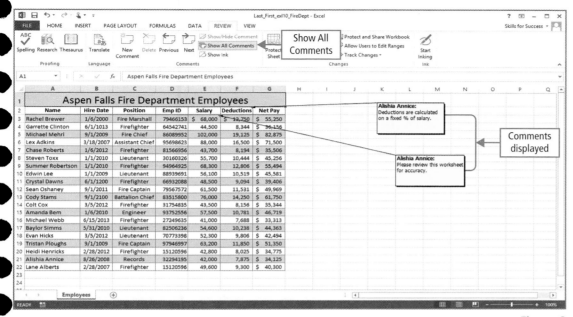

Figure 3

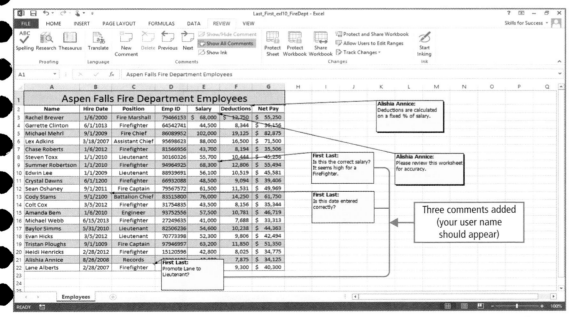

Figure 4

4. On the **Employees** worksheet, point to cell **F2** so that the comment from Alishia Annice displays.

   Cells with comments display a **comment indicator**—a small red triangle in the upper right corner of a cell.

5. Click the **Review tab**, and then in the **Comments group**, click **Show All Comments**. Compare your screen with Figure 3.

   Showing all comments allows you to read all of the comments at one time.

6. Select cell **B13**, and then in the **Comments group**, click **New Comment**.

7. In the comment box, type Is this date entered correctly?

8. With the comment attached to cell **B13** still selected, point to the comment box border, and then with the [pointer icon] pointer, drag so that the upper left corner of the comment box is positioned in cell **I13**.

9. Select cell **E9**, and then click **New Comment**. In the comment box, type Is this the correct salary? It seems high for a Firefighter.

10. With the comment attached to cell **E9** still selected, point to the comment box border, and then with the [pointer icon] pointer, drag so that the upper left corner of the comment box is positioned in cell **I8**.

11. Select cell **C22**, and then click **New Comment**. In the comment box, type Promote Lane to Lieutenant? Select cell **A1**, and then compare your screen with Figure 4.

12. In the **Comments group**, click **Show All Comments** to hide the comments from view.

13. **Save** [save icon] the workbook.

■ **You have completed Skill 1 of 10**

▶ **EXL 10-2 VIDEO**

▶ ***Data validation rules*** place restrictions on the types of data that can be entered in cells.

1. Select the range **B3:B22**. Click the **Data tab**, and in the **Data Tools group**, click the **Data Validation** button.

2. In the **Data Validation** dialog box, on the **Settings tab**, click the **Allow arrow**, and then click **Date**. Click the **Data arrow**, and then click **greater than**. In the **Start date** box, type 1/1/1975 Compare your screen with **Figure 1**.

3. In the **Data Validation** dialog box, click the **Input Message tab**, and then in the **Title** box, type Hire Date In the **Input message** box, type Hire date cannot be before 1975

> An ***input message*** is a data validation message that informs the data entry operator about the types of data that can be entered in the cell.

4. Click the **Error Alert tab**. If necessary, click the **Show error alert after invalid data is entered** check box. In the **Title** box, type Invalid Hire Date In the **Error message** box, type The hire date must be after 1/1/1975 Click **OK**, and then select cell **A1**.

> An ***error alert*** is a data validation message that tells the data entry operator that invalid data has been entered in the cell.

5. In the **Data Tools group**, click the **Data Validation arrow**, and then click **Circle Invalid Data**. Compare your screen with **Figure 2**.

> When a data rule has been applied to a cell, Excel indicates invalid data by circling a cell whose value does not match the rule.

■ **Continue to the next page to complete the skill**

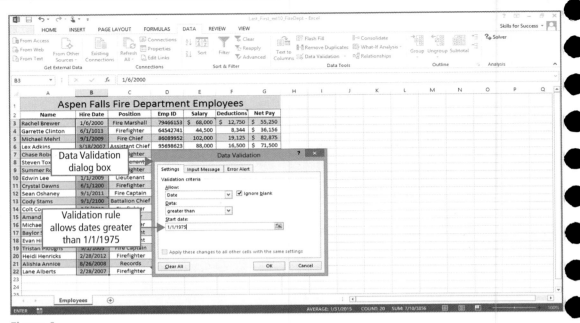

Figure 1

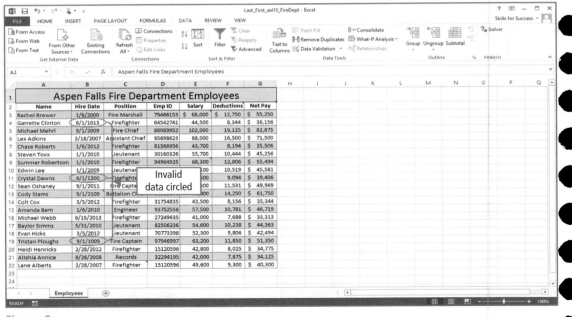

Figure 2

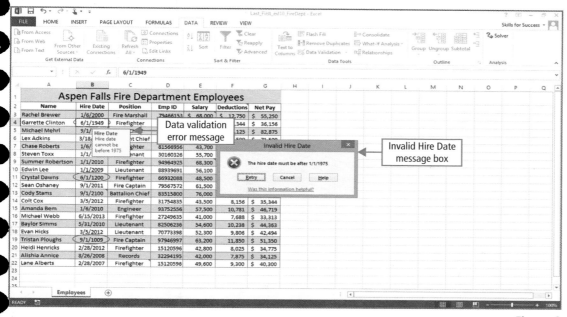

Figure 3

Error Message Styles

Type	Purpose
Stop	Prevents users from entering invalid data in a cell. This message has two options: Retry or Cancel.
Warning	Warns users that the data entered is invalid, without preventing them from entering it. When a Warning message appears, users can click Yes to accept the invalid entry, No to edit the invalid entry, or Cancel to remove the invalid entry.
Information	Informs users that the data they entered is invalid, without preventing them from entering it. This type of error alert is the most flexible. When an Information alert message appears, users can click OK to accept the invalid value or Cancel to reject it.

Figure 4

6. Select cell **B4**, and then verify that the input message displays.

7. Select the range **E3:E22**, and then click the **Data Validation** button. In the **Data Validation** dialog box, click the **Settings tab**. Click the **Allow arrow**, and then click **Decimal**. With the **Data** box set to **between**, in the **Minimum** box, type 25000.00 In the **Maximum** box, type 110000.00

   This validation rule specifies that decimal numbers between the minimum and the maximum should be entered.

8. In the **Data Validation** dialog box, click the **Error Alert tab**. Click the **Style arrow**, and then click **Warning**. In the **Title** box, type Salary Alert In the **Error message** box, type Salary should be at least $25,000 and no more than $110,000 Click **OK**.

9. Click cell **B4**, type 6/1/1949 and then press [Enter]. Compare your screen with **Figure 3**.

   The Invalid Hire Date message box displays because the date entered is before 1975.

10. Click **Retry**, type 6/1/2011 and then press [Enter]. Change cell **B11** to 8/12/2010 Change cell **B19** to 9/1/2009

11. In cell **E9**, change the salary to 483000 and then press [Enter].

    When the Error style is set to *Warning,* you are given the option to proceed when the data is invalid. The three error message styles are summarized in the table in **Figure 4**.

12. Read the **Salary Alert** error message, and then click **No**. In cell **E9**, change the salary to 48300 and then press [Enter].

13. **Save** 🖫 the workbook.

- **You have completed Skill 2 of 10**

▶ When you are collaborating with others, you can see each reviewer's changes by enabling *change tracking*—a feature that tracks all the changes made to a workbook.

1. Select cell **A1**. On the **Review tab**, in the **Changes group**, click **Track Changes**, and then click **Highlight Changes**. Compare your screen with **Figure 1**.

   To track changes, the workbook must be a *shared workbook*—a workbook in which multiple users on a network can make changes at the same time.

2. In the **Highlight Changes** dialog box, select the **Track changes while editing** check box to track changes and share the workbook. Select the **Who** check box. Compare your screen with **Figure 2**, and then click **OK**. In the dialog box that displays, click **OK**.

   The Excel title bar displays the text *[Shared]* to indicate that the workbook is currently being shared with others.

3. Click the **File tab**, and then click **Save As**. Save the workbook in your **Excel Chapter 10** folder as Last_First_exl10_FireChanges

4. Click the **File tab**, and then click **Options**. In the **Excel Options** dialog box, change the **User name** to Alishia Annice and then click **OK**.

   You will now be editing the worksheet as Alishia Annice.

■ **Continue to the next page to complete the skill** ▶

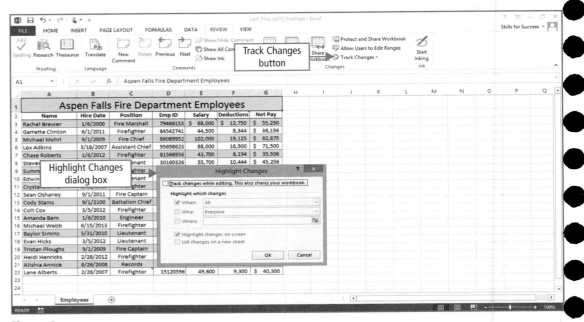

Figure 1

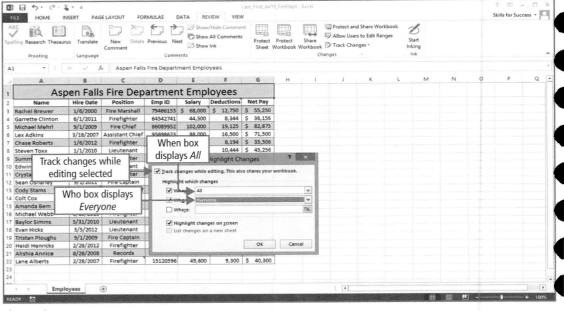

Figure 2

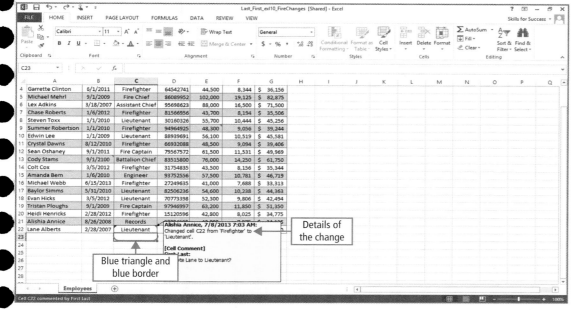

Figure 3

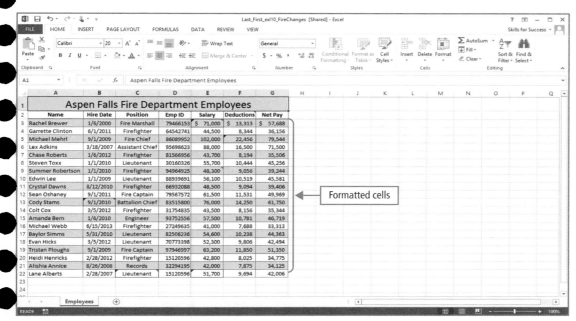

Figure 4

5. Select cell **C22**, type Lieutenant and then press Enter. Scroll down, and then point to cell **C22** to display the comment box, as shown in Figure 3.

When a change is tracked, a blue line displays around the changed cell, and a blue triangle displays in the upper left corner of the cell. When you point to the cell, details about that change display such as the date and time of the change and the original values.

6. Select cell **B13**, type 9/1/2010 and press Enter. Continue in this manner to make the following changes:

Cell **E3**	71000
Cell **F5**	22456
Cell **E22**	51700

7. Select the range **G4:G22**. On the **Home tab**, in the **Number group**, click **Comma Style** ⟨,⟩, and then click **Decrease Decimal** two times. Select cell **A1**, and then compare your screen with Figure 4.

Notice that there are no blue lines around the range G4:G22. Only changes that affect the cell data are tracked. Formatting changes applied to ranges are not tracked.

8. **Save** 💾 the workbook.

■ **You have completed Skill 3 of 10**

▶ Excel maintains a record of tracked changes in the ***change history***—a log that records each data change, who made the change, and when the data was changed.

▶ When changes are tracked, you can choose to accept or reject each change.

1. Click the **Review tab**. In the **Changes group**, click **Track Changes**, and then click **Highlight Changes**. In the **Highlight Changes** dialog box, select the **List changes on a new sheet** check box, and then compare your screen with **Figure 1**.

2. Click **OK**, and then compare your screen with **Figure 2**.

   A temporary worksheet—*History*—is added to the workbook. The History worksheet displays the entire change history. All of the changes made by Alishia Annice are listed (your dates and times will be different).

3. With the **History** worksheet tab displayed, press ⊞, type snip and then press Enter. Using the Snipping Tool, create a full-screen snip. **Save** 🖫 the snip in your **Excel Chapter 10** folder as Last_First_exl10_FireSnip and then **Close** ✕ the **Snipping Tool** window.

   The History worksheet is dynamic and will not automatically display when the workbook is opened again.

4. **Save** 🖫 the workbook.

   Notice that the History worksheet no longer displays.

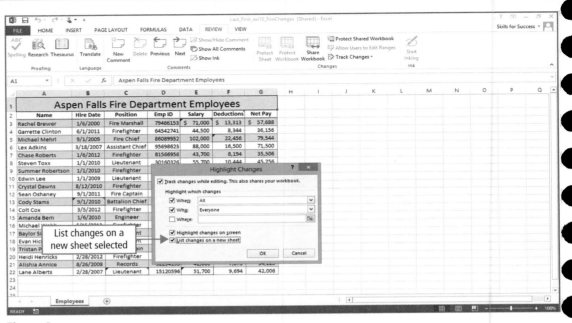

Figure 1

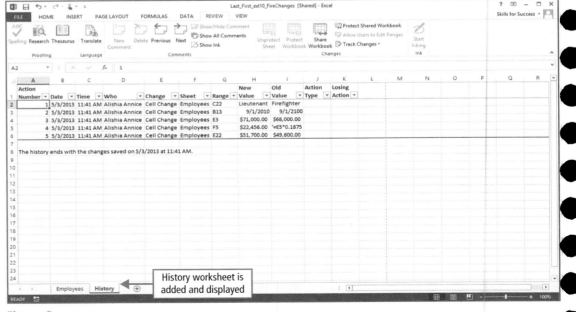

Figure 2

■ **Continue to the next page to complete the skill** ➤

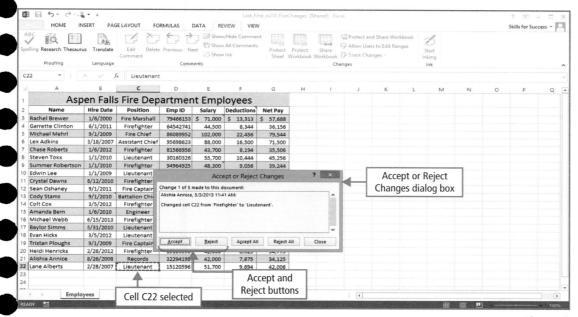

Figure 3

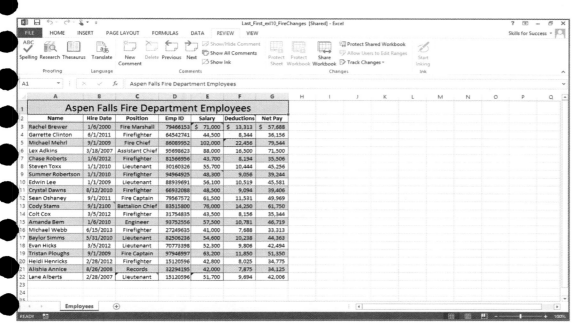

Figure 4

5. On the **Review tab**, in the **Changes group**, click **Track Changes**, and then click **Accept/Reject Changes**.

6. In the **Select Changes to Accept or Reject** dialog box, verify that the **When** box displays *Not yet reviewed*, and then click **OK**. Compare your screen with **Figure 3**.

   The Accept or Reject Changes dialog box selects changed cells one at a time so that you can accept or reject each change. Cell C22 is selected, and the details of the change display in the dialog box. Your date and time will be different.

7. In the dialog box, click **Accept** to change the value in cell **C22**. Read the change details for change 2 of 5—cell **B13**—and then click **Accept** to change and override the original value.

8. Read the change details for change 3 of 5—cell **E3**—and then click **Reject** to revert to the original value.

9. Click **Accept All** to accept all the remaining changes. Compare your screen with **Figure 4**.

10. **Save**, and then **Close** the workbook.

■ **You have completed Skill 4 of 10**

▶ **Compare and merge** is a process that combines the changes from multiple copies of a workbook into a single copy.

▶ To use compare and merge, the Compare and Merge button must be added to the Quick Access Toolbar.

1. Open **Last_First_exl10_FireDept**. Using the skills practiced previously, open the **Excel Options** dialog box, and then change the **User name** to your own first and last names.

2. In the left pane of the **Excel Options** dialog box, click **Quick Access Toolbar**.

3. Under **Customize the Quick Access Toolbar**, click the **Customize Quick Access Toolbar arrow**, and then click **For Last_First_exl10_FireDept.xlsx**.

4. Click the **Choose commands from arrow**, and then click **Commands Not in the Ribbon**.

5. Scroll down the list, click **Compare and Merge Workbooks**, and then click **Add** to add it to the Customize Quick Access Toolbar list. Compare your screen with Figure 1.

6. Click **OK** to close the **Excel Options** dialog box, and then compare your screen with Figure 2.

   In this manner, you can add buttons to the Quick Access Toolbar.

7. On the **Quick Access Toolbar**, click the **Compare and Merge Workbooks** button ⊙. Read the message that displays, and then click **OK**.

■ Continue to the next page to complete the skill ▶

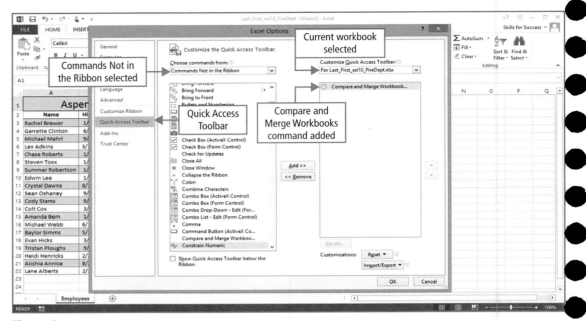

Figure 1

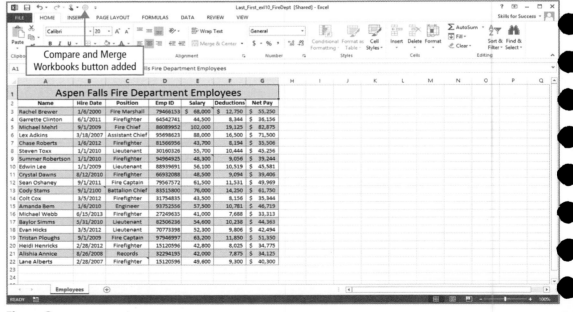

Figure 2

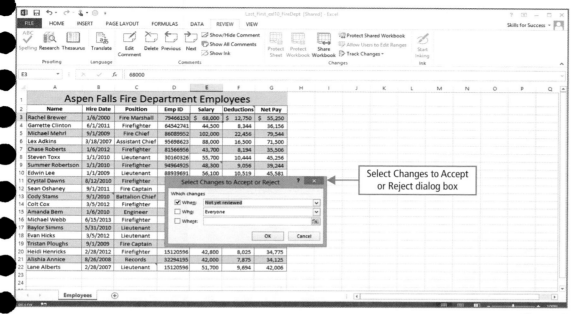

Figure 3

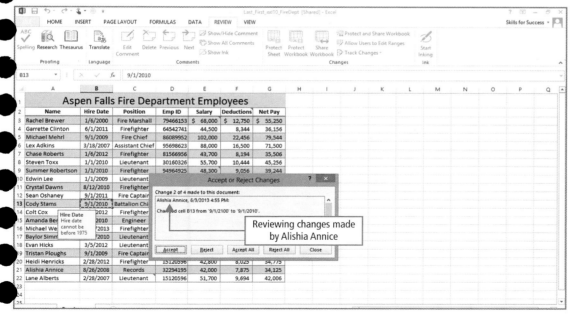

Figure 4

8. In the **Select Files to Merge Into Current Workbook** dialog box, open your **Excel Chapter 10** folder, click **Last_First_exl10_FireChanges**, and then click **OK**.

9. Select cell **E3**. On the **Review tab**, in the **Changes group**, click **Track Changes**, and then click **Accept/Reject Changes**. Compare your screen with **Figure 3**.

10. Verify that the **When** box reads *Not yet reviewed*. Select the **Who** check box, and then verify that the **Who** box reads *Everyone*.

11. Click **OK**. Review the information in the **Accept or Reject Changes** dialog box, and then click **Accept**. Compare your screen with **Figure 4**.

    You are now reviewing the changes made by Alishia Annice.

12. In the **Accept or Reject Changes** dialog box, click **Accept All**.

13. In the **Changes group**, click **Track Changes**, and then click **Highlight Changes**. In the **Highlight Changes** dialog box, clear the **Track changes while editing** check box, and then click **OK**.

14. Read the message, click **Yes**, and then Save ☐ the workbook.

- **You have completed Skill 5 of 10**

▶ **Document properties** are details that describe a workbook file. For example, the author name, company name, or comments may be stored in the document properties.

▶ Before sharing a workbook, you should search for and remove any personal information that may be stored in the file.

1. Click the **File tab**, and compare your screen with Figure 1.

   The Document Information Panel displays the file's **metadata**—information that describes the data in an Excel file. Here, the metadata has personally identifiable information, such as a name in the Author Property.

2. In the **Info group**, click **Check for Issues**, and then click **Inspect Document**. If necessary, read the message, and then click **Yes**.

3. In the **Document Inspector** dialog box, clear the **Comments and Annotations** check box, and compare your screen with Figure 2.

   The Document Inspector is used to search for comments, metadata, headers, footers, and other elements that may be hidden from view.

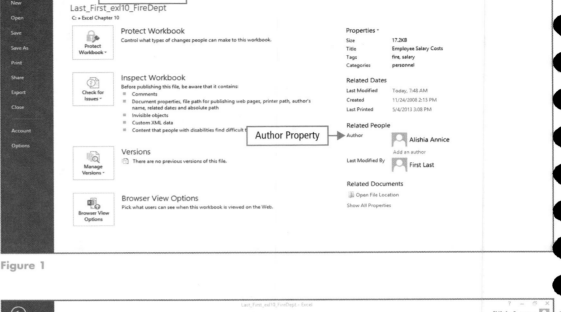

Figure 1

Figure 2

■ **Continue to the next page to complete the skill** ▶

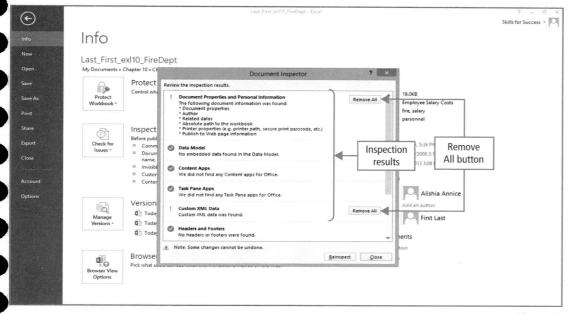

Figure 3

Figure 4

4. In the **Document Inspector** dialog box, click **Inspect**. Wait a few moments, and then compare your screen with **Figure 3**.

> If an item is found in the Document Inspector, the Remove All button displays. In this workbook, document properties and personal information, and custom XML data were found.

5. To the right of **Document Properties and Personal Information**, click the **Remove All** button, and then click **Reinspect**.

6. In the **Document Inspector** dialog box, click **Inspect**. Note that the **Document Properties and Personal Information** section does not show any results.

7. Click **Close**, and then compare your screen with **Figure 4**.

> In the Document Information Panel, under Properties, both the Title and Tags are cleared because items were removed with the Document Inspector. Under Related People, the **Author** has been cleared and **Last Modified By** has not been saved.

8. On the **Info** page, under **Related People**, click **Add an author**. In the **Author** box, type your first and last name, and then press Enter. In the **Check Names** dialog box, click **Cancel**.

9. Save 🖫 the workbook.

■ **You have completed Skill 6 of 10**

▶ *Hypertext Markup Language (HTML)* is used to mark up text files so that they can be viewed on the Internet.

▶ You can save all or part of a worksheet as an HTML web page.

▶ HTML text files are typically given an *.htm* or *.html* file extension so that they can be viewed in a web browser.

1. Click the **File tab**, and then click **Save As**.

2. Navigate to your **Excel Chapter 10** folder. In the **Save As** dialog box, click the **Save as type arrow**, and then click the seventh file type—**Web Page**.

3. In the **Save As** dialog box, click in the **File name** box, and then type Last_First_ exl10_FireWeb Compare your screen with **Figure 1**.

4. In the **Save As** dialog box, click the **Change Title** button.

5. In the **Enter Text** dialog box, under **Page title**, type Fire Department Pay Compare your screen with **Figure 2**, and then click **OK**.

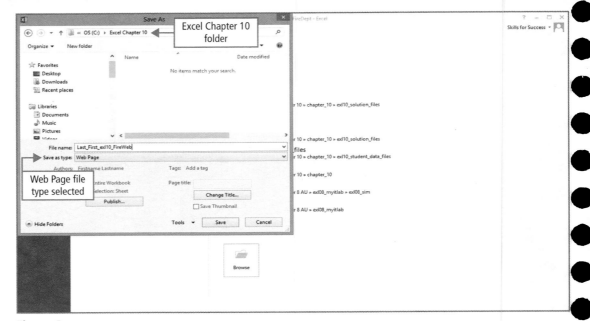

Figure 1

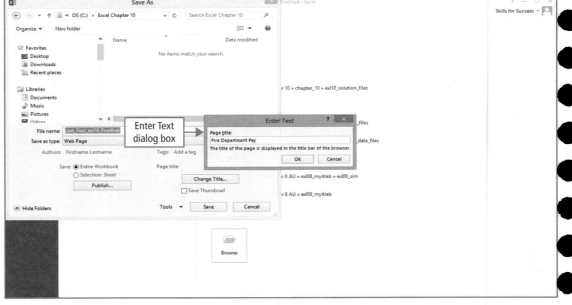

Figure 2

■ **Continue to the next page to complete the skill** ▷

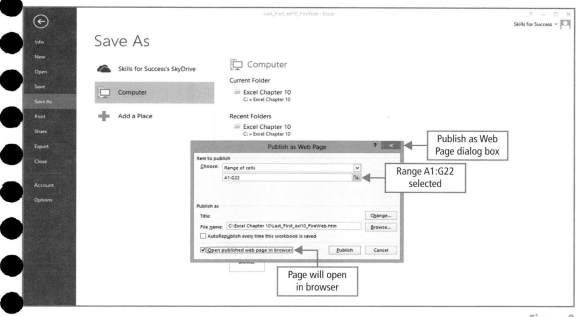

Figure 3

6. In the **Save As** dialog box, click **Publish**.

7. In the **Publish as Web Page** dialog box, click the **Choose arrow**, and then click **Range of cells**. In the second **Choose** box, type A1:G22 Under **Publish as**, check the **Open published web page in browser** check box.

8. Compare your screen with Figure 3, and then click **Publish**. If the message **How do you want to open this type of file (.htm)?** is displayed, select **Internet Explorer**. Maximize ☐ **Internet Explorer**, and then compare your screen with Figure 4.

   The title displays at the top of the page and in the page's tab.

9. **Close** ☒ your web browser.

■ **You have completed Skill 7 of 10**

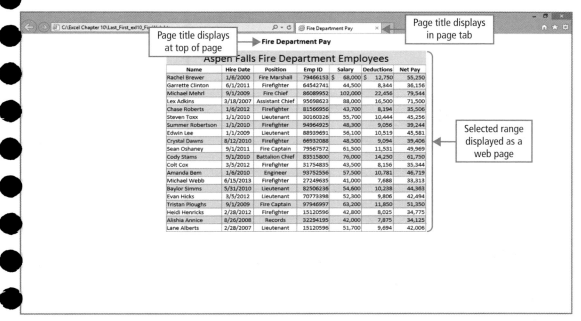

Figure 4

▶ **Protect Sheet** prevents unauthorized users from making changes to a worksheet.

▶ To allow revisions to parts of a protected workbook, you must first unlock the cells you want to change.

1. Exit **Backstage view**. Select the range **A3:E22**. On the **Home tab**, in the **Cells group**, click the **Format** button, and then in the list, verify that **Lock Cell** is toggled on, as indicated by the green color around the icon. Compare your screen with **Figure 1**.

   All cells are locked by default, but the lock is not enforced until worksheet protection is enabled.

2. In the **Format menu**, click **Protect Sheet**.

3. In the **Protect Sheet** dialog box, in the **Password to unprotect sheet** box, type Success13!

4. Under **Allow all users of this worksheet to**, verify **Select locked cells** and **Select unlocked cells** are selected, and then select the **Format cells** check box. Compare your screen with **Figure 2**, and then click **OK**.

   When protecting workbooks, use a **strong password**—a password that contains a combination of uppercase and lowercase letters, numbers, and symbols. In this exercise, the selected protection options will allow individuals to select cells and format cells. No changes to formulas or cell data will be allowed.

5. In the **Confirm Password** dialog box, type Success13! and then click **OK** to confirm the password.

■ **Continue to the next page to complete the skill**

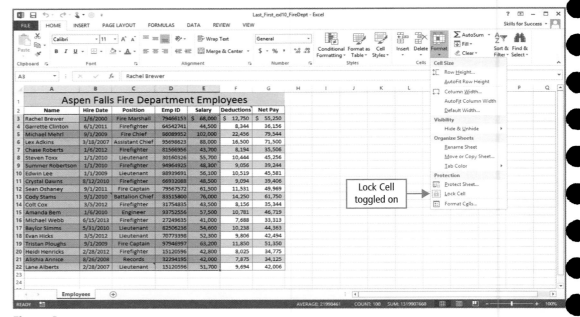

Figure 1

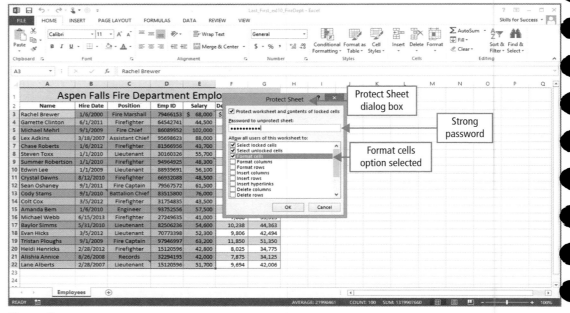

Figure 2

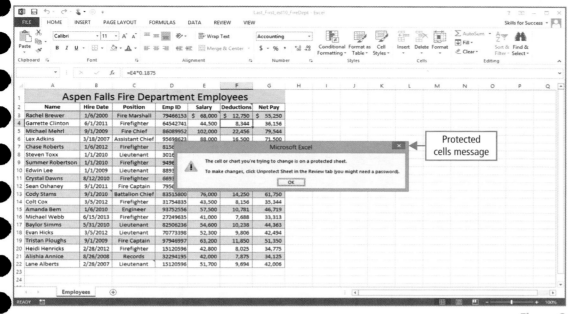

Figure 3

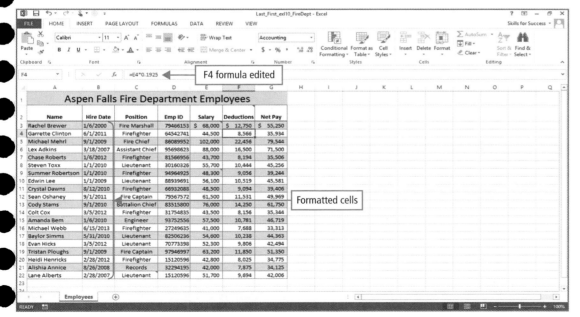

Figure 4

6. Select cell **F4**, attempt to type 8232 and then compare your screen with **Figure 3**.

   The message informs you that the cell is protected and cannot be changed until protection is removed.

7. Click **OK** to close the message. On the **Home tab**, in the **Cells group**, click **Format**, and then click **Unprotect Sheet**. In the **Unprotect Sheet** dialog box, in the **Password** box, type Success13! and then click **OK**.

8. Select the range **F3:F22**. In the **Cells group**, click **Format**, and then click **Lock Cell** to toggle off the lock of the selected range.

9. Select the range **A3:G22**. Use the techniques you just practiced to toggle on protection for the range using the password Success13!

10. Click cell **E4**, and attempt to change the value. Read the message, and then click **OK**.

11. Click cell **F4**. In the **formula bar**, select the existing text, and then type =E4*0.1925 Press `Enter` to change the formula.

    When a cell's lock is toggled off, you can make changes to the cell when protection is on.

12. Select the range **B3:B22**, and then in the **Alignment group**, click the **Align Left** button ≣. Select cell **F4**, and then compare your screen with **Figure 4**.

    Because formatting changes were allowed in the Protect Sheet dialog box, the formatting change was accepted.

13. **Save** 🖫 the workbook.

- **You have completed Skill 8 of 10**

▶ A *macro* is a stored set of instructions that automates common tasks.

▶ The macro recorder creates a macro by recording the steps you perform in a routine activity. The recorded steps are then performed whenever the macro is run.

1. Click the **File tab**, and click **Save As**. Navigate to your **Excel Chapter 10** folder, and then in the **Save As** dialog box, click the **Save as type arrow**. In the list, click the second choice, **Excel Macro-Enabled Workbook**. In the **File name** box, type Last_First_exl10_FireMacro and then click **Save**.

2. Click the **File tab**, and then click **Options**. In the **Excel Options** dialog box, click **Customize Ribbon**. Under **Customize the Ribbon**, if necessary, select the **Developer** check box. Compare your screen with **Figure 1**, and then click **OK**.

3. Select cell **A1**, and then on the **Developer tab**, in the **Code group**, click **Record Macro**.

4. In the **Record Macro** dialog box, in the **Macro name** box, type InsertInfo In the **Shortcut key** box, type m In the **Description** box, type Inserts the name and date in cells A23:A24 Compare your screen with **Figure 2**, and then click **OK**.

5. Select cell **A23**. On the **Home tab**, in the **Cells group**, click the **Format** button, and then click **Unprotect sheet**. Enter the password Success13! and then click **OK** to unprotect the worksheet.

6. In cell **A23**, type your first and last name, and then press [Enter]. In cell **A24**, type =NOW() and then press [Enter].

■ **Continue to the next page to complete the skill**

Figure 1

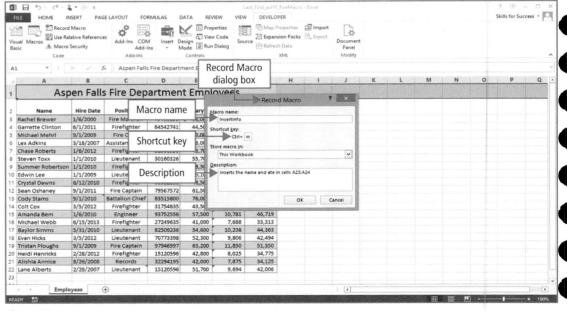

Figure 2

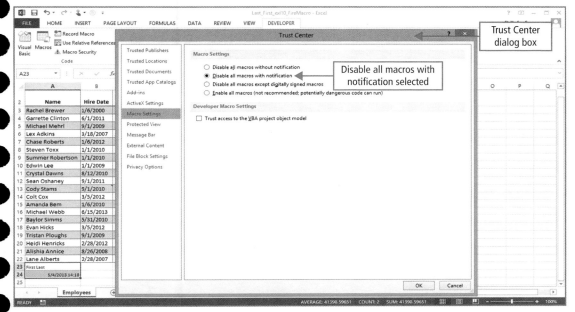

Figure 3

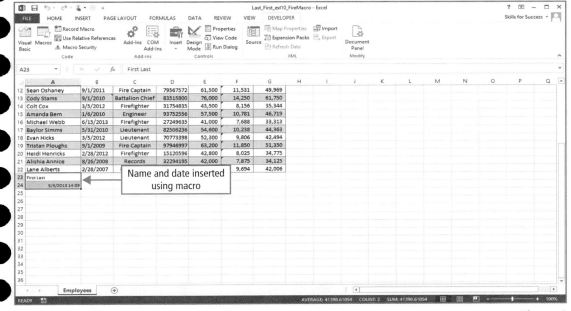

Figure 4

7. Select the range **A23:A24**. In the **Font group**, change the font size to **8**. Click the **Font Color arrow**, and then under **Standard Colors**, click **Dark Blue**.

8. On the **Developer tab**, in the **Code group**, click **Stop Recording**.

9. In the **Code group**, click **Macro Security**. In the **Trust Center** dialog box, verify that **Disable all macros with notification** is selected. Compare your screen with **Figure 3**, and then click **OK**.

   The security setting requires your permission to execute a macro. Macros can be used to spread *malware*—software that is designed to harm a computer—so you should enable only macros from trusted sources.

10. Delete **rows 23** and **24**. Select cell **A1**, and then click **Save** 🔲. Read the message, click **OK**, and then **Close** ✖ the workbook.

11. Navigate to the **Excel Chapter 10** folder, and then open **Last_First_exl10_FireMacro**. In the **Message Bar**, click **Enable Content**.

    When you open a workbook with a macro, the Security bar informs you when the workbook contains a macro. You can then choose to enable or disable the macro.

12. On the **Developer tab**, in the **Code group**, click **Macros**. In the **Macro** dialog box, select **InsertInfo**, and then click **Run**. Compare your screen with **Figure 4**.

13. Delete **rows 23** and **24**, and then select cell **A1**. Press Ctrl + M to verify that the assigned shortcut key runs the macro. Click **Save** 🔲. Read the message, and then click **OK**.

■ **You have completed Skill 9 of 10**

▶ *Visual Basic for Applications (VBA)* is a high-level programming language that can be used to write and modify macros.

▶ VBA macros are entered and edited in the Visual Basic Editor (VBE).

1. Select cell **A1**. On the **Developer tab**, in the **Code group**, click **Visual Basic**.

2. In the **Microsoft Visual Basic for Applications** window, click the **Insert menu**, and then click **Module**. Compare your screen with **Figure 1**.

    The *Code window*—the window in which VBA code is written—for Module2 displays.

3. In the **Code** window, type the following sub and comments. Be sure the last two lines begin with a single quotation mark, as shown:

    Sub InsertFileName()

    'Created by First Last

    'Inserts the file name in the footer

    A *sub* is a group of instructions that is a subset of a program. After you press [Enter] to go to the next line, *End Sub* will display and remain at the end of the code. In VBA, all subs end with *End Sub*. Each line will have different colors associated with it. The *InsertFileName* sub has two *programming comments*—statements that document what the code does—which display in green.

4. After the last comment, press [Enter], and then type the following statements:

    ActiveSheet.PageSetup.LeftFooter = "&F"

    ActiveWindow.View = xlNormalView

5. Compare your screen with **Figure 2**.

    The sub has two *programming statements*, which are instructions. The statements insert the file name in the left footer and then return the worksheet to Normal view.

■ **Continue to the next page to complete the skill** ▶

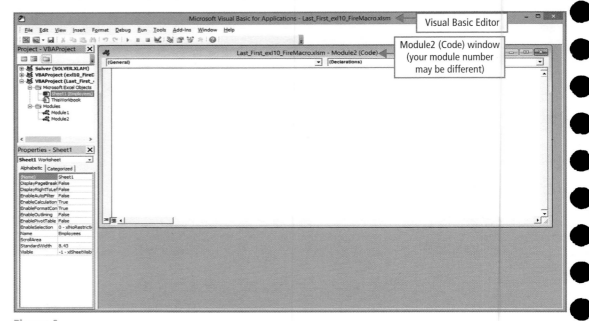

Figure 1

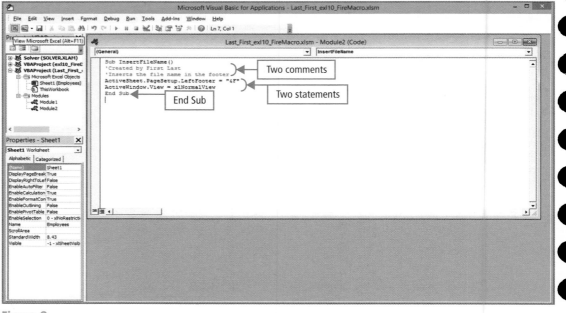

Figure 2

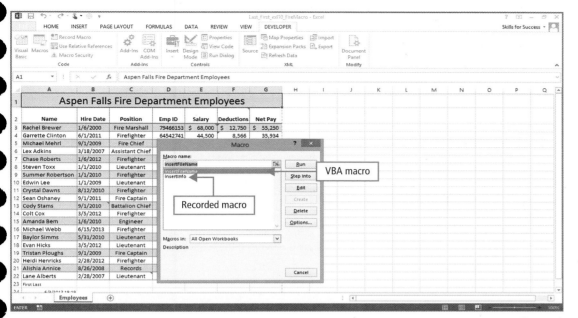

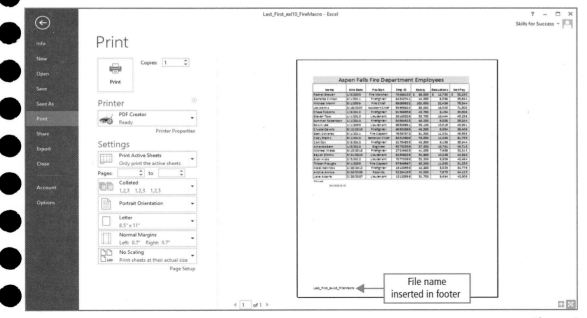

File name
inserted in footer

Figure 4

Figure 3

6. From the **File menu,** click **Close and Return to Microsoft Excel.**

7. On the **Developer tab,** in the **Code group,** click **Macros.** Compare your screen with **Figure 3.**

   The Macro dialog box displays two macros, the recorded macro and the VBA macro.

8. In the **Macro** dialog box, ensure **InsertFileName** is selected, and then click **Run.**

9. If an error message displays, click the **Debug** button, and then on the VBE Standard toolbar, click the **Reset** button. In the **Code** window, carefully check your typing, and then return to Excel.

10. Click the **File tab,** click **Print,** and then compare your screen with **Figure 4.**

    The VBA macro inserted the file name in the footer.

11. On the **File tab,** click **Options.** Click **Customize Ribbon,** and then in the **Customize the Ribbon** area, clear the **Developer** check box. In the left pane, click **General,** and then, if necessary, restore the Excel user name to the value you recorded in Skill 1. Click **OK.**

12. Select cell **A1,** and then **Save** 🖫 the workbook. Read the message that displays, and then click **OK.** Submit the files as directed by your instructor.

13. **Close** ⊠ Excel.

✔️ **DONE! You have completed Skill 10 of 10, and your workbook is complete!**

More Skills

The following More Skills are located at **www.pearsonhighered.com/skills**

More Skills Insert Form Controls

Form controls can be added to worksheets to provide style and require users to choose the options provided.

In More Skills 11, you will edit a worksheet and create check box and button form controls.

To begin, open your web browser, navigate to www.pearsonhighered.com/skills, locate the name of your textbook, and then follow the instructions on the website.

More Skills Add Macro Buttons to the Quick Access Toolbar

When you have created a macro that you use regularly, you can add a shortcut to the Quick Access Toolbar that allows you to run the macro without having to display the Developer tab on the Ribbon.

In More Skills 12, you will use a macro and add a custom command to the Quick Access Toolbar to run the macro.

To begin, open your web browser, navigate to www.pearsonhighered.com/skills, locate the name of your textbook, and then follow the instructions on the website.

More Skills Modify the Ribbon

As you continue to use Excel 2013, you will discover that you begin to regularly use the same tools. Excel allows you to modify the Ribbon by creating a custom tab that contains any commands that suit your needs.

In More Skills 13, you will modify the Ribbon by creating a custom tab and adding commands to the tab.

To begin, open your web browser, navigate to www.pearsonhighered.com/skills, locate the name of your textbook, and then follow the instructions on the website.

More Skills Assign Macros to Command Buttons

When you have created a macro that you use regularly and you want it to be available to others collaborating on the workbook, you can assign the macro to a command button so that anyone who edits the workbook on any computer can use it.

In More Skills 14, you will create a macro and then add a custom command button to run the macro.

To begin, open your web browser, navigate to www.pearsonhighered.com/skills, locate the name of your textbook, and then follow the instructions on the website.

Please note that there are no additional projects to accompany the More Skills Projects, and they are not covered in End-of-Chapter projects.

The following table summarizes the **SKILLS AND PROCEDURES** covered in this chapter.

Skills Number	Task	Step	Icon
1	Personalize Microsoft Office	File tab → Options → Personalize your copy of Microsoft Office	
1	Add comments	Review tab → Comments group → New Comment button	
1	Delete comments	Review tab → Comments group → Delete button	
1	Show all comments	Review tab → Comments group → Show All Comments button	
2	Validate data criteria	Data tab → Data Tools group → Data Validation button → Data Validation dialog box → Settings tab	
2	Create validate data message	Data tab → Data Tools group → Data Validation button → Data Validation dialog box → Input Message tab	
2	Create validate data error alert	Data tab → Data Tools group → Data Validation button → Data Validation dialog box → Error Alert tab	
2	Circle invalid data	Data tab → Data Tools group → Data Validation arrow → Circle Invalid Data	
2	Clear validation circles	Data tab → Data Tools group → Data Validation arrow → Clear Validation Circles	
3	Track changes	Review tab → Changes group → Track Changes button → Highlight Changes → Track Changes While Editing	
4	Accept/reject changes	Review tab → Changes group → Track Changes button → Accept/Reject Changes	
5	Merge changes	Quick Access toolbar → Compare and Merge Workbooks button → Select workbooks	
6	Inspect workbook	File tab → Info → Check for Issues button → Inspect Document	
6	Remove personal information from properties	File tab → Info → Check for Issues button → Inspect Document → Document Properties and Personal Information → Remove All	
7	Save workbook as a web page	File tab → Save As → Save as type → Web Page → Publish	
8	Lock/unlock cells	Home tab → Cells group → Format arrow → Lock Cell	
8	Protect/unprotect worksheets	Home tab → Cells group → Format arrow → Protect Sheet	
9	Create macro	Developer tab → Code group → Record Macro button → Macro dialog box	
9	End macro	Developer tab → Code group → Stop Recording button	
9	Run macro	Developer tab → Code group → Macros button → Select Macro name → Run	
10	Create VBA macro	Developer tab → Code group → Visual Basic button → Insert tab → Module	

Key Terms

Online Help Skills

1. Start **Excel 2013**, and then in the upper right corner of the Excel window, click the **Help** button ? . In the Help window, click the **Maximize** ⬜ button.

2. Click in the search box, type track changes and then press Enter . In the search results, click **Track changes in a shared workbook**.

3. Read the article's introduction, and then below **In this article**, click **Changes that Excel does not track or highlight**. Compare your screen with **Figure 1**.

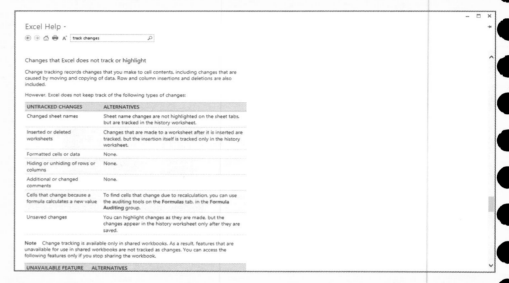

Figure 1

4. Read the section and answer the following questions: What are three changes that Excel does not track? What are three features of Excel that cannot be used when you share a workbook?

Matching

Match each term in the second column with its correct definition in the first column by writing the letter of the term on the blank line in front of the correct definition.

___ **1.** Descriptive text added to cells that does not modify the data in the worksheet.

___ **2.** A rule that restricts the type of data that can be entered in a cell.

___ **3.** A box that displays when data is entered in a cell that specifies what types of data can be entered in the cell.

___ **4.** A feature that tracks any modifications that are made to the data in a worksheet.

___ **5.** The log that records tracked changes.

___ **6.** Information about a workbook file, such as author and company names.

___ **7.** The feature that removes personal information from a workbook.

___ **8.** A language used to write web pages.

___ **9.** A group of stored instructions that perform with a single click.

___ **10.** A high-level programming language that can be used to write and modify macros.

A Change history

B Change tracking

C Comments

D Data Validation

E Document Inspector

F Document properties

G HTML

H Input message

I Macro

J Visual Basic for Applications

Multiple Choice (MyITLab®)

Choose the correct answer.

1. A blue or red triangle in the upper right or upper left corner of a cell.
   A. Input message
   B. Document Inspector
   C. Comment indicator

2. This process combines the changes from multiple copies of a workbook into a single copy.
   A. Compare
   B. Join
   C. Compare and Merge

3. This term refers to a workbook in which multiple users on a network can make changes at the same time.
   A. Common
   B. Shared
   C. Master

4. A data validation message that informs the data entry operator that invalid data has been entered in the cell.
   A. Error alert
   B. Input message
   C. Comments

5. This term is another way of referring to document properties.
   A. Metadata
   B. File information
   C. File data

6. Prevents unauthorized users from modifying the worksheet.
   A. Document Inspector
   B. Protect Sheet
   C. Data validation

7. What uses a combination of uppercase and lowercase letters, numbers, and symbols to protect a workbook?
   A. User name
   B. Password
   C. Malware

8. VBA code is written in this window.
   A. VBE
   B. Module
   C. Code

9. These lines in the programming code document what the code does.
   A. Programming comments
   B. File notes
   C. Instructions

10. These statements are instructions stored in a subroutine.
   A. Informational
   B. Comment
   C. Programming

Topics for Discussion

1. What types of common tasks might a business worker want to automate by recording those tasks' steps in a macro?

2. In a worksheet that you plan to give to others to use, what types of cells should be locked and what types should be unlocked?

Skills Review

MyITLab®
Grader

To complete this project, you will need the following file:

- exl10_SRTransit

You will save your files as:

- Last_First_exl10_SRTransit
- Last_First_exl10_SRTransitChanges
- Last_First_exl10_SRTransitWeb
- Last_First_exl10_SRTransitMacro

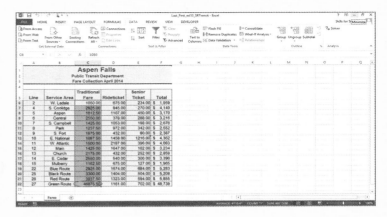

Figure 1

1. Start **Excel 2013**, and then open the file **exl10_SRTransit**. Save the file in your chapter folder as Last_First_exl10_SRTransit

2. On the **File tab**, click **Options**. If necessary, in the **User name** box, type your own name. Click **OK**.

3. Select cell **E13**. On the **Review tab**, click **New Comment**, and then type This seems too high. Select cell **A1**, and then toggle on then off the **Show All Comments** button.

4. Select the range **C6:C22**. On the **Data tab**, click **Data Validation**. In the **Data Validation** dialog box, on the **Settings tab**, click the **Allow arrow**, and then click **Decimal**. In the **Minimum** box, type 1000 In the **Maximum** box, type 5000

5. Click the **Error Alert tab**, and then in the **Title** box, type Transit Fare In the **Error message** box, type Invalid Fare and then click **OK**. Click the **Data Validation arrow**, and then click **Circle Invalid Data**. Compare your screen with **Figure 1**.

6. On the **Review tab**, click **Track Changes**. Click **Highlight Changes**, and then select the **Track changes while editing** check box. Click **OK** two times. **Save** the workbook in your **Excel Chapter 10** folder as Last_First_exl10_SRTransitChanges

7. On the **File tab**, click **Options**. Change the **User name** to Ann McCoy Change cell **C22** to 4875.50 Change cell **E13** to 216.00

8. On the **Review tab**, click **Track Changes**. Click **Accept/Reject Changes**. Click **OK** two times. Click **Accept All**. **Save** and then **Close** the workbook.

9. Open **Last_First_exl10_SRTransit**. On the **File tab**, click **Options**. Change the user name to your name. In the left pane, click **Quick Access Toolbar**. Click the **Customize Quick Access Toolbar arrow**, and then click **Last_First_exl10_SRTransit.xlsx**. Compare your screen with **Figure 2**.

Figure 2

10. Click the **Choose commands from arrow**, and then click **Commands Not in the Ribbon**. Click **Compare and Merge Workbooks**, click **Add**, and then click **OK**.

■ Continue to the next page to complete this Skills Review ▶

11. On the **Quick Access Toolbar**, click **Compare and Merge Workbooks**, and then click **OK**. Click **Last_First_exl10_ SRTransitChanges**, and then click **OK**. On the **Review tab**, click **Track Changes**, and then click **Accept/Reject Changes**. Click **OK**, and then click **Accept All**.

12. Click **Track Changes**. Click **Highlight Changes**. Clear the **Track changes while editing** check box, click **OK**, and then click **Yes**. **Save** the workbook.

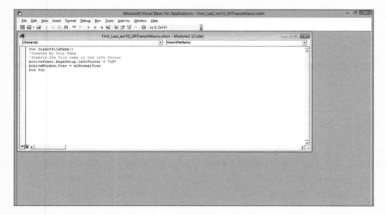

Figure 3

13. On the **File tab**, click **Check for Issues**. Click **Inspect Document**. If necessary, clear the **Comments and Annotations** check box, and then click **Inspect**. Click the **Remove All** button beside **Document Properties and Personal Information**. **Close** the Document Inspector.

14. Select cell **A1**. Click **Save As**, navigate to the **Excel Chapter 10** folder, and in the **File name** box, type Last_First_exl10_SRTransitWeb Click the **Save as type arrow**, and then click **Web Page**. Click **Change Title** and in the **Page title** box type Transit Fares and then click **OK**. Click **Publish** two times. Compare your screen with **Figure 3**, and then **Close** the web browser.

15. In the **Last_First_exl10_SRTransit** workbook, on the **Home tab**, click **Format**, and then click **Protect Sheet**. In the **Password to unprotect sheet** box, type Success13! Click **OK**, and then type Success13! and click **OK**. **Save** the workbook.

16. Save the file as an **Excel Macro-Enabled Workbook** in your **Excel Chapter 10** folder as Last_First_exl10_SRTransitMacro

17. If necessary, to show the Developer tab, click the **File tab**, and then click **Options**. Click **Customize Ribbon**. Select the **Developer** check box. Click **OK**. Select cell **A1**, and then on the **Developer tab**, click **Record Macro**. In the **Macro name** box, type InsertInfo Click **OK**. On the **Home tab**, click **Format**, and then click **Unprotect Sheet**. Type Success13! and click **OK**. Right-click **Row 1**, and then click **Insert**. In cell **A1**, type your name. Click cell **A2**. On the **Developer tab**, in the **Code group**, click **Stop Recording**.

18. On the **Developer tab**, click **Visual Basic**. If necessary, in the **VBE window**, click **Insert**, and then click **Module**. In the **Code** window, type the following, and then compare your screen with **Figure 4**:

Sub InsertFileName()

'Created by Your Name

'Inserts the file name in the left footer

ActiveSheet.PageSetup.LeftFooter = "&F"

ActiveWindow.View = xlNormalView

19. Click **File**, and then click **Close and Return to Microsoft Excel**. Click **Macros**, click **InsertFileName**, and then click **Run**.

20. If necessary, restore the Excel user name and hide the Developer tab. **Save** the workbook, click **OK**, and then submit the files as directed by your instructor. **Close** Excel.

 DONE! You have completed the Skills Review

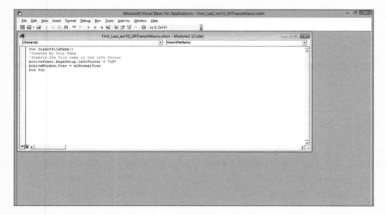

Figure 4

Skills Assessment 1

MyITLab®
Grader

To complete this project, you will need the following file:

- exl10_SA1Bonds

You will save your files as:

- Last_First_exl10_SA1Bonds
- Last_First_exl10_SA1BondChanges
- Last_First_exl10_SA1BondsSnip
- Last_First_exl10_SA1BondsMacro

1. Start **Excel 2013**, and then open the student data file **exl10_SA1Bonds**. Save the file in your chapter folder as Last_ First_exl10_SA1Bonds Change the user name to Cyril Shore

2. In cell **C7**, insert the following comment: Can bond be resold? If necessary, hide all of the comments.

3. In the range **C6:C9**, write a data validation rule that requires a decimal value that is less than or equal to .04 Create an input message titled Interest Rate that displays The interest rate should not exceed 4.00% Create a **Warning Style** error alert with the title Excessive Rate and the message Interest rate is too high!

4. Turn on **Track Changes**. Save the workbook as Last_First_exl10_SA1BondChanges Change the **User name** to your first and last names. Change cell **C7** to 3.3% Change cell **F8** to Clubhouse

5. Accept all changes. **Save** and then **Close** the workbook.

6. Open **Last_First_exl10_SA1Bonds**. Add the **Compare and Merge Workbooks** command to the Quick Access Toolbar. Merge **Last_First_exl10_BondChanges** with the open document. Accept all changes. Stop sharing the workbook.

7. Use the **Document Inspector** to remove all document properties except the comments.

8. Publish the entire workbook as an HTML web page file named Last_First_exl10_SA1BondsWeb **Title** the page Aspen Falls Bonds **Save** as Last_First_exl10_SA1BondsSnip, and then **Close** the workbook. Compare your browser with **Figure 1**.

9. Open **Last_First_exl10_SA1Bonds**. Save the file in your **Excel Chapter 10** folder as an **Excel Macro-Enabled Workbook** named Last_First_exl10_SA1BondsMacro

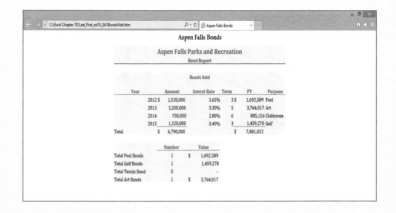
Figure 1

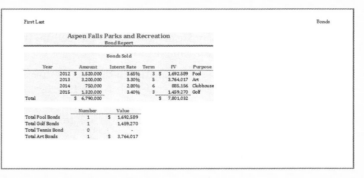
Figure 2

10. If necessary, add the **Developer tab**. Record a macro named FileInfo While recording, complete the following three tasks, and then stop recording: in the right header section, add the **Sheet Name**; in the left header section, type your name. Select cell **A1** and return to **Normal view**.

11. Delete the header text, and then run the macro to verify that it runs correctly.

12. Use the **Visual Basic Editor** to create a macro, using the code from Skill 10 as your guide, to type a VBA statement that inserts the file name in the left footer. **Close** the **Visual Basic Editor**, and then run the macro.

13. Preview the worksheet and then compare your screen with **Figure 2**.

14. If necessary, restore the Excel user name and hide the **Developer tab**. **Save** the workbook, and then submit the files as directed by your instructor.

 DONE! You have completed Skills Assessment 1

Skills Assessment 2

To complete this project, you will need the following file:

- exl10_SA2Truck

You will save your files as:

- Last_First_exl10_SA2Truck
- Last_First_exl10_SA2TruckChanges
- Last_First_exl10_SA2TruckMacro
- Last_First_exl10_SA2TruckWeb

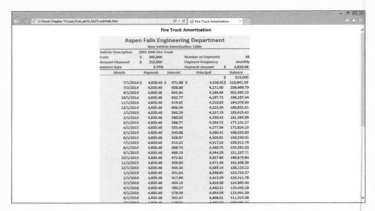

Figure 1

1. Start **Excel 2013**, and then open the student data file **exl10_SA2Truck**. Save the file in your chapter folder as Last_ First_exl10_SA2Truck

2. Change the user name to Leah Kim Insert a comment in cell **B6** that reads Can we get a better rate? Hide all comments.

3. In cell **E4**, write a data validation rule requiring a decimal value less than or equal to 48 Create the input message Fire Truck Loan that displays Loan term cannot exceed 48 months Create a **Warning Style** error alert titled Excessive Term with the message Truck term should not exceed 48 months

4. Turn on **Track Changes**. Save the workbook as Last_First_exl10_SA2TruckChanges Change cell **B5** to 215,000 cell **B6** to 3.75 and cell **E4** to 60 In the warning box, click **Yes**. **Accept** the change in cells **B5** and **B6**. **Reject** the change in cell **E4**. **Save** and then **Close** the workbook.

5. Open **Last_First_exl10_SA2Truck**. Add the **Compare and Merge Workbooks** command to the Quick Access Toolbar. Merge **Last_First_exl10_SA2TruckChanges** with the open workbook. **Accept** all changes. Stop sharing the workbook. Use the **Document Inspector** to remove all of the document properties and personal information.

6. Publish the workbook as a web page titled Fire Truck Amortization Save the file as Last_First_exl10_SA2TruckWeb **Close** the workbook. Compare your screen with **Figure 1**. Close the web browser.

7. Open **Last_First_exl10_SA2Truck**. Unlock the range **A6:E6**, and then protect the worksheet using Success13! **Save** the workbook, and then save the file as an **Excel Macro-Enabled Workbook** named Last_First_exl10_SA2TruckMacro Activate and then click the **Developer tab**. Open the **Visual Basic Editor**. Insert a new module. In the **Code** window, type the following:

Sub AddFooter ()

Figure 2

'Created by Your Name

'Adds the file name to the left footer

8. Use the code from Skill 10 as your guide to type a VBA statement that inserts the file name in the left footer. **Close** the Visual Basic Editor. Run the macro.

9. If necessary, restore the Excel user name and hide the **Developer tab**. Compare your worksheet with **Figure 2**. **Save** the workbook, and then submit the files as directed by your instructor.

✔ **DONE! You have completed Skills Assessment 2**

Visual Skills Check

To complete this project, you will need the following file:

- exl10_VSDisputes

You will save your files as:

- Last_First_exl10_VSDisputes
- Last_First_exl10_VSDisputesSnip

Start **Excel 2013**, and open the student data file **exl10_VSDisputes**. Save the file in your chapter folder as Last_First_exl10_VSDisputes If necessary, change the **User name** for the workbook to your name. Apply comments and the validation rules necessary to mark the circled invalid data as shown in **Figure 1**. In **column C**, the **Usage** should not be more than 50,000. In **column F**, create an **Input Message** as shown and apply the settings as appropriate to the message for **Late Fees** over $200. Show all comments (moving as needed), circle the invalid data to match the figure, and select the range F4:F14. Using the skills you previously practiced, create a full-screen snip. **Save** the snip in your chapter folder as Last_First_exl10_VSDisputesSnip and then **Close** the **Snipping Tool** window. **Save** the file, and then submit the files as directed by your instructor.

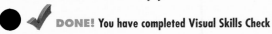 **DONE! You have completed Visual Skills Check**

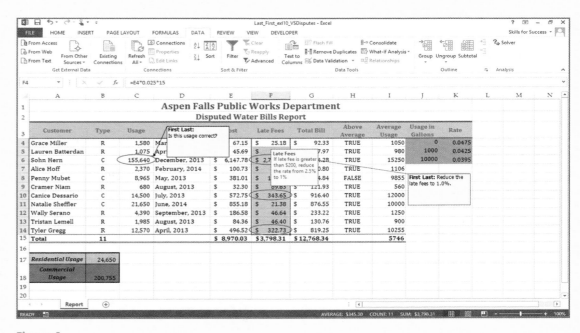

Figure 1

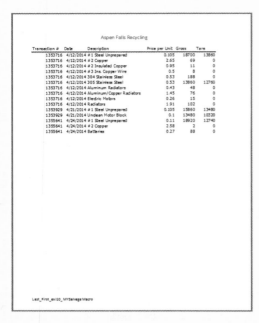

Last_First_exl10_MYSalvageMacro

Figure 1

My Skills

To complete this project, you will need the following file:

- exl10_MYSalvage

You will save your workbook as:

- Last_First_exl10_MYSalvageMacro

1. Start **Excel 2013**, and save the file in your chapter folder as a macro-enabled workbook with the name Last_First_exl10_MYSalvageMacro

2. Record a macro named SalvageHeader and assign the shortcut key as s

3. Select **rows 1** and **2** and insert two blank rows. In cell **A1**, enter Aspen Falls Recycling

4. Change the font size to 14 the font color **Dark Red**, and then **Merge** and **Center A1:F1**.

5. **Stop Recording** the macro, and then delete **rows 1** and **2**. **Run** the macro by pressing Ctrl + S.

6. Create a macro in the **Visual Basic Editor** that will enter the file name in the left footer using the following comments and statements:

Sub InsertFileName ()

'Created by Your Name

'Inserts the file name in the left footer

ActiveSheet.PageSetup.LeftFooter = "&F"

ActiveWindow.View = xlNormalView

7. **Run** the macro.

8. **Save** the workbook. Preview the worksheet and then compare it with Figure 1. Submit the workbook as directed by the instructor.

 **DONE!** You have completed My Skills

Skills Challenge 1

To complete this project, you will need the following file:

- exl10_SC1Classes

You will save your files as:

- Last_First_exl10_SC1ClassesWeb
- Last_First_exl10_SC1ClassesSnip

Start **Excel 2013**, and then open the student data file **exl10_SC1Classes**. If necessary, Enable Content. Save the file in your chapter folder as a web page with the name Last_First_exl10_SC1ClassesWeb Change the title of the page to Enrichment Classes Publish the workbook. Maximize the browser and

create a full-screen snip. Save the file as Last_First_exl10_SC1ClassesSnip Save the workbook, and then submit the files as directed by your instructor.

 DONE! You have completed Skills Challenge 1

Skills Challenge 2

To complete this project, you will need the following file:

- exl10_SC2Budget

You will save your files as:

- Last_First_exl10_SC2Budget
- Last_First_exl10_SC2BudgetSnip

Start **Excel 2013**, and then open the student data file **exl10_SC2Budget**. Save the file in your chapter folder as Last_First_exl10_SC2Budget Using the skills you have practiced in this chapter, ensure the user name is your first and last names. Review the displayed comments, and then turn on Track Changes to track the changes while you are editing the worksheet. Turn the comments off to see the cells. Using the

comments as your guide, edit the cells. Accept all changes and then create the list of changes as a new sheet. Create a full-screen snip using the name Last_First_exl10_SC2BudgetSnip Save the file, and then submit the files as directed by your instructor.

 DONE! You have completed Skills Challenge 2

CAPSTONE PROJECT

To complete this project, you will need the following files:

exl_CAPFarmMarket
exl_CAPFarmOfferings

exl_CAPFarmData
exl_CAPFarmSales

You will save your files as:

Last_First_exl_CAPFarmMarket
Last_First_exl_CAPFarmWeb

Last_First_exl_CAPFarmMacro

1. Start **Excel 2013**, and then open the file **exl_CAPFarmMarket**. Save the workbook in a new folder named Excel Capstone as Last_First_exl_CAPFarmMarket

2. In the **Offerings** worksheet, in cell **A1**, using all the wizard defaults, import the data from the delimited text file, **exl_CAPFarmOfferings**.

3. In cell **E2**, **TRIM** the data from cell **B2**, and AutoFill the function through cell **E47**. Copy the selected text to cell **B2** using the **Paste Values**, **Values (V)** option.

4. Sort the range **A1:D47**, **A to Z** by **FarmID**. Apply a custom filter to **Farm** to display data for **M & M Hills** and **Alexis Acres**. Compare your screen with Figure 1.

5. On the **Sales** worksheet, in cell **B3**, use the custom number format -yyyy-. Use the **Format Painter** to copy the format to **C3**. **Save** the workbook.

6. Open the **exl_CAPFarmSales** workbook, and then switch to the **First_Last_exl_CAPFarmMarket** window.

7. **Consolidate** the data from the **June**, **July**, and **August** worksheets in the **exl_CAPFarmSales** workbook to **A4** in the **Sales** worksheet. Use **Sum** as the **Function**, and **A4:B23** as the range for each worksheet. Include the **Farm** labels in **Left Column**.

8. In cell **D4**, insert an **AND** function, entering **Logical1** $B$3>$C$3 and **Logical2** B4>C4 AutoFill the function down through **D23**.

9. In cell **D24**, insert a **SUMIF** function, entering **Range** D4:D23 **Criteria** TRUE and **Sum_Range** B4:B23

10. In the **Sales** worksheet, add a **Legend** to the **Bottom** of the **Farm Sales** chart. Edit the **Horizontal Axis Labels** to include the range **A4:A23**. Edit the **Legend** so that **B3** and **C3** are the labels. Edit the **Series value** using the range **B4:B23**. Select **Chart Style 9**. Compare your screen with Figure 2.

11. Using **PowerPivot**, import the **Farm_Sales_Week1** table from the **exl_CAPFarmData** Access file.

Figure 1

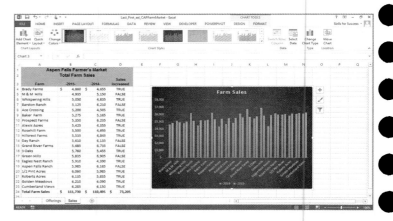

Figure 2

12. In **PowerPivot**, add three calculated fields: one named Total Sales/lb that multiplies the **Costlb** field by **QtySold**, one named Total Sales/piece that multiplies the **Costpiece** field by **QtySold**, and one named Total Sales that adds the **Total Sales/piece** and **Total Sales/lb** fields. Format the fields as **Currency** with **2** decimal places.

▪ Continue to the next page to complete the skill

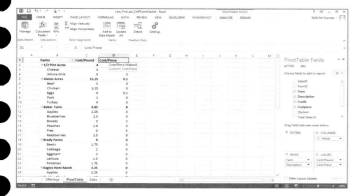

Figure 3

Figure 4

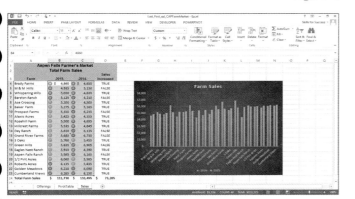

Figure 5

13. In **PowerPivot**, using the **Farm_Sales_Week1** table as the data source, insert a PivotTable report into a **New Worksheet**. Rename the sheet as PivotTable Delete **rows 1** and **2**.

14. For the PivotTable, add **Farm** and **Description** as the row labels, and **Costlb** and **Costpiece** as values. In cell **B1**, replace **Row Labels** with Farms In **C1** replace **Sum of Costlb** with Cost/Pound In **D1** replace **Sum of Costpiece** with Cost/Piece Compare your screen with **Figure 3**.

15. Save and publish the worksheet as a web page with the title Farmer's Market Save the file with the name Last_First_exl_CAPFarmWeb and ensure the **Item to Publish** is set to **Sheet**.

16. Remove the **Costlb** and **Costpiece** fields and add **QtySold** and **Total Sales** as values. In cell **C1** replace **Sum of QtySold** with Quantity Sold and in **D1** replace **Sum of Total Sales** with Total Farm Sales Collapse all of the **Farms** except for **Alexis Acres** and **M & M Hills**.

17. Use a slicer to display **Description**. Move the upper left corner of the slicer to cell **F1** and then drag the lower right corner through **H25**. Show the value **Cheese** and apply the **Slicer Style Dark 2** style. Ensure the **Farms** are expanded. Compare your screen with **Figure 4**. Select cell **A1**.

18. Change the user name of the workbook to your first and last names. In the **Sales** worksheet, insert a comment in cells **B7**, **B15**, and **B17** that reads Please recheck sales total

19. Apply the conditional formatting **Indicators** set **3 Symbols (Circled)** to the range **B4:C23**. Compare your screen with **Figure 5**. Select cell **A1** and **Save** the workbook.

20. If necessary, show the **Developer tab**. In the **Offerings** worksheet, record a **Macro** using the name InsertInfo and shortcut key i that will insert your first and last names in **B50** and =NOW() in **B51**. To the same cells, apply font size **10**, font color **Standard Color Green**, and **Bold**. **Save** the workbook as a **Macro-Enabled Workbook** with the name Last_First_exl_CAPFarmMacro **Close** the workbook.

21. Open the **Last_First_exl_CAPFarmMarket** workbook. Protect each worksheet in the workbook using the password Success13!

22. If necessary, restore the Excel user name and hide the **Developer** and **PowerPivot tabs**. **Save** the workbook, and then submit the files as directed by your instructor. **Close** Excel.

 DONE! You have completed the Excel Capstone Project

Using Excel Web App to Create a Worksheet

▶ ***Excel Web App*** is a cloud-based application used to create, edit, and format basic worksheets using a web browser. Excel 2013 does not have to be installed on your computer to use Excel Web App.

▶ SkyDrive, a free cloud-based service from Microsoft, allows you to save your work to the cloud from an Internet-enabled computer, and then work on the file from any other computer connected to the Internet.

▶ Using the Excel Web App and SkyDrive, you can easily collaborate with colleagues on workbooks. You have full control over who accesses your workbooks and what they can do with them.

▶ Excel Web App provides a minimal number of features. If you need a feature that is not available, you can open your workbook in Microsoft Excel, make the changes you need, and save the workbook on your SkyDrive.

© Yvan Reitserof /Fotolia

Aspen Falls Volunteer Fire Department

In this project, you will create a worksheet for Jim Holt, Fire Chief of the Aspen Falls Volunteer Fire Department (AFVFD). The AFVFD recently sponsored a rummage sale to raise funds for the purchase of new lifesaving equipment. The department exceeded its goal of raising $10,000. The worksheet you create will compare the recent fund-raiser results with the results of fund-raisers held over the past five years to determine which type of event is most effective.

Anyone with a Microsoft SkyDrive account can use Excel Web App to create or open Excel workbooks from any Internet-connected computer or device. In addition to basic text and numbers, you can add formatting and styles to text and cells. You can create workbooks on your SkyDrive, and then open the files in Excel 2013 to access the features not available in the Excel Web App. In Excel Web App, workbooks are edited in ***Editing view*** and viewed to see what they will look like printed in ***Reading view***.

In this project, you will use Excel Web App to create a workbook with formatted and styled text, basic formulas, and a chart. You will open the workbook in Excel 2013 to add formatting to the chart, add a formatted 3-D pie chart, and save the file back to your SkyDrive.

Time to complete this project – 30 to 60 minutes

Student data file needed for this project:

New blank Excel Web App workbook

You will save your workbook as:

Last_First_exc_WARummageSale

Outcome

Using the skills in this project, you will be able to create and edit a Excel Web App workbook like this:

SKILLS MyITLab®

At the end of this project you will be able to:

► Create new Excel workbooks
► Type text in Editing view
► Create a clustered column chart
► Format text
► Switch to the desktop Excel to complete editing
► Apply Totals Style
► Create a 3-D pie chart
► Format the charts
► Save workbook to SkyDrive
► Open the file in SkyDrive
► View workbook in Reading view
► Print a worksheet

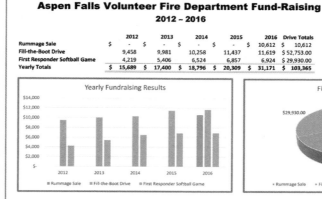

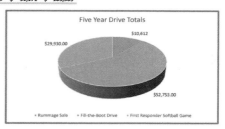

1. Start **Internet Explorer**, navigate to skydrive.com and log on to your Microsoft account. If you do not have an account, follow the links and directions on the page to create one.

2. After logging in, navigate as needed to display the **SkyDrive** page, and then compare your screen with **Figure 1**.

   Due to the volatile nature of web pages, the formatting and layout of some pages in SkyDrive may display differently than the figures in this book. If the SkyDrive web page has changed, you will need to adjust the steps in this assignment to complete the actions specified.

3. On the toolbar, click **Create**, and then click **Excel workbook**. In the **New Microsoft Excel workbook** dialog box, name the file Last_First_exc_WARummageSale and then press [Enter] to save the workbook and start **Excel Web App**.

   You can also click the Create button to save the workbook and start Excel Web App.

4. If necessary, click in cell **A1**. Type Aspen Falls Volunteer Fire Department Fund-Raising Click in cell **A2**, and then type 2011 – 2016 Press [Enter].

5. Click in cell **B4**. Type 2012 and then press [Tab]. Type 2013 Select cells **B4** and **C4**. Use the fill handle to fill the years through cell **F4**.

6. Click in cell **A5**. Type Rummage Sale and then press [Enter]. With cell **A6** active, type Fill-the-Boot Drive and then press [Enter]. Type First Responder Softball Game and then press [Enter]. Compare your screen with **Figure 2**.

■ **Continue to the next page to complete the skill**

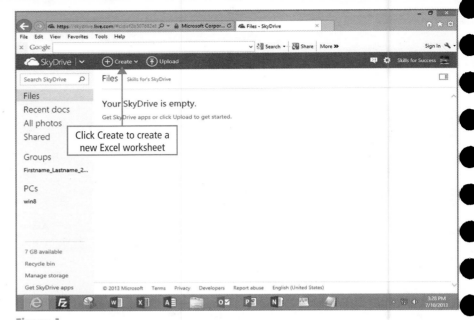

Figure 1

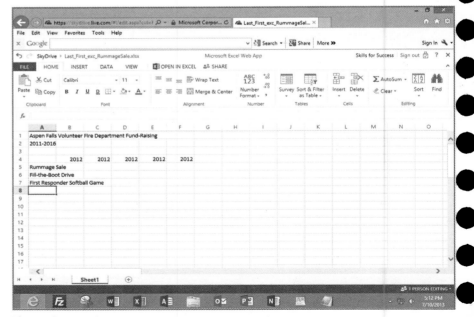

Figure 2

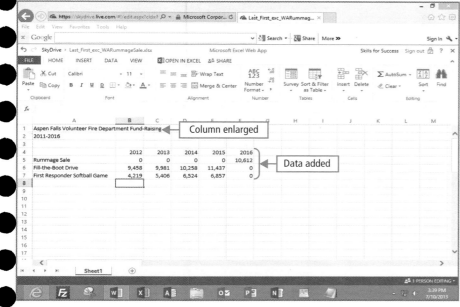

Figure 3

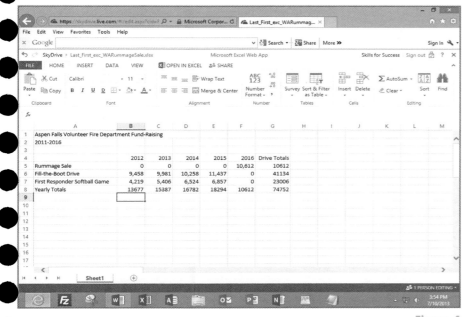

Figure 4

7. Put your pointer on the bar between the **A** and **B** column headers, press and hold the left mouse button, and then drag the bar to the right until the first column is wide enough to contain *First Responder Softball Game.*

8. Type the following data into your worksheet:

	2012	2013	2014	2015	2016
Rummage Sale	0	0	0	0	10,612
Fill-the-Boot Drive	9,458	9,981	10,258	11,437	0
First Responder Softball Game	4,219	5,406	6,524	6,857	0

Compare your screen with Figure 3.

9. In cell **A8**, type Yearly Totals and press Tab . With the pointer in cell **B8**, on the **Home tab**, in the **Editing group**, click **AutoSum**. Verify the range summed is **B4:B7**, and then press Tab . Use the fill handle to fill the SUM formula across to cell **F8**.

10. In cell **G4** type Drive Totals and then press Enter . On the **Home tab**, in the **Editing group**, click **AutoSum**. Use the fill handle to fill the formula down to cell **G8**.

11. Autofit **column G**. Compare your screen with Figure 4.

12. Select cells **B5:G5**. On the **Home tab**, in the **Number group**, click the **Number Format** button, and then click **Accounting**. Select cells **B8:G8**. Use the previous step to format the selected cells as **Accounting**.

In Excel Web App, using the Ctrl button to select noncontiguous ranges does not work.

■ Continue to the next page to complete the skill

13. Select cells **A4:F7**. On the **Insert tab**, in the **Charts group**, click the **Column** button. Click **Clustered Column** (the first chart style). Move the chart until the top left corner is at the top left of cell **A10**.

14. On the **Chart Tools Chart tab**, in the **Labels group**, click **Chart Title**. Select **Above Chart**. In the **Edit Title** dialog box, in the **Title text** box, type Yearly Fundraising Results Compare your screen with **Figure 5**, and then click **OK**.

15. After viewing the chart, you realize you left out the figures for 2016 for the Fill-the-Boot Drive and the First Responder Softball Game. In cell **F6**, type 11,619 In cell **F7**, type 6,924 If necessary, AutoFit columns **F** and **G** to display all the text.

    The chart automatically updates with the new values.

16. Click in cell **A1**. On the **Home tab**, in the **Font group**, change the font to **Arial Black**. Change the font size to **18**. Select cells **A1:H1**. In the **Alignment group**, click **Merge & Center**.

17. Select cells **A2:H2**. **Merge & Center** the selection. Change the font to **Arial Black**. Change the font size to **14**. Between the **Row 2** and **Row 3** row headers, double-click the bar to increase the height of cell **A2** to fit the text. Compare your screen with **Figure 6**.

■ **Continue to the next page to complete the skill**

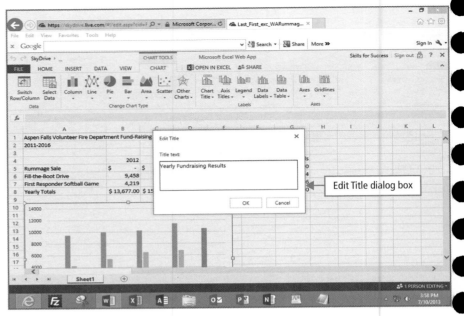

Figure 5

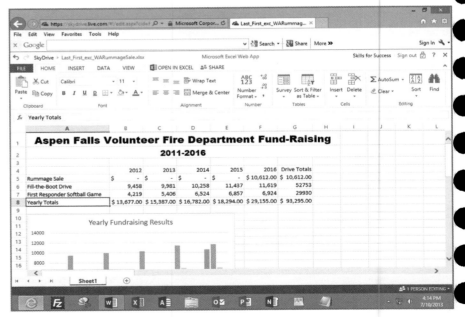

Figure 6

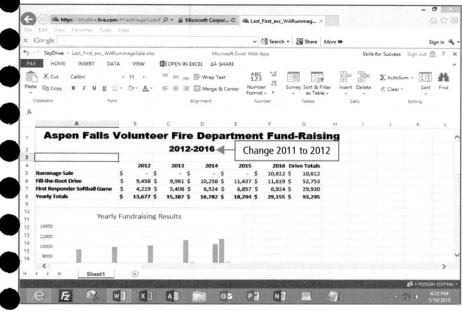

Figure 7

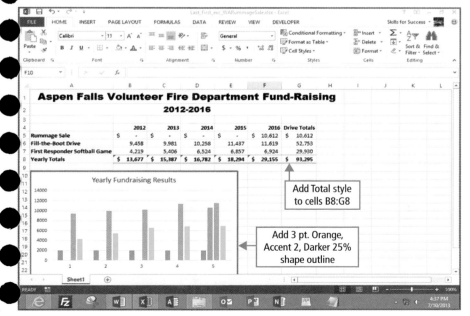

Figure 8

18. Select cells **B4:G4**. On the **Home tab**, in the **Font section**, click the **Bold** button.

19. Select cells **A5:A8** and apply **Bold** formatting. Select cells **B8:G8** and apply **Bold** formatting.

20. Select cells **B6:G7**. On the **Home tab**, in the **Number group**, click the **Comma Style** button. Select cells **B5:G8**. In the **Number group**, click the **Decrease Decimal** button twice.

21. You realize there is an error in cell A2. Click to select **A2**. On the formula bar, change *2011* to *2012* Compare your screen with **Figure 7**.

22. You would like to add some formatting that is not available in Excel Web App. Click the **Open in Excel** tab. Click **Yes**. If necessary, provide your SkyDrive login information.

23. Select the **Clustered Column Chart**. On the **Chart Tools Format tab**, in the **Shape Styles group**, click the **Shape Outline arrow**. Below **Theme Colors**, select **Orange, Accent 2, Darker 25%**. Click the **Shape Outline arrow** again, rest your pointer over **Weight**, and then click on **3 pt**. Click outside the chart to deselect it and see the chart border.

24. Select cells **B8:G8**. On the **Home tab**, in the **Styles group**, click the **Cell Styles arrow**. Below **Titles and Headings**, click the **Total** style. Click outside the selected cells. Compare your screen with **Figure 8**.

■ **Continue to the next page to complete the skill**

25. Select cells **A4:A7**. Press and hold the `Ctrl` key while selecting **G4:G7**. On the **Insert tab**, in the **Charts group**, click the **Insert Pie or Doughnut Chart** button. Below **3-D Pie**, click the **3-D Pie** button. At the top right corner of the pie chart, click the **Chart Elements** button. Click the **Data Labels** check box.

26. Move the pie chart so that the top left corner is in the top left corner of cell **F10**. With the pie chart still selected, on the **Chart Tools Format tab**, in the **Shape Styles group**, click the **Shape Outline arrow**. Below **Theme Colors**, select **Orange, Accent 2, Darker 25%**.

27. Click the **Shape Outline arrow** again, rest your pointer over **Weight**, and then click on **3 pt**. Click outside the chart to deselect it and see the chart border. **Save** the workbook. Compare your screen with **Figure 9**.

28. One of the data labels is formatted as an Accounting number, while two are not. To correct this, select cells **G6:G7**. On the **Home tab**, in the **Number group**, click the **Number format arrow**, and select **Accounting**. Click outside the selected cells.

29. Click on the **Pie Chart title**. Change the title to Five Year Drive Totals. Click anywhere outside of the pie chart. On the Quick Access Toolbar, click the **Save** button. Compare your screen with Figure 10.

■ Continue to the next page to complete the skill ▶

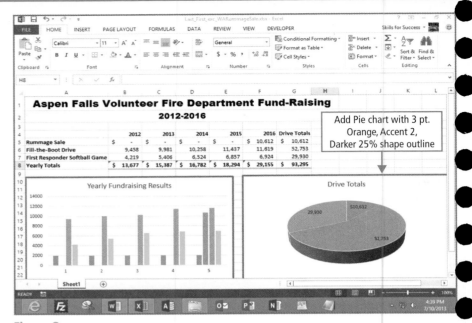

Figure 9

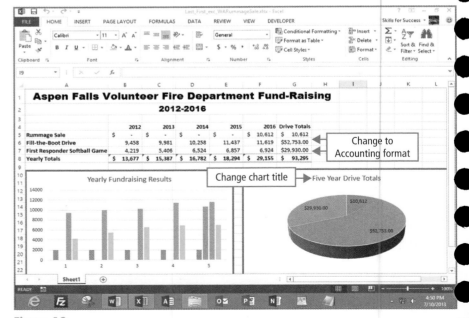

Figure 10

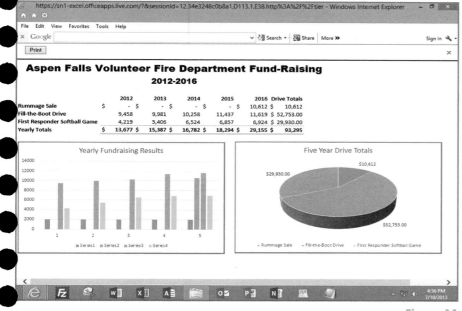

Figure 11

30. Save your workbook and then **Close** Excel 2013. Navigate to your SkyDrive account in Internet Explorer. Open the **Last_First_exc_WARummageSale** file in Excel Web App.

31. You decide the data values on the pie chart are too hard to read. Select the pie chart. On the **Chart Tools Chart tab**, in the **Labels group**, click the **Data Labels arrow**, and then click **Outside End**.

32. On the **View tab**, in the **Document Views group**, click **Reading view**. After reviewing the worksheet, click the **Edit Workbook tab**, and then click **Edit in Excel Web App**.

33. Click the **File tab**, and then click **Print**. Click the **Print** button. In the **Print Options** dialog box, if necessary, select **Entire Sheet**, and then click **Print**. The worksheet will open in Print Preview. Compare your screen with **Figure 11**.

34. If instructed to print the worksheet, click the **Print** button. Otherwise, in the top right corner, click the **Close** button. Submit your workbook as directed.

DONE! You have completed Excel Web App Project

Glossary

3-D Short for three-dimensional.

Absolute cell reference The exact address of a cell, regardless of the position of the cell that contains the formula, and that remains the same when the formula is copied. An absolute cell reference takes the form $A$1.

Active cell The cell outlined in green in which data is entered when you begin typing.

ActiveX controls Objects such as check boxes and buttons that provide interactive options or run macros.

Add-in A file that adds functionality to Excel, usually in the form of new functions.

Amortization table Tracks loan payments over the life of a loan.

AND A function that evaluates two conditions. When both conditions are true, the displayed value is TRUE.

Area chart A chart type that emphasizes the magnitude of change over time.

Argument The values that a function uses to perform operations or calculations.

Arithmetic operator A symbol that specifies a mathematical operation such as addition or subtraction.

Array A collection of data typically arranged in multiple columns and rows. Most spreadsheets arrange data in arrays.

Array formula A formula that can perform calculations across multiple items in an array. For example, you can calculate the sum of the values in one column multiplied by the values in another column.

AutoFit A command that automatically changes the column width to accommodate the longest entry.

AVERAGE function A function that adds a group of values, and then divides the result by the number of values in the group.

AVERAGEIFS A function that averages cells in a range that meet multiple criteria.

Axis A line bordering the chart plot area used as a frame of reference for measurement.

Background color Shading assigned to a cell.

Backstage view A collection of pages on the File tab used to open, save, print, and perform other file management tasks.

Bar chart A chart type that illustrates comparisons among individual items.

Button A control that typically starts a macro when it is clicked.

Calculated column A column in an Excel table that uses a single formula which adjusts for each row.

Calculated field A data field whose values are derived from formulas that you create.

Calculation The process that Excel uses to compute formulas and functions and to display the results.

Category axis The axis that displays the category labels.

Category label Nonnumeric text that identifies the categories of data.

Cell A box formed by the intersection of a row and column into which text, objects, and data can be inserted.

Cell address The column letter and row number that identify a cell; also called the cell reference.

Cell border Decorative lines applied to worksheet cells that can be added to differentiate, emphasize, or group cells.

Cell fill color Shading assigned to a cell.

Cell reference The column letter and row number that identify a cell; also called a cell address.

Cell style A prebuilt set of formatting characteristics, such as font, font size, font color, cell borders, and cell shading.

Change history A log that records each data change, who made the change, and when the data was changed.

Change tracking A feature that tracks all the changes made to a worksheet.

Chart A graphical representation of data used to show comparisons, patterns, and trends.

Chart layout A prebuilt set of chart elements that can include a title, legend, or labels.

Chart sheet A workbook sheet that contains only a chart and is useful when you want to view a chart separately from the worksheet data.

Chart style A prebuilt chart format that applies an overall visual look to a chart by modifying its graphic effects, colors, and backgrounds.

Chart template A custom chart type that you can apply like any other chart type.

Check box A control that allows a user to select one or more values in a group of choices.

Clipboard A temporary storage area for text and graphics.

Clustered bar chart A chart type that is useful when you want to compare values across categories; bar charts organize categories along the vertical axis and the values along the horizontal axis.

Code window The window in which VBA code is written.

Color scales A conditional format that uses color to help the user visualize data distribution and variation.

Column chart A chart type useful for illustrating comparisons among related numbers.

Column heading The letter that displays at the top of a column.

Comma-separated values Text that uses commas to separate each column of text.

Command button A control that runs a VBA macro.

Comment Descriptive text that you can add to cells without modifying the data in the worksheet.

Comment indicator A small red triangle in the upper right corner of a cell.

Compare and merge A process that combines the changes from multiple copies of a workbook into a single copy.

Comparison operator Compares two values and returns either TRUE or FALSE.

Compatibility mode A mode that limits formatting and features to ones that are supported in earlier versions of Office.

CONCATENATE A text function that is used to join the text in two cells into one cell.

Conditional formatting Formatting that changes the appearance of a cell or range when one or more conditions are true.

Consolidate A command used to summarize and report results from separate worksheets.

Content Underlying formulas and data in a cell.

Contextual tab A tab that displays on the Ribbon only when a related object such as a graphic or chart is selected.

Copy A command that places a copy of the selected text or object in the Office Clipboard.

COUNT function A function that counts the number of cells that contain numbers.

COUNTA function A function that counts the number of cells containing values that are specified.

COUNTIF function A function that counts the number of cells in a range that meet a specified criteria.

Criteria The condition that is specified in the logical test.

Cube function A function that connects to and manipulates data in an online analytical processing (OLAP) cube.

CUBEMEMBER function Defines the categories and how the data should be aggregated.

CUBEVALUE function Defines the value derived from the cross-tabulation of the categories.

Data bar A format that provides a visual cue to the reader about the value of a cell relative to other cells. The length of the data bar represents the value in the cell.

Data marker A column, bar, area, dot, pie slice, or other symbol that represents a single data point.

Data model A collection of tables with relationships.

Data point A chart value that originates in an Excel worksheet cell, a Word table cell, or an Access field.

Data series Related data points that are plotted in a chart, and that originate from worksheet columns.

Data table A range of cells that is set up to show how changing one or two values in a cell will affect the results of the formula.

Data validation rules Place restrictions on the types of data that can be entered in cells.

Decrease Decimal A tool that displays rounded values, although Excel uses the unrounded values in all calculations.

Default printer The printer that is automatically selected when you do not choose a different printer.

Delimited text file A file in which the data in each column is separated by an identifying character such as a comma, a space, or a tab stop.

Delimiter The character used to separate columns of text in a data table.

Dependent Any cell value that depends on the value in a given cell.

Detail sheet A worksheet with cells referred to by summary sheet formulas.

Displayed value Data displayed in a cell.

Document Information Panel A panel that displays above the worksheet window in which properties or property information is added, viewed, or updated.

Document properties Details about a file that describe or identify the file, such as the title, author name, and keywords.

Double-click To click the left mouse button two times quickly without moving the mouse.

Double-tap To tap the screen in the same place two times quickly.

Drag To press and hold the left mouse button while moving the mouse.

Drag and drop A method of moving objects, in which you point to a selection and drag it to a new location.

Dual axis chart One or more data series is plotted on a secondary vertical axis.

Edit To insert, delete, or replace text in an Office document, workbook, or presentation.

Embedded chart A chart that is placed on the worksheet containing the data.

E-mail attachment A file that is sent with an e-mail message so that the recipient can open and view the file.

ENCODEURL A web function that returns a URL-encoded string.

Error alert A data validation message that informs the data entry operator that invalid data has been entered in the cell.

Error indicator A green triangle that indicates a possible error in a formula.

Error value A message that displays whenever a formula or function cannot perform its calculations.

Excel add-in A tool that adds features and commands to Excel, extending Excel's capabilities as if the tool were part of Excel.

Excel table A series of rows and columns that contains related data that have been formatted as a table.

Exponential trendline Data points that create a symmetric arc.

Fax service provider A company that receives faxes sent to them from the Internet and then relays the fax to the recipient using phone lines. Fax service providers typically charge fees for their service.

Field In a PivotTable, a cell that summarizes multiple rows of information from the source data.

Fields Categories of data organized into columns.

File type A standard way that information is encoded for storage in a computer file, and is designated for that version.

Fill handle The small black square in the lower right corner of the selection.

Filter A command to display only the rows of a table that meet specified criteria. Filtering temporarily hides rows that do not meet the criteria.

Filtering Displays only the data that satisfies conditions you specify.

FILTERXML A web function that returns specific data from the XML content by using the specified XPath.

Font A set of characters with the same design and shape.

Form A database object that is used to find, update, and add table records.

Form Controls Objects such as buttons or check boxes that are added to a worksheet.

Format To change the appearance of text—for example, changing the text color to red.

Format Painter A tool used to copy formatting from one place to another.

Formatting The process of specifying the appearance of cells or the overall layout of a worksheet.

Formula An equation that performs mathematical calculations on number values in the worksheet.

Formula AutoComplete A feature that suggests values as you type a function.

Formula bar A bar below the Ribbon that displays the value contained in the active cell and is used to enter or edit values or formulas.

Freeze Panes A command used to keep rows or columns visible when scrolling in a large worksheet. The frozen rows and columns become separate panes.

Function A prewritten Excel formula that takes a value or values, performs an operation, and returns a value or values.

Future value (Fv) In a loan, the value at the end of a period of time, or the cash balance you want to attain after the last loan payment is made. The future value for a loan is usually zero.

Gallery A visual display of selections from which you can choose.

General format The default number format. It does not display commas or trailing zeros to the right of a decimal point.

Goal Seek A what-if analysis tool used to find a specific value for a cell by adjusting the value of another cell.

Gridlines The lines that run horizontally and vertically across a worksheet and intersect to create cells.

Hyperlink Text or a graphic that you click to go to a file, a location in a file, or a web page on the World Wide Web or a web page on an organization's intranet.

Hypertext Markup Language (HTML) Used to mark up text files so that they can be viewed on the Internet.

Icon sets Classify a range of data into three to five categories and display small graphics in each cell depending on that cell's value.

IF function A logical function that checks whether criteria is met, and then returns one value when the condition is TRUE, and another value when the condition is FALSE.

Information function A function that provides information about a cell's contents.

Input message A data validation message that informs the data entry operator about the types of data that can be entered in the cell.

Inquire add-in Assists with analyzing and reviewing workbooks to understand their design function and data dependencies, and uncover a variety of problems including formula errors or inconsistencies, hidden information, and broken links.

Insertion point A flashing vertical line that indicates where text will be inserted when you start typing.

Interest The charge for borrowing money; generally a percentage of the amount borrowed.

ISERROR function A function that evaluates a cell to determine whether the cell contains an error message.

ISODD function A function that returns the value TRUE whenever it evaluates a cell with an odd number.

Keyboard shortcut A combination of keys that performs a command.

Label Text data in a cell that identifies a number value.

LEFT function A text function used to return a specified number of characters starting from the left side of the data.

Legacy objects Objects that are compatible with earlier versions of a program.

Legend A box that identifies the patterns or colors that are assigned to the data series or categories in a chart.

Line chart A chart type that illustrates trends over time, with time displayed along the x-axis and the data point values connected by a line.

Linear Forecast trendline Data points that follow a straight line with a two-period forecast.

Linear trendline Data points that follow a nearly straight line.

Live Preview A feature that displays what the results of a formatting change will be if you select it.

Logical function A function that applies a logical test to determine if a specific condition is met.

Logical test Any value or expression that can be evaluated as being TRUE or FALSE.

Lookup function A function that is used to find values stored in a lookup table.

Lookup table Data organized into rows and columns in such a way that values can be easily retrieved.

Lync A hosted service that lets you connect with others through instant messaging, video calls, and online meetings.

Macro A stored set of instructions that automate common tasks.

Malware Software that is designed to harm a computer.

Markup language A method for describing text that is separated by special characters.

MAX function A function that returns the largest value in a range of cells.

Metadata Information that describes the data in an Excel file.

MID function A text function used to return a specified number of characters starting from a specified position in the data.

MIN function A function that returns the smallest value in a range of cells.

Mini toolbar A toolbar with common formatting commands that displays near selected text.

Moving Average trendline Data points that follow a smooth curve to show data fluctuations.

Name A word that represents a cell or range of cells that can be used as a cell or range reference.

Name Box An area that displays the active cell reference.

Nested function A function placed inside another function.

Non-native files File formats that are not current Excel 2013 files, including previous versions, text files, and data tables.

Normal view A view that maximizes the number of cells visible on the screen.

NOW function A function that returns the serial number of the current date and time.

Number format A specific way that Excel displays numbers.

Number value Numeric data in a cell.

Office 2013 RT A version of Office optimized for working on portable devices with touch screens such as Windows phones and tablets.

One-to-many relationship A relationship in which a single record in one table can have many associated records in a second table.

One-variable data table Changes one value in a formula using input from either a row or a column.

Online analytical processing (OLAP) cube Extends a two-dimensional worksheet to three or more dimensions, where each dimension is a separate category.

Operator precedence The mathematical rules for performing calculations within a formula.

OR A function that evaluates two conditions. If one condition is true, the displayed value is TRUE.

Or A logical operator that evaluates two conditions.

Organization chart A chart that graphically represents the reporting relationships between individuals and groups in an organization.

Page Layout view A view used to adjust how a worksheet will look when it is printed.

Parameter A quantity whose value is selected for particular circumstances and in relation to which other variable quantities may be expressed.

Paste A command that inserts a copy of the text or object from the Office Clipboard.

Paste area The target destination for data that has been cut or copied.

PDF document An image of a file that can be viewed using a PDF reader such as Adobe Acrobat Reader instead of the application that created the original document.

Pie chart A chart type that illustrates the relationship of parts to a whole.

Pinch Sliding two fingers closer together to shrink or zoom out.

PivotTable report An interactive, cross-tabulated Excel report used to summarize and analyze data.

PivotTable values Fields for which summary statistics are calculated.

Placeholder A reserved, formatted space into which you enter your own text or object. If no text is entered, the placeholder text will not print.

PMT function A function that calculates the payment amount required to pay off a loan for a given amount, a given number and frequency of payments, and a given interest rate.

Power View An interactive data exploration, visualization, and presentation experience that encourages intuitive ad hoc reporting.

PowerPivot An Office Professional Plus Excel add-in used to perform powerful data analysis and to create sophisticated data models.

Precedent Any cell value that is referred to in a formula or a function.

Present value (Pv) The total amount that a series of future payments is worth today, often the initial amount of a loan.

Principal The initial amount of the loan; the total amount that a series of future payments is worth today. Also called the present value (Pv) of a loan.

Programming comments Statements that document what a code does.

Programming statements Instructions stored in a subroutine.

PROPER function A function that converts text to title case—the first letter of each word is capitalized.

Protect Sheet Prevents unauthorized users from making changes to a worksheet.

Protected View A view applied to documents downloaded from the Internet that allows you to decide if the content is safe before working with the document.

Query A database object that displays a subset of data in response to a question.

RAM The computer's temporary memory.

Range Two or more cells in a worksheet that are adjacent or nonadjacent.

Range finder An Excel feature that outlines all of the cells referenced in a formula. It is useful for verifying which cells are used in a formula and it can be used to edit formulas.

Rate The percentage that is paid for the use of borrowed money.

Records A collection of related information that displays in a single row in a database table.

Relative cell reference Refers to cells based on their position in relation to (relative to) the cell that contains the formula.

Replace A feature that finds and then replaces a character or string of characters in a worksheet, or in a selected range.

Report A database object that presents tables or query results in a way that is optimized for onscreen viewing or printing.

RGB values Colors constructed from combinations of red, green, and blue.

RIGHT function A text function used to return a specified number of characters starting from the right side of the data.

ROUND function A function used to round numbers to a specified number of digits.

ROUNDDOWN function A function that always rounds down to the next decimal value.

ROUNDUP function A function that always rounds up to the next decimal value.

Row heading The number that displays at the left of a row.

Row labels Fields used to categorize the data by rows.

Scenario A set of values that Excel can save and automatically substitute in cells.

Screen clipping A picture of a portion of the computer screen that can be inserted into a worksheet. It can be very small or as large as the entire screen.

Screen shot An image of the computer screen.

Serial number A sequential number.

Series A group of things that come one after another in succession; for example, the months January, February, March.

Shared workbook A workbook in which multiple users on a network can make changes to the workbook at the same time.

Silverlight A powerful development tool for creating engaging, interactive user experiences for web and mobile applications.

SkyDrive A secure online application used to store and share files.

Slicer A tool that is used to filter data in PivotTable views.

Slide (PowerPoint) An individual page in a presentation that can contain text, pictures, or other objects.

Slide (touch screen) Touching an object and then moving the finger across the screen.

SmartArt graphic A visual representation of information you can use to effectively communicate your message or ideas.

Software version A software release or format.

Solver A what-if analysis tool used to find solutions to complex problems. It looks for solutions to achieve a desired goal.

Source data The data that is used to create a PivotTable.

Sparkline A chart contained in a single cell that is used to show data trends.

Special characters Characters, such as the degree symbol and trademark symbol, that are not found on the standard keyboard but are included on a shorter list of frequently used symbols on the Symbols tab.

Spreadsheet The primary document that you use in Excel to store and work with data; also called a worksheet.

Statistical function A predefined function that describes a collection of data; for example, totals, counts, and averages.

Stretch Sliding two fingers apart to enlarge or zoom in.

String Any sequence of letters and numbers; it is designated by quotation marks.

Strong password A password that contains a combination of uppercase and lowercase letters, numbers, and symbols.

Style A group of formatting choices that can be applied in a single step.

Sub A group of instructions that is a subset of a program.

SUM function An Excel function that adds all the numbers in a range of cells.

SUMIF function A function that adds the cells in a range that meet a specified criteria.

SUMIFS function A function that adds the cells in a range that meet multiple criteria.

Summary sheet A worksheet that displays and summarizes totals from other worksheets.

Symbol A character such as font symbols or a bullet character that is not found on a common keyboard.

Tab scrolling buttons The buttons to the left of the worksheet tabs used to display Excel worksheet tabs that are not in view.

Table A database object that stores the database data so that records are in rows and fields are in columns.

Table style A collection of table formatting options that can be applied to a range with a single click.

Template A prebuilt workbook used as a pattern for creating new workbooks; used to build workbooks without having to start from a blank workbook.

Text box A rectangular object on a worksheet or chart into which you type text.

Text file A file that stores only the text characters, not the formatting or tables.

Text format Treats the cell value as text even when the cell contains numbers.

Text value Character data in a cell that labels number values.

Text wrap A format that displays text on multiple lines within a cell.

Theme A prebuilt set of unified formatting choices including colors and fonts.

Three-color scale A conditional format that compares a range of cells and applies a gradation of three colors; the shades represent higher, middle, or lower values.

Three-dimensional Refers to an image that appears to have all three spatial dimensions: length, width, and depth.

Thumbnail A small sample image of a style located in the gallery.

TODAY function A function that returns the serial number of the current date.

Top/Bottom Rules A conditional format used to apply formatting to the highest and lowest values in a range of cells.

Total row A row that displays as the last row in an Excel table and provides summary functions in drop-down lists for each column.

Trendline A graphic representation of trends in a data series, used for showing predictions.

TRIM function A text function used to remove all spaces from a text string except for single spaces between words.

Truncated Cut off.

Two-color scale A conditional format that compares a range of cells and applies a gradation of two colors; the shade of the color represents higher or lower values.

Two-variable data table Uses two inputs—one from a column and one from a row.

Underlying formula The formula as displayed in the formula bar.

Underlying value Data displayed in the formula bar.

Value Data in a cell.

Value axis The axis that displays the worksheet's numeric data.

Visual Basic for Applications (VBA) A high-level programming language that can be used to write and modify macros.

VLOOKUP function A function that finds values in a table where categories are organized by columns.

Volatile The result of a function that does not remain as entered, but is updated each time the workbook is opened.

Watch Window Displays cells and the formulas in those cells when they are not visible on the screen.

Watermark A graphic inserted into a workbook background. Watermarks are typically inserted into the header.

Web query A query that retrieves data stored on your intranet or the Internet.

Web service A method of communication between two electronic devices over the web. It can offer application components such as currency conversion, weather reports, or even language translation.

WEBSERVICE function A web function that returns data from a web service.

What-if analysis A set of tools that change the values in cells to show how those changes affect the outcome of other formulas on the worksheet.

Word wrap Words at the right margin automatically move to the next line if they do not fit.

Workbook A file that you can use to organize various kinds of related information.

Worksheet The primary document that you use in Excel to store and work with data; also called a spreadsheet.

Worksheet tabs The labels along the lower border of the workbook window that identify each worksheet or chart sheet.

Worksheet template A workbook with content and formatting that you use as a model to create similar workbooks or worksheets.

X-axis Another name for the horizontal axis.

XML/eXtensible Markup Language A method of storing data in a text file.

XML Paper Specification A file format that preserves formatting and embeds its fonts in such a way that it can be shared on many different devices and programs.

XML schema Describes the structure of an XML document and is used to validate and format XML data.

XPS An acronym for XML Paper Specification.

XSD files Files that define which elements and attributes are permitted in a file, and in which order.

Y-axis Another name for the vertical axis.

Index

CW The internet icon represents Index entries found within More Skills on the Companion Website: www.pearsonhighered.com/skills